DREW SMITH'S
GOOD
food

DREW SMITH'S
GOOD
food

The ultimate critical guide to what we eat

HarperCollins*Publishers*

NOTES

Nearly all the foods tested for this book were bought independently from supermarkets and delicatessens. A small number were tasted at exhibitions or tastings organised by third parties.

The prices quoted are those charged or displayed to us as consumers. The tasting notes are my own, from batched comparison tastings usually in conjunction with one or two colleagues with specialist knowledge.

The nutritional analysis is based on packet information or from the Ministry of Agriculture tables laid down by down by McCance and Widdowson's Composition of Foods.

First published in 1996
by HarperCollins*Publishers*, London
© Drew Smith 1996

A catalogue record for this book is available from the British Library.

ISBN 0 00 412725 0

Editor: Lewis Esson
Editorial Director: Polly Powell
Commissioning Editor: Barbara Dixon
Illustrations by Tony Hannaford
Designed by Drum Design, Hampshire

Printed and bound in Great Britain by
The Bath Press, Bath

For Sue, Grace and Oliver

ACKNOWLEDGEMENTS

A great many people have helped in the putting together of this book:
answering questions, checking facts or just allowing me to put ideas and
thoughts to them. There are special thank-yous due to Juliet Harbutt,
Patrick Rance and Randolph Hodgson for the dairy sections; Paul Fry for
the fruit and vegetables; Simon Watson, Lawrence Alderson and Alastair
Cuthbertson for the meat; Dr Eric Edwards for shellfish; Alan Davidson,
Ninnette Lyon and Rick Stein for their excellent writing on fish; Helen
Conn, Charles Carey and Judy Ridgeway for the larder section;
John Lister for bread. There are smaller, but no less grateful, thanks to
George Benyon, Colin Boswell, Tim Clarke, Sue Cloke, Colin Creese,
John Dewesbury, Wilson Dyer, Mike Ford, David Frost, Peter Hadaad,
John Hassal, Dorothy Hollingsworth, Peter Hudson, Martin Keeble,
Monica Lavery, Trevor Paveley, Miriam Polunin, Nick Reed, Ron Smith,
William Tullberg and Adam Wells. Also thanks to a number of specialist
shops that unwittingly have been supplying much of the better produce:
Camisa, Carluccio's, I Camisa, Fromagerie, Harvey Nichols, Harrods,
Jeroboams, Langman's, Lena's, Loon Fung, Mortimer & Bennett,
Neal's Yard, Tom's, William's Kitchen, Wing Yip, Wild Oats, and to
everyone at Billingsgate, Nine Elms and Smithfield Markets.

On a personal level my thanks go to Emma Bland and to Sam Dobson,
who did some heroic shopping trips; to Lewis Esson for his noble efforts in
organizing and editing the text, and to Polly Powell and to Robin Wood
for having the vision to commission it in the first place.

CONTENTS

INTRODUCTION

This is a book about the foods we eat, how they are produced and why they are made. It is a book about good foods. Some have long traditions and have stamped themselves on the way we survive on this planet; others are new and are changing the way we eat, the way we cook and the way we live.

SHOPPING

TRENDS

THE READY-ROASTED POTATO

The statistics suggest that our diet is changing at a rate of 10 to 20 per cent a year. That is an incredible rate of change. Some of these changes are simply cosmetic alterations of packaging or slight variations in recipes or price; but others are fundamental.

One of the great achievements of a supermarket culture has been to offer customers, perhaps for the first time in history, a choice of what to eat. And that choice is really what this book is about.

I have set out to write a simple book that could make sense of the huge choice of foods in the modern supermarket. A book that would save you money – and it can save you a lot of money – and point you towards those kinds of foods that you would be likely to enjoy. It is a book about good foods. If I had tried to detail every innovation that has taken place in the last two years since the first edition was published then this book would have weighed more than a sack of potatoes. The speed of change in the supermarkets is awesome.

Tesco produced a neat little brochure to highlight some of the new products that were in store one month. There were:

2 new egg pastas from Italy
a rare virgin olive oil
an instant coffee
risotto rice
jasmine rice
bottled hot pepper sauce, fruit sauce, jerk sauce
4 new marinades for fresh pork

4 new sachets of own-label salad dressings
6 new ready-made fish dishes
2 new kinds of frozen fish fingers
4 new ranges of pizza
the introduction of the Swedish breakfast cheese, Arla Morgon
a range of aerosol oils for cooking
a range of 5 new spreads
monster munch packs to contain 5 kinds of new crisp
a whole range of own-label chocolate
Power Ranger lollipops, mini wine gums, Lion bar ice-creams
5 kinds of newly decorated cakes
2 kinds of roulade, a date and walnut loaf cake, chocolate eggs
a revolutionary new sugar from Silver spoon using half sugar and half
    artificial sweetener
Sunblest launched Tropical Coconut Cornflakes
and there were new ranges of dog and cat food.

Never mind a partridge in a pear tree, these new lines just tack on to the list of more than 17,000 items currently on sale in the stores. At about the same time, Sainsbury launched its innovative new Special Selection of high-quality own-label larder products that previously could only be found in a handful of delicatessens. Other retailers have also been innovating at the same pace.

The diversity is, on the face of it, amazing. Even discounting those foods that are no more than changes of packaging, the wheel of change is spinning at a mind-boggling rate.

The quest for ever more convenience has seen **Marks & Spencer** (who else) develop oven-ready chips packaged with ready-battered fish; and thoroughly awful ready-roasted potatoes.

In ready meals, the trends have been solidly towards old-fashioned English cooking of the kind that most of us have abandoned – especially puddings – and in the area of Indian food, where the supermarkets seem to want to rival the take-away. Both genres perform passably well, being robust and solid and undamaged in the handling process. Chinese food is typically less successful because it relies so heavily on the last-minute heat of the wok. Thai food is the rising new star. The vegetarian options are expanding apace on the back of the success of the **Linda McCartney** range (disappointingly stodgy and imitative of meat cooking) and the huge effort behind Quorn dishes which has also allowed tofu to get into the supermarket. Dwarfing even these trends has been pizza, bearing out the thought that what the British food industry really wants is the lowest possible cost base.

Pasta has become chic. While many supermarkets have been happy to bring in pasta with sauce mixes, at the same time Italy and authentic durum wheat has been flavours of the month. Odd shapes like cellentani and pipe rigate have been dressed in elegant designer packages. The approach has been one of 'I've got more egg in my pasta than you' – not necessarily a be-all-and-end-all of quality because it is easy enough to add an egg to pasta at home. **Sainsbury** and **Tesco** have even gone to the lengths of bringing in designer names like **Cipriani**, though the real breakthrough in dried pastas is still waiting to happen when short shelf-life unpasteurized pastas arrive.

For so long rice has languished happily without too much attention on the bottom shelves of the aisles. In the last year the modules have been augmented by the arrival of little sachets of flavoured rices – ready, with their dried ingredients, for kedgeree and biryani, often at three times the price of good-quality basmati. More positively, some of the more fashionable stores have begun also to bring in variations of risotto rice and to concentrate on Thai fragrant rice. Equally, the large bags which represent the best value have not lost their listing.

Diet remains the other obsession. The variations of fromage frais and yoghurt, seemingly with ever less and less fat, are breathtaking. **Petit Danone** has targeted children with its **Super Fromage Frais**, claiming that 'more of the vitamins and minerals essential to a child's healthy growth are retained'. **Ski** has got the calorie level down to only 50 per 100 g, with its **Fruit Light** range, virtually fat-free. The improvements in the **St Ivel Shape** range are also said to have boosted the flavour with a higher fruit content and all are now bio.

The ultimate dream of the low-fat double chocolate gateau has apparently been scaled by **McVitie** who have been in expansionist mood, with a 95% fat-free variation and also with low-fat cheesecakes. Doubtless the digestive magnates have been spurred on by the arrival of the neatly long boxes of **Entenmann's** of not just New York but also Miami and Chicago, with a 97% fat-free chocolate fudge brownie.

Aerosol cooking sprays present a mind-boggling new dimension. **Sunbee** claims to use ecologically friendly propellant. Vegetable, soya and even olive oils are available.

Appealing to the same mentality but in a rather different way have been wafer-thin hams and meats. Reputedly these now account for 30% of sales of all cooked meats. The latest arrival from **Safeway** is **Wafer Thin Bacon** slices which can be grilled or microwaved in 2-3 minutes, a snip at 89p per 150g (enough to cover four sandwiches, we are told). In the same vein, there are now wafer-thin turkey slices that look – and are sold like – bacon.

In-store bakery sections are deceptive. **Sainsbury** has moved to centralizing production and just allowing the stores to finish off the breads. **Safeway** seems to be more concerned with getting the smell of freshly baked bread to waft down the aisles.

The bakery products' sense of tradition is not always matched by their respect for the original article. Nevertheless, **Safeway** has been marching forward with the revival of Simnel cake for Easter. **Safeway** actually suffered pretty badly from Easter last year, offering duck and chicken marshmallow shapes, Easter chick doughnuts and – apart from selling hot cross buns six weeks early – was also cooking a variation of Raisin and Treacle hot cross bun. Naan and pittas have become mainline products in many stores.

For all the healthy eating messages, the loyalty of the bakery sections still tends to be largely towards the cream doughnut rather than interesting breads in their own right. Celebration cakes pioneered by **Jane Asher** and **Sainsbury** three years ago have moved up to the mainstream, reflecting the trends of the moment. *Care Bears, Snow White, Power Rangers* – once the province of inspired home cake decorators are now widely available. Grown-ups may prefer the **Marks and Spencer** ranges of French pâtisserie.

Tinned spaghetti variations are the other home of the trend of the moment, with TV personality endorsement. *Gladiators* may be on **Frosties** and *Bay Watch* on **Coco Pops**, but *Thomas the Tank Engine* has signed up with **Heinz** while *Lion King, Sonic the Hedgehog* and *Power Rangers* have gone with **HP**.

What are we to make of all this? Read on…

SHOPS

ASDA

Walking into a large **Asda** is like going back in time. There are innovative ideas, such as its own FM Radio station pumping out Rod Stewart or the clucking machine by the eggs, but the overall vision is of too much space and not much idea of what to do with it. Half the average **Asda** is devoted to hardware. The ideal **Asda** customer is a woman with two children who is planning a long expedition into the wilderness and who needs to stock up on non-perishables and cds. The fact that the big stores tend to be a very long *walk* is good training.

Asda was formed in 1965 out of a small supermarket chain and a dairy group. It grew swiftly into one of the most powerful chains by the late seventies but was badly hit by its move away from good value to value added, a point even accepted in the company report.

Asda excels at stocking the kind of brand names that dominated the '50s and '60s. This is where names like **Vesta**, **Tyne**, **Fray Bentos** and **HP** ended up, a sort of graveyard for empire foods. The thinking behind what is stocked is depressingly old-fashioned – 38 yards of shelving devoted to breakfast cereals compared to two yards of space for flour; ten yards of shelving for margarine spreads against two yards for butters. The organization on the shelves can be pretty mindless, with **Branston Pickle** next to ice-cream and gimmicky novelties like **HP's Power Rangers** pasta shapes and **Sonic the Hedgehog Sausages** lost in the myriad of other tins back on aisle 17.

Fruit and vegetables are mediocre in both choice and quality. Fresh meat is sold with all the finesse of Desperate Dan.

Pasta is mostly own-label, supported by **Buitoni** and **Barilla**; rice is mostly **Tilda** and **Uncle Ben**, with as much space given over to value-added rices as to generic. There is a surprisingly good pulses section and strong showings for old-fashioned things like dried and marrowfat peas. Anonymous hams and cured meats occupy most of the delicatessen.

Cheese is disappointing, ranging from the very gunky, such as the Five Counties Slice, the Pineapple Gateau (which is in fact a cheese) and the self-explanatory Orange Grove, which is also called a cheese. The rest of the selection is pedestrian, except the own-label farmhouse Lancashire, Cheshire, Cheddar and Leicester, innovatively packed in thick greaseproof paper, and admittedly priced at more than the own-label (and usually premium) Shropshire Blue.

The freezer aisles are equally well stocked with the big brands. There seems to be no room for any small producers or any company without a significant marketing budget. Wines are unexpectedly well chosen and show a level of discernment not evident in the food buying. In terms of nutrition, **Asda** increasingly looks bottom of the class.

READY MEALS

The **Asda** ready-meal ranges are better than you might expect or perhaps it is just a flash of modern thinking amid the old-fashioned hangar philosophy. There is own-label fresh pasta, a good range of Indian meals, including packages (like **Tesco**) for single meals of different dishes for one. Balti dishes, chicken masala and rogan gosh make the chill cabinet feel like the local tandoori menu. The range is surprisingly innovative, varying from enchiladas to Yorkshire pudding with chilli con carne. There are practical elements such as egg fried rice and lasagne, matched also by a good range of Quorn variations. Sweets are fashionably old-school, even a bit more dinner party than usual, with Pineapple Upside Down Pudding, Marbled Chocolate Sponge, Raspberry Jam Sponge and Custard.

CO-OP

The **Co-op** is the fifth largest retailer, although in practice it is run by an assortment of different management teams. It has taken a strong ethical stance on eggs, insisting producers label factory-farm eggs as 'intensively produced', albeit it still stocks them at 26p less for half a dozen than for free-range. Its right-to-know policy is absolutely correct and in keeping with its founding principles, but how far it is window dressing and how far real policy is an open question.

The fate of the **Co-op** is depressing. A quick run through the Christmas press releases reveals **Co-op** Prawn cocktail, **Co-op** mini potato waffles, **Co-op** Chocolate Meringue Gateau, **Co-op** Fishburgers. How far this is removed from the original founding zeal of finding honest fresh nutritious whole foods at reasonable prices. Was the vision they had of a better world nothing more than Nut Meringue Gateau? The big stores are a passable imitation of other big supermarkets, but the smaller branches are in disarray.

The **Co-op** was started in 1844 by 28 disaffected workers fed up with adulterated food in the Rochdale area. The first shop, in Toad Lane, is now a museum. Not only was the food fresh, but profits were shared out among members at the end of the year, according to how much people had spent. It still claims to be the largest retailer in the UK, with eight million members, but each region now has separate policies. Beyond its 1,000 plus stores, it also does the biggest milk round, delivering to one-third of homes, and is also the largest undertaker, doing a quarter of all funerals. There are membership forms in each branch, which probably should be used to launch a huge consumer protest.

MARKS AND SPENCER

M&S is probably the only supermarket that has really thought about what the customer wants. It is all own-label, which cuts out the unnecessary fuss about choosing from myriad different packets which are largely the same foods in different guises. Vegetables are sold in different states of convenience: from trimmed; to combined in pairs, say baby sweetcorn and asparagus, or baby cauliflowers with baby broccoli; to shredded in a bag ready to go straight in the microwave. Many of the newer innovations have concentrated on using the microwave to good effect.

In a sense **Marks and Spencer** does not properly qualify to be listed alongside other supermarkets, because its contribution is much smaller in the area of the weekly shop. It is one-day shopping, not stock-up shopping, unless you are very extravagant and have a large freezer. The quality of the shops varies widely. The showpiece Marble Arch store is perhaps a rival for any food shop in Britain, the pioneer of chilled foods and convenience. Other branches lack the same dedication. The problem can be compounded by the commitment to fresh foods, so that when stocks run out the shelves seem even more empty.

The butchery sections of stores that have them are superb examples of presentation, with the styles drawn neatly between English and French and some convenience elements coming in; for example, ready-to-cook Beef Wellington.

Fruit is in first-class condition, always labelled by variety, and at different times of the year there are ready-made-up fruit salads offering six variations on a single day; or picturesque fruit rings in jelly for Christmas.

Baking is also notable in the bigger stores, ranging from Bath buns and teacakes to the simply Yum Yum – an American twisted doughnut. Look also for walnut and stilton rolls or the hazelnut and saffron rolls.

The sandwich range has started to look more pedestrian compared to the brilliance of the **Prêt à Manger** chain, but is still solid and there has been a move to diversify into different breads – say tomato-flavoured, or stuffed pittas. There is usually a better range of fruit drinks to go with them than at most other outlets.

READY MEALS

M&S remains clearly the leader in chilled ready meals, though the ready meals do include: vegetables packed in twos, potatoes sold as Lyonnais, ready-blanched as chips, or even as chips paired with breadcrumbed cod or haddock in one package; potato wedges with cheese and tomato sauce for the microwave; ready-cut vegetables, complete with their sauce ready for the microwave.

There are big ranges of Chinese – not always successful because of the nature of the cuisine – and Indian, which can be first-class because they are more robust. New ranges include Lite dishes and six variations on fruit salads. The whole thesis is energized with new concepts within existing ranges cropping up on a rolling basis. Classics like the salmon ring filled with salmon mousse survive, otherwise the themes change, with a preponderance of chicken and potato variations in all guises. The ready-cooked roast potato with rosemary seems a dubious advance. Some of it is so convenient you can almost flop in to the armchair with jacket potatoes already filled with chilli or ready-made macaroni cheese. Equally there are also some brilliant innovations, like the parsnip and Gruyère bake or aubergine and tomato filo parcels.

There is no shying away from fast-food trends, with hand-held hot sandwiches like bacon and mushroom or, the frustratingly disappointing, microwavable hamburgers.

Some of the ready-to-cook meat dishes are not as good as the fresh meat available where there are butchery counters. Fish has not had the same vision applied as that evident in other areas. Usually it just comes breaded with the ready-cut and -blanched chips. Party snacks are a strength: cheese and garlic bites, mini quiches; mini pizzas; mini Indian bites; mini salmon en croûte; even bacon and sausage rolls and the rather more clever bacon wrapped around processed cheese.

Desserts are another area of excellence, varying from white chocolate torte and egg custard tarts to American fudge cake and the spectacular tarte aux citron in its own box. English sweets tend to the tradition of bread and butter pudding – ordinary and luxury versions – lots of sponge puddings and Bramley apple tart; or, in the cold section, mini fruit tartlets filled with crème pâtissière. Standards fluctuate – especially in terms of choice between stores – but the energy behind it all is invigorating.

SAFEWAY

Of all the big supermarkets, **Safeway** appears to have lost its way. Much of the innovation is superficial. Newer stores are a mish-mash of ideas. The fresh foods, like bakery, delicatessen, butchery, fish, dairy and wine, are wrapped around aisle upon aisle of branded dry goods which more resemble an **Asda** than anywhere else. **Safeway** was the corporate raider of the supermarkets, born out of the vicious price wars of the late seventies, assembled by acquisition of small retail outlets and industrialized food businesses. It appears to have run out of ideas.

Fruit and vegetables are consistently of good quality, with the emphasis towards variety, although the zeal to bring in new varieties of apple, carrot and tomato evident a few years ago seems to have disappeared. In its place there are odd mixes – salad creams in the middle of the lettuces and chocolate bars over the cheeses.

There are good Italian breads from **La Fornaia**, recognitions of other styles like soda and scofa breads, naans and pittas, but the thrust of the bakery is firmly towards rolls, rolls and more rolls – bran, soft, burger, cobble, salad, split, petit pain, soft papless things of questionable value; or lots of cream buns in the ilk of sponges, turnovers, choux buns, profiteroles, Florida orange pie etc.

The delicatessen counter seems the most impressively large of all supermarkets. Big branches offer freshly roast chicken, DIY pizzas, Indian and Chinese takeaways, party services, salads of potato, cheese and pineapple, even a choice of olives, square hunks of cheese and thin slices of cured meat. However, the commitment to any notion of quality is absent and there is little discernment.

The pasta range of branded names like **Buitoni** and **Dolmio** also includes **Bachelors** (with sauce) and **Galliana Blanca** (with sauce), although the own-label has gone on holiday to Italy, with strange shapes like cellentani, pipe rigate, tricolore and fusilli. If rice was once good value in the supermarket, **Safeway** have overseen the introduction of kedgeree at 65p per 100g and biryani at 75p per 100g, compared to **Easycook** at 9.9p per 100g or even Basmati at 21p per 100g.

What **Safeway** is actually good for are things like biscuits and innovation via manufacturers, hence **McVitie Mini Cheddars** flavoured with Marmite; **Jacobs Ritz Hitz**; **Crawford's Allstars**, New York hot-dog flavour, and **Tuc's** barbecue flavour all find their outlet with **Safeway**. The original American company was the first to bring purpose-built supermarkets to Britain in 1963. After promising much, however, it now appears badly in need of some radical re-thinking.

READY MEALS

If **Safeway** has actually understood the idea of convenience and ready meals then they tend to keep it to themselves. It seems stuck in a time-warp of lobbing a gunky bottle of 1000 Additive dressing in among the fresh salad leaves. The delicatessen counter has gone off on a bizarre tack of its own, offering ready party meals or DIY pizzas. **Safeway** has got pizza particularly badly, even offering pizza of the month and a DIY topping service with brick ovens in some stores

The other selections of Indian and Chinese are small and usually found at the back of the store. The meats tend to prefer the idea of poor-quality bread products and other innovations are stuck on quiches and old-fashioned mega pies, steak pies, and beef and onion pie, which are often bizarrely stocked in among the meats. It all looks very old-fashioned and dull.

The boast of its publicity brochure is horribly prophetic: '**Safeway** are always looking to develop our range... we have just launched chicken casserole.' Wow. **Marks and Spencer** will be really worried about that. Or 'the latest exciting addition to **Safeway's** range of traditional puddings for the whole family is Chocolate Chip Pudding'; which tradition is that? To compensate, the delicatessen counters offer salads and ready-meals but the same dead tongue seems to be on the job.

SAINSBURY

The entrance of the newly revamped showpiece **Sainsbury** on Gloucester Road, West London is marked by stands selling ready-roast chicken pieces, a stand of pot noodles ('light') and a pic'n'mix counter for sweets. This says as much about the store as its brilliant advertising. Most of **Sainsbury's** main virtues are on the first aisle – fruit, vegetables, rice, pasta and (in some stores) fish. Beyond this, the aisles are filled with endless variations of seemingly identical foods in different packages and prices. More than other supermarkets **Sainsbury** seems to specialize in selling one example of something very good and one example of something very gunky in the same range. The support and enthusiasms for own-label – even with many variations within one product range – is manifest.

The brilliant advertisements of famous people cooking and the homely values projected in its good value magazine – headed by Delia Smith – need to be read against an equal support for convenience packets and labels where the value is wholeheartedly questionable. As much space is given over to value-added rices in tiny packets as it is to indigenous whole rices. Beyond very good own-label pastas there are smaller showings for **Barilla** and **Buitoni**. Ready meals are way back in the field, though innovation is promised. The delicatessen counter is a poor mish-mash, confusingly selling many of the same foods as are found chilled without any clear indication of which is better or cheaper. The bulk of the choice is illusion: more than 20 Cheddars; more than 50 variations on low-fat yoghurt; yards of bacon, where price bears little relation to quality. Commitments to dry-cure and some free-range are there, although they appear to be rather tentative.

Through the veal outcry **Sainsbury** was bravely sticking to its stand of selling English veal raised outdoors. In other fresh meats the extra-matured ranges tend to be worth the extra money in terms of flavour. The showpiece stores have good fish counters, the one at Gloucester Road being especially notable. Other stores are content with frozen.

Typical of the schizophrenia is the Special Selection trialed in 11 major stores and now rolled out to more than 200 stores. This is a shop within a shop, a bijou collection of designer foods that range from hand-made chocolates by **Melchior** and **Sarah Jayne's Venus Nipples**, preserves of raspberry, banana, apricot and almond, AA-grade Kenya coffee, Gunpowder Green Tea, Formosa Oolong, single packets of spices including the rare black-roasted sesame; interesting diversions of quality virgin olive oils to gimmicky oils and vinegars with herbs. In some shops there is also a cook shop. It is at once astounding and atypical of what **Sainsbury** really stands for. This should be the future, but there is a nagging doubt that it will ultimately be dismissed as a minor event. The jury is out.

Sainsbury is the oldest of the supermarkets, originating out of a north London dairy in the 1860s and is perhaps the longest in the tooth too. It has consistently pursued a policy of own-label since then and has remained a family-owned and -run business. It excels at French products, notably wine, dairy and even sometimes bread – stotty cakes being sold as a speciality line in South Kensington will bring a wry smile to Geordie readers. The new bake-off plant has been very successful in speciality areas such as chollah and scofa, but less so in main lines, though the brown loaf made with 60% wholemeal flour is an honest triumph.

Fruit and vegetables are extensive, if not always in as good nick as they might be. It is proud of its integrated crop management, for example introducing wasps (*Encarsia formosa*) to tomato greenhouses (the wasps lay their eggs in the eggs of the pest whitefly), where previously pesticides were used. These pesticides also killed the bees and pollination had to be done artificially. With the introduction of the wasps, the bees happily pollinate again.

Some of the modern stores, notably at Camden Town and at Plymouth are also brilliant attempts to break the mould of box-like superstore architecture.

Against this there is a certain matter-of-fact cynicism – the same potatoes sold as baking at a premium, the lettuce with the least amount of vitamin C being sold as 'high in vitamin C', own-label corn flakes sold as 'Low in Fat' when the difference with Kellogg's is 0.1%. Its new range of baby foods happily accepts the principle that babies can be brought up on maltodextrin – a sugar derivative used to deliver additives in grown-up foods.

What it seems to lack is any discernment or philosophy behind why it stocks some foods and not others.

READY MEALS
Despite John Cleese's superb advertisements for **Sainsbury's** convenience foods, the ready-meals section lags some way behind the other supermarkets. The choice is uninventive and clearly aimed at the comfort sector. That said there are promises of improvement, with new Italian ranges and others. Vegetarian meals concentrate on the kind of dishes that are oh-so-easily put together, with ingredients found elsewhere in the store: broccoli mornay, cauliflower cheese, vegetarian lasagne. Or else the unbelievably inept, like corned beef hash or roast potatoes with garlic butter and rosemary. The Indian range is exempt from criticism, and probably the market leader. There is a pervading sense of old-fashionedness about the range of meat pies and pasties. The desserts positively flaunt the idea of olde Englande – apple and rhubarb crumbles, jam roly-poly, deep-filled apple pie, jam sponge pudding and chocolate fudge pudding.

SOMERFIELD
This is the new look for what used to be the **Gateway** chain. The move across is fundamental not cosmetic. Where **Gateway** dealt mostly in cheap lesser brands that could not find a home anywhere else, **Somerfield** has improved the fresh foods, brought in some surprisingly good own-label, kept up much of the value and been a breath of fresh air for many small towns. It is hard to argue with clementines being sold for 10p per lb the week after Christmas.

The stores tend to be smaller than those of rivals and usually centred in town rather than out of it. In the last edition I said the stores had taken on much of the character of small **Safeways** and that still holds good. Indeed, **Safeway** could learn quite a few lessons from what **Somerfield** is doing.

Few of the ranges could claim to be market leaders, but they are usually good-value middle-of-the-road. The meat buying is often surprisingly shrewd. There is limited space for chill counters but the range of branded dried goods is no worse than at **Asda**. Quite why they want to sell yards of brown sauce is unclear, but the special offers of two for the price of one have brought back some fun to shopping.

TESCO

Tesco is looking the most dynamic of all the supermarkets and the one most in control of its own destiny. It offers the most genuine choice of all the big stores, without being too flashy about it. Around half the lines are own-label, with all the price benefits that brings. Equally, however, there is a sense of selection about the brands it stocks to give real variety, although some of the range of this choice is obscured.

The newer stores tend to be laid out almost as stores within stores, so pasta or ready-meals can appear in two or three different places. The freezer cabinets are improved versions of horizontal chill cabinets so the frozen foods look as interesting.

The new generation of **Tesco Metro** stores, mostly in London and big regional cities, are starting to look like the first real competition **Marks and Spencer** has had. They are also a fitting riposte to the charge of out-of-town stores destroying inner cities. The choice is scaled down and aimed at one or two night's shopping. **Justin de Blank's** new range of sandwiches is the equal of the independent **Prêt à Manger** chain, but was a short-lived innovation. There are fresh fruit and vegetables and ample space given over to ready-meals, freshly baked items, and wine; with less room given to traditional grocery areas and non-foods. The effect is a 'greatest hits' repertoire culled from the bigger stores.

Out-of-town in the new bigger stores there are welcome breakthroughs in terms of convenience – some of the best sampling pick-and-mix sections, not just for cheese, but also pâté and chocolate. As with **Marks and Spencer**, the move has been to offer carrots whole, shredded, washed in batons, in microwavable packets combined with swede, or with courgettes and garlic butter.

The deli counter now includes genuinely rare and exceptional cheeses, such as **Quicke's Cheddar** or Manchego, and tubs of clotted cream. The bakery has got out of the rut of thinking the only difference between breads is their size. The French section includes ficelles, baguette, pain de campagne and Grande Rustique. Equally, there are naans and pittas and pizza bases. Traditions like crumpets – even square ones – muffins, pancakes and potato cakes have been brought back to prominence.

The own-label pastas from Italy are notably good, though as with rice, the selection is not vast. The fruit and vegetables are mainline and good quality, though some of the enthusiasm for exotics and unusual varieties seems to have waned. Fish is smaller than **Waitrose** and less adventurous, but typically sensible and mainline. The new initiative on meat last year has improved quality considerably for pork, lamb and beef. All this is done in tandem with the razzmatazz of 4% fat oven-ready chips and the Christmas Double Cream with Cointreau or Thomas the Tank Engine Baked Beans or more variations on pizza than seems possible.

Tesco seems more thorough than some competitors – its bread flours for example have sufficient protein in them to bake a sound loaf. It's major ethical stances on healthy eating and a positive approach to the environment are not without some commitment. Improvements are introduced across the board and not just lobbed in as extra-high-premium earners. Amazingly, the Swindon branch has been selling Sevruga caviar at £11.99 an ounce.

READY MEALS

Many **Tesco** stores spread their ready-meals across the aisles. They have followed the **Covent Garden Soup Company** with their own and excellent range of new soups. Otherwise there is a huge choice in different styles, be it frozen or chilled. The main themes are English, such as Family Chicken Pie, Teviot Pie and, similarly in desserts, Spotted Dick and Bread and Butter Pudding. The desserts tend to be more dinner-party: Pineapple Upside Down or Apple Amber or the Danish range, such as Woodland Fruit Strudel.

There is no shying away from innovation, especially with the microwave: for example, egg and bacon muffins (pretty stodgy) or **Mighty White Pizza** slices or **McCain Pizza Rollas**.

Pizza is an obsession and reappears in different parts of the store. On one aisle there may be **Chicago Town**, **GoodFellas**, **Pizza Feast**, **San Marco**, and two variations of **Tesco** own-label, Thin and Crispy or Deep and Crispy. Three aisles later a whole section might be given over to other **Tesco** pizzas. Thai dishes have begun to appear on the chilled meals and there is also a good Indian range.

WAITROSE

The smallest and most quality conscious of the big five. The bigger stores have wide aisles and a sense of trying to create a less frantic atmosphere. There have been innovations towards convenience, with chickens roasted in store, and a few good cheeses on the deli counters. Of all the supermarkets, the branded goods seem to be chosen with some discernment. There is a cohesive sense of philosophy about the whole package that is welcomingly reassuring; not so much of the jungle of the down-market pile-it-high shops, rather an orderly garden. Even the recipe leaflets are rather elegant.

Probably the best supermarket for fish, in meat it has been selling whole sirloins and loins of pigs. Fruit and vegetables are high-quality and varied; it is certainly the best supermarket for exotic fruit. The bakery is probably the most interesting of all the supermarkets, barring only a top-line **Marks and Spencer**, and the quality of the branded goods is high. There is a sense of innovation – a flower delivery service and salad bars, for instance.

The pricing policy is bizarre and unnerving. Where the other supermarkets mark up consistently, **Waitrose** can sell Valencia oranges for three different prices on the same day; baked and ordinary Estima potatoes for 85p in the bag for 750g or loose at 16p for 454g. Bacon prices seem completely arbitrary and illogical. Fresh herbs are sold at a single price with the adjustment made by adding or subtracting a few leaves here or there, though why there should be any difference at all is not that clear. All of which can make the bill something of a surprise.

It has a reputation for being expensive. However, the chain claims to sell 150 basic lines as cheap as anywhere else. The problem is that there is more temptation to buy them in other stores.

READY MEALS

Waitrose are more sensitive to trends and fashions. Thai meals lead the innovation – green chicken curry, coconut rice, beef rendang with rice, chicken satay – matched with forays into safe Japanese areas like teriyaki and Singapore for noodles.

The traditional lines include ready-to-cook lamb casserole – which still takes an hour's cooking – or a stab at the ultimate populism of Chicken Tikka Lasagne or **McVitie's** Low Fat Double Chocolate Gateau, which claims to be 95% fat-free.

As with **Sainsbury**, there seems to be a lingering distaste for too much convenience when all the ingredients are there for cooking. Even the Raymond Blanc endorsement centres on recipes to make use of own-label and well-chosen branded goods in store.

On the other hand, **Waitrose** has been happy to leap on the luxury dip bandwagon, with perhaps the wackiest assortment of all an all-singing pack that includes tropical mango and lime, Caribbean pineapple and coconut; smoked salmon and dill, and tuna and sun-dried tomatoes.

FOODS OF THE YEAR

Inevitably, in putting together a book like this there are new discoveries and innovations that stand out. Here are my personal plaudits for foods that have come to light since the last edition:

Marfone potatoes – brilliant for mashing
Domaine do Souvio olive oil – a superb Provence oil
Red basil – sold in the pot, beautifully aromatic and decorative
Loseley's Gin & Tonic ice-cream – a great gimmick done with élan
Sainsbury's Special Selection – a brilliant initiative into quality
Baby Organix – for revitalizing the baby food market
Tesco's square crumpets – well, they don't have to be round
The Fresh Olive Company of Provence's balsamic vinegar – for finding an inexpensive but genuine example in a discredited market
Mrs Kirkham's Lancashire Cheese – Supreme Champion at the British Cheese Awards in 1995
Waitrose breads – reasonable quality at mass-market prices

I would also like to credit three shops that have set and maintained standards: the Food Halls at **Harrods** and at **Harvey Nichols**, both in Knightsbridge; **Carluccio's** in Neal Street for an inspired version of all things Italian; **Neal's Yard**, custodian of Artisanal UK cheeses; **Bakers & Spice** in Walton Street for demonstrating what bread should be like; and **E & F** on Frith Street for consistently questioning the whole idea of what a food shop should be, with weird and wonderful examples from another cuisine.

Throughout the book, foods marked with ** are defining examples of the best of their kind; those marked * offer particularly good value or interest in their sector.

NAFF FOOD OF THE YEAR

This could have been quite a long list, but ultimately what could be more naff than:

Old Fashioned Foods microwavable **Squeeze Cheese**, declaring itself as 'mature Cheddar' and 'real' from Maryville USA. It is actually as much Cheshire cheese, anyway.

SHOPPING BY POST

Mail-order shopping for food has been well established in America for many years. Here a number of small companies have started to sell direct, mostly expanding their ranges from around one or two mainline specialities. The best have access to individual products that are hard to find. Hampers, as a rule, tend to be highly marked up.

GROCERS DIRECT

Chocolate Society tel 01423 322230
Not just **Valrhona** chocolates but also a good covering of other French larder products. The emphasis is on quality rather than price – oils, champagne vinegars, olives, saffron, fleur du sel from the Guerande, **Wynad** black pepper; also fruit purées and extracts. Membership is not compulsory.

Conservas Rainha Santa (Portuguese foods) tel 0171 737 4101
Importers with a shop at Spitalfields market selling a good range of hams, chorizos, stuffed olives, Elvas plums, quince curd cheese and unpasteurized ewes'- and goats'-milk cheeses.

Fresh Food Company tel 0181 969 0351
Dedicated mail-order specialist with two main lines: deliveries of fresh boxes of excellent quality fish direct from Cornwall overnight and a newer service providing a box of organic foods, fruit and vegetables delivered on a weekly basis. At Christmas there are free-range bronze turkeys and both free-range and organic geese.

James & John Graham tel 01768 62281
Old-fashioned purveyors of fine foods and wines, with shops in Carlisle and Kendal. Notably suppliers of good northern cheeses; home-cured hams and bacon; good olive oils and vinegars; **Valrhona** chocolate and endless jams and preserves.

Jeroboams tel 0171 727 9792
Superlative specialist cheeses sent out in collections of four. Also wines, hams, pâtés, **Couderec** foie gras and **Caviar House** caviar.

Morel Bros, Cobbett & Son tel 0171 384 3345
Superb brochure for a company that pretends to have a history but is, in reality, a new concept. The range is small but excellent. Caviar, foie gras in tins, **Oil Merchant** olive oils, **Beaufor** vinegars and mustards, a range of five Portuguese olives from the Elvas region, dried mushrooms,

Connetable sardines, a sensational range of 10 unusual peppers, **Savoy** coffees and **Weiss** chocolates.

The Olive Grove, Bristol tel 01275 332671.
A short specialist list includes **Edmond Fallot's** wine vinegars and mustards; single estate Umbrian olive oils; **Nyonsiad** virgin oil from Provence; and nut and seed oils.

Rosslyn Too tel 071 794 9210
The popular Hampstead, London, delicatessen also does foods by post. Much of it is own-label, with strong ranges in teas, preserves, oils and spices. Look also for the range of 16 different honeys, the American selection and good names like **Innes** for breads, **Bizac** for tinned foie gras, **Connetable** for tinned fish, and **Mezzetta** from California for hot peppers and salsas.

A-Z OF MAIL-ORDER SUPPLIERS

ARBROATH SMOKIES:
R. R. Spink & Sons tel 01241 72023. From one of the original family firms.

BLACK PUDDING:
Morris's tel 01204 71763. Award winning sausages.

CHEESE:
Neal's Yard tel 0171 379 7646. Specialists in traditional UK cheeses.
Wells Stores tel 01235 535978. Good English cheeses both new and traditional and imports from France weekly.
   (See also Jeroboams listed on previous page.)

CHOCOLATES:
Chocolate Society tel 01423 322230 (see previous page).
Melchior tel 01769 540643. Hand-made liqueur chocolates.
The Nuns of Daventry tel 01327 702569. Contemplative order made famous when John Gummer ordered the slaughter of their chicken flock and who have since turned to chocolates instead.
Sara Jayne tel 0181 874 8500. Hand-made truffles with voluptuous fillings.

CLOTTED CREAM:
A. & M. Piggott tel 01579 370270.

CRAYFISH:

Whistley Crayfish tel 01747 840666. The American Signal crayfish is farmed in ponds and dispatched overnight by courier.

DUCKS:

Hereford Duck Company tel 0198 121 767. Specialist breeders of the Trelough duck, a variation bred from the Rouen and kept outside in water pens.

GEESE:

G. B. Geese tel 01476 870394. Grass-fed and hung 10 days, available from Michaelmas.

Holly Tree Farm tel 01565 651835. Specialist duck and geese farm. The birds are kept outdoors.

Pipers Farm tel 01392 881380. Reared in orchards and dry-plucked. Also free-range bronze turkeys.

Seldom Seen Farm tel 0153755 742. Free-range geese hung 10 days, available from Michaelmas.

HAGGIS:

Macsween tel 0131 229 1216 Legendary Edinburgh butcher will mail-order Scotland's most famous meat product.

HAMS:

Abberley Farm tel 01299 896704. Wild boar to order.

Ashdown Smokers tel 01229 718324. Traditional smokers, also do the unusual lamb 'ham' Herdwick Macon (see page 156).

Country Victualler tel 01636 86465. Alderton hams.

Denhay Farm tel 01308 22770 Cheddar and pig farm, selling its own produce, notably air-dried hams.

Emmett's tel 017287 9250. Suffolk hams.

Heal Farm tel 01769 574341. Hams and sausages from rare breeds and also other small Devon products.

Richard Woodall tel 01229 717237. Famous for Cumberland sausages and air-dried hams.

Sutherlands tel 01794 68158. Farm a Wild Blue pig, a cross between a boar and a Hampen Blue gilt. Good sausages.

HERBS:

Cheshire Herbs tel 01829 760578. More than 200 varieties.

The Herbary Prickwillow tel 01353 88456. Mostly organic, posted freshly cut. Also edible flowers.

Iden Croft tel 01580 891432. Has specialist variations of mint. Also edible flowers.

Sawyers tel 01787 228498. Specialists in unusual varieties.
Sellet Hall tel 015242 71865. Plants only.

HONEY:
Struan Apiaries tel 01349 61427. Only supplier of monoculture honey, including raspberry, clover and, more predictably, variations of heather.

KIPPERS:
Cley Smokehouse tel 01263 740282. Norfolk kippers, also bloaters.
George Devereau tel 01624 673257. Isle of Man kippers.
Robson & Sons tel 01665 576223. Craster kippers smoked in same kiln since 1865.
Swallow Fish tel 01665 721052. **Seahouses** kippers lightly smoked over oak.
Summer Isles tel 0185 482 353. Northerly Scottish smokery runs a kipper club. Also smoked eel.

ORGANIC MEATS
Craig Farm tel 01597 851655. Includes rare sources of mutton and goat. Also tuna and groupers from St Helena.
Home Farm, Nanpantan tel 01509 23922. Hereford beef and Dorset Down lamb.
Eastbrook Farm, Freepost SN12, Swindon tel 01793 790460 Good sausages, hams and also smoked products.
Leigh Farm tel 0171 377 8909/ 0171 375 1554. Devon farm with London butchers in Commercial Road, keeps mainly rare breeds of pig, Poll Dorset, Portland and Jacob sheep and Aberdeen Angus and Hereford beef. Some Norfolk black turkeys.
Longwood Farm tel 01638 717120. Wide range of unspecified (but guaranteed organic) meats, also various cheeses. Free delivery on orders over £150.
Meat Matters tel 0181 442 0658. Nearly all the meat from this specialist butchery is from Soil Association-approved farms. The lamb is Downland; the pork English Saddlebacks. There is also a range of ready-prepared dishes. Sampler packs from just under £30.
Pipers Farm tel 01392 881380. Sells meat only from small family farms with high welfare values, mostly in Devon. The preference is for old-fashioned breeds but modern butchery tricks of ready-stuffed meats. The beef is Red Devon hung for four weeks. Introductory packs from £40. Delivery £10.
Mrs Potters Perfect Pork tel 01603 611156. Free-range Gloucester Old Spot, 'no farrowing pens, no teeth clipping, no tail cutting, early weaning or castration'.
Real Meat Express tel 01985 840436. Campaigning supplier of

hormone-free, humanely reared meats. Quality, purity and welfare are the company's watchwords. There are nearly 50 affiliated shops, but also a delivery service.

Swaddles Green Farm tel 01460 234387. A complete range of organic meats raised near Chard in Somerset, as well as pies and ready-prepared dishes. Their chickens won the Soil Association Organic Food Award in 1995. Orders over £80 delivered free.

Oysters:
Abbotsbury, Weymouth tel 01305 788 867.
Butley Orford Oysterage tel 01394 450277. Mostly Pacifics from east Anglian beds.
Carew Osyters tel 01646 651452. Pacific oysters farmed 20 miles inland so they tend to be less salty. The bay is also a naturist sanctuary.
Company Shed tel 01206 382700.
Cuan Sea Fisheries, County Down tel 01238 541 461.
Loch Fyne Smokehouse tel 014996 217. Very good Pacifics taken from the rich waters of the loch.
Rossmore, County Cork tel 0101 353 21 883248. London delivery. Also have developed an oyster cracker to open oysters.
Seasalter, Whitstable tel 01227 272003. Revival of historical industry very near the site at Reculver where the Roman industry was centred. Pacifics, also supplier of spat.

Potted shrimp:
James Baxter tel 01524 410 910. Morecambe Bay originals.

Seaweed:
Clokies tel 0186287 272. Collected from Inverness to Sky and dried for reconstituting. Also easily available in Japanese shops.

Smoked eel:
Brown and Forrest tel 01458 251520. Gathered from around the country, frozen and then hot-smoked over beech.
Teviot Game Fare tel 01835 5253. Taken from the Tweed.
Inverawe Smokehouse 01866 2446. Taken from Loch Awe.

Smoked mackerel:
Cornish Smoked Fish Company tel 016726 72356.
Salcombe Smokers tel 01548 852006.
Seasalter tel 01227 272003.

Smoked salmon:
Forman tel 0181 985 0378

Ghillie & Glen tel 01467 625 700
Inverawe tel 01866 822446
Joseph Johnson tel 01674 672666
Loch Fyne tel 01499 600264
Minola tel 01367 860391
Pinney's tel 01576 300777
Robson & Sons tel 01665 576223
Salmon & Seafood Ltd tel 00353 9521278
Strathaird tel 01463 715123

SNAILS:
L'Escargot Anglais tel 01432 760218. The smaller *petit gris*, *Helix aspera*.
French's tel 01458 252246. Reared outdoors in polytunnels.

VENISON:
Holme House Farm tel 015396 24618. Cumbrian farm specializing in red deer. Does its own butchery.

WHOLEFOODS:
Alara Wholefoods tel 0171 387 9303. Wholesale supplier of all ranges of wholefoods. Will take orders over £100.

FOR WHAT WE ARE ABOUT TO RECEIVE

The era of the street market has passed. With them has gone the only real opportunity for small or seed food producers to establish their businesses. There are also serious doubts as to the future of wholesale markets like Nine Elms and Billingsgate.

Some people may still romantically hold to the notion that the countryside is full of old ladies making jam or cheese or curing their own bacon; but for the most part that is really a fiction. The food industry is dominated by a handful of conglomerates who enjoy a special relationship with the bit supermarkets, mainly just because of their size. What we eat in the next decade may well be decided by less than a dozen men.

The only realistic competition to this monopoly comes from what is perhaps a surprising quarter – the dynamic growth of eating out. In some cities planners have already written off corner shops and food manufacturing in favour of theme restaurants. Brewers rush to convert pubs to brasseries. Already people like Terence Conran, Anthony Worrall-Thompson, Rick Stein and Antonio Carluccio have tacked food shops on to their restaurants. More mainstream, a chain like **Prêt à Manger** has used retaurant values to compete directly with the likes of **Boots**, **M&S** and **BHS** in sandwiches.

Amid all this change there are questions that have not been asked.

The debate has become hysterical. Witness the political ineptitude over fishing rights, over the EU agricultural policy, over BSE. Witness the consumer campaigns against infant formula milks or transporting animals huge distances in cramped lorries. Witness the rise of anorexia among children or the lingering obesity. Witness the jolly chefs on TV, Ryan Giggs advertising Quorn burgers. Witness the hysterical response to out-of-town supermarkets thirty years too late. The whole food discussion has become a rather bizarre pantomime.

There is a need for change, and a change in philosophy, and a new idea of where food fits in our society. And one thing is certain, that there will be change. There already is. The danger is that the more important social issues will not be on the agenda. The furtive self-interested nature of the food industry will win out again and nothing will happen. Yet the outcome of these changes must fundamentally influence the quality of life in the UK into the new millennium.

When I began writing this series of books – this is now the third, and a fourth reference volume is planned – I wanted to keep a reporter's distance from the issues. I wanted to be free to put both sides of the arguments. And invariably in food there seemed to be two sides, if not three, to every issue. In pulling together all the different strands of history and research that have gone into compiling this edition, the contradictions in food and how we see what we eat have become stark.

On the one hand, you might argue that we have never had such a spectacular array of foods to choose from in this country. Supermarkets bring foods from around the planet and deliver them inexpensively to a depot near you. Wonderful. On the other hand, if you were to conduct a MORI poll on the kind of foods that most people would deem to be good foods – foods that were beneficial socially, that were nutritionally sound, that have flavour – then you might find that it is very much these kind of foods that are in retreat as Europe industrializes its food economy. You might also argue that much of the abundance that we are offered is cynically superficial. That huge investments have been made in cheap addictive junk foods that demean not just the quality of our diet, but also the quality of the way we live in terms of the jobs in those industries and their contribution to the community and their role in the diet.

Of course, commercial market places are always messy places that never fully conform to the aspirations anyone might have for them. The difference with food is that it is not in anyone's interest for it to be a mess.

Whether we are consumers, producers or retailers, there are huge gains for all of us to be made in terms of the quality of life and the economy in having clear goals for where and how this labyrinthine industry should best sit amongst us. The issues are often poorly understood. I want to try to bring some focus to bear on them.

The Right to Know

There is – or there should be – a basic right for all of us to know what we are eating – what goes into it, why it is added and what it does to the food and us. Unless we as consumers are prepared to settle down for an afternoon a week surrounded by heaps of textbooks, it is becoming increasingly difficult to have any idea of what is done in our name. E numbers are a horrible fudged compromise and scientific jargon adds another layer of mistrust. How many people could say, without looking it up in the appendix of this book, what lecithin is? And most of us have eaten it almost daily for a generation.

Few of us can know what we eat. This is wrong and it needs righting. Freedom of choice demands that consumers have proper access to untampered-with information. It is this right that needs to be re-asserted. And that is one reason I wrote this book. There is a simple way to enforce this consumer right. Food makers are expected in law now to show that they have been duly diligent in ensuring their foods are safe to eat. The same principle should equally apply to a manufacturer making due effort to explain what they are selling. A gourmet might be expected to know the difference styles of caviar, but why should a young mother be expected to know the implications of maltodextrin in her baby food or any of the rest of us be aware of the negative implications of hydrogenation?

The language of food is, of course, corrupt. Different foods claim all manner of virtues. Advertising portrays foods as sorts of super quasi drugs. Never mind the acid or the ecstasy, look what these wot-sits can do. These can turn your hair orange, those little tubs can get you dancing on the kitchen table.

M&M's 'trip your trigger' and will turn you into a basketball star. 'The only chicken worth eating is a **Birds Eye**.' 'Turn to **McCain** to fill them'.

Forgive my sense of humour failure but this is just yobbism. These are messages that are the direct opposite of what anyone ought to be allowed to claim for foods. If they were not such nonsense they might be legislated against. They provide no real information on which the consumer might make a rational choice. The weight of this propaganda simply destabilizes the whole argument about what is good food.

Behind the mask of this fiction there are serious issues. But even legislators have become befuddled. The good intentions of labelling both ingredients and nutritional values have at best produced results that are incomprehensible and at worst have been deliberately subverted. Ingredients because no one knows what E312 stands for; nutrition because, as the tables in this book show clearly, the issue is fudged.

As consumers we are perpetually bombarded with ideas that we know to be fundamentally unsound – that we crave fat; that if we eat chocolate we will feel sexy; that sugar is not a carbohydrate; that Cheddar is Cheshire; that night is day. All of this you might be tempted to think is a part of a dynamic and entertaining market.

Is the Customer Always Right?

From a simplistic consumer perspective, provided you live near one of the more enterprising supermarkets there is plenty of choice and opportunity for a varied diet. However, the consumer perspective is flawed when it comes to food. Because food is an essential component of the way we live, and unlike cars or washing machines, it is not practicable to disassociate oneself from the wider implications either in terms of the effects of diet on the economy or the quality of life. We are not just consumers. We also live amongst and are dependent on this mess we call the food industry.

Then there is the question of what the customer wants. Who actually wants a choice of 15 margarines? Did housewives in Huddersfield actually go out and ask for it? Of course not.

The cynical view is that supermarkets are no longer food businesses. They are simply financial operations that buy in on x days credit and sell for cash. Their stocking policies then just become a matter of choice for choice's sake. So long as the shelves are full, what does it matter what they are full of? Of course, I would argue that it does matter. Retailers, however, keep a commercial distance from the issues. This allows them to pursue fruitless policies of setting up own-label brands to prevent competition from small businesses; cynically to espouse good causes – currently apple varieties – when it was, in practice, the supermarkets that caused the orchards to be grubbed up in the first place; and not to commission small or fledgling business.

It is interesting to wonder why supermarkets do not employ subject experts. There are, of course, a few token consultancies, but there is, unfortunately, nothing in areas like bread or fruit or fish equivalent to a master of wine, many of whom have been employed by supermarkets to assist in their wine buying and the resulting move to a greater understanding of wine has galvanized the market. My point is that there is no visible investment in the knowledge base, nor in the industry is there any appreciable investment in research and development compared to, say, pharmaceuticals, except at the very extremes of plant varieties... and this is the biggest industry in this country. The result is that the only genuine technological breakthrough of recent years has been the **Mars Bar** ice-cream and subsequent variations.

The Impact of Shopping

Somewhat belatedly, the Department of the Environment has recognized that building massive out-of-town supermarkets may have a detrimental effect on the inner cities and town centres. This argument was well thrashed out in the '30s in the USA, where small traders even managed to get referenda held on the issue. In France, where the construction of the food economy is completely different from that here, there has been a moratorium on out-of-town building.

The irony in a democratic society is that many such small traders were also the same local councillors who fought against the big retailers coming to their towns and who also failed to see the potential impact of lack of parking. From the customer's point of view, one-stop, once-a-week shopping is a great asset, saving time and petrol. The sheer size of modern large supermarkets has also brought the cost of the weekly shop down. Already the new facades of the **Tesco Metros**, **Marks & Spencers** and probably also the smaller **Somerfields** taking over inner-city sites could bring many of these benefits back into the towns. That will then raise serious questions for the future of any corner shop that cannot compete on quality or price.

There is a real proposition that supermarkets will soon be able to offer a complete service, from postage stamps through to credit and financial services. **Asda** in Bristol holds 'Singles Nights'. The most important development, in food terms at least, is **Sainsbury's** introduction of its Special Selection of high-quality larder items – many of which might have been culled from the first edition of this book. Whether this is just a marketing ploy, or a genuine attempt to allow small producers into supermarkets, remains to be seen. If a supermarket goes for quality in that way, what is left for the independent?

The issue that has finally managed to percolate its way through to one side of Government (Environment) has still to find an answer on the other side (Agriculture, or what ought really to be called 'Food').

And government has looked increasingly stupid as all these changes have unfolded. Who, one wonders, defined the strategy for a positive food economy? Brussels or MAFF?

The Ministry of Agriculture revealed its position when questioned by Channel 4's *Despatches* over why trans-fatty acids in the diet are not being labelled. The answer was that it was no longer its responsibility, but an EU responsibility. Agriculture has become an EU issue, as the decommissioning of fishing boats, the giving over of the high seas to Spanish boats and countless other examples show.

The complexity of the grant structure is such that consultants who can find their way through the systems are becoming an industry in themselves. Why should Hull get grants but not London? Why Wales but not Hereford? Why farmers but not fishermen? Why wine and not apple juice? I am not arguing against the idea of grants. I am arguing that without a cohesive strategy on food where it fits into our society, public money is being spent without accountability.

In the late 20th century there is arguably no need to have a Ministry of Agriculture – it might as well be incorporated with trade. The need is for a ministry that can use food as an agent of social advantage, that can rescue inner city areas from blight, that can regenerate the countryside, that can use diet to promote the welfare of the country's health.

BLUEPRINTS FOR DISEASE

The Government's own COMA report on Nutritional Aspects of Cardiovascular Disease illustrates just how deep the schism is between what the medical world knows about interaction of diet and health and what most of the food industry in this country is producing.

We know now, as increasing surveys prove the point time and again, that the era of the British diet that relied on wheat, fat and sugar has created serious social diseases from obesity to heart problems. A twelve-year study of 11,000 adults in this country by the Department of Public Health at the London School of Hygiene and Tropical Medicine revealed that people eating a non-meat diet might be 40% less likely to contract cancer. Research at Harvard into trans-fatty acids, which are one product of hydrogenation of oils to make them more malleable in the production of things like biscuits, cakes and spreads, may also be the time-bomb that triggers many diseases – making mother's breast milk run so thin they cannot breast-feed or, even worse, laying down hereditary blueprints for disease in later life.

The overall science points clearly to the idea that many of the foods we produce in this country are contributing to our ill-health. This is not idle speculation. You only have to go to Middle America to see the full impact an industrialized food economy can have on a population. It is called obesity.

Demonstrably, the food industry at large does not work in the national interest – there is a huge import/export imbalance; many of the practices of different industries are concealed for good reason, the quality of our diet lags way behind what it could be, the quality of jobs in food industries is often menial and lowly paid, whole communities have been undermined by short-term policies, the countryside is being abandoned, we have very little viable food culture to export to other parts of the globe who have their own very real needs.

The pollution of the environment has been well publicized. It makes depressing reading to learn the practical details of how brown trout are nearly wiped out, native crayfish extinct, how bans on wild salmon are imminent, how the North Sea is in danger of becoming a dead sea capable only of supporting amoebae. There is also the question of the unmitigated fumigation of the land by pesticides and how that may impact on the diet. And what of the mass-production techniques which have brought into focus the risk of salmonella in chickens and BSE in cattle? Already we have to pasteurize almost all milk to make it safe. What do we think we are doing?

RECALCITRANT TENDENCIES

To provide a sense of perspective, let me offer a visual image of what we might generally agree to be good food. Much of the answer can be found along the first aisle of most major supermarkets – fresh fruit, fresh vegetables, pasta, rice, fresh fish, good quality bread. It is the other 16 to 26 aisles that pose the problem. Quality has become the issue.

For all the positive signs of change, one is equally conscious of the back-sliding. One might have thought that breaded-and-crumbed products were a thing of the past, consigned to oblivion by the move away from fried foods, with poor-quality coatings and depending on cruel farming methods. Their revival is surprising, yet even **Marks & Spencer** has been majoring its fish range on bread coatings, often matched with chips. Turkey products have been more innovative in a pop way, with Flintstones turkey shapes, some clever innovation also in the vegetarian areas from **Bernard Matthews**, and also using turkey and cheese in fast-food variations of *wiener schnitzel*.

FOOD SAFETY

For the first time last year there were more complaints to Trading Standards Offices about food than about second-hand cars. At the same time there were nearly 80,000 cases of food poisoning reported for the year ended 1994, the highest since records began. Fast-food and outside catering were the biggest culprits.

Gosh how dreadful. Consider for a moment: given that only a percentage of the population are buying second-hand cars at any given time, but everyone is eating food three times a day, the surprise is perhaps that there are not more cases of food poisoning, not less. If anything, the short-term danger of an upset stomach for one in 800 is being overshadowed by the long-term implications of consistently eating a junk-food diet over many years. It seems to me that in a nation of 55 million people it is unlikely that we would have sufficient conformity of physiology ever to hope to get the figure down any lower for food poisoning. Safety is just the headline issue. In truth it is a symptom and the real issue is diet. In an era where most of us expect now to live into our 70s and 80s and longer, however, the accumulated effects of diet-related diseases in later years is far more significant and asks much deeper questions about our society and how we want to live.

CHEAP FOOD?

We are told that we are seeing a price war. Surveys tend to show that the differences between shopping in one supermarket as against another could amount to around 5-10%. The discounter **Netto** is said to be the cheapest, followed by **Kwik Save**. Rationalizing prices across different shopping baskets is highly complex. Even a survey for *Which?* calculated the price of Cheddar at £2.22 when, in reality, on the day of publication most supermarkets were selling it for less than £1.50. These surveys don't reflect the true picture of everyday shopping. They tend to be accurate for people who only buy branded goods like **McVitie's Digestives**, **Kit Kat** and **Coca Cola** and are widely off beam with the more healthy items like fresh fruit and vegetables, pasta or rice, where market forces tend to offend the statistician's sense of control. It is quite possible – as even **Safeway** has conceded in its advertising – with an idea that could easily have been taken from the first edition of this book – to buy exactly the same foods in the same store for almost half the price, often without any real difference in quality. Ask perhaps not why one is so cheap, but why the other is so expensive?

The other factor in comparing supermarkets with discounters is that the big supermarkets offer a genuine choice in the areas where it matters for a healthy diet. The discounters seem mainly concerned with the kind of foods that most of us are trying to get out of our diet. For the most part discounters are not innovators in the food sense. They are just piggy-backing on systems set up by more enlightened retailers.

Another comic turn has been the fuss over the demise of pounds and ounces. There has been a huge reluctance to follow the EU directive and move over to labelling foods in grams so as not to confuse the customer. Former ministers have been persuaded to write emotional tomes about how it is anti-British to sell in grams not ounces. It is also anti-consumer to confuse the market by selling the same product at one price in grams and another in pounds, especially where the packaging concentrates on the most mathematically complex weights. Who can compute in their head in a supermarket whether 364 grams of tinned peaches at 64p is cheaper than 14 ounces of fresh peaches at 67p per lb?

In the old interpretation of a free market, where shops just bought at the price they could find, there may have been some justification. Today, however, when retailers are fundamentally involved with their suppliers, there is no justification for exploiting the market in this way.

The issue is not price, but competition and a fair market – which food, of course, is not. It is not fair because some foods receive subsidies from their governments where others do not; some companies receive special patronage that others do not; and others pay to have their foods stocked in certain shops.

It was always said – before we married into Europe – that the UK had a Cheap Food Policy. Cheap food is not an end in itself. As a policy it had its time, which has now passed. In the '50s, it was a reasonable strategy to get as many different foods as inexpensively as possible into the market place after two decades of austerity. In the '90s there is a need for a new approach. That approach might be called acting in our own or the national interest. It is hardly enough to say that getting the price of turkey down to 35p per lb is in itself a success. At what cost to the welfare of those animals and the dehumanizing of the people who work in that trade?

The campaigns to stop the trade in veal and other animals have a clear message. What this says is that due diligence as laid down to ensure that food producers are responsible for safe food, also extends to producers being mindful of the welfare of the animals they bring up. The time will come – if it has not come already – when customers will not put up with battery chicken farms or hauling living animals thousands of miles, and all the other practices that have been kept quiet for decades. It is an insult to an intelligent society.

The only common ground is high welfare standards, respect for animals and their individuality, a return to smaller more specialized, quality production. If we have to pay more for it and eating meat becomes an occasional luxury, then so be it. We have to re-think what we want to do with the land, if it is not going to produce food.

Adapting to Change

It is useful to get some form of historical perspective on all of this. Often the first evidence of change is seen by the cook who has to handle the foods. In that sense cooking is a great practical art. It is what links us to the earth. This is how we have survived as a species. At times of austerity this has sometimes thrown up examples of man's greatest ingenuity. At times of peace and abundance it has raised new questions of how we housekeep the world for future generations. There is no shortage of examples of countries and nations that have ignored this basic message to their ultimate disaster and destruction, e.g. Russia and Somalia.

Britain's history is unusual. It has always been a fight and a struggle in a northern climate to produce the foods we need to survive. Across centuries we have brought in new foods and adapted them into our diet. If there were foods indigenous to this island at one point, then for the most part they have been usurped by immigrants. As a nation we have always adapted to change, or we certainly have since the 17th century.

Our climate has meant that agriculture is more frail for some foods than others. From a historical point of view one must question the abandoning of those foods that do prosper here – say oats in Scotland or apples in Kent or farmhouse Cheddar – in favour of the abundance of new foods brought in from abroad.

The Global Food Market has given us the chance to redefine where and what foods fit with our society. It is a change as important as the advent of the Industrial Revolution. Ironically, because our culture has been so weak, we are perhaps one of the first countries in Europe to respond to this change. As in other areas, it is highly likely that this country's future will depend largely on technical innovation.

The Link to the Land

However, any such technical innovation must have some link to the geography of this country or any benefits will be lost. Consumer opinion has often been battered into submission on the grounds that flavour and taste are subjective and therefore have no value. However, is it not possible that flavour and taste are in fact our bodies responses to what we eat? We are arguably not learning to understand the signals they send us. As science uncovers more about the nature of foods, we discover that perhaps our instincts were right after all? Analysing vanilla samples, the Department of Food Science at Rutgers University, New Brunswick discovered that the 'characteristic vanilla flavour and aroma was made up of a wide variety of organic compounds... which varied according to geographic origin'. The fact that we are only just beginning to understand the composition of some foods and their relation to the ground does not make our judgements subjective. It may well be that our judgements are in fact highly objective but that the evidence does not fit the perceived wisdom on the subject. Is it not feasible that the perceived wisdom is wrong and that we lack the vocabulary to express what is self evident?

If wine tasters can freely discuss the flavour characteristics of grape varieties and different processes, why is it that baked bean manufacturers cannot do the same? One answer is that there is not much to talk about with a factory and a balance sheet. Industrialization strangles the argument at birth. There is no producer with a stake in the land, no craftsmen with a stake in the process to argue differently.

There is a self-evident need to relate the qualities of the land we have to the food chain. Glasshouse growing of salads may be the way ahead, but ultimately that can be done anywhere. It is the uniqueness of these green and pleasant lands that needs to be preserved. For example, British lamb remains some of the finest in the world because of the quality of the climate and the grazing. The same claim can hardly be made for beef any more, where its birthright has been sold off and mated with French stock.

Need for Diversity

The immense diversity that has come from craft cheese production, from man's ingenuity with the cocoa bean and the soya bean, or from the making of olive oils, argue rather differently and suggest there is another way of using foods to maintain the quality of life. In a wider context, communities are better off if they protect these crafts, which is why the BBC goes off to make romantic films about the cooking of the Mediterranean and India, where some of these crafts and ways of life still survive.

On balance, some of the European culture is considerably more attractive than some of the imported American ideas that have been shovelled over here in the last 40 years. Even in areas like California, the culture has moved more to the European example, based around wine, and fresh foods, freshly prepared.

What are we to make of all this? What do we think? Is food like any other commodity best left to supposedly (but not) free market forces? Or is it so central to the welfare of the nation in terms of our diet, community, quality of life and economics that it deserves more attention?

The food industry is pressing its foot to the floor and accelerating ahead of legislation. It is moving at such a speed that statisticians or even dieticians are barely keeping up. What impact is that having on trade, on our health, on the communities that rely on these businesses that have either opened to meet the new demand or closed to make way for the new?

SO WHAT DO WE THINK?

I am persuaded to the idea that a food industry is necessary and that it should serve the community in a way that improves the quality of life. I am also persuaded to the idea that the world is full of governments that have not dealt with these issues which may have led to their downfall, but far worse is the legacy of poverty and famine that has followed them.

I am not suggesting Britain is in that situation. I am suggesting that we have had successive governments which have been happy to duck the issues.

Food is immensely complicated. But it is mainly complicated because it is such a large subject that covers so many various interests. All these interests have succeeded to a lesser or greater degree in packaging their areas up under terms like agriculture, technology, economy, weights and measures, nutrition or retail and tend to present the arguments in different ways. This book presents another perspective, that of the consumer, although at times I have felt more like a partisan.

In France there is a ministry responsible for preserving the culinary arts that sponsors classes for schoolchildren on how to eat and where foods come from and where they fit in the world. In other European countries the trade qualifications for crafts like baking and cheese-making are institutionalized and considerably more stringent than here. In some countries you are not allowed to deal with food without four or more years approved apprenticeship and examination. In this country you can get your food handling certificate in a day. Food is not part of the school curriculum.

There may be some merit in having a lax system that allows innovation, but there is little merit in carrying on without recognizing the huge losses that are being incurred socially and economically in and around the food arena. Compiling parts of this book have been like chronicling an unfolding tragedy.

Perhaps we are content just to be customers at the Global Food Restaurant. But how long before we have to go into the kitchen and wash the dishes to pay the bill?

There needs to be a political recognition that communities depend on food and the quality of life in the 21st century is going to judged by that criterion. There needs to be a recognition that in a Global Food Market the only companies that will survive will be producing foods of higher quality than we see today. There needs to be a recognition that different parts of the country have natural advantages that have to be protected and exploited. There ought be to be a recognition that food is a better trade than guns or even money itself. The reason being simply that food is for everyone.

Drew Smith, Foxley, December 1995

HIDDEN FATS

The Committee on Medical Aspects of Food, known as COMA, published its most recent review of the national diet and how diet impacts on heart disease in late 1994. Since it first reported 20 years before, the incidence of heart disease in the UK has fallen, albeit not by the same degree as in Australia or America. The UK has the same high level of heart disease as the other dairy nations like Denmark and Ireland, and considerably higher than countries like Greece and France.

The main theme of the report was to encourage a move away from eating fats – especially saturated fat – and replacing the calories by eating more carbohydrates as in bread, potatoes, pasta and rice.

These are obviously broad brush strokes which are complicated by the changing eating patterns and by the fact that each of us performs slightly differently, but they give a broad perspective on the kind of targets anyone might set for themselves. The key areas are:

SATURATED FATS, found mainly in meats, dairy products and fat spreads, should be reduced to provide around 10% of the calories we eat.

MONOUNSATURATED FATS, as found in olive oil, were generally deemed to be better for us but as most of our diets have too much fat in them in the first place the committee held back from recommending them outright. The deficiency in calories would be better supplied by carbohydrates found in foods like potatoes, rice, pasta, etc.

POLYUNSATURATES were split into two different groups. Intake of the N6 family – mainly seed oils and polyunsaturated margarines – should not be increased and should only supply 10% of the calories in the diet. The N3 group – mainly from the oily fish like mackerel, herring and trout – should be eaten more. 'There is evidence that increasing intake reduces risk of death'. It suggests we should eat fish twice a week and one of those meals should be an oily fish.

TRANS-FATTY ACIDS, from foods with hydrogenated fats in them like cakes, biscuits and especially margarines and cooking fats, 'may have undesirable effects'. COMA suggests they should be restricted to 5g a day or 2% of the total energy. Other research has shown that because many of these trans-fatty acids are hidden in convenience foods, many people may be consuming more than recommended levels.

TOTAL FATS in the diet currently supply an average of around 40% of the calories we need. COMA suggests a reduction to 35%, but also notes that in some diets fat intake can be reduced below 10% 'with evidence of benefit', although a figure of 20% is probably more realistic without a wholesale change in the way we eat.

CHOLESTEROL levels are linked to eating saturated fats. Reducing dietary cholesterol – principally from eggs, which supply almost half the amount in the diet, the rest coming from dairy products – is principally important for people with family tendencies to high blood cholesterol. Two eggs a week is judged a good level.

CARBOHYDRATES, from bread, potatoes, rice, pasta, and the natural sugars found in fruits and vegetables, should be increased to make up the energy gap in reducing the fat. Carbohydrates should make up 50% of the diet.

SALT intake should be reduced from 9g average a day to 6g. Much of the salt in the diet is coming from convenience foods and just taking the salt off the table at home is not enough in itself to achieve that level of reduction.

FINDING THE FAT

Much of all this jargon can be computed out of the nutritional labelling on packet foods, although it takes some mathematical dexterity.

Nutritional labelling is compulsory in four areas of energy – calories, protein, carbohydrates and fat – and optional in four other pertinent areas: whether the carbohydrates are sugar (bad in excess) or starch (good); whether the fat is saturated (bad) or not; how much salt; and how much fibre. It covers all packaged foods, but not unpacked foods or alcoholic drinks – which are another source of calories.

Most, but by no means all, foods now comply. Supermarket own-labels tend to be much more diligent in giving all eight categories, while brands often only give the first four and avoid the confessionals of sugar or saturated fats.

The important equation in this country is the interaction of calories and fat. Most people today eat enough protein, so it is not regarded as an issue. An average woman might expect to need 1,800 calories a day against an average man who might need 2,000 calories, although research suggests many eat as much as 2,300. The COMA advice is to try and get at least half of those calories from carbohydrates.

In other words, a healthy diet for an average man would have less than 90 grams of fat in it a day and for a woman less than 70 grams. One effect of moving over to carbohydrates is that you actually need to eat more, because carbohydrates have less calories than fat. One gram of carbohydrate equals four calories, where one gram of fat equals nine calories.

The fallacy of nutritional labelling is that it does not actually give you the amount of fat you are eating in the percentage terms that are needed to compare easily the targets laid down by the nutritionists.

The two codes might have been dreamt up by separate groups of experts who had never met each other, and matters are further complicated by little asides such as listing calories as energy, kcals and cals etc. That huge vested interests have at different times ensured that the real levels of fat or sugar in their products should be obscured by the labelling is fairly self-evident.

Throughout this book I have followed the idea of calories being the important figure, because they are a measure of the energy we get from food. They are expressed as for a 100g serving as they are normally listed on the packet. By using the formula it is possible to identify where the fat in your diet comes from.

To calculate from the label how much fat you are really eating as a percentage of any given food you have to multiply the fat figure by nine (i.e. how many calories) and then divide it by the calorie level. This gives the real percentage of fat in 100g of any given food. That is:

$$\frac{Fat \times 9}{calories} = \text{total percentage fat in 100g}$$

For example a **Sainsbury Thick and Creamy Yoghurt** lists only 3.5g of fat on the label, but 3.5 x 9 divided by 131 calories equals 24% fat. Or, for example, a **Mars Bar** has 17.5g of fat; times 9 equals 157.5 divided by 452 cals equals 34 % fat. Take a combination of both, such as the newly released **Aero Chocolate Mousse**: 13.2 x 9 equals 118.8 divided by the calories of 240 equals 49% fat. Or take **Diet Clover**, with fat at 39.9: multiplied by 9 equals 359 divided by 383 equals 93%.

So much for 'Diet' you might think, but there is also the question of how much of these things we actually eat. With spreads and butters, the percentages are high but the quantities are small. The new generation of aerosol cooking fats may register in the realms of 100% fat but, because they are designed to put only a thin film on the pan, the total amount is actually very low. Equally, something like a pesto sauce is very high in fat but only a small amount is used to flavour a very high carbohydrate dish, like pasta, so the overall effect is arguably positive.

The best laid equations are further thrown into the maelstrom of daily cooking, where they feature only as part ingredients in different foods. Breakfast cereals give the breakdown not just as an average 100g and a notional portion at 30g, but also with a portion in skimmed milk.

Some of the most obvious pitfalls surround so-called Diet foods, where the nutritional labelling has encouraged claims that such and such food is lower in fat; it may still, however, be a high-fat food. The total percentage fat in **I Can't Believe It's Not Butter Light** is actually higher than in the ordinary version, although it does contain less fat.

Much of all this smacks of intellectual compromise. The supposition is that by weaning us on to lower-fat foods there will be a beneficial effect on the diet overall, which is fair enough. What it does not do is reduce the scale of the problem.

When nutritionists talk about a balanced diet they are, for the most part, talking about the first aisle in a supermarket, not aisles two to sixteen.

To give you some striking examples, here are tables on the nutritional values of some potato and corn snacks. It is salutary to compare them to similar analyses of potatoes themselves, see pages 204-5 and 229.

Crisps

The fat as a percentage of calories in crisps

	Calories	Protein	Carbos	Fat	% Fat of Cals
McCoys (BBQ)	518	6.8	49.5	32.5	56
Quavers (cheese)	565	3.2	53.2	37.5	59
Wolf Intersnacks	551	2.5	61	32	52
Walkers (salted)	552	6	46	38	61
Hula Hoops	520	3.7	56	31	53
Kettle	484	6.7	53.9	26.7	49
Potato Sticks	519	5	65	30	52
Smiths	543	1	44	39	64
KP Solo	473	6.2	60.5	22.7	43
Roysters	521	6.2	51	32.4	55
Highlander	501	6.3	40	35.7	64

Some companies detail the level of saturated fat. In **Kettle** it is only 3.9 or 7%, compared to **Potato Sticks** at 12 or 20% or **Hula Hoops** at 14 or 24% saturated.

Corn

The deepest penetration of the UK diet for corn is through denatured cooking oils and as snack alternatives to potato crisps. Labelling side-steps the issue of how much sugar or how much of the fat is saturated.

	Calories	Protein g	Carbos g	Fat g	% Fat of Cals
Monster Munch (pickled onion)	493	6.3	60	25	45
Dorito (Safeway)	508	7	63.5	25	44
Prawn Cocktail Snack	520	4.2	59.8	28	48
Wotsits (cheese) (Safeway)	546	2.2	52	33.1	54
Bacon Streaks	483	8.4	59	22.6	42

A 30g pack of corn snacks represents nearly one-tenth of a day's calories.

ORGANIC FOOD: WHERE IS IT ALL?

The idea of organic food has outstripped the reality. Much is made of the fact that the Ministry of Agriculture gives grants to farmers who want to convert to organic methods. Superficially this may seem politically laudable and is often presented as such, but as the maximum amount of grant available is £100 per hectare a year, in reality it hardly pays for a pair of decent working boots and is a lot less than they would get if they just set the land aside.

There are commercial reasons that have blocked the progress of the movement, often still presumably the very reasons why organic methods were dropped in the first place. Without protection from pests, crops fail. The result is that, in practice, many producers adopt a halfway-house approach.

There are two areas where the organic movement has made serious in-roads. Wine, because it is a bottled and identified commodity in which added value for quality is recognized, has shifted perceptibly away from pesticides. In California, the **Fetzer** wine company has set up a project to persuade all of the region to go organic by the year 2000. The showpiece is a cookery and gardening school that grows varietals of different herbs and salads. Last year's winner of the Organic Wine Challenge was in fact one of Australia's leading producers, **Penfolds**. Here in Britain the **Henry Doubleday Research Association** now runs its own mail-order organic wine club.

The other area is baby food. The advent of **Baby Organix** showed up the multinational reliance on low-priced ingredients and asked basic questions about why things like maltodextrin should be fed to babies at all? **Boots**, **Heinz** and others responded with semi-organic ranges. Here the word organic has come to be taken as a symbol of sound nutrition, good sense and food – as they used to say, but for different reasons – that was not mucked about with.

A case could, or should, also be made for dairy products, where the care smaller producers take can also translate into quality. Ice-cream from **Rocombe Farm**, of Newton Abbot in Devon (see page 32) has managed to find a welcome niche beneath the corporate razzmatazz of the **Ben and Jerry's** etc. through a strict adherence to organic Jersey milk, organic double cream and free-range eggs and an imaginative use of flavourings – 2,200 at the last count, from Lemon Meringue to Drambuie Chocolate Truffle. Equally, the late Douglas Campbell's **Ty'n Grug** Cheddar-style cheese made at Lampeter alongside his better known **Pencarreg** was a model of how the disciplines of organic production can be married with those of the food craftsmen to produce an important new cheese.

The hub of the movement is now the **Ryton Organic Gardens** at Ryton-on-Dunsmore outside Coventry (tel 01203 303517), a 20-acre green-field site translated into a series of showpiece gardens, shop and research centre. A second centre is planned for Yalding in Kent. It is owned and run by the **Henry Doubleday Research Association**. This is a vision on a grand scale and set in a hard part of the country for garden-ers – there has been a frost every month for ten years. There are upwards of 30 aspects of the work, from displays of making compost to a 250-plant herb garden, an ornamental showpiece kitchen garden, a seed library and programme for preserving old varieties (notably potatoes), and soft- and top-fruit gardens. Further afield, the HDRA has helped develop reforestation schemes in Africa and India, as well as tropical organic pro-jects.

Many farmers who have gone over to organic methods run thriving mail-order services, usually with a £40 minimum for free delivery. (See the Mail-order section on pages xvi-xxi for phone numbers.) Often the diversity of the farm holds some of the more interesting foods. For example, **Craig Farm** at Dolau, Llandrindod Wells is a rare source of goat and mutton, as well as tuna and grouper fish imported from St Helena. **Home Farm** at Loughborough sells Dorset Down lamb and the pigs roam on woodland. This concentration on variety and breed is surely the wise route forward, rather than the gimmicky ready-made burgers or lemon-stuffed chicken which any butcher could do themselves.

The other area that has annexed the organic movement, rightly or wrongly, is that of the importers who specialize in trading with countries too poor to have got into pesticides. Hence Sicilian olive oil is deemed organic, as are flavoured teas from the Seychelles. Some, like the Seyte brand from the Port Glaud Tea Garden, are eminently worthwhile and carry the Fairtrade Foundation symbol (see page 366). Only the Evernat range (contact via Brewhurst Health Food Supplies, Abbot Close, Oyster Lane, Byfleet, Surrey) claims to offer a comprehensive range of organic foods.

BREADS & CEREALS

The miller's influence has stretched far wider than just bread. The pies, pastries, buns and cakes of the first half of the century point to an alliance with the other great Victorian industrialized food processes in sugar, dairy and fat that stamped itself over the national diet. Breakfast cereals are another offshoot. These powerful monolithic – often government-funded – agencies represent the last great food barons of the Victorian era: sugar dominated by two companies; flour-milling by three; milk, until this year, a national monopoly since the '30s. It is only the power of the supermarkets in the last decade that has begun to threaten the status quo.

FLOUR

WHITE FLOUR · SELF-RAISING FLOUR · STRONG
FLOUR

From the 1880s onwards, America, Canada and Australia supplied all
our flours. These came from hard high-protein wheats. The deep, rich,
loamy soil of the Prairies produced high-quality wheats against which
the thin overworked top soils of Europe could not compete, except in
isolated patches like East Anglia. It was not for 100 years – until Britain
joined the EU and work on wheat varieties and the use of nitrates on the
soil, and punitive levies on imports – that the pendulum swung back to
home production. Today most breads might only contain 10%
Canadian wheat, the rest is all home-grown – or at least European. The
EU now produces a surplus of wheat.

Half a dozen varieties of wheat are used to make flour, of which two –
Mercia and Avalon – are by far the most common. The seed is registered
and approved by the Ministry of Agriculture, Fisheries and Food. More
than 60 types were registered in 1986. Standardization, in practice,
remains a stern discipline. Of the 32 milling businesses in this country,
three supply 80% of the flour for our bread.

The combine-harvester thrashes off the straw and chaff and leaves
simply the berry of the wheat. On a traditional STONE-GROUND
mill, the berry is squashed and worked out into ever smaller particles.
Millers still using stone grinds tend to specialize in more unusual batches
of wheat, quite often some of it organic, although the distribution tends
to be localized. Good names to look for are **Downfield Windmill** of Ely,
Shipton Mill of Tetbury, **Crowdy Mill** in Totnes, **Letheringsett
Watermill** at Holt, **Newnham Mill** of Tenbury Wells, and the **Water
Mill at Little Salkeld**, Penrith.

On the roller-grind factory system, the teeth actually cut the berries.
As the wheat moves through different – ever-decreasing – rollers,
different products are extracted: wheatgerm, bran, middlings, semolina,
special high-performance flours designed for branded products like
cakes, and even pet food.

WHITE FLOUR

This flour has always been popularly perceived as the best although in
reality it has had the most taken out. The trade in what has been ground
out of the wheat has inexorably involved the miller with other large-
scale food products, such as sugar, and has been an influence on large
areas of the national diet and how – and what – we cook. The innocent

FLOURS FROM OTHER GRAINS

Stone-grinding is not confined to wheat. **Doves Farm** specializes in different grains, producing flours for different styles of baking or for people with gluten tolerance problems. The brown rice flour is a good value alternative to commercial baby starter foods. There is a pale yellow gram flour (widely used for batters in Indian cooking , notably *bhajis*). Spelt is an old variety of wheat that fell out of fashion at the turn of the century because it was more difficult to thresh. The bread is less likely to crumb than with ordinary flour. Some research has suggested that although it contains gluten, spelt may be tolerated by people with gluten allergies. There are also rye and malthouse. They are sold in wholefood shops or by mail order (01488 684880).

tubby little bags of flour on the supermarket shelf seem increasingly like tombstones to different – now mostly dated – eras of cooking.

SELF-RAISING FLOUR

This is is a low-protein, highly refined flour to which a raising agent, usually sodium bicarbonate and an acid are added (see page 12). Variations might be still weaker and more refined for, say, cake flours. Self-raising is also the flour for soda bread. Self-raising is still said to be the biggest seller, which is perhaps a statistical nicety and paints an unlikely vision of whole tracts of suburbia bent over their ovens baking marble squares, sticky date puddings, gingerbread and peach melba sponges. Can this really still be the case?

STRONG FLOUR

This is, or should be, for bread-making, although most of the examples in the supermarkets would appear at the bottom of a list of good bread flours. Sometimes vitamin C is added to improve the strength of the protein. If the flour is not strong enough – ie it does not have enough protein – then when the yeast creates carbon dioxide, the protein strands snap and the bread will collapse in the oven.

BEST BUYS **Waitrose organic plain flour** has a protein level as low as 8%. Bakers would regard 11% protein as low-grade white and expect to bake with a protein level of 12%. Wholemeal flour would be 13.5% in a bakery. An independent analysis for this book of six flours bought off the supermarket shelf revealed the following protein contents:

THE NATIONAL LOAF

For more than a decade the quality of the national loaf was the centre of a huge row between the nutritional experts on one side and millers on the other. The issue was simple: should there be a standard unadulterated loaf in which the goodness of the wheat was left untouched and which the country could rely on as safe source of good nutrition? This had been the practice through the war years and subsequent rationing to great effect. Or should bakers and millers be allowed to refine the flour as much as they chose, provided they put back into it afterwards any missing vitamins.

The decision finally fell to Henry Cohen who was then the Minister of Agriculture. On January 10, 1956, Cohen over-ruled his own advisers and did what the millers asked. He told Parliament. 'The conclusions of the panel differ from those presented in their evidence by the Government's medical and scientific advisers and by the Medical Research Council. These advisers have been admirably zealous and eminently successful in guarding the nutritional well-being of all sections of the population (in the War and rationing years) and their scientific arguments have not been disproved...'

Inadvertently Henry Cohen had opened the door on the era of additives and supplements in the national diet.

Sainsbury strong white flour	9.4%
Allinson's strong white, soft-grain	10.99%
Somerfield strong white	9.2%
Homepride strong white	10.7%
Sainsbury strong wholemeal	11.9%
Sainsbury strong brown bread flour	12.5%

Neither of the ordinary supermarket white flours were strong enough to bake a loaf and, almost without exception, the branded flours were around the 11% mark. It is probably not too cynical to suggest that a retailer might prefer customers to pay for the added convenience and expense of a ready-baked loaf; or that a miller will make more profit supplying a baker than he will encouraging end-users to bake their own bread. In the case of **Waitrose**, the strong white flour – which one would expect to be the bread flour – only declares a protein level of 10.1% and you would have to go to wholemeal at 12.6% to be confident of a good loaf. **Tesco** flours are strong enough to bake bread. The strongest flour is probably **Granary Malted Brown** at 14%, which takes some of its strength from the added malt.

Krupczatka is a Canadian flour which carries a premium price as an import to EU. Canadian bread flours tend to have much more protein, usually 14%. Users report enthusiastically on its performance, especially the quality of the bread crust and in Italianate variations of pizza and foccacia.

BREAD

BLOOMER · SANDWICH LOAF · FRENCH BREAD ·
SOFT LOAVES · BROWN BREAD · WHOLEMEAL
BREAD · SPECIALITY BREADS · TEABREADS

Ordinary bread is a mix of 60% water with flour, salt and yeast kneaded by hand or machine and left to ferment. During the fermentation, alcoholic and carbonic gases are produced and this makes the dough swell. As it rises so the flavour matures, or the insolubles are converted to soluble proteins and the gluten sets with the starch. Good bread therefore needs a high gluten content – or what is called strong flours (see above). Industrial breads have shorter fermentation periods. As it is the fermentation that breaks down the gluten, there have been suggestions that there may be a connection with the rise in gluten allergies.

Breads provide one of the most efficient forms of consuming the complex group of carbohydrates. The idea that they were fattening has now been completely discredited. Work at the Institute of Food Research in Reading has even indicated that eating enough of the complex carbohydrates can have an important affect on moods. Eating bread increases the blood concentration levels of the amino acid tryptophan, which in turn helps synthesize the brain chemical serotonin, that regulates appetite, sleep and mood. Psychobiologist Dr Peter Rogers argues that the effects of eating these complex carbohydrates may be longer-lasting than that achieved from chocolate and sugary foods. The government guidelines on a healthy diet suggest we should be eating 6 slices of bread a day. Half of men fail to reach this target, while women on average eat only 3 slices, and 2 out of 5 women eat no bread at all.

Although we have the cheapest form of bread in Europe (even cheaper now that bread is one of the loss-leader items in the price war, with a loaf sometimes selling for less than 20p), we eat less than any other European nation. Perhaps there is a connection? The array of supermarket breads is to some extent a deception. For all the Bloomers, Hedgehogs, Parisiennes, Danish and Cobs, the flours conform, the sizes conform strictly to factory batches of 400 g or 800 g, and the factory technologies are broadly similar. Variety has been tightly focused so, for the most part, breads are different mainly because of their shape.

Good bread depends on the flour, how it is mixed, and how long the yeast and dough are allowed to mature. As with white flour, the popular perception of quality runs against the known evidence. Most of the flavour of bread is found in the crust and much of if its goodness derives from its hardness. However, soft – even bouncy – and crustless breads have become the norm.

Breads in a supermarket divide into three philosophies. The freshly baked unpacked loaves tend to take their names from their shape. The BLOOMER is baked on the floor of the oven so that it has crusty top and bottom. A SANDWICH LOAF is baked in a tin with a lid on, so it has minimal crust.

BEST BUYS FRENCH BREAD has suffered badly from this definition – it is merely English bread in a *baguette* shape. However, **Sainsbury's Traditional French** and others are part-baked loaves imported from France, which are more faithful, using French flour which has shorter-keeping qualities. Some traditional loaves will also indicate that the dough has been matured and the flavour will be improved as a result. Some of these innovations are more than cosmetic. **Tesco** French range, which includes *baguettes*, *ficelles*, *Grande Rustique* and *pain de campagne* are first-class. **Waitrose** also does a more than passable rendition of traditional French bakery, with its *baguettes* and *pain de campagne*. These are conspicuous diversions away from the norm of shape being everything. **Marks and Spencer** has followed suit, but in many cases the fillings seem to have become more the stars of the show than the bread itself. The range of novelty goes much wider than just using good quality French flour.

The packeted and well marketed breads in the section that includes **Mighty White** or **Weight Watchers** are largely aerated to make them softer. The extra benefit in low calories is more air and less bread. Actual SOFT LOAVES, by contrast, use emulsifiers and fats rather than air to create the softness. BROWN BREAD is no longer a term with much meaning. The trade gives strict definitions for white and WHOLEMEAL bread, while brown just inhabits anywhere it chooses in between. Established as far back as 1886, **Hovis** was originally a brown bread flour into which some bran had been put back, but is now a brand name covering any kind of loaf from wheatgerm to granary, country grain to wholemeal. Unfortunately, the language of bread no longer makes much sense.

Speciality breads have become increasingly prominent, although the section is more of a tourist's guide to what bread might have been somewhere once upon a time. The runaway success CIABATTA was originally made with sunflower oil. It was the innovative bakery **La Fornaia** in King's Cross that started to use olive oil to make it seem more authentic. It attracts a premium not just because of its fashionability but because the dough is so sticky it has to be kneaded by hand. It has spawned a generation of sunny Mediterranean-style breads in which authenticity seems again to be mostly to do with shape. Ciabatta itself is also sold stuffed with olives, sun-dried tomatoes or rosemary.

Bread

Types of bread compared for percentages of fat and carbohydrates

	Calories	Protein g	Carbos g	Fat g	% Fat of Cals	% Carbos of Cals
Brown bread	218	8.5	44.3	2	0.8	81
(toast)	272	10.4	56.5	2.1	0.6	83
Chapati	328	8.1	48.3	12.8	35	58
(with fat)						
Hovis	212	9.5	41.5	2	0.8	78
Pitta	265	9.2	58	1.2	0.4	87
Rye	219	8.3	45.8	1.7	0.6	83
White bread	235	8.4	49.3	1.9	0.7	83
Mighty White	230	7.6	49.6	1.5	0.5	86
French stick	270	9.6	55.4	2.7	0.9	82
Wholemeal	215	9.2	41.6	2.5	1	77

The carbohydrates also need to take account of fibre levels, higher in wholemeal. Brown bread samples vary widely, through the spectrum of wholemeal at around 9g and white sliced at a low of 3.7g of dietary fibre (Southgate method) or 6 and 1.5 (Englyst method).

Bread, Butter and Jam

An average slice of bread weighs approximately 33g, then presume a generous covering of butter at 5g and jam at 10g.

	Calories g	Protein g	Carbos g	Fat	% Fat of Cals
Bread (Hovis)	77	3.3	15	8	9
Butter	37	0.025	0	4	97
Jam	26	0	6.9	0	0
Total	140	3.325	22.9	12	7

FOCACCIA seems to be the same thing but flatter, while PUGLIESE and the so-called Spanish version GALLEGO are round. There are some very disappointing Italian-style breads around. The variety of other breads is often down to the addition of a few seeds or in the case of **Marks and Spencer** just about anything else from walnuts to saffron.

There are some glorious exceptions to all this bland uniformity, for example the **Manoucher** breads imported from Canada and **Innes** sourdough breads. In London, **Sally Clarke's** breads represent the true art of bread-making, which is unfortunately in decline, as do, in the French tradition, **Baker & Spice** of Walton Street.

RYE BREADS were made in this country up to the 17th century. Often the rye was mixed with other cereals, usually wheat, to improve the gluten levels. In northern Europe rye bread is the main bread rather than wheaten. The old recipe was for the rye meal to be kneaded with boiling water. As with sourdough breads, some of the dough from the day before was held back to help the fermentation. The soldier's bread was *Kommisbrod*; the more everyday was simply *Schwartzbrod*, which can be excellent; while the Pumpernickel is stickier and darker and usually sold in square packets. They are hard to find outside of specialist north-European delicatessens

SPROUTED WHEAT BREADS claim to be older than yeast baked breads. They are made without any of the traditional additives, like yeast or dairy products, and were originally developed for people on diets. Nutritional analysis shows they have more fibre (at 10g) than wholemeal (at only 7g) and less than 0.8g fat compared to 7g. The loaves are made by sprouting the wheat and then grinding it, fashioning it into oblong bread shapes and then slow baking. The texture is moistly sticky, like a wet parkin. Under the **Sunnyvale** label, **Everfresh** produces a range of seven flavoured with dates, raisins, onions, fruit and almonds, stem ginger and sunflower seeds. Wholefood of year? Contact Everfresh at 01296 25333 fax 01296 22545 or Mary Nicholson on 0171 385 3940.

Older definitions of bread were more concerned with quality. VIENNA ROLLS were always made with highest-grade white flours and baked in moist ovens at lower temperatures to create the glaze on the outside. The glazing has come to be imitated by brushing with egg wash. MILK ROLLS were defined as being 200 parts flour to 65 parts water to 50 parts milk. Other regional loaves varied considerably in the proportions of flour to water to yeast. SURREY LOAVES were very large and dry, using a minimum amount of water and lot of yeast. YORKSHIRE BREAKFAST BREAD used only a teaspoon of yeast warmed in 1 pint of hot milk to 2lb of flour.

Most of the tradition for fancy breads such as YORKSHIRE TEA BREADS, LONDON CURRANT LOAVES and DEVON AND CORNISH SAFFRON CAKES stems from farmhouse baking. A piece of dough was kept back from the main bread-making batch and mixed with spices and currants and any other sweet things that were available. BARA BRITH (Welsh currant bread) originally was half flour and half oats mixed with half as much lard as fruit and peel. ROEHAMPTON ROLLS used a basic bread mix into which three egg whites were whipped. LARDY CAKES Dorothy Hartley in her brilliant *Food in England*, attributes to the length of the chalk-line from Wiltshire through Oxfordshire as far as Cambridge. The dough was trolled out and dotted with dabs of 'cold stiff lard about the size of walnuts' and crystallized sugar and strewn with 'barely a breath of nutmeg or a suspicion of cinnamon or allspice'. LONDON BUNS, which have now come to be the long large finger-shaped buns covered with icing sugar, originally used a mix of lard and warm water to activate the yeast into which dried currants, caraway seeds, nutmeg and sugar was kneaded in. Similar recipes exist for HOT CROSS BUNS, where GOOD FRIDAY BUNS used candied peel and beaten eggs.

MUFFINS, CRUMPETS or PIKELETS and SCONES were bought from bakeries. Making these was a specialist task because individual stones had to be set in the brick ovens. They use soft flours and yeast mixed with bicarbonate of soda and cream of tartar to help the aeration. Crumpets usually used milk, where muffins were often made using part water and sometimes even potato. For muffins the batters were quite gloopy and were actually beaten. They were baked originally inside muffin stones, and then inside rings on a hot iron plate. Pikelets are thought to have been associated with Lancashire and Yorkshire, where crumpets were more a Midland style. Over the years crumpets acquired more yeast and became thicker. Scotch scones use buttermilk as well as water. SALLY LUNN BUNS are subject to much story-telling. Whether there was a buxom Sally at all or that was just, as Dorothy Hartley says, because the buns were split and 'embosomed in clouds of cream' is unclear. There were various suggestions that either the name referred to the French *sol et lune* (sun and moon, i.e. day and night) because they took so long to rise or even someone completely different, such as Solemena as in Liza Acton's recipe dated 1855. The buns authentically are made in two parallel fermentations – the first using fresh milk and yeast. This is then folded into a second mix of yeast, flour and milk, and the two allowed to rise together overnight – hence the 'day and night' references. The baking was always improved by brushing with egg yolk. The whites went to whip up with the cream to go in the cleavage of the freshly split bun. However *Law's Grocer's Manual* of 1933 gives a completely different account, recognizing that they were sold on the streets by a pastry cook called Sally Lunn at the end of the 18th century. The recipe is totally different. In this version it is supposedly a sweet spongy teacake 'eaten hot, well buttered, and cut into three slices'. The seasoning for the dough is butter, sugar, eggs, lemon and spice.

BEST BUYS Breads in supermarkets are a strange hotch-potch of philosophies. The move, some years ago, to create in-store bakeries might have been a great leap forward for the craft but has somehow got caught freeze-framed in mid leap. Taking the talent from the high street in to the store was more of a loss for the craft baker than a gain for the big store. The smell of freshly baked bread may waft out across the front door of new **Safeway's** shops, but it seems as if the smell was what was important, not the bread itself. **Safeway** is very big in pappy rolls and

STOTTY CAKES

These were traditionally made with left-over dough baked on the sole – the coolest part – of a coal-fired oven. The slow cooking gives the yeast longer to act, producing a chewy texture. 'Stotting' refers to the practice of dropping of the newly baked roll on the floor to see if it bounced and was therefore cooked. In the '20s and '30s they were, according to local chef Terence Laybourne, 'a pillar of poverty cuisine and the cakes could be seen lining windowsills in working-class terraces throughout Newcastle'. This is his mother's recipe:

Crumble 15 g (^{1}/2 oz) fresh yeast in to a bowl. Add a pinch of pepper, ^{1}/2 teaspoon sugar and 3 tablespoons tepid water. Mix and leave for 15 minutes until frothy.

Sieve 350 g (12 oz) plain white flour and 1 teaspoon salt into another bowl. Pour in the yeast and 250 ml (8 fl oz) tepid water. Mix to a firm dough. Knead until smooth and glossy. Cover and allow to rise for an hour in a warm room, or until doubled in size.

Roll the dough out on floured boards and shape into 12 rounds, about 2.5 cm (1 in) thick. Put on a greased baking sheet and bake 20 minutes at 200C/400F/gas 6, turning after 15 minutes. Eat warm with butter and jam.

gimmicks like hot cross buns. It takes most of the innovative range from **La Fornia** to compensate. **Sainsbury** has switched tack and invested heavily in a national plant at Milton Keynes to part bake and then distribute for the in-store bakeries to finish off. The investment is huge, but it remains to be seen whether it can produce any decent breads, although it is promised that baking will go on through the day, so it may be that buying a loaf at 6.00 pm to eat that evening could be the smart thing to do. Some of its innovations, like selling stotty cakes in South Kensington, are just plain odd. To date the most successful products have been in the speciality areas: a very good chollah, interesting scofa; also a good brown loaf with a discernible and high wholemeal content. The larger **Marks and Spencers** seem to be baking to save the nation, with Bath buns, tea cakes, malt loaves, walnut and sultana rolls, hazelnut and saffron rolls. The sun-dried tomato bread seems to have as much tomato as flour. Typical of its desperate quest for convenient luxury are the American variation on twisted doughnuts, christened (as if out of late-night desperation) simply Yum Yum. The best work is probably in the French loaves and those that surface elsewhere as part of the sandwich collection. Main-line **Asda** shops can position the bakery in the furthest point of the store, which is self defeating, if there was anything worth finding. **Tesco** have been forthrightly pursuing a policy of tradition mixed with innovation – potato cakes, square crumpets, pikelets, an excellent French range - that deals mainly with bread and not the other artery of the craft, the cream bun. None of these is really a match for the quality of the sandwiches at the excellent **Prêt à Manger** chain.

Biscuits

The percentage of fat in calories of leading biscuits

	Calories	Protein	Carbos	Fat	% Fat
		g	g	g	of Cals
Crispbread (rye)	321	9.5	70.5	2	5.6
Digestive (chocolate)	493	6.8	66.5	24	43
(plain)	471	6.3	68.6	21	40
Gingernut	456	5.6	79	15	29.6
Jaffa	363	3.5	68	10.5	26
Custard Cream	513	5	69	26	45
Rich Tea	457	6.7	75	16.5	32
Shortbread	498	6	64	26	47

The percentage fats in biscuits are comparable to chocolate bars.

Buns

The percentage of fat to calories in buns

	Calories	Protein	Carbos	Fat	% Fat
		g	g	g	of Cals
Chelsea bun	366	7.8	56	14	34
French horn	435	3.8	26	36	74
Crumpet	199	6.7	43.5	1	4.5
Danish pastry	374	5.8	51	17.6	42
Doughnut (jam)	336	5.7	49	14.5	38
Doughnut (ring)	397	6	47	21.7	49
Eccles cake	475	4	59	26.4	50
Eclair	396	5.6	26	30.6	69

Rolls

Percentage differences between different rolls

	Calories	Protein	Carbos	Fat	% Fat	% Carbos
		g	g	g	of Cals	of Cals
Brown roll						
(crusty)	255	10.3	50.5	2.8	0.9	79
(soft)	268	10	52	3.8	12	77
Croissant	360	8.3	38	20.3	50	42
Hamburger bun	264	9.1	50	5	17	75
White roll						
(crusty)	280	11	57	2.3	0.7	81
(soft)	268	9	51.5	4.2	14	76
Wholemeal	241	9	48	3	0.7	79

Notice the difference between soft and crusty rolls.

RAISING AGENTS

BAKING POWDERS · YEAST

BAKING POWDERS

Baking powders have been used to remove the smells from fridges and even as toothpastes in America – and now relaunched over here – as well as for making cakes rise. Their mix of alkali and acid sets up the reaction which releases carbon gases into the mix through the cooking and makes cakes and pastries rise. The acids were traditionally provided by tartaric acid and cream of tartar, the alkali from bicarbonate of soda. The mixing has always been a professional process to ensure that each tiny particle is properly covered with the other and then left to mature.

YEAST

Yeast was always the province of the brewer's wife who sold it to the farmers' wives at market. A small piece of fresh yeast was fed on mixes of boiled waxy potatoes, pounded with treacle and their own water which was enough for a week's baking. It was kept in a covered jar on the back of the stove.

German yeast, first brought here from Hamburg around 1850, was always considered the best. It was the barm collected from distillers' vats after the fermentation of grain to make spirits. The barm was mixed with water and washed through a series of ever finer sieves, then allowed to settle and put into cloths and pressed. The result was a pasty, putty like mass that smells like the yeast in beer.

Yeast is a microscopic plant that lives on sugar and starchy substances. As it grows, it ferments and gives off carbon dioxide that swells up the dough. Fresh yeast is hard to find, except from professional bakers, and even the trade has moved towards dried yeasts. The main differences between yeasts are now in the drying. Bakers use compressed cake yeasts, whereas yeasts sold in the supermarkets are either pellets, which need mixing with water and sugar, or increasingly easy-blend for 'quicker simpler home-baking', which can be added straight to the flour. Yeast is a main influence in the flavour of bread and all the haste promised on the packet is not likely to encourage well-flavoured bread. By contrast, breads sold on the next aisles have begun to declare the virtue of their matured dough. *Allinson's dried pellets of yeast produce a more responsive and sensual dough. Packet recipes encourage the speeding up of the process, but the yeast needs time to ferment and allow the flavours to develop – preferably mixed with a small quantity of flour, then left overnight and the rest added the next day.

BREAKFAST CEREALS

CEREALS · MUESLI · PORRIDGE

CEREALS

The extraordinary rise of the breakfast cereal began with the recycling of the 'miller's offal'. As the miller ground purer and purer for white flour, so he was left with the husks, nibs and rusks and had to find a use for them. The irony of the British and American breakfast is that cereals which now constitute such a part of it are the goodness milled out of the bread which we then go on to eat with butter and jam to make it more palatable. If we baked harder breads out of wholemeal flours there might be no nutritional role for cereals – or, arguably, even butter and jam.

The best thing to be said about the razzmatazz of breakfast cereals with their stupid names, ridiculous offers for ridiculous toys and artificial additions of vitamins and minerals, is that the labelling is impeccably clear and in **Kellogg's** case there are so many vitamins added nobody can really complain. Most of the answers to their precise contents are listed on the sides of the packets.

The trend continues to be eccentric, with new launches as varied as the dinosaur models or free trolls inside. Of this year's releases from the cereal 'fun factory', **Cheerios** worthily mix corn, oats, rice and wheats – albeit with 22.9% added sugar. In practice, they are last year's flavour, **Start**, with added rice. **Squares** offer an unlikely promise of packets filled with hazelnuts and chocolate – at 34.2 % sugar, not quite as cardinally sucrose as some. **Tesco** responded by cleverly adding **Apricot Squares**, which round off the health message more successfully than chocolate. On the other hand, **Corn Pops** from **Kellogg's** represent a huge gulf between protein at 5% and sugar at 41%.

Kellogg's have been so concerned about the potential risk of anaphylactic shock brought on by allergies to peanuts in some people (see page 363) that **Corn Flakes** and **Frosties** carry labels declaring the risk. Neither actually contain peanuts or peanut (groundnut) oil, but they are made in the same factory as **Crunchy Nut Corn Flakes,** which do.

BEST BUYS Nutritionally, the most admirable cereals are ***Puffed Wheat**, ***Weetabix**, and ***Shredded Wheat**, which provide good benchmarks against which to assess other cereals.

FIBRE: In principle, high fibre content in cereals is good – above 10% on the more commonly used Englyst scale. The best in this respect are **All Bran** at 24.5%, **Bran Buds** at 22%, **Bran Flakes** at 13%, **Common Sense Oat Bran Flakes** at

10%, **Sultana Bran** at 10%, **Weetabix** at 9.7% and **Shredded Wheat** at 9.5%. The lowest, at under 1%, are **Ricicles**, **Honey Bears**, **Frosties**, **Rice Krispies**, **Crunchy Nut Corn Flakes**, and **Corn Flakes** at 1%.

PROTEIN: Protein content is less of a nutritional issue than it was, because most of us get enough from the rest of our diet. Although in an ideal world there should be more protein than sugar. The cereals which are the best protein sources are **Special K** (where it is added), **All Bran**, **Puffed Wheat**, **Bran Buds**, **Ready Brek**, **Weetabix**, **Swiss Style Muesli** and **Shredded Wheat**.

SUGAR: Predictably the sugar levels in cereals span an enormous range, from 0.5% in **Shredded Wheat** through to **Sugar Puffs** at a staggering 56.5%.

SALT has crept up as one of the more controversial issues in cereals. Manufacturers argue that salt adds a necessary flavour, which given that they are not working with very much in the first place is probably true. Their claims serve to underline the poverty of the nutritional thinking behind many of the leading brands. One serving of any of the following would provide an adult's complete daily requirement of salt: **Rice Krispies**, **Special K**, **Bran Flakes**, **Kellogg's Corn Flakes**, **All Bran**, **Farmhouse Bran**, **Weetos**, **Crunchy Nut Corn Flakes**, **Coco Pops** and **Ricicles**.

MUESLI

Swiss Doctor Bircher-Brenner first introduced muesli to patients at his clinics in 1897. He wanted a mix that created a strong pattern of B vitamins, a range of A, D, and E vitamins and a blend of cereals that covered the amino acids.

Today's all-singing and all-dancing views of Swiss mountain tops or designer polystyrene packets are exuberantly miscalculated. The notion of luxury derives more from the concept of an Alpine health clinic than a top-of-the-line diet. The sugar levels are alarmingly high

COOKING: *Dr Bircher-Brenner's original muesli recipe was:*

1 tbsp rolled oats
3 tbsp water
1 tbsp Nestlé's sweet condensed milk or single cream and honey
juice of half a lemon
1 peach or some strawberries
1 small apple, grated with the skin on
1 tbsp chopped nuts, such as almonds, walnuts, hazelnuts, cashews

PORRIDGE

Low in protein and susceptible to individual additions of salt and/or sugar, porridge oats are still rich in important fats that are recognized to be positively healthy – or certainly more healthy than wheat. The outer husk is milled off, because it is deemed indigestible. Oats grow best in

Breakfast Cereals

The healthier cereals like **Shredded Wheat** or all **Quaker** products avoid adding extra vitamins and minerals. **Weetabix** adds a smaller cocktail of B1, B2, niacin, folic acid and iron.

Nestlé puts as many as nine extra vitamins in its cereals, usually up to the full 100% recommended daily intake of B1, B2, niacin, B6, C, folic acid, B12, pantothenic acid and iron. **Kellogg's** add vitamin D as well, but not the pantothenic acid.

Because of restrictions on advertising foods as medicinal, the bigger claims for health tend to be made by cereals with added vitamins rather than those made of whole brans. Some claims are quite spurious. **Sainsbury's** has claimed that its own-label corn flakes are 'Low in Fat' when, in reality, the difference compared to **Kellogg's** is 0.1%.

The trend of the new cereals has been clearly to sugared versions of old favourites. **Frosted Wheats** have 21g of sugar compared to **Shredded Wheat** at 0.7g, **Frosted Shreddies** have 37g compared to 15.3g in **Shreddies**. **Nestlé's** apparently healthy **Cinnamon Toast Crunch** has nearly 34g sugars. Predictably **Nesquick Cereal** has 41g sugars; **Kellogg's Banana Bubbles** 39g; **Frosted Chex** 32g. Even **Quaker**, who for the most part have resisted the lure of sugar, allow 19g on its **Wholegrain Feast**.

	Calories	Protein g	Carbos g	Fat g	% Fat of Cals	% Carbos of Cals
All-Bran	261	14	46.5	19	34	11
Bran Flakes	318	10	69	19	2	5.6
Coco Pops	384	5.3	94	38	1	2
Common Sense	357	11	74	17	4	10
Corn Flakes	360	8	86	8	0.7	1
Frosties	377	5.3	94	42	0.5	1
muesli (Kellogg's)	363	10	72	26	6	15
Porridge (with water)	49	1.5	9	0	1	18
Puffed Wheat	321	14	67	0.3	1.3	3
Ready Brek	373	11.5	69.5	2	8	19
Rice Krispies	369	6	90	10.5	1	2.5
Ricicles	381	4.5	96	42	0.5	1
Shredded Wheat	325	10.5	68	1	3	8
Sugar Puffs	348	6	84.5	56.5	1	2
Weetabix	352	11	76	5.2	2.5	6

cold climates on poor soils, but also at higher temperatures than other grains. Scotland was known as a prime grower, especially East Lothian. The Scottish dependence on oats was akin to the Irish on the potato and was not confined to porridge, as traditional dishes such as herring fried in bacon fat and oatmeal shows.

Oats respond differently in cooking, which renders meaningful comparison of different brands difficult. They are best cooked long and slow with regular rhythmic stirring to break down the starch and bring out the flavours. Larger grains take longer cooking. Porridge keeps poorly, losing its taste and taking on flavours from around it, so it is best kept sealed in a dark dry place.

DAIRY PRODUCE

The story of milk might be the story of food in the 20th century. From the replacement of the milk maid at the turn of the century, no other foodstuff has so accurately encapsulated the effect of man on the food chain – from massive subsidies and political chicanery to the impact on the countryside, down to its effect on diet, both good and bad.

The ending of the 60-year monopoly of the Milk Marketing Board was a trauma. The price of milk panicked the industry. One victim may well be the milkman; some pundits suggest 2 out of 3 bottles of milk will soon be bought in the supermarket. Change was well overdue. The protests against selling calves into the Dutch veal-crate industry are symptomatic of an industry that has been allowed to become too big, too impersonal, too inhuman. The issue is one of scale and values. Using modern medicines and technology to extract the last drops of milk from a cow; pasteurizing this milk to make it safe; and then producing row upon row of meaningless lumps of fatty protein in factories that employ a minimum number of people in meaningless jobs hardly qualifies as progress. As the endless acres of set-aside farmland testify, there is a real need to bring the craft and skills back to the countryside on a local level in a way that will create new jobs and bring the countryside back into use. Supporting those dairy products that reflect a real commitment to communities and their history, to the welfare of the animals, and to the proper husbanding of the land is an articulate means of protesting against factory-farming and the obscenity of its excesses.

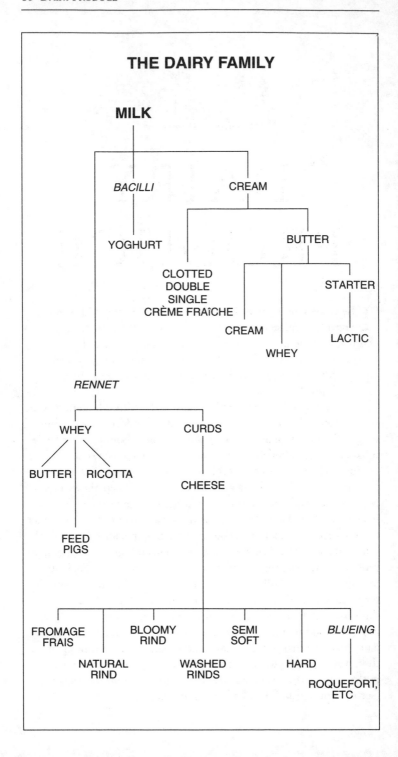

THE DAIRY FAMILY

MILK

BACILLI

CREAM

YOGHURT

BUTTER

CLOTTED
DOUBLE
SINGLE
CRÈME FRAÎCHE

STARTER

CREAM

WHEY

LACTIC

RENNET

WHEY

CURDS

BUTTER | RICOTTA

CHEESE

FEED
PIGS

FROMAGE
FRAIS

BLOOMY
RIND

SEMI
SOFT

BLUEING

NATURAL
RIND

WASHED
RINDS

HARD

ROQUEFORT,
ETC

MILK

SKIMMED MILK · SEMI-SKIMMED MILK ·
WHOLE OR FULL-CREAM MILK · HIGH-FAT MILK ·
PASTEURIZED MILK · RAW OR UNPASTEURIZED
MILK · HOMOGENIZED MILK · UHT MILK ·
CHANNEL ISLANDS MILK · EVAPORATED MILK ·
CONDENSED MILK · OTHER MILKS · MILK
ALTERNATIVES

It is only in this century – and mostly in this country – that fresh milk has come to the fore. Before, the difficulty of moving fresh milk around the country prohibited its mass sale. Cow sheds in and around Victorian cities were reviled as dirty places selling potentially dangerous, disease-carrying liquids.

To the British nutritional movement, milk has provided two great *causes célèbres*. The nutritional importance of milk is its calcium, riboflavin, protein and zinc content. The vitamins – A, D and E – are mostly in the cream and are mostly skimmed off. In the '20s and '30s, milk was seen as one cornerstone of a diet that could nourish the mal-nourished. In the '80s, the fat in this same milk was depicted as a dietary villain, a harbinger of heart disease. Friesian cattle, first introduced from Holland in 1922, undermined the standing of the traditional dual-purpose 'meat and milk' cow, especially the Hereford, by producing more milk than any other breed. The growing universality of pasteurization – which destroys the differences in flavour between milks from one breed of cattle to another, and from one area to another – means Friesian cattle now supply 8 out of every 10 pints of milk sold nationwide.

From the late '20s, this country inexorably adopted policies which meant that fresh milk was favoured over other milk products. The creation of the Milk Marketing Board, initially on a government subsidy in 1933 to provide milk in schools, centralized milk policy. In 1940, the Ministry of Food extended the policy to ensure all under-fives and their mothers had cheap or free milk. The production of cheese and butter withered under these decrees and the supremacy of the Friesian. Neither have ever properly recovered. Fifty years on and much of this commitment remains. But the nutritional arguments which were so strong in the '30s are less relevant now that the diet is supplemented by so many other foods. Mothers are actually warned against giving babies fresh milk because of the imbalance of vitamins. That half the nation can switch from full-cream to skimmed milk in the space of a few years suggests also that our habit of milk with everything can be broken. Ironically, much of this surplus now finds its way into the diet as cheap powder bulking for junk foods.

GOODBYE TO THE MILKMAN AND ALL THAT

The political commitment to the dairy industry in the UK has had a big down side. It has failed to maintain a form of farming that has kept people on the land in skilled jobs. It has skewed the free market in favour of a whole raft of foods of questionable nutritional value. This great industry has been maintained at huge public expense over decades in a way that has inhibited other craft food industries from growing. Public money has been used to subjugate another species as if it were a machine, not an animal.

Millions of pounds have been frittered away in pretending this is not happening; in campaigns about friendly milkmen, sponsoring football matches and bike rides, and archaic advertising campaigns that pretend that drinking a pint of milk a day will be the answer to everything.

Half the milk drunk in this country is delivered to the door, but by 1998 this is expected to have fallen to 1 pint in 3. The milkman's days may be numbered, despite being one of the oldest, most effective and possibly most popular distribution systems in the world. Both Unigate and Northern Foods blame dwindling demand on shoppers defecting to supermarkets, but this seems a fairly feeble excuse given the milkman's ability to deliver other foods as well. Sales of the *Dairy Crest Cookery Book* are still the highest of any cookbook and suggest customers would be happy to buy direct if they were offered the chance. At the same time, the milk bottle itself may be under equal threat – not from the industry's own (and seemingly waning) move into milk cans, but with the arrival of re-sealable cartons.

Milk is a peculiarly British food. Despite its obvious virtues, there is little to suggest that its role might not have been better played by other foods. It is an artificial enthusiasm that has been sold to us, a legacy of the great Victorian ideas of how to sell food – have it with tea; have it with cornflakes; have it with rice... all the great imperial imports. Milk belongs to an era when the British diet was dominated by three raw materials – the other two being flour and sugar. Even when it could not take up a central position, it always made a case for itself in a cup of tea to sit alongside the jam doughnuts. The very images of comfort food are redolent of the '50s and the war years. This culture has passed.

The interesting milk products now are artisanal cheeses, especially the revivalist British cheeses, and some of the great French AOC cheeses; whacky innovations with fromage frais; the return of clotted cream; the increasing validity of Greek yoghurt over its new generation of imitators; the subtlety of crème fraîche; and the unexpected return of using cream in ice-cream. These products represent a more civilized way forward. They are a better use of fat in the diet; they are economic for an industry in turmoil, and they have a much greater value in the kitchen. As with meat, going back to working with individual breeds rather than just numbers on a test tube is probably the only way to ensure the welfare of the animals themselves.

Milk Grades

SKIMMED MILK has 0.3 % fat or less; SEMI-SKIMMED MILK has 1.5-1.7% fat; FULL-CREAM MILK has at least 4% fat; HIGH-FAT MILK (from South Devon, Jersey and Guernsey cattle) has 4.8% fat or more. The caps of bottled milk are colour-graded: **BLUE** for skimmed; **RED-AND-SILVER** for semi-skimmed; **RED** for homogenized; **SILVER** for full cream; **GOLD** for high-fat milks from South Devon, Jersey and Guernsey cattle; **GREEN** for unpasteurized. However, some supermarkets have their own codes.

Pasteurization

As early as 1768 it was known that heat preserved foods. Milk was heated and canned by Nicholas Appert in 1795. Louis Pasteur's experiments in the 1850s and '60s explained how bacteria soured milk, wine etc.

Pasteurized milk is nowadays heated to 71.7°C (160°F) for 15 seconds to kill bacteria, principally tuberculosis. Farms with accredited bacteria-free herds still sell UNPASTEURIZED or 'RAW' MILK but, as our diets have become more sanitized, so the risk of our not being able to cope with the kind of bacteria found in unpasteurized milk has risen. Writing, in 1943, in *The Living Soil* Elizabeth Balfour was unequivocal about the pros and cons of pasteurized and unpasteurized milk: 'Nutritionally there is a world of difference between the two. Pasteurization, and of course cooking, injure both the vitamin and calcium content of milk, and the beneficial lactic acid bacteria, which attack disease organisms (and in the process cause souring) are killed by heat.'

Homogenization

Homogenization spins the fat molecules through a narrow tube which evenly distributes them through the milk, creating a smoother, more consistent texture. Homogenized milk is usually therefore whiter.

UHT Milk

LONGLIFE is the most widely available UHT, or ultra-high temperature milk. The milk is heated to above 132°C (270°F) and held there for a few seconds. This process was developed in the '40s and milk thus treated first sold in 1965. Heating to such a high temperature creates off flavours (usually said to be caramel), but it extends shelf-life to up to six months when sealed (but no more than fresh milk once opened) and there is minimum nutrient loss. MILK CANS contain milk processed using a new form of UHT technology that heats the milk more swiftly and cools it instantly to minimize off flavours. **Halo** is a milk alternative launched by **Express Dairies**. It is 97% milk but only 0.2% fat, and the use of sunflower oil to replace natural fat reduces cholesterol to zero compared to 7% for ordinary semi-skimmed milk.

CHANNEL ISLANDS MILK

Jersey and Guernsey cows survived the move to the one-cow policy because of the higher fat levels of their milk and cream and, to a lesser extent, because the male calves went for veal. Jersey cows were originally called Alderneys, after the Alderney Packets, or steamboats, which brought them from the Channel Islands. The first herd was established on the mainland in 1811 to decorate the parklands of the Audley End estate in Essex. Guernsey cows are descended from two French breeds originally taken to the island around the 11th century.

EVAPORATED MILK

The water content is reduced by about 45% (and must contain 7.8% fat) and is then canned.

CONDENSED MILK

Reduced to under 33% of its original volume and has added sugar as a preservative.

OTHER MILKS

HORSES' MILK contains the least fat – at 1.2% – of all animal milk, while guinea pig milk contains the most, at 45.8%. Human milk is close to cows' milk, at 3.7%.

EWES' MILK is hard to find and usually frozen. It will keep for three days once open.

GOATS' MILK contains less folic acid, but is otherwise similar in composition to cows' milk. There have been cases of anaemia in babies fed solely on boiled goat's milk. Neither are therefore advised for young children.

BEST BUYS **NEW MILKS** The remorseless trend to diversification has seen the insitutionalizing of whacky milks on the supermarket shelves. **Frizz** has led the way with lurid milk shakes in banana, strawberry and chocolate flavours at the equivalent of 71.6p per pint – nearly twice the price of organic milk. For a few cheap flavours and some different packaging this seems excessive in the extreme. Older brands like **Yazoo**, **Breaktime** and **Stripes**, sold in down-market stores, tend to be better value. The mould-breaking **Wild Jack Chaser Milk** (using maple syrup and a whiff of bourbon) seem to be losing shelf space. HEALTHY MILKS, enriched with vitamins A and D, are another avenue which has begun to open up, despite the fact that most breakfast cereals already have blasts of these vitamins as well.

MILK ALTERNATIVES

Some people have an intolerance to the lactose in milk. Soya milk is often used as a basis for an alternative, the hulls mixed with water. In the unsweetened version it is fairly puritanical and the effect in real (not instant) coffee is cosmetic – coffee meeting soya beans is an unusual head-on collision. The sweetened version, built up with apple juice and calcium, tastes pleasantly of what it is and has potential as a genuine alternative drink rather than a substitute.

LACTOLITE is cows' milk in which the lactose has been reduced by adding an enzyme that transforms it into glucose and galactose. Conspicuously sweet, despite its fat level of 4g per 100 ml, it has the thinness of poor skimmed products.

CREAM

HALF CREAM · SINGLE CREAM · DIET EXTRA-THICK CREAM · WHIPPING CREAM · DOUBLE CREAM · CLOTTED · CREAM · SOUR CREAM · CRÈME FRAÎCHE

Cream in this country was always sold fresh, not ripened as for butter or the French crème fraîche. The advent of pasteurization further rendered this idea obsolete as it destroyed the bacteria that create the sourness.

The labelling of types of cream is strict but confusing. Nutritional labelling weighs cream in grams, but cartons are sold in mls and pints. Easy translation in the supermarket is about as difficult as it could be. Price goes up with fat level, roughly $\frac{1}{2}$p per g. Double cream is almost £2 per 600 ml (1 pt), compared to milk at 30p.

The fat content determines what cream is called, and usually this is indicated now by coloured tops to the cartons (**BROWN** for half cream; **RED** for single; **GREEN** for whipping; **BLUE** for double; **ORANGE** for clotted cream; **PURPLE** for sour cream.).

HALF CREAM (12% FAT)
Designed for pouring and for coffee. Of limited use, it is irritatingly packed in half-pint cartons rather than quarter-pints like other creams.

SINGLE CREAM (18% FAT)
Useful for pouring or in cooking where there is a lot of liquid (soups, casseroles or quiches). Mix in a little of the hot liquid first to blend it evenly. It will not whip or freeze.

DIET EXTRA-THICK CREAM (23.5% FAT)
The ultimate in marketing tautology. It has more fat than ordinary cream and costs slightly more than whipping cream.

WHIPPING CREAM (35% FAT)
The cream absorbs the air for whipping. Under 35% fat and there would not be enough to absorb the air properly. Whipping by hand you are unlikely to create more than a 70% air-to-fat ratio with either whipped or double cream, but machines can now achieve ratios close to 100% for commercial sweets. Whipping cream was pioneered as a cheaper alternative to double cream – usually about 5p per 150 ml ($\frac{1}{4}$ pint). It will double its own volume on whipping, and when lightly whipped can be frozen for up to two months. It can be used to give bulk to soufflés and mousses. It can have added sugar, clotted or canned cream, or emulsifiers

and stabilizers. Nisin is a common preservative, usually found in ready-made cream dishes rather than straight whipping cream.

DOUBLE CREAM (48% FAT)

Supremely versatile in cooking as it withstands higher temperatures. To whip, first thin it down with a little milk to increase the volume – probably marginally less expensive than buying whipping cream. It should whip to 1 1/2 times its volume and will keep frozen for up to two months.

CLOTTED CREAM (55-60% FAT)

Unlike the rest of the English dairy tradition, this was ripened and heated in huge wide pans, either for the clotted cream itself or for what seems to have been a very fine – but now extinct – butter. The practice was thought to have been introduced to Cornwall by the Phoenicians trading in tin. It produces unpredictable results in cooking, but will keep frozen for up to a month. It used to be difficult to find but now **Hobb's** clotted cream is sold in **Asda**, and **Tesco** have begun to sell an own-label.

SOUR CREAM (18% FAT)

Has a starter added and has been ripened. This adds outrageously to the price – which can be on a par with crème fraîche. It is, however, still cheaper – but fattier – than Greek yoghurt which is its most obvious other rival. Either way it is poor value.

CRÈME FRAÎCHE (30-47% FAT)

The French allow a natural sour nuttiness to develop the character of their cream, as if making butter. Good crème fraîche is thick enough to hold its shape in the pot if turned upside down. The high fat content makes crème fraîche versatile in cooking, especially in sauces and casseroles. Like double cream, it is multi-purpose. As the fat levels descend, so the cooking applications become more restrictive. The best examples are sealed in foil-topped tubs and unopened will keep up to three weeks in the fridge, but will not freeze.

We are unusually fortunate in getting nearly all our crème fraîche from Isigny in Normandy, which produces the best in the world and holds an *appellation contrôlée* for it. There is a premium of about 20p against double cream.

Some rather pointless low-fat crème fraîches have insinuated their way into the market, but tend to be vanilla-ish sludges that lack the distinction of the original article and acquire severe graininess from the bulking agents. The list of ingredients used to stabilize them tell their own story. A full-fat Greek yoghurt is possibly a better alternative.

BEST BUYS ****Isigny** from Sainte-Mère in Normandy has an *appellation contrôlée*, as for its butter. Found in clean red-and-blue-lettered pots, sealed with foil, fat levels are higher than own-brands, around 40%. Creamy in colour, with a sublime silky texture, it has a long-lasting flavour edged with flowers and nuts, and the sourness works as a flavour rather than being all-pervasive. **Sainsbury** sell it notably cheaply, being proud of introducing it.

*Waitrose own-label has reduced the fat content to 30% without destroying the quality. Thick and immovable, it is very good, with an immediate flavour of lovely sour lemons and edges of almonds.

**Neal's Yard rightly calls its version 'slightly soured cream'. The fat content is a swaggering 47% (still 1% off double cream). With a beautiful thick texture devoid of wateriness, it again has hints of nuts and lemons.

More commercial versions come from **Yoplait**, made in France for **Dairy Crest**, with 30% fat and a culture added to speed up the ripening. It has a pronounced accent of sourness, lemons with nuts, and a texture that tends towards graininess rather than smoothness. **Yoplait Light**, as well as containing a starter culture, has added skimmed milk in order to reduce the fat by half, plus starch, gelatine and pectin to stabilize, and potassium sorbate to preserve. The effect is looser and creamier in texture, the sourness is muted, more of a diluted version of the real thing with some unattractive grainy after-tastes. **Yoplait Épaisse**, with 30% fat, is for cooking and is more solid than the ordinary crème fraîche, with a resulting concentration of its sours. **Yoplait Gastronomique**, with 40% fat, is designed for hot cooking and is very solid, very rich and has a defined accent of sour lemons, but is dull and one-dimensional.

YOGHURT

SET YOGHURT · STIRRED YOGHURT · STRAINED
YOGHURT · BIO OR LIVE YOGHURT · WHOLE-
MILK YOGHURT · LOW-FAT YOGHURT ·
FLAVOURED YOGHURT · GREEK YOGHURT ·
EWES'- AND GOATS'-MILK YOGHURT · YOGHURT
ALTERNATIVES

As a viable low-fat alternative to other dairy ingredients, yoghurt makes sense – even the new generation of frozen yoghurt ice-cream alternatives are outstandingly successful.

Before 1960, there seems to be hardly any evidence that yoghurt was ever made in this country. Yet it is one of the oldest foods, found widely around the Mediterranean rim, certainly used by the Egyptians and Israelites and taken east to India by Arab traders. Its first arrival in mainland Europe is thought to have been around 1600, but it was then mostly confined to monasteries and Bulgaria where it has been held, rightly or wrongly, as contributing to amazing local longevity. Unfortunately, common-sense suggests there is quite a distance between the Bulgarian monk and his sheep's-milk yoghurt on the one hand and a diet bio raspberry flavour with added sugar and 'fruit' on the other.

Yoghurt-making is distinct from cheese-making. The curds and whey are not separated. It remains a milk product. Milk needs the bacilli *Lactobacillus bulgaricus* and *Streptococcus thermophilus* to turn it into yoghurt. These bacilli first scientifically identified at the start of the century in the Pasteur Institute, feed off the milk and detrimental bacteria it contains which might otherwise cause decay and so postpone the breakdown and help preserve it. The first commercial factory making yoghurt was opened in Barcelona in 1925 for **Danone**.

The explosion in the yoghurt market has perversely knocked ordinary yoghurt out of the ring. Most supermarkets stock Greek yoghurt at one end of the spectrum, low-fat at the other. Ordinary yoghurt is now out of the ordinary. Supermarkets classify yoghurt and fromage frais as part of the dessert aisle rather than the dairy, which has led to a headlong rush into novelty flavours and 'fun-packs'.

BEST BUYS Prices are, however, reassuringly consistent . **Safeway** has been undercutting most of the supermarkets by a few pence. Added flavours are only charged at one or two pence more, compared to the practice in fromage frais, where mark-ups are much greater. Yoghurt prices are infamously difficult to compare, with cartons ranging widely in size. Supermarkets seem to take the comfortable levels of 100, 125 150g, etc., where brands are left with awkward equations like 227g or 340g.

SET YOGHURT

The yoghurt is poured straight into the pots in which they are sold. For this reason they are, it is argued, more natural, or less likely to have anything added.

STIRRED YOGHURT

The yoghurt is poured into a large tub, mixed and then poured into the individual pots, possibly with some additions like milk or whey powders to extend them. The general effect is to make it more cream-like.

STRAINED YOGHURT

The water is drained off to concentrate the fats. The effect is to make it creamier.

BIO LIVE YOGHURT

Sold on the benefits of the bacteria, reputedly to clean out the gut. The lettering BA stands for *bifidus* and *acidophilus*. These bacilli can be beneficial to people whose natural resources may be run down. Their addition also supposedly creates a less acid taste.

BEST BUYS   Occasionally it is possible to find organics like **Dairy Farm**, a thick set yoghurt. **Sainsbury** do a bio, allegedly with active cultures, and an 'extra mild' with 5% fat. **Little Swallow Bio** is 3.5% fat, has a loose double-cream texture and a piercing good cool flavour. Compare that to **Onken**, often said to be the main market influence, which has a clean, strong, attractive impact and a distinctively creamy aftertaste.

WHOLE-MILK YOGHURT

Currently out of vogue. Farmers can sell on the cream and therefore have been happy to follow the trend to skimmed-milk products.

LOW-FAT YOGHURT

Low-fat has become the standard. They are made from skimmed milk and the fat levels fluctuate from about 5% to only 1% as in VIRTUALLY FAT-FREE, or DIET. Oddly, many adjust the health balance by adding sugar. The saving from not using the cream is passed on in this case, unlike the prevailing practice with milk.

GREEK YOGHURT

This was first introduced by **Total** as recently as 1985. It is thick and creamy, with a relatively high fat content of around 10%, compared to 18% for single cream. It bears favourable comparison with other mainstream dairy products, both in terms of price, honesty of the marketplace, quality and interest.

Yoghurts etc

The diversity in yoghurt is awesome. **Sainsbury** alone lists seven variations of own-label, each with its own sub-permutations of flavouring and pricing. There is a big difference in the %age fats of calories. Crème fraîche yoghurt is a notable oddity, with the fat level more equivalent to Greek yoghurt than crème fraîche. The lower the fat levels, the more desperate can be the flavour. Note also the high levels of sugar even in low-fat yoghurts. Levels of saturated fat are usually 2:3. For all the health messages, many are just fat and sugar.

	Calories	Protein g	Carbos g	Sugar g	Fat g	% Fat of Cals
Sainsbury:Thick & Creamy Yoghurt	131	5.7	19	18.7	3.5	24%
Raspberry Bio Yoghurt	108	3.9	16.9	15.9	2.7	22%
Diet Strawberry Bio	44	4.9	5.8	5.4	0.1	2%
Custard-style	146	4.2	20	19.3	5.3	32%
Low-Fat + real fruit	85	5.4	14.2	14.2	0.7	7%
Crème Fraîche Yoghurt	141	3.3	14.5	14.5	7.7	49%
French, Low-Fat Smooth	81	4.1	14.2	14.1	0.9	1%
Loseley BA Yoghurt	49	3.9	5.9	Nil	1.5	27%
Loseley BA Yoghurt (vanilla)	87	3.6	11.6	Nil	1.3	13%
Loseley BA Whole Milk Yoghurt	97	7.8	6.4	Nil	5	46%
Total Greek Yoghurt	106	4.4	5.6	5.6	7.5	63%

There is a wide variation in percentage fats, even in single ranges of products.

GREEK-STYLE YOGHURT is made here in the same manner, although some examples have higher levels of sugar and are not as thick.

BEST BUYS   Brands suffer a steep mark up – **Total** and **Loseley** at more than 30p, and deli prices of **Neal's Yard** or **Raines** at around 35p. The fat level of Neal's Yard is lower than usual, at 7.5%, but it is gloopily creamy and thick-textured compared to a typical **St Michael** Greek-style at 10% fat, which seems to want to imitate cream. **Raines** Greek-style yoghurt has 10% fat and claims live cultures; it is good, clean, creamy, coolingly thick, with an attractive acid taste.

EWES'- AND GOATS' MILK YOGHURT

Presumably the original yoghurt would have been made with sheep's milk rather than cows'. These are now rare. Fat levels are around 5-6%.

BEST BUYS   One example is **Live**, with 5.8% fat. **Robert Acidophilus**, a natural live goats'-milk from **Anchor End Farm**, Brandon Bank, Norfolk, is soft and slidy in texture, with a tart lemon milk flavour. **Sussex High Weald Dairy** sheep's-milk yoghurt from Duddleswell is 99p for 225 g; it is distinctly more solid in texture and less alternative than other versions. Henrietta Green in her *Food Lovers' Guide to Britain* recommends the hard-to-find **Yan-tan-tethera**, made on Llugwy Farm, Powys, from a herd of Frieslands, whose milk in spring can give a fat content as high as 8%.

YOGHURT ALTERNATIVES

There are some radical alternatives on the market, mostly in health-food shops. For example, there is **Sojasun**, a fermented soya-bean-and-water product at £1.39 for four 100 g pots. It tastes mainly of the sour beans, with a sweet aftertaste. Most such products bear little relation, beyond texture, to the original article.

ICE-CREAM

Farmers originally sold ice-cream on market days in summer, often employing strings of boys on bicycles to peddle it around the towns. The Ministry of Food banned all ice-cream containing cream in 1940 and even after the War it could only be made with skimmed milk powder. Originally ice-cream was literally frozen cream, but custard-style recipes were also used. The health risks of old ice-cream were well known and it was a frequent source of food poisoning. Even now soft ice-creams sold from vans and kiosks both here and in Europe consistently fail health checks. The main risk areas are the dispensing machines if they are not thoroughly cleaned, ice-cream that has been refrozen (usually noticeable from the river patterns on the surface and the larger crystals), and staff with dirty hands or hair.

The freezer counter has become the summer confectionery store. Brand names like the revived **Spangles**, **Skittles**, the disappointing **Kit-Kat** and very fatty Bounty etc have ambushed the more conservative old codgers like **Walls**. Supermarket own-labels, notably those at **Sainsbury**, **Marks & Spencer** and **Tesco** have also followed the lead of the more upmarket specialist names like **Häagen-Dazs**, **Ben & Jerry's** and **Steve's**. In this area, the quality is really down to the flavourings themselves. Chocolate in all guises seems to be considerably better than the more marginal flavours, such as **Mint Magnum** and **Häagen-Dazs's Baileys**.

The gimmicky exception is **Loseley's** brilliant Gin and Tonic ice-cream – made with real gin and therefore breathalizable – a stunningly brilliant marriage with **Gordon's**.

BEST BUYS **Ben & Jerry's** ice-cream is a fable of the business pages: how two hippy-looking drop-outs went into ice-cream and finally raised enough equity from Vermont farmers to go world-wide. The ice-cream itself is smooth and sugary but lent some individuality by the quality of the vanilla, It is more of an iced milk product than an ice-cream. Flavours are the main thing: Chunky Monkey (with banana and walnuts); Rainforest Crunch (with brazils and cashews); or New York Super Fudge Crunch.

**Bowman's farm near St Albans in Hertfordshire began making ice-cream in 1989, and it is available from the farm-shop, run by Bruce Luffman at junction 22 off the M25. The ice-cream has one of the highest fat contents, at 18%, and an overrun of 40%, with the resulting benefit of silky smoothness.

**Godiva, the Belgian chocolate company, has diversified into a range of superb ice-creams made with crème fraîche, whole milk, egg yolks and a great range of high-quality flavours: vanilla, praline, chocolate, passion fruit, apricot and raisin, fruits of the forest. The fat content is 20-22% and it is sold in original and sensible

ICE-CREAM GROWS UP

The duopoly of **Walls** and **Lyons** in the '60s persisted in keeping the cream out of ice-cream. By infiltrating corner shops with their own chillers, they strangled the market and invented a new generation of ice-cream in which the dairy qualities were devalued to save money. The health arguments for using non-dairy ice-creams are somewhat spurious – even the highest fat contents are lower than single cream. Although regarded here for many decades as a children's food, in Sweden, Russia and America ice-cream is aimed at adults. This trend really only began to be evident here in the mid '70s with the opening of the **Dayville** ice-cream parlours.

Two things have rejuvenated ice-cream: the arrival of the American giant **Häagen-Dazs** – blatantly exploiting the fact that the big dairy companies had abandoned cream – and the imposition of milk quotas which have forced farmers to find other outlets for their cream (not least because of the rising sales of skimmed milk). Proper ice-cream is based on a custard made from eggs, sugar and a cream-enriched milk and, generally, the higher the fat content the better the product. Air is added in the whipping and the trade term for this is 'overrun'. Something very foamy – like a **Mr Whippy** – has a high overrun: quality ice-cream has a low overrun. The other key factor is the quality of the flavouring agents used. Few companies are consistent across the range in this respect.

hexagonal polystyrene tubs, designed to keep the ice-cream frozen for up to four hours.

Häagen-Dazs, created by Reuben Mattus in 1961, redefined the American market-place, and now the British. The fat content is 16% and the overrun about 30%. It is inclined to egginess and sweetness, but has brilliantly selected flavours. The boxed choc-ice on a stick is covered in Belgian chocolate and was the forerunner to **Walls' best-selling but (marginally) inferior **Magnum**. With many of the other brands, there is the suspicion that their reputation hangs on the quality of the flavours rather than the ice-cream

*Hingston's ice-cream is most notable for its inventive range. Made by Andrew Hingston, an ex-Wall-Street lawyer who settled in Dunmow, Essex, the fat content is sometimes as high as 17.5% and the overrun under 30%.

Norfolk County ice-cream is very sweet, with the vanilla only used to underpin the honeyed creaminess.

*Rocombe Farm ice-cream, from Newton Abbot in Devon, is made not just with Jersey milk but using organic eggs and milk powder. The result is very richly creamy, almost inviting comparison with malt drinks, while the texture is classic English brick. Opinions vary: some say it is among the best on the market, others are less impressed. The style is, however, faithful enough to what might have been an old-fashioned ice-cream.

Steve's is the other big new American player. Using raw cane sugar, it is not as smooth as **Ben & Jerry's**. In effect, the flavour is very close to that of the cream on top of coffee.

Other good names that have shown well in comparisons of vanilla ice-creams have been **Loseley, New England, Criterion** and **Marks & Spencer**.

ICE-CREAM ALTERNATIVES

Some of the ice-cream alternatives introduced in the last two years have been surprisingly successful. Two stand out and, interestingly, both use very different techniques. Neither seem to taste of what they are. **Häagen-Dazs**'s range of fruit frozen yoghurts are widely found, even in **Gateway**.

Swedish Glace are completely non-dairy, using organic soya milk which transforms miraculously into a superb imitation of ice-cream. Three flavours are available: vanilla, strawberry and chocolate.

Calorie for calorie these compare well against attempts at slimming ice-cream from people like **Weight-Watchers** which tend to take their progeny from the fats industry. Those who have put themselves through the deprivation of eating only slimming foods report that they are no worse than other such foods. Other people were less complimentary

BUTTER

FRESHLY CHURNED BUTTER · BLENDED BUTTER ·
CHANNEL ISLANDS BUTTER · COUNTY BUTTERS ·
WELSH BUTTER · SPREADABLE BUTTER · WHEY
BUTTER · LACTIC BUTTER · FRENCH BUTTER ·
ITALIAN BUTTER · BUTTER ALTERNATIVES

In the 19th century, good butter was deemed to be yellow – supposedly because the cows had grazed on grass, though usually it was coloured – in this country with carrot juice or anatto dissolved in hemp or sesame oil; in Holland, America and Australia with coal-tar yellow. It was also highly salted, often containing as much as 7%.

Butter from fresh milk has little flavour and a poorer yield, so the milk was always ripened to allow the bacteria in the dairy to influence the flavour. All this was a bit haphazard. There were good and bad bacteria in the dairy. Part of every Victorian grocer's duty was to check his consignment after two weeks to see if it had gone rancid – if it had, it was sent to the bakers.

The nutritional labelling on the butter packets suggests 100 g (3½ oz) per day supplies an adult's vitamin A requirements and one-third of the necessary vitamin D. However, anyone eating that amount of butter in a day would have a serious dietary debility in the first place. Manufacturers only have to comply with nutritional labelling if they are making health claims.

UK butter must be at least 80% fat. Farmhouse butters often reach levels of 85-87%. The colour comes from the grazing pastures and the level of fat in the milk: the higher the fat, the more yellow the colour. Butter from Friesian herds will be paler than Guernsey or Jersey, because of the lower fat content.

UK butter has become so standardized that the main differences are in the packaging not the product. A few are still highly salted. British, Irish and Commonwealth butters are made without a starter culture. European lactic butters are made, like cheese, with a culture.

FRESHLY CHURNED BUTTER
The milk has come directly to the creamery after milking. Butters without this label tend to be blends of different milks which may have been stored and possibly frozen.

BLENDED BUTTERS
Blending butter was known to produce a lesser product. W A. Robinson writing in 1928 declared: 'If butter is worked after the first manufacture,

MASS-PRODUCED BUTTER

In 1891, the bacteriologist C. O. Jensen discovered a maverick bacteria in the dairy and cow sheds at the Dueland Estate Dairy in Denmark. He could kill it if the milk was heated to 70°C (160°F). Following the principles of cheese-making, he added a small quantity of good butter or yesterday's ripened milk from another – clean – dairy and produced excellent butter. If Jensen did not invent pasteurization, he had found its commercial application and his idea was to change dairy-farming forever.

The new pasteurized butters won every show medal. Within six years of his report, 97% of Danish dairies had gone over to pasteurizing all milk for butter. In 1906 it became Danish law to pasteurize all milk, and all butter had to be marked with the national Lur-brand and dated.

Jensen's discovery coincided with R. S. Woodwell's invention of a centrifugal cream separator in Orange County, New York (it was first shown here at the Royal Agricultural Society Show in Kilburn in 1879). The separator increased the yield by 10-20%. This was the end for the dairy-maid. The centrifuge was more efficient in extracting the water from the butter – where lingered many of the impurities which would otherwise cause the butter to go off – and this made it possible for the creamery to take milk from surrounding farms and mass-produce butter. Co-operative farming became possible. The first European creamery was set up in Denmark in 1882, three years later there were 84, and in the next five years another 595. The Danes and the French sent huge exports to Britain.

British farmers sold their butter piecemeal to blenders who would batch the lot and package it for market. It was only with the creation of the **Milk Marketing Board** in 1933 (see page 18), that we moved over to the Danish system of collecting the milk directly from the farm and delivering it to larger creameries. In Normandy, by contrast, farmers sold their butters to factors who graded the best to be sent Paris and London and only blended the lesser butters. The difference in the trade has meant that many more individual butters have survived in France than here.

such working or blending tends to weaken the texture and destroy that smooth silkiness of touch that is so pleasing.'

BEST BUYS   Supermarket blends tend to be the cheapest butters at around 63p per 250 g, followed by generic English at 69p and Danish at another 4p more, then Normandy at a minimum of 20p more.

CHANNEL ISLANDS BUTTER

The Jersey and Guernsey herds and the lush pastures on which they graze, produce a higher-fat milk. It is usually sold as a log, a habit previously used in Normandy after the co-operatives were set up to mark out butters of distinction. Of all the mass-market butters this stands out. Marigold-yellow in colour, it has the taste of buttercups.

COUNTY BUTTERS

Devon and Somerset once produced what was recognized as some of the best butters in the world. Even at the start of the century, however, they were being blended with other butters outside of the counties to meet the demand. The fresh milk was poured into wide shallow pans and left for 24 hours to let the cream rise to the top. It was then heated until the first bubble appeared, the heat then turned off and the milk left to stand for a further 12 hours. The cream formed a dense, clotted layer on the surface which was collected in a crock and used either as cream on the farm or stirred by hand into butter. A Devon dairy-maid was always said to need cool hands to do this well. One explanation for this practice has it that the Phoenicians may have traded tin with the Cornish and introduced this way of making cream and butter which was otherwise unique in Europe.

BEST BUYS Today Cornish butter retains some individuality; mostly sold in round pats and usually freshly churned, it is a beige-yellow in colour, with 1-2% salt and a mild good clean flavour. **Kerrygold** matches it for colour, if not flavour. As you travel east, even as far as Somerset, the bland hand of uniformity takes over; the butter is the colour of Brie, and is discernibly inferior to that from Cornwall. More spurious geographical claims, such as the vapid **Scottish** butters are more of an exercise in marketing imagination than flavour or quality.

WELSH BUTTER

A throwback to feeding the miners. Famously high in salt with levels as high as 7%, which outstrips even some specialist salt products.

BEST BUYS *Rachel's Diary, Brynllys, Dyfed is a solitary UK entry in the specialist butter market. Its organic farmhouse salted butter is made in the lactic style (see below) but is churned in a wooden churn, using milk from a Guernsey herd. Deep saffron-yellow in colour, the salt disguises the texture and the flavour is mild and mainstream.

SPREADABLE BUTTER

This was first introduced by **Anchor** in late '91 and sales have been spectacular. Others have followed, noticeably Danish giant **Lurpak** and **Tesco**. **St Ivel** tested the market but withdrew. Different techniques are used: **Anchor** extracts the hard fats from the butter, using a technology borrowed from other parts of the fat industry. The butter is treated in New Zealand and then shipped. An alternative approach, employed by

Tesco and others, is to use early summer milk, when the concentration of hard fats in the butter is at its lowest. The butter is then frozen and worked to improve its spreadability. The difference in flavour compared to other mass-market butters is marginal, but the spreadability is significantly improved by both processes.

WHEY BUTTER

A by-product of cheese-making. The whey will be taken off after the starter culture for the cheese has been added and there is, therefore, a distinct cheesy edge to the flavour. Little is actually made, but examples can sometimes be found in specialist cheese shops.

BEST BUYS The best examples are from: ****Quicke's**, who are better known for their Cheddar cheese. ****Appleby's** of Hawkstone, Shropshire, who are better known for their Cheshire cheese. ****Duckett's**, of Wedmore, Somerset, known for their Caerphilly cheese. Also good is that from **Mrs Montgomery** of Manor Farm near Yeovil, Somerset, who also makes Cheddar.

LACTIC BUTTER

The big Danish creameries introduced pure lactic cultures to start their milk ripening more swiftly. In a few years the butters – which previously had been subject to the diet of the cow, the light and bacteria in the individual dairy, and the diligence of the milk-maid – had become a blank canvas on which the creameries could paint any flavour they desired. The flavour is more uniform and predictable. The best of these butters taste of reduced cream, which is what they really are. French sauce cooking is based on their lactic butters, so they should be used for French recipes, especially for sauces. The European custom is not to add salt. Only **Sainsbury**, perversely, charge more for salted than unsalted. Most Danish generic butters taste the same with only fractional differences in lushness from brands like **Lurpak**, **Wheelbarrow** and, more so, **Cornflower** organic.

FRENCH BUTTER

Round the coast to Normandy, the sense of the pastures in the flavour becomes more pronounced. In a blind tasting you could spot a French butter against a Danish one, even if you couldn't spot the difference between two Danish ones. The best individual butters tend to come from France.

BEST BUYS **Beurre au Sel de Mer de Noirmoutier** is more of a promotion for the island of Noirmoutier and its salt industry. Ironically, the saltiness is less marked than ordinary Welsh. **Tesco** has also been selling the plain version.

    **Échiré from Deux Sèvres is sold in distinctive blue-lined wrappers or small

BUTTER VERSUS MARGARINE

The butter industry has spent the best part of the century behaving like some stuck-up floosy who thinks she is too good to talk to anyone else at the party, while her brasher, no-flies-on-me competitor, the margarine industry has flirted outrageously with all and sundry, quite prepared to prostitute herself under any fashionable cause that happened to be in vogue principally value or health, even to the point of completely reformulating products without so much as changing the names on the packet.

At the end of '94, the Butter Council stepped off its pedestal with a direct attack on its rival, funded by the EU, which underlines the sense of irritation at the cheap tricks of the margarine industry and also the power of the European farming lobby.

In graphic detail, full-page adverts listed the 12 chemical steps involved in the creation of bog-standard margarine – much of which would have been pretty obvious if we had not been conditioned into believing over a period of time that the addition of vitamin A (by law) suggests it could be a healthy product or that extending margarine formulas with water (which used to be banned before the slimming industry got going) is a good deal.

The word margarine lovingly derives from the Greek margaros, meaning a pearly oyster, describing the clear pearl globules of fat. It has masqueraded under names as various as Dutch butter, Bull butter, **Butterine** and **Oleo** as well as its more up-to-date counterparts such as **I Can't Believe It's Not Butter**.

Margarine was invented by the French chemist Mege-Mouries in 1869, using animal fats pounded inside a cow's udder. The first production was in the village of Oss in Holland three years later. The emergent meat-packing industry in America found a new market for its fatty by-products (Oleo). Later it was recognized that vegetable fats could also be used. It was in 1903, however, with the discovery by Sabatier that liquid oils could be hardened through hydrogenation that the modern industry was created. Later, in the Great War when animal fat was scarce, the margarine industry established itself.

Today seeds are crushed so they exude an oil which is de-gummed and filtered. This is washed with sodium hydroxide, bleached, filtered and deodorized. It is then hydrogenated and filtered again. This oil will be blended with a vegetable, animal or fish oil, coloured, flavoured, bulked out with a cheap extender like whey, and vitamin A added to comply with the law. It then has to be emulsified with lecithin and monoglycerine to make it spreadable.

wooden tubs. Widely used in top-class restaurants and often put up as a candidate for *appellation contrôlée*, its flavour is resonant with elements of sea breezes.

Isigny in Normandy has been recognised as the premier butter-making district of France since early this century. The butter from here was the first to hold *appellation contrôlée* status. It is rarely found over here, where **Échiré** has made a determined bid for the quality market, although **Harrods** and selected branches of **Sainsbury** do stock it. There is an unpasteurized version in a gold wrapper which does not carry *AOC* status, but still bears a hefty premium. It is lushly creamy, like unctuous clotted cream. The **Extra Fin** is pasteurized, cheaper at £1.80 per 250 g, and lighter and more delicate. It has a lovely lactic edge to the flavour, with hints of flowers and ending in echoes of Camembert. Novelty butters from the area, impregnated with caviar and sea salt, are beginning to be sold.

Lescure is a *grand cru* butter from Charentes. The legend of the butters of the last century survives here. Charentes claimed its butters were superior to those of Normandy because Norman butter was a by-product of cheese-making. Sold in a long gold log with a white label bearing blue lettering, this good solid, above-average butter has a deep creamy taste and the best is said to taste of hazelnuts.

President, in its gold and white wrapper, is only sold by **Waitrose** at a premium price. Of those widely available, it is an outstanding example of a French supermarket butter, with a deep, intense lactic creaminess.

Surgères, from Charentes, has been made since 1889, albeit not quite in the same way. Its flavour is intense and long-lasting with hints of nuts. A good surviving example of the style of Charentes butter, it is hard to find here but it is widely available in France.

Other French butters worth looking for include: **Pampile** from Deux Sèvres, with a cheesy edge and muted butteriness; clear-tasting **Paysan Breton** from Brittany; and **Paquette Normande** from Normandy, with a deep sweet-cream lactic mix of richness.

ITALIAN BUTTER

This rarely surfaces here. The cows tend to be kept indoors and fed on hay, and produce an almost lard-white butter. One example is **Buro Montanaro**, which is white, sweet, milky and very different.

BUTTER ALTERNATIVES

The quest for purity in butter opened the door to other fats and spreads. Many of these are simply fats diluted with water, so less goes further. The invention in 1911 of the process of hydrogenation – which turns liquid fats like vegetable or fish oils into hard, workable substances for industry – meant that butter could be widely and cheaply imitated. Hydrogenation also meant that other oils could replace butter in biscuits and cakes and this led to the industrialization of the bakery. The disadvantage from a health point of view is that hydrogenation turns unsaturated fats into saturated ones.

Alternatively, by buying more interesting bread you could dispense with spreads altogether. The real 'fatless' dairy product is, in fact, not a butter or a spread but low-fat fromage frais.

BEST BUYS Attempts to produce a 'fatless fat' have so far proved unsuccessful. Van den Bergs released **Promise**, a 97% fat-free product made up principally of modified starch and water to which cream is then added to give the flavour (this accounts for the fat level). The taste is of a cheesy margarine, but the texture is convincing. **Anchor** has produced a half-fat butter (only 40%), the rest of the bulk made up with hydrogenated vegetable oil; this seems self-defeating – the worst of both fats. **Flora** has a fat level of 38%. **Sainsbury** has been selling a low-fat alternative at only 60% fat, bulked out with whey powder. Unilever has developed **I Can't Believe It's Not Butter**, which has a relatively high fat content, at 70% and contains hydrogenated vegetable oil. For the same fat levels you could smear clotted cream on the bread.

Butter Versus Margarines and Spreads

	Calories	Protein g	Carbos g	Fat g	% Fat of Cals
Butter	737	0.5	0	81.7	99
Diet Clover	383	7.1	0	40	93
Clover	684	0.8	0	75	98
Delight	359	2.8	0	39	97
Asda Olive Gold	538	0.2	0	60	100
Asda Soy Margarine	740	0	0	83.5	100
Blue Band	730	0.1	0	82	100
I Can't Believe It's Not Butter	675	0.8	0	70	93
I Can't Believe It's Not Butter Light	370	3	0	40	97
Dripping	891	0	0	99	100

Even diet products contain high levels of fat. The saving is usually water in the product in place of calories.

FROMAGE FRAIS

By rights fromage frais ought to be listed under cheese, but modern versions make it more relevant next to yoghurt.

Fromage frais was originally fresh, low-fat unripened cheese potted and eaten within a week. The sense of creative adventure in the trade has created a spectrum of innovative fromage frais, very few of which anyone might guess to be cheese at all: **Munch Bunch, Pot Shots** and **Hippopots** for children; **Shape** and **Delight** for slimmers; **Quark** in Germany is eaten with fruit for breakfast; **Chambourcy** in France; **Valfrais** for dips. The dairy industry has discovered a product that has very little fat, no taste and can do with it what it likes. The fat content is graded into three categories: ordinary at 6.8%, low-fat at 3% and diet at 0.1% or even less. Low-fat varieties lack the flavour of full-fat versions. The taste goes granular and unattractive, so it is usually disguised with flavours. Larger, 500 g pots are cheaper all round. Premium prices – as much as 20p – tend to attach themselves to brands and to organic.

Factory versions take off some of the water, which produces a glossy 'pot of emulsion' effect. Craft versions tend to be creamy, firm but gloopy, coarse and structured unlike yoghurt.

MULTIPACK CONFUSION

As the fat content drops, the games begin. Flavours are introduced and the pop-art packaging comes on line. Sizes of pot vary from 60 g to 400 g. Multiply the confusion by multi-pack offers, x 6, x 12, x 18 etc, and by any reasonable standards, the pricing structure is mesmerizingly incomprehensible. This is food sold as a TV game show. Ordinary fromage frais is 25p for 100 g. Compare that to the prices per 100 g from the same week from different packaging shown in the table below. Safeway seem intent on hiding their best buy by putting it in 41 g pots. Onken at 25p for 100 g, sold in 500 g cartons, not only tastes the best but is nearly the cheapest.

Sainsbury	30p
Petit Fromage Frais (in packs of 6 x 360 g)	18p
Petit Fromage Frais (in packs of 18 x 60 g)	21p
St Ivel	31p
Ski	31p
Yoplait (in packs of 6 x 60 g)	38p
Country Love (in 150 g pots)	16p
Petit Danone (in packs of 12 x 60 g)	26p
*Safeway (in packs of 6 x 41 g)	15p
Tesco	30p

BEST BUYS **Neal's Yard unpasteurized fromage frais is a fine example of its historical origins. **Sainsbury** import fromage frais from France which is very distinctive; denser and stickier, it has a yoghurt-like flavour and a resounding sweet mild vanilla finish, very imitative of cream. Also, there is **Sainsbury's La Faisselle**, billed as a French country-style natural fromage frais. The differences are marked, La Faisselle being intrinsically white, more cheesily granulated than the smoothness of the own-label, and discernibly with an ancestry in cheese-making. The low-fat version, however, is a eunuch by comparison to either. Some good ewes'-milk versions, notably **Sussex High Weald Farm**, are sold through health shops.

CHEESE

TRADITIONAL ENGLISH CHEESES · NEW BRITISH
CHEESES · DUTCH CHEESES · FRENCH AOC
CHEESES · OTHER TRADITIONAL FRENCH
CHEESES · ITALIAN CHEESES · SPANISH
CHEESES · SWISS CHEESES

Three out of four cheeses sold in supermarkets are called Cheddar. The
rest just make up the weight, providing a mere veneer of choice, and
more likely a device to divert farmers' subsidies to supermarket bottom
lines. The great abundance is a mirage. Great names like Camembert are
prostituted and abused. A supermarket probably wouldn't sell a ripe
Camembert, so instead they sell something else that they call
'Camembert', which at its best is unripe and at its worst is just sponge
protein.

The biggest difference between cheeses is just price not quality,
especially in Cheddar where there is no logic to price. It is predictable
that the scale of supermarkets means all cheese will be factory-made.
The mistake supermarkets made was to cut out the *affineur*, who took
cheeses from the farms and ripened them before sale.

'Sell-by' or 'consume-by' dates on cheeses need to be read with
caution. Many cheeses will not have reached full maturity by the date
given. Chilling regulations mean most cheeses are sold in more

---

CHEESEBOARDS

Cheesophiles argue that a proper
cheeseboard should contain examples of all seven different styles of
cheese: fresh (Ricotta, Feta); natural rind (goats'); bloomy rind
(Camembert); wash rind
(Milleens, Langres); semi-soft
(Gubbeen, Reblochon); hard
(Cheddar) and blue (Stilton). At
the Paris restaurant of the great
cheese factor Androuët, a whole
meal is constructed around the
seven styles, with two or three trays
of different cheese of each type
offered in ascending order, from
fresh right through to blue – with
Roquefort, symbolically, offered on
its own at the end. As a compromise, perhaps, three cheeses – a
hard, a blue and a goat – will cover
most eventualities. The plasticization of cheese has encouraged people to serve a great number of different cheeses. A proper farmhouse cheese deserves to be taken
more seriously and given a course
of its own, with fresh bread and perhaps a salad. The British habit is
taking of cheese to finish a meal.
The French custom of having the
sweet after cheese provides a better
grammar for the end of the meal.

stabilized conditions, but these will not help them ripen. The best place to store cheese is in the salad compartment of the fridge, ideally in a plastic container; take them out two hours before serving. Soft farmhouse cheeses can be ripened swiftly by keeping them at room temperatures for a few days.

Cheese
Percentage fat of calories in leading cheeses

	Calories	Protein g	Carbos g	Fat g	% Fat of Cals
Brie	319	19.3	0	27	76
Camembert	297	21	0	23.7	71
Cheddar	412	25.5	0.1	34.5	75
Danish Blue	347	20	0	29.6	76
Edam	333	26	0	25.5	68
Feta	250	15.5	1.5	20	72
Gouda	375	24	0	31	74
Parmesan	452	15.6	0	32.7	65
Philadelphia	313	8.6	0	31	89
Stilton	411	22.7	0	35.5	77
Lancashire	376	23.4	0.1	31.3	74

TRADITIONAL ENGLISH CHEESES

CAERPHILLY · CHEDDAR · CHESHIRE · DERBY ·
GLOUCESTER · LANCASHIRE · RED LEICESTER ·
STILTON · WENSLEYDALE

The nine English territorial farmhouse cheeses represent some of the last links with the foods that people have eaten on this island for hundreds of years. Records of Cheshire cheese go back to the Domesday Book, Cheddar was revered by the Elizabethans and others can trace their roots back to at least the 1700s. Abused, imitated and adulterated, these nine cheeses can at least claim to be our heritage. They are, at their best, some of the finest hard cheeses found anywhere in the world, though what is normally found in plastic wrappers in supermarkets bears little relation to the original article.

There are signs of a change in attitude. **Tesco** has taken on Juliet Harbutt, the creator of the British Cheese Awards (BCA), to advise on cheese. **Sainsbury** has started to pack hard crumbly cheese in waxed paper. There is still quite a way to go before any idea of quality and genuine choice takes hold. Pick'n'mix selections are where the Industry's heart lies. Hopefully, however, these sampling exercises will be effective enough that most people will not be fooled twice by emulsions of fat with pineapple pieces.

Many factors undermined farmhouse cheese-making. In 1940, the Ministry of Food unilaterally declared fresh milk was to have priority over cheese-making. This war-time edict was never properly repealed. The post-war Labour government preferred, or understood, industrialized production better and was in no mood to favour the traditionally Conservative farmers. The pasteurization of all milk robbed the cheese-maker of the individuality that raw milk offered, so too did the standardization of breeds of cattle. The supermarkets were happy to preside over the plasticization of cheese in neat vacuum packs and, more recently, to encourage the growth of novelty lines. The now defunct Milk Marketing Board unashamedly tried to pass off factory cheeses as if they were farmhouse; trying to give these some claim to regionality or tradition when they transparently did not was to the detriment of any cheese that did.

The current revival in British cheese-making, it has to be said, has come about despite these successive acts of genocide. Somewhat late in the day, supermarkets have begun to package traditional cheeses in parchment rather than plastic. A big step forward — especially for the crumblier cheeses like Lancashire.

CAERPHILLY

This was the miner's cheese, only made west of the Usk. Now the best is made in Somerset and some new farms in Dyfed. Good Caerphilly is magnolia-white.

Caerphilly is a simple cheese. Morning milk is mixed with some from the night before and warmed, with the whey from the day before's cheese used as a starter. Before salting, the curd should be soft enough to retain the imprint of a hand. It is moulded for 30 minutes, salted again, pressed and then washed in brine. Factories have tended to go for higher acidities, which is safer and quicker, usually by increasing the level of starter.

Caerphilly can be eaten after a week, but becomes smoother and sharper with age. It is best taken out of its vacuum pack, wiped dry and left to breathe and recover. It is a cheese that loses most of its character in mass-production. Unpasteurized versions are much closer to the character of the original.

BEST BUYS **Duckett's Caerphilly** made by Chris Duckett at Walnut Tree Farm, Wedmore, Somerset, has a whole cellar given over to it exclusively at **Neal's Yard Dairy** in Covent Garden. Aged properly, Caerphilly alters its complexion quickly. The fresh cheese is bready, pliable, fresh and pleasant; by four weeks it will have acquired that distinctive effervescence and hints of primrose; by six weeks the acidity mellows dramatically; after 8-12 weeks, the crust will go peachy grey and then it behaves more like a Brie, losing its magnolia whiteness, going a deep cream with orange hues and developing an intense creaminess, like a French cheese. Other typical tasting notes on a fresh Caerphilly are: 'friable lemons, crushed with bracken, hints of stone walls'. Duckett's also make a **Wedmore**, with a band of chives through the centre, and an intense **Torville**, matured for six weeks and washed in cider.

Other good examples from Dyfed include the smooth wax unpasteurized rounds from **Caws Cenarth** of Pontseli (there is also a smoked version); **Glynhynod Caerphilly**, unpasteurized and organic from John and Patrice Savage-Onstwedder; and **Welsh Farmhouse Caerphill**y, made by Peter Sayer with pasteurized milk, to be eaten young. He also smokes a variation and the **St Ishmael** is with laver bread.

CHEDDAR

Cheddar was almost certainly first made with sheep's milk. By early Tudor times, however, co-operatives were making gigantic tall Cheddars from cows' milk. The use of common land meant that each family put its cows' milk into the co-operative and was paid back in cheese. Although most of Somerset made Cheddar cheese (as did East Devon, Dorset and, later, Wiltshire), the parish of Cheddar and nearby

Mere produced outstanding cheeses. The cattle used were probably Dairy Shorthorn.

In Elizabethan times, Cheddar was rare and fetched high prices; it was regarded both here and in Europe as one of the finest cheeses in the world. In 1724 Daniel Defoe visited Cheddar: '(on the large common) in which the whole herd of the cows, belonging to the town, do feed; the ground is exceedingly rich, and as the whole village are cow keepers, they take care to keep up the goodness of the soil, by agreeing to lay on large quantities of dung for manuring and enriching the land.' Ironically it was to be 150 years before such ideas on improving the pastures took hold for the dairy industry at large. It also questions the assumption that the British can never work effectively in co-operatives. Defoe said these Cheddars were 'the best cheese that England affords, if not, that the whole world affords'.

In the middle of the 19th century, the expansion of farmhouse cheese-making was further limited by a cattle plague combined with the growing demand from the new cities for fresh milk and, by 1870, further by imports from new cheese factories in Denmark, Holland, France and America. In 1939, the last year before the Ministry of Food centralized production, 513 farms in the South-west were registered as makers of cheese, of which 333 were making Cheddar. By 1948 there were only 57. By 1974 there were 33. By 1988, only 11 farms were making Cheddar in the traditional way and only four were still using unpasteurized milk. In Cheddar itself no Cheddar is made any more, although there is a touristy farm-shop museum nearby. Residents even raised a petition against the setting up of a creamery in the '80s.

Cheddar takes its name from 'cheddaring', the traditional hand turning and stacking of the curds to release the whey. In the traditional recipe, the rennet is added to the milk and starter at 29°C (84°F). The curds are cut, placed in a vat, the whey expressed out and the curds heated to 32-38°C (90-100°F) for 40 minutes. (The two scaldings of the milk are distinctive: overcooked, it goes rubbery.) The whey is drawn off again, the curds cut and stacked in 8-12 inch blocks, and turned by hand to work out more whey (cheddaring). This smoothes the rubbery, spongy curds. These are broken again, salted, milled for uniformity, moulded and pressed. It is then kept at 13°C (55°F) – the ideal storage temperature for the cheese.

Cheddar today is made across the world in massive machines with names like Cheddarmaster or the Bell-Siro system that takes the milk at one end and produces 18 kg (40 lb) blocks at the other. Sealed in plastic rather than the traditional cloth (in which it could breathe), these will be matured for 5-12 months depending on the strength of flavour required. The technology was the result of the collusion between big dairies and supermarkets in the '50s that led to mass uniformity. Another factor was that to make bulk cheese, the starter culture had to be used in ever greater concentrations. Professor Barry Law at the Institute of Food Research at Reading has pointed out that the modern cultures are very efficient but have produced bland cheeses.

Nevertheless, Cheddar is the biggest-selling supermarket cheese. Its success lies in its robustness: better than other cheeses it can withstand the industrial mauling.

Safeway, **Tesco** and, this year, **Sainsbury** have introduced different grading levels to encourage Cheddar buyers to experiment with other cheeses of similar strengths. Canadian cheddar is **Safeway's** strongest at 5, where a mature **Davidstow** from Somerset is a middling 3. **Sainsbury** equates the strength code to maturity – mild being 3 months, very strong being up to 2 years.

Where the precise taste is reminiscent of proper Cheddar, the lack of texture and variety in these vacuum-packed slabs places them nearer to the confectionery counter. The zeal for something novel has seen two separate generations of sub-Cheddars sold in the past few years. First there were the plastic, technicolour derivatives invoking quasi-historical names – ALBANY with cumin; APPLEWOOD, smoked and rolled in paprika; CHARNWOOD smoked; CHEVIOT with chives; ILCHESTER with beer; NUTWOOD with raisins and nuts; RUTLAND with garlic, beer and parsley; and, most vivid of all, WINDSOR RED following the old practice of adding elderberry wine. The flavours have no significant interaction with the cheese and are purely cosmetic.

Last Christmas, a second generation arrived which bends the mind further: Cheddar with smoked garlic; Cheddar with Marmite; Cheddar with Christmas pudding in neat little triangles. A bizarre marriage with pineapple pushes the price up to £2.55 per lb. As outrageous as these may be, they are not horrible – they are intriguing. What they have very little to do with at all is Cheddar.

The word 'farmhouse' has also been devalued. Proper Cheddars made on a farm with milk from specific herds and grazed on specific fields change by the season and the maker: sweet or sharp, moist or hard. Put these cheeses into factory production with uniform milk and machinery and it is a different product. Factory cheeses still win prizes at cheese shows, but often these are judged by factory graders, or they are often special cheeses made solely for the occasion, or the prizes are only for factory Cheddars. They will be sold to specialist cheese shops or to supermarkets as premium brands. They are the exceptions which are supposed to delude the market place into believing such artisan practices are still the rule. Traditional Cheddar was round. Factory cheese was oblong, to suit the cutting mechanism for the supermarkets, but even this dividing line is being eroded. To protect themselves from this corruption, many of the new generation of cheese-makers using Cheddar techniques are calling their cheeses by other names, for example Llanboidy or Gospel Green (see New British cheeses, page 59).

BEST BUYS The following seven examples – all but the last made in Somerset – are possibly the only surviving, genuinely traditional Cheddar cheeses. Some of the unpasteurized versions lean towards what are deemed today as faults – most commonly an eggy sulphurousness – but nonetheless underline their supreme individuality and potency. A specialist cheese shop or factor will mature the cheeses for more than a year to bring them to maturity. It is this art, as much as anything else, that the culture of the supermarket has destroyed – to the detriment of us all.

***Chewton Cheddar** is made by Nigel Pooley at Chewton Dairy Farms, Chewton Mendip, in 4, 6 and 56 lb rounds, using vegetarian rennet. It was over-all Best Cheddar winner at the 1995 British Cheese Awards.

***Cricket Cheddar** is made by Derek Butler of Cricket Malherbie Farms, in 36 lb rounds using only local milk and vegetarian rennet.

****Green's** is made by John Green, at Newton Farm, third-generation Cheddar-maker. Richly buttery, it has extraordinary depth of flavour and composed intensity. Their Traditional Mature Farmhouse Cheddar was a Gold Medal winner at the 1995 British Cheese Awards.

Unpasteurized ****Keen's Cheddar** is made by George and Stephen Keen of Moorhayes Farm, in smaller 3-7 lb or 60 lb cloth-bound rounds. Dry, intense and full-bodied, it is nutty and sweet, with hints of liquorice and green grass. It was a Silver Medal award winner at the BCA.

Unpasteurized ****Montgomery's Cheddar** is made by J. A. & E. Montgomery at Manor Farm, North Cadbury, using milk from their own Friesian/Holstein cows. Known as a wet 'gummy, clammy, chewy' cheese, it is superbly rich, explosive, complex, with an almost curried acidity. It was a Silver Medal award winner at the BCA.

Unpasteurized ****Quicke's** is made by Mary Quicke and partners in Devon from milk of a single herd. Intense and tangy, with hints of almonds to hazelnuts, it has a searing acidity. It was a Gold Medal winner at the British Cheese Awards. They also do a pasteurized version.

Other good makes of Cheddar who have won awards at the British Cheese Awards are **Denhay**, **Pilgrim's Choice** from North Downs Dairy Co, **Gowrie** from **Ingle Smokehouse**, **Longman**, **Barber**, **Nuttalls** (smoked); **Lockerbie Creamery**, **Horlicks**; **Campletown**, **Bagborough Farm**, **South Caernarfon**, **Loch Arthur Creamery** and **Kirkwall's Orkney**.

CHESHIRE

Cheshire claims to be one of the oldest identifiable cheeses, thanks to its mention in the Domesday Book. Properly, it should come from within a 20-mile radius of Whitchurch; and for centuries it was the major industry of the area. The cheese's saltiness came from the ground: Cheshire is, and was, also the centre of the salt industry. Ironically the

Nantwich Cheese Show, now a Mecca each July for makers and admirers of myriad cheese concoctions, was originally just for the local Cheshire cheese.

The recipe is a variation on Cheddar (or the other way round), but the temperature at which the curds are set is lower and the cheese is not pressed. This makes it a more difficult cheese to keep (it needs turning daily) and it was usually sold young. Creameries are inclined to make raw wet cheeses to get extra weight.

Two types of Cheshire are made: the original white, and an orange version dyed with annatto. Both types are sold young, from about 2-3 weeks. The crumbliness has worked against it in the supermarket, where a denser product survives better in vacuum packs.

The traditional ways of making Cheshire have been maintained by two women: Christine Appleby, and the late Mrs Bourne of Bank Farm, Malpass. Today there are only perhaps 10 farms making traditional Cheshire, where 20 years ago there were 50 or 60 and in 1939 there were 400. Cheshire cheese is an endangered species.

Tom Hassal, who runs the cheese section of the Cheshire Show gives these instructions to judges on looking for a winning cheese. 'Use all the senses: first, sight: the colour should be clean throughout, a buttery waxy, cream to yellow. It should fill the iron without breaking at the edges. The back of the iron should be clean. Second, touch: break a piece off in your fingers and it will become friable – but should not be so sticky that it would stick to the ceiling. Third, listen: hold the iron to the ear and squeeze the sample and you can hear how moist it is. Fourth, taste: it should be silky, rich, warm, with a little bitterness/sourness, chewy and grassy'. Professional cheese tasters will often use Cheshire to cleanse the palate after tasting other cheeses.

BEST BUYS **Appleby** from Hawkstone Abbey Farm, Weston, Shropshire, is handmade, unpasteurized, bound in calico, and uses annatto for a deep salmon colour. The milk is from their own herd of Friesian and Holsteins, and they use a minimum amount of starter, which slows the process. The cheese is kept on the farm for 6-10 weeks, but some factors will mature it much longer – for up to a year. The white cheese is a British Cheese Awards silver medallist.

Bourne from Bank Farm, Malpass, first won the Cheshire Show prize in 1933 and repeated the victory in 1993. It is not as well distributed as Appleby's, but just as good.

Other good names are **Butlers**, a BCA gold medal winner; **Windsor** of Whitchurch; **Hares** of Whitchurch, winners of the BCA bronze medal (a family farm for 35 years on the Shropshire/Cheshire border with 160 Friesians, their cheese is grassy, lemony, and usually sold after 2-3 weeks but can improve with age); **Beltons**, which also won a BCA bronze medal; and **Overton Hall** from Mr and Mrs Barnett at Overton Hall, Cheshire.

DERBY

One of the great cheeses that distinguished itself, like Cheshire, early on from the wealth of Midlands cheese-making. The original cheese was 35-40 cm (14-16 inches) across and 10-15 cm (4-6 inches) high, weighing nearly 13.5 kg (30 lb), the best wrapped in calico, though some were kept in paste and flour. This cheese died out around 1925, partly due to the excessive secrecy among makers. The traditional recipe was similar to Cheddar and Cheshire, very akin to the Scottish Dunlop, and made in Gouda-like rounds with the salt added to the outside after moulding. A variation lived on because Derby was also the pioneer of large-scale factory dairies set up in the town and at Longford. Following a grant in 1862, the first cheese factory was set up in Siddals Road, Derby, using the steam from next-door's silk mill. By 1876 there were 10 factories devoted to cheese, serving five counties. Even this softer version, however, has declined into oblivion.

More familiar to look at – if not similar in taste – is SAGE DERBY, which is about half the size but vividly green. Traditionally these were the spring cheeses, mixing the curd with the strained juice of sage leaves (quite brown) and young spinach or potato tops (for greening). The moulds were filled with alternating layers of the green cheese and the white to produce a spectacular combination which was brought out for the harvest workers at the end of summer. The vivid emerald waxed rounds sold as traditional in supermarkets are just poor processed sweaty cheeses, with odd bits of stalk and leaf inside, which brings out the worst of the sage in its 'dirty-football-socks' mode.

GLOUCESTER

A mild cheese that lends itself to abuse, Gloucester is relatively easy to make – and easy to make poorly. It is often sold too young. There were no gold awards to Gloucester in the British Cheese Awards, only silvers. Sometimes called 'the orphan' because it was made with the milk from Gloucester cows which are now a rare breed. Proper production came to a halt in 1983 with the closing of Watercombe Creamery in Somerset. It was made with the skimmed evening milk added to the morning, as with Cheddar, but washed in beer after a month to give it colour (though now it is achieved by adding annatto).

A good Gloucester should be more solid than Cheshire, less flaky and more waxy than Cheddar. Single Gloucester was made with the skimmed milk from the farms, with the cream going for butter and for the farmer's table. Double gloucester, made with whole milk, was the premium cheese for selling at market and its reputation grew as the barges took it north to Birmingham and south to London. Some is still made out of a sense of tradition by other cheese-makers.

Like Cheddar, Gloucester has spawned a number of gimmicky children of dubious parentage: ABBEYDALE with onions and chives; COTSWOLD with chives; the popular HUNTSMAN, layered with Stilton; and SHERWOOD with sweet pickle.

BEST BUYS **Appleby's of Hawkstone Abbey Farm, Shropshire, are as well-known for their Cheshire, but also make this lightweight cheese (compared to Cheddar). They do a beautifully orange version of double.

*Martell's by Charles Martell, of Laurel Farm, Dymock, is made from the milk of one of the only surviving Gloucester herds (his first love). He no longer makes the Double Gloucester, only the single – 'a good cooker', sometimes bound with nettles.

**Quicke's by Mary Quicke of Devon, who is famous for her Cheddar, but also makes 'enigmatic toffee-like versions of both single and double Gloucester', underlining the link between the two processes.

**Smart's by Diana Smart of Old Ley Farm, Gloucestershire, is made using milk from their own herd. The double is matured for seven months, 'like double fudge with citrus zest'; the single is paler, made with the full-cream milk of the previous day added to the day's skimmed milk, to give a flavour of double cream and scorched caramel.

LANCASHIRE

This was a kitchen cheese, first differentiated from Cheshire around 1700. The best was said to come from the south of the county and two kinds were made – acid and fatty. The acid, like a Cheshire, uses one-day-old curd and was made for a fast sale. The fatty uses the curd from two days' milkings and matures into a softer, stickier, creamier cheese. This was the prime cheese for cooking as it falls away under the heat and does not go stringy like Cheddar. Today the farmhouse label should apply to fatty cheese.

In the old recipe the milk was left overnight to let the acidity rise, then heated and the rennet added. The curd forms in an hour, is cut and the whey drained off after another 30 minutes. It is then cut again (cheddared) to remove more whey. This fresh curd is mixed with the day before's curd (with its higher acidity), ground, salted, moulded and pressed to extract the last drops of whey. It is bandaged after 24 hours and pressed again for 6 hours. It is eaten from 1-6 months old. Until the '60s, the rind of most Lancashire was buttered, but now they are waxed. As a result they have become wetter. **Neal's Yard Dairy** is the only factor currently buttering its Lancashires.

Unlike Cheshire, a good Lancashire should be moist enough to stick to your fingers, crumbly, soft, fatty and mellow: tasting notes include 'lemons, acid body, buttery, tons of grapefruit'. Most is now factory-produced.

It is argued that the more acid cheeses were encouraged as an expedient by the Ministry of Food in the war and this led to the decline of sales in the '70s. There has also been a trend to build up the levels of starter to make them faster-ripening.

BEST BUYS Few supermarkets sell more than one variety of Lancashire. **Nuttal's** initiative in packing crumbly cheeses more appropriately marks a major breakthrough.

**Kirkham's from Goosnargh, Lancashire, uniquely use the unpasteurized milk from three days' milkings to produce a lighter buttery cheese with more complex flavours and peppery overtones. It was voted Supreme Champion at the 1995 British Cheese Awards.

*J.M. Nuttal, a brand of **Dairy Crest**, has introduced a new form of brown paper packaging backed with cellophane, that allows the cheese to breathe more happily and retain its 'sense of crumbly lemons'.

Other good names to look for include: **Carron Lodge** and **Joseph Heler**, both BCA gold medallists; Carron Lodge also won a silver for its fatty Lancashire; **Sandham's** of Preston, which is very sweet, fruity and supple; **Butler's**, which is soft and buttery with hints of grapefruit; **Centurion**, which is buttery and excellent for cooking; and **Dewlay**, which is often a classic cheese 'wetter, yeasty and pungent'.

RED LEICESTER

Leicester used to be made alongside Stilton, using up the leftover milk. It was widely established and acclaimed in the 1700s. The first factory opened in 1875 and farmhouse production died out by the 1920s. The lavish use of annatto actually indicated attempts to conceal faults in the cheese, but these faults also contributed to the flavour. The addition of annatto was stopped as an economy in the war and hence the coloured cheese became known as RED LEICESTER to differentiate it from the more anaemic version.

The rennet is added at 23-24°C (74-76°F) and the curds are cheddared smaller than for Cheddar, which makes it flakier. It is packed in the widest hoops of any English cheese, 50 cm (20 in) across, and left to ripen until a blue mould develops. It is normally kept for three months, but is better after six when it develops a nuttiness.

BEST BUYS Red Leicester is a widely abused cheese, but some good versions are still made by **Tuxford and Tebbutt** at Melton Mowbray (a one-time gold medal winner at the BCA), after a valiant rearguard action to preserve it by Patrick Rance and Elizabeth David in 1983. Cheddar-specialists **Quicke's** make some in Devon, as do Cheshire specialists **Overton Hall** in Cheshire.

BRITISH CHEESE AWARDS

The British Cheese Awards, now in their third year, are a uniquely validated competition open to all producers. The judging is split between cheese experts and authorities from other food disciplines The winners in 1995 were:

Supreme Champion:
Mrs Kirkham's Lancashire

Cheese Lovers Trophy and Best New or Experimental:
Doolin from Waterford Foods

Best Scottish:
Mature Cheddar from The Cheese Company, Lockerbie

Best Speciality Cheese:
Hereford Hop from Malvern Cheesewrights

Best Blue:
Cropwell Bishop Blue

Best Cheddar:
Chewton extra mature

Best Semi-soft:
Oria (Organic Sheep's) from Manch Estate

Best Soft White Rind Cheese:
St. Killian

Best Fresh Young Cheese:
Godraevy Plain in Herb Oil

Note: The awards are not definitive because they only refer to the best cheeses on the day and to those (more than 400) who entered. They provide a good guide to the quality of the makers and cheeses displaying the gold, silver and bronze awards are worth seeking out.

STILTON

Stilton is the only British cheese to have protected its name – by court judgement in 1969, affirming the Stilton-makers' definition laid down in 1910 that Stilton has to be made in the district of Melton Mowbray and surrounding areas within the counties of Leicestershire, Derbyshire and Nottinghamshire. It was never made in Stilton itself. A local cheese, known as QUENBY, was sold at the Bell Inn (now restored) at Stilton and its reputation and name spread with the coaching parties that passed through.

Patrick Rance attributes its parentage possibly to Lady Beaumont's cheese at Quenby Hall, Hungarton, just outside Leicester. It was certainly made around 1722 and its development was probably down to Elizabeth Scarbrow, a housekeeper at the Hall. She married a farmer called Paulet who gave her the milk. They had two daughters, one who helped her make the cheese and one who married Cowper Thornhill, the landlord of the Bell Inn. As late as 1756, Stilton still seems to have been sustained by this family link. By the end of the century, however, Stiltons were being made across the district.

These would have been potent creamy cheeses, often called 'English Parmesan', which suggests they were kept much longer than the fresh-faced creamy versions now sold. Defoe gorily points out in his *Travels*

Around England (and this was the origin of scooping) that two spoons were given to eat a Stilton, one to dig out the centre and one to eat the maggots and mites that lived in the crust (this was deemed the point of ripeness). Sometimes the rind was washed in beer, or wine was added to the curds – hence the tradition of pouring Port into a Stilton. The serving of Stilton at Christmas stemmed from making the best cheeses from September milk.

Good Stilton looks like shattered porcelain and should never have a brown rim inside the crust. The streaking of the needle marks for the bluing can be seen like spoke scorches going from the outside in. The cheeses are not pressed and as the whey drains it leaves cavities where the air can penetrate and create the bluing. Good Stilton is hard and buttery, with streaks of salt and a smell of flowers. It is matured for 3-4 months. Factors point out that the pasteurized versions are ripening quicker than unpasteurized versions. Fifteen weeks' keeping is generally regarded as a peak. To keep a Stilton, the surface should be covered with cling film or a damp cloth.

WHITE STILTON, originally preferred by Nottinghamshire miners, is still made in the same way, but without the added mould or *Penicillium roqueforti*. The rennet is added at 29-30°C (84-86°F) and the curds set in about an hour. It is then sliced, drained for an hour, lightly squeezed and left for 12 hours. Next the curd is broken and salted and the cheese is ready for the mould.

The enthusiasm of the past year has been to sell White Stilton with dates and pecans or apricots, which underlines the trend to move cheese out of the dairy and into the novelty area. The king has been put into pantomime.

SHROPSHIRE BLUE, the same cheese only with added annatto, is marked up often by £1 more again. However, in its different clothes it is a reminder of the aristocracy of the genre. The annatto, as with some Gloucesters, serves to eke out different elements.

BEST BUYS There are six Stilton makers, all of whom might claim to produce excellent cheese. The protection of the name and the weight of the cheese's reputation have allowed them to uphold the principles. Cheeses from the same day, the same dairy, and the same milk can still vary noticeably. Good Stilton will become buttery and explosive; under-ripe, a common criticism, it will be just cream and blue, unseparated.

**Colston Bassett has been made by Mr Wagstaff in Nottingham for the last 25 years. It was the last of the dairies to give up unpasteurized milk, but seemingly with only a marginal difference in quality. The broadest cheeses measure 26 cm (10½ in) across and have an intense flavour of herbs and white wine. They also make a definitive Shropshire Blue.

Long Clawson, in Melton Mowbray, began as a co-operative for local farmers. Its cheeses are not quite so broad as Colston Basset and are inclined to firmness.

J. M. Nuttal of Hartingdon, although owned by Dairy Crest, is still capable of producing brilliant cheese, which can be golden-crusted, with a wide variation in textures. A good example has won silver at the British Cheese Awards.

Tuxford and Tebbutt, of Thorpe End, Melton Mowbray, is the dairy closest to Stilton's birthplace, eight miles north of Quenby. Although it comes under the umbrella of a large concern (**Express Foods**), the quality and notable creaminess of their Stiltons survives. It has been conspicuously successful at the British Cheese Awards, winning gold for its mature cheese.

Milway Foods of Melton Mowbray supply much own-label supermarket Stilton. **Cropwell Bishop** is made at the Somerset Creamery, in fact in Nottinghamshire. They also do a credible Shropshire Blue which won the 1995 BCA Best Blue.

STILTON PRICES Supermarkets mark up mature Stilton against ordinary cheese with enthusiasm – from 30p to almost £1. There is some weight loss and improvement in flavour, nevertheless the extra cost seems rapacious. Equally **Sainsbury** sell vegetarian Stilton at a 20p mark-up, which is exorbitant.

WENSLEYDALE

Wensleydale, or cheeses like it – possibly made with goats' milk – are mentioned in the Domesday Book. The recipe was well adapted to making cheese from small amounts of milk. In that sense it was true farmhouse cheese. It is a simple cheese, dependent on the quality of the raw milk. Its decline is traceable precisely to the arrival of bulk milks by train to the Dales and, later, the impact of pasteurization.

The original cheese, made from spring and September milk was round and flat, 30x10 cm (12x4 in). Summer cheese was tubby, like Stilton (and, in some cases, naturally allowed to develop a blue mould), designed for the Christmas market. The rennet is added at 36°C (97°F) and the curds form within 15 minutes. They are cut and then heated again, pressed and salted. The taste should be of wet curds, milk and grass. 'Once tasted by epicures, Wensleydale is not likely soon to be forgotten,' said Law's Grocer's Manual grandly in 1950.

Alas it was already being forgotten. **Dairy Crest** stopped production of Wensleydale at Coverham and Kirkby Malzead in 1983. A management buyout of the dairy at Hawes is possibly a last lifeline, but so far there has been more hype than evidence of a determination to re-establish the virtues of true Wensleydale.

Mark Robertson at **Redesdale Dairy**, Northumberland, still makes an unusual variation, mixing cows' and sheep's milk. A more accurate reincarnation of traditional Wensleydale may well be another Dales cheese, **Swaledale**. The aromatic, cream caramel **Malvern Ewe**, made since 1988 at Worcester, employs a Wensleydale recipe using, untraditionally, sheep's milk.

NEW BRITISH CHEESES

BEENLEIGH BLUE · BOSWORTH · BUTTON ·
CORNISH YARG · DUDDLESWELL · EMLETT ·
GOLDEN CROSS · GOSPEL GREEN LANARK BLUE ·
LITTLE RYDINGS LLANGLOFFAN · SPENWOOD ·
TYMSBORO' · WATERLOO · WELLINGTON ·
YORKSHIRE BLUE

The revival in farmhouse cheese-making over the last ten years has been encouraging. The quality of many of these new cheeses is as good as anything that has been seen before. However, the cheese-makers remain an individualistic and private band of people, and only very rarely will any one shop sell more than a few varieties.

The Specialist Cheese-makers' Association lists around 250 new cheeses, though many are variations on the same themes. They are all individually made, using traditional craft techniques. It is no coincidence that the same maker is responsible for a number of the cheeses.

Revival remains in the air. A number of first-class new cheeses emerged at the British Cheese Awards which are worth seeking out. Notably BERKSWELL from Ram Hall Dairy; Laddiswell AVONDALE; JOUVENET and also CORINNA from Gedi; and PILGRIM'S CHOICE from North Down Dairy. Another gold medallist was the revived DEVON GARLAND, now made by Jeremy Frank-Pitt under instruction from its creator Hilary Charnley.

CHURNTON was advertised on television as the first new English cheese since Lymeswold, although the label stoically is a black-and-white photograph of a 1920s cloth-capped milkman and also suggests – always a bad sign – that it is 'best served straight from the fridge'. Churnton looks like Cheddar, has a faint lemony smell like Lancashire and has the bouncy soft texture of a processed cheese triangle. It is not quite the total waste of time that Lymeswold was, but it is still a factory-made lowest-common-denominator cheese on the marketing of which far too much money has been spent which could have found a better use with any of the other cheeses listed here. **Waitrose** politely suggests it is 'excellent for cooking'.

**BEENLEIGH BLUE

First made 11 years ago by Robin Congdon in the Dart Estuary, Devon, but only in May and June because after that the character of the sheep's

ENGLISH WASHED RIND CHEESES

The trouble with white rind cheeses is that they suggest a Camembert- or a Brie-type of cheese and invariably English cows'-milk cheeses have been bitter. The sweetest is Pencarreg; Bonchester can be good, sometimes excellent, and is often put up as a prime example of modern UK cheese-making. The pick of the style at the BCA was a **Somerset Camembert** from **Lubborn** which won a silver medal. As a sector, however, they have yet to achieve the excellence of the hard cheeses or the far more successful variations using goat and sheep's milk rather than cow's.

milk changes. About 1,500 cheeses are made a year. They are turned six times and kept at 22°C (72°F) for the first day to encourage the bacteria to develop. They are then spiked – to allow the air in for the bluing – and salted. The cheese are matured for four months, though the flavour will improve for eight or nine. The new year's cheeses are first sold in September. They are steely blue, tangy, rich and – unusually – slightly sweet. Congdon also makes HARBOURNE BLUE from goats' milk and sometimes produces variations to order, including a very good DEVONSHIRE BLUE.

**BOSWORTH

Hugh Lillingstone makes this series of equally outstanding pocket-sized goats' cheeses, 9 cm (3½ in) across, in Staffordshire. Superbly packaged with leaves from the estate, they are firm and dry when young, but develop a sensational burnt caramel flavour with a wonderful subtle citrus finish as they age. They are very intense, so only a little is required for the full effect. Lillingstone also makes CLIFTON, a smaller version of Bosworth.

BUTTON

Both Bosworth and Button were out shadowed in the British Cheese Awards by this tiny fresh cheese, which scooped not only the Best Fresh Cheese award but the Supreme Champion in 1994. A pure, floral, brilliantly refreshing example of the cheese-maker's craft.

CORNISH YARG

This is made in Liskeard, Cornwall and named after Mr Gray (spelt backwards) who discovered the old recipe. Now made by Mike Horrell in 3.2 kg (7 lb) rounds, it is wrapped in nettles, which begin to turn pink and crinkle with age. Young Yarg resembles Caerphilly. After 4-6 weeks it develops into a softer, creamier cheese. Often said to be one of the best cheeses to go with wine, it is now widely available in supermarkets. It has a subtle blandness, with edges of sooty grey from the rind which is also eaten.

DUDDLESWELL

Started in the early '80s by the Hardy family at the Sussex High Weal Dairy, who also make very good Haloumi, Feta and soft ewes'-milk cheeses. Made from local ewes' milk, the small truckles are 20 cm (8 in) tall. The skin is mottled pale orange, the paste parchment yellow. Sweeter than Spenwood, it has an intense dryness with walnut edges and verdant tones.

EMLETT

Made by Mary Holbrook in Timsbury, Avon, this is a round craggy cheese, 7x3.5 cm (2¾x2 in), with white flecks on pallid shades of cream. When it is young it stands out white and pure and firm, but when properly matured it wrinkles and the orangey-pink pigment comes through as the curd softens. Tasting notes include, 'burnt cream, very strong, very spiky, a concentrated sensation of burning'.

GOLDEN CROSS

A goats'-cheese log made by Kevin and Alison Blunt of Lewes, East Sussex. Notable as it is, it is not widely available.

GOSPEL GREEN

James and Cathy Lane started making cheese in Petworth, Sussex, in the early '80s. Gospel Green is one of the most admired of the new cheeses, 'because it tastes as if it might have been around for 400 years'. It is a small production, using local unpasteurized milk, made in 18x14 cm (7x6 in) truckles. A cross between Cheshire and Cheddar, it is cloth bound (which leaves an imprint), a deep buttery yellow, and quite springy when young. Tasting notes include, 'supple, smooth, grasses, lemons, even grapefruit'.

LANARK BLUE

Made by Humphrey Errington in, predictably, Lanarkshire from a single flock of sheep that graze on the moorland heather, this cheese is herbaceous in flavour and at its best when young and creamy rather than flaky. It shot to national prominence when a zealous Environmental Health Officer alleged it was contaminated. The case has become a *cause célèbre*, going all the way to the House of Lords, who have ordered up the said stock for their dining room.

**LITTLE RYDINGS

A ewes'-milk cheese also made by the outstanding Mary Holbrook in Timsbury. It is sour rather than bitter and has much of the unctuousness of a Camembert. The rind is floral and the taste is very long.

LLANGNOFFAN

Leon and Joan Downey make this unpasteurized Cheddar-style cheese from Jersey milk at Castle Morris, Haverfordwest, Dyfed, between March and December. They sell it by mail order or from the farm gate. Fine and crumbly in texture, it is also at the same time dense and creamy, and grassy in flavour with a touch of English mustard.

SPENWOOD

Made in Reading, Berkshire, by Anne Wigmore, the production of this ewes'-milk cheese alternates with Wellington (below). The mould is white-brown with clouds of red, the hard paste is pale lemon. Vegetarian rennet is used. It has a beautiful nutty grapefruit flavour; it is not as tart as Wellington, but still makes the eyes water.

**TYMSBORO'

Mary Holbrook's third cheese is an outstanding goats' cheese. The ashed white pyramid grows a Camembert-style mould on top. With age it dries out and an orange pigmentation appears in the rivulets. The flavour concentrates to a unique and magnificent creamy sharpness. It just tastes of flowers. You would be hard pressed to think of another goats' cheese in Europe to match this.

**WATERLOO

Ann Wigmore in Reading washes the rind of this cheese to take off the rancidity. Made at 6.5x5 cm (3x2 in), it has a grey smoky skin and buttery paste. Soft, crumbly and tart, it is an outstanding cheese, and won a gold medal and category at the BCA. She also makes a WIGMORE, with washed sheep's curd.

PASTEURIZED V UNPASTEURIZED

The romance of unpasteurized cheese is as much to do with history as with taste and quality. Before the pasteurization of all milk, cheese was an individual and specialist craft – in France, women were married on the basis of their cheese-making.

Subtle differences as simple as what straw a cheese might be ripened on, which room, the mean temperature of the year, the bacteria in the storeroom or – most famously – in the caves for Roquefort, created cheeses as distinct as one person to another.

The difference in hard cheese is less marked than it is in soft cheese, where many great names no longer live up to their reputations.

In a blind tasting for the Covent Garden delicatessen Mortimer & Bennett, an independent panel of food writers and experts rated unpasteurized cheeses against their pasteurized counterparts. Unpasteurized outscored pasteurized by 75-25% for goats' cheese; 82-18% for Pont l'Évêque 53-47% for St-Augur; 57-43% for Petite Munster; 67-33% for mountain ewe; 73-23% for St-Paulin and 56-44% for triple cream.

WELLINGTON

The Guernsey cattle on the Duke of Wellington's estate provide the milk for this cheese made again by Anne Wigmore. The rough skin is pink to orange, while the paste is a smooth clean orange. The colour derives from the richness of the milk, and vegetarian rennet is used. It is a dry cheese, with creamy and nutty overtones.

YORKSHIRE BLUE

Made by Judy Bell of Shepherd's Purse, North Yorkshire; she also does a good silver-medal-winning Feta and the more gimmicky OLD YORKE flavoured with herbs.

DUTCH CHEESES

GOUDA · EDAM · MAASDAM

Ninety-eight percent of all Dutch cheese-making is now done in factories. Nearly all the cheese are neatly codified by the colour of their waxed jackets. The Netherlands has one of the longest known histories of cheese-making in Europe, with pots and vessels used in cheese-making having been found in Friesland dating back to the second century BC. There was extensive trade in the Middle Ages, with bargees paying their tolls in cheese. Most of the dairy markets seem to have been set up in the century from 1266. The Dutch were known as 'cheeseheads' from the moulds they used and these were also used as helmets in battle.

The Netherlands was also the first country to respond to the dramatic changes in production with the discovery of mechanized skimmers for milk and pasteurization, and went swiftly from a farm-based economy to co-operative creameries. Today there is a certain frightening rigidity to the cheesemaking. Where the towns still tell tourists about the weighhouses used to check the new cheeses, nearly all today's production is not just colour-coded but seemingly season-co-ordinated, with the added flavour of cumin very much in the ascendancy.

GOUDA

The weigh house at Gouda, south of the Hague, dates back to 1668 and is still used. Sixty percent of all Dutch cheese is now Gouda – usually round, but squares and blocks can be found. The fat level must be above 48%. There is a variation using cream, which must have a fat content of 60%. The young cheeses are waxed in yellow; mature cheese, which can be excellent when as old as two years, are waxed in black. Other colours denote flavourings: green for herbs, mahogany for peppercorns, browny orange for cumin.

EDAM

The town of Edam used to be the export centre for all Dutch cheese. Now the cheese that bears the town's name is made across the country. It is distinctively round and waxed red. The fat content, at 40%, is lower than Gouda . It is usually sold after six weeks, but black-waxed versions can be matured for longer. Other colour codings follow the Gouda litany of green for herbs, or orange for cumin.

MAASDAM

A modern cheese for the modern European market, with distinctive holes and a nutty flavour to emulate Emmenthal. Sometimes it goes by other names, such as LEERDAMMER, FRICOTAL and WESTBERG. The fat level is low at 28%. It has been very successful commercially in Europe.

Other Dutch cheeses are not often found. The town of Leyden makes a skimmed milk cheese flavoured with cumin, again with a fat content at 40% which drops to 20% in mature versions. FRIESIAN CLOVE is seasoned with cumin and clove and matured for 4 months, sold cut off great orange wheels. KERNHEM is a 60%-fat wet cheese with a bright yellow paste and label. ARINA is a goats' cheese made like Gouda in a factory. Fresh soft cheeses are branded MON CHOU. Predictably quick on the uptake, there is also a new generation of light cheeses with the fat content under 30%, mostly made to Gouda specifications.

IRISH CHEESES

CASHEL BLUE · DURRUS · GUBBEEN · MILEENS

A few exceptional Irish cheeses are sold in this country. As with the new revivalist British cheeses, they are individual and hand-made.

**CASHEL BLUE

Made by Louis Grubb in Cashel, County Tipperary, this is unusually creamy for a blue cheese. The rind is eaten. It is at its peak in a state of semi-collapse, when it explodes like a bluing sunset and brings water to the eyes.

*DURRUS

Jelta Gill has been making Durrus by hand since 1979, using unpasteurized morning milk from a Friesian herd in County Cork. It is sold at 3-5 weeks, but will mature for 12. It is a mellow cheese, with hints developing of field mushrooms, apples and mustard as it ages.

**GUBBEEN

Gin Ferguson in County Cork makes this semi-soft washed-rind cheese using pasteurized milk in 1-3 lb lots. Somewhat akin to Pont l'Évêque (see page 170), it has a loose dog-skin-like rind, which is pinkish-orange, very supple and bouncy. The flavour has a dense, earthy vegetal finish.

**MILLEENS

Made by Norman and Veronica Steel in Beara, County Cork, this washed-rind cheese is quite firm when young. The moon crater crust is eaten. Pink to white, it has a sweet farmyard taste.

FRENCH AOC CHEESES

ABONDANCE · BEAUFORT · BLEU D'AUVERGNE ·
BLEU DE CAUSSES · BLEU DE GEX-HAUT-JURA ·
BRIE · CAMEMBERT · CANTAL · CHAOURCE ·
CROTTIN DE CHAVIGNOL· FOURME D'AMBERT ·
LAGUIOLE · LANGRES · LIVAROT · MUNSTER ·
NEUFCHÂTEL · PONT-L'ÉVÊQUE · REBLOCHON ·
ROQUEFORT · SAINTE-MAURE ·
SAINTE-NECTAIRE · SALERS · SELLES-SUR-CHER ·
VACHERIN

The French system of *appellation contrôlée*, developed for wine, was extended to more than 30 cheeses from the end of the '70s. It recognizes the tradition and the craft of making a food on a specific and identified piece of land or region in a particular way. Age and progeny may not, however, be a complete guarantee of quality in themselves, but they have history on their side. In some cases the boundaries have been enforced elastically to include large commercial creameries. Pasteurized milk is allowed to the detriment of some cheeses. Nevertheless in the main, AOC cheeses are fine examples of crafts that may go back a millennium.

The French have protected their cheeses where we have failed. There is another reason for the quality of French cheeses. The French trade of the *affineur* is different to that of the English factor. An *affineur* is not just a trader, but a maturer of cheese. They will buy direct from the farm and allow the cheeses to ripen, often in specifically designed cellars, so they are sold in different stages. Some shops – like **Jeroboam's** and **Neal's Yard** for English cheeses – may follow the practice if they have the space, but to a more limited degree. Supermarkets do not, which is one reason why great soft cheeses are so rarely found in larger retailers.

ABONDANCE

A fine cheese, but whether it deserves recognition over other mountain cheeses is questionable. It needs to age to develop its distinction. Large, at 20x6 cm (8x2½ in), with a hide-pink skin and the occasional pock mark. The flavour has a pure and deep creaminess unusual in a hard cheese.

BEAUFORT

Among the oldest recorded cheeses, dating back to pre-Roman times, these are huge cheeses co-operatively made, with the farms receiving scaled payments according to the quality of their milk. The cattle graze above 2,000 metres (6,500 ft) in the south of the Savoie. The BEAUFORT HAUTE MONTAGNE will be marked with a green oval plaque. Milder and more delicate than the other big mountain cheese, COMTÉ (see page 74), unless allowed to mature. It melts well in cooking and would have been one of the original cheeses for fondue (half and half with Emmental or Comté) and is also used in raclette. *Al dente* in texture and floral in flavour, it has hints of freshly crushed nuts.

BLEU D'AUVERGNE

This was badly hit by the rise of the new blues from Bresse and also the move to pasteurization allowed by the AOC in 1976. Kept in caves for three months, the bluing is more olive-to-green. Dusty of rind, with squarish crenellations, it is sold in distinctive gold paper. The flavour is creamy, sour and softish. A good second to Roquefort, more reliable than distinguished.

BLEU DE CAUSSES

From Rouerque, these are blued in separate caves to Roquefort. Made from cows' milk, with 45% fat, 25x10 cm (10x4 in) in size, large injection marks under the wrapping indicate where the veining marks were made. It is the most immediate of all blues: beautiful, sea surf salt on the first taste; creamy and vanilla as the taste ebbs away slowly like a tide.

BLEU DE GEX-HAUT-JURA

Unusually light for a blue cheese, 'like a Cézanne portrait of a southern Pyrenean skyline', the surface has clouds of small pocking. It is probably more than 700 years old. Tasting notes include, 'digs deep into the wells of the creaminess to pull out the blues, gains sharpness and intensity, cheek puckering, violent, later bitterness'.

BRIE

Brie was not known to the Romans, but Charlemagne certainly knew of a famous cheese from the same area around AD744. Brie was served at the French court right up to the revolution. Although its reputation survives, it is probably not as important a cheese now as it was 250 years ago. Nevertheless, Magritte once painted its label for **Dinkla**.

Appellation contrôlée was given to both Brie de Melun and Brie de Meaux in 1980, Although the Melun is less common, it was probably the original Brie. See also COULOMMIERS (see page 75).

BEST BUYS **BRIE DE MELUN is sharper than the Brie de Meaux and deeper, consequently it always has a fine, slightly chalked centre and never softens as much. The texture is more grainy, though it becomes runny next to the rind.

**BRIE DE MEAUX is brilliant. The skin white with terracotta streaks, the paste smooth, gold and swelling, like solid seaside sunshine. Tasting notes include, 'white skin, traces of orange, the paste going fluid and smooth on the outsides, but still a line of pock marks, chalky inside, the smell is of mushrooms, tart, long finish'.

In both cases, the unpasteurized version is infinitely more complex and rewarding. Occasionally there are interesting combinations of cows' and goats' milk, sold as Brie-style, the skin is usually more ashen grey-white and goat-like, with a flavour of herbs and primroses, but the inside is soft and surprising.

CAMEMBERT

The creation of modern Camembert is credited to Marie Harel, née Marie Fontaine. In 1789, she took in a priest, Abbé Gobert, who was fleeing the Terror. He told her what he knew of how Brie was made – patience with the curd and leaving it unbroken before going into the mould – and she adapted the recipe from there. She sold her cheeses at Vimoutiers market, where they went so well that she enlarged the mould to its modern size of 11 cm (4½ in) across. Its meteoric rise to fame coincided with the advent of the railways and also the neat wooden boxes which allowed it to travel.

Camembert became high fashion; the round boxes took labels that were art: in the early part of this century there was 'King Kong Camembert', 'Mini Mouse Camembert', 'Cowboy Camembert', 'Charleston Camembert'... even, later, 'Sputnik Camembert' and 'War Veteran Camembert'.

In 1910 *Penicillium candidum* was introduced to replace natural surface blue *P. glaucum*, which must have fundamentally altered the cheese. Like Cheddar in Britain, it was widely imitated and manufactured in factories across France and abroad. The AOC protection since 1983 extends only to CAMEMBERT DE NORMANDIE as the last vestiges of what real Camembert was about. The high fat content of the milk from the Normandy cattle is critical.

With 45% fat, it is ready to eat when all traces of white disappear from centre – though some say a few shafts are good – it should never be chalky. As with Brie, unpasteurized versions have much more developed flavours.

The art of the *affineur* is taken to extremes by Henry Pannec with his

CAMEMBERT VOLUPTUEUSE APHRODITE, which he macerates in cider and sells with a cork embedded in the skin into which is poured Calvados as a variation on the *trou Normande*. It is a brutally strong cheese, like a ripe Livarot, but matched with the softness of the Camembert.

BEST BUYS Price tends to be a reasonable indicator of quality. Unpasteurized versions will only be worth the premium if they have been properly looked after. A good example is *La Petite Normande, Moule a la Louche, unpasteurized and twice the price of a supermarket version. The full-blooming smell of clean citrus and flowers comes through immediately. There are also elements of the cellar, as if you could smell the room itself. All of which gives way to a crystal-clear, almost caramel flavour, rather than the nuttiness of pasteurized versions.

In pasteurized Camemberts, the elements of nuts seem to be more pronounced. Bouncy and mild, just a deep sticky hint of what it might be: 'That socks and smoky railway carriages taste is in the rind, the paste is like springy butter with elements of oily richness. There is a big uplift in flavour at the end'.

CANTAL

Probably one of the oldest of all cheeses, Cantal is often produced by the same makers as Salers. The AOC does not insist on raw milk and there has been a tendency to blandness and commercialism. The best remain unpasteurized and dry with age, though it is sold at different degrees of maturity. The paste is smooth, ivory in colour and gets nuttier after six months (*vieux*). It is a warm rich cheese, with a slight metallic taste from the volcanic soil of the Auvergne.

CHAOURCE

Records go back to Louis X eating Burgundian Chaource. It is bright and creamy, with a white chalky exterior, running fresh and rich inside. A light-hearted richness like no other cheese in the world, it needs to be ripe and this is difficult because of the deep coat and broad drum-like shape. The cheeses are made in different shapes, but smaller versions tend to be more reliable for an even ripeness. If it is too young, the texture is Caerphilly-like and chalky, but it turns into a Brie-like creaminess after four weeks. It should be unpasteurized, but AOC permits the use of pasteurized milk and there are a number of factory versions which lack the true potential of a great Chaource. The milk is ripened before renneting, and the Chaource matured for 14 days on rye straw. Good Chaource tastes of lemon essences, of double cream, with a long tang and has the puckering bite of mature Parmesan or Cheddar.

CROTTIN DE CHAVIGNOL

Goats' cheeses were first mentioned in the area in 1573. Crottin (meaning 'dung', which they resemble as they age) was adapted from the Franks around 1500, and first officially adopted as the cheese's name in 1829. It was awarded the AOC in 1976, but this allows frozen curd, some of which can be imported from the UK. If the cheeses are left to age, as is the French practice, they go from a soft creamy white rind to bluish grey to dark grey to black.

FOURME D'AMBERT

Fourme is the old word for a mould for cheese. A kind of Fourme d'Ambert was certainly made prior to the Romans. The Auvergne caves where they ripen for three months are naturally infected with *Penicillium glaucum*. The AOC allows pasteurized milk to be used, so the old nutty flavour has given way to standardization closer to Gorgonzola. With 45% fat, it has pock marks of yellow, a drift of penicillin across marble. A good Fourme will have a lovely, intense creamy-flowery taste, sweet not overly strong blue, like a blue soup. Poor examples tend to be one-dimensional, with a wet, sour texture and a very salty taste with hints of nettles.

LAGUIOLE

Pronounced 'la yole', this is a very old hard cheese, though records are not specific. Made from the milk of fabled Aubrac cattle (which some say produce the best meat in France), which is well suited to cheese-making, it was brought into *appellation contrôlée* in 1976.

LANGRES

Made on the highland plateau on the Burgundy borders, this unpasteurized washed-rind cheese is made to be eaten within six weeks. The flavour is immense, and not for the faint-hearted when it goes over the top. Creamy when young, it quickly goes soft – sometimes even liquid – in the centre. The flavour is also mild when young, but later gives way to a smooth, rampant cream, tasting of concentrated oranges. It is stronger than Livarot, but not as strong as Munster, and stands out in the cheese shop as a bright orange chef's hat with a sunken head. Some are washed in Mirabelle and acquire a sweet pungency. 'The rind smells of pussy-cat fur. Smoky acorns, chestnuts, woody clothes around an intense centre of milky cream.

**LIVAROT

Despite its reputation as one of the strongest cheeses, it is quite mild when young and much of the pungency comes from the skin rather than the flesh. Related to, but possibly not exactly the same as, the ancient Norman cheese ANGELON (or ANGELOT), it is first mentioned around 1693.

Inside the round box, a proper Livarot will have five orange bands of sedge grass, designed originally to hold softer cheeses in shape, hence the French nickname, 'le Colonel'. With a firmer and stronger paste than Camembert, it is a plump, rosy big drum of a cheese, twice the height of a Camembert.

Livarot is made from two days' milking, lightly skimmed, to give 40% fat, and then washed in brine three times during 48 days maturing. The AOC was given in 1976 for cheeses from the Pays D'Auge, between the rivers Touques and Dives.

BEST BUYS   A good version will have a marbled, rust-and-white crust, the flesh will be creamy golden and smooth with tiny pock marks. Softly sweet in flavour, it is in fact milder than Langres, although the smell of the skin is deceptively strong. **Graindorge** is a good example. Going to old hay and bitterness. Intense, distinct earthy farmyard, full-bodied.

*MUNSTER

One of the strongest of all French cheeses, the name derives from the word for monastery, where similar cheeses were probably made from the 6th century. The AOC has lumped it together with the second cheese of the area in Alsace, the larger, GÉROMÉ. Géromé traditionally comes from the western slopes of the Vosges mountains, and Munster from the east. Most of the milk will be organic as the cattle graze above the level of the vines. The orange rind is neatly lined, like a tiled roof, and sometimes turns shades of pink (historically this was from drying in the sun). Morning and evening milk are used and the cheese fashioned by hand. The smell is inherent in the crust, taking on the bacterium linens from the maturing caves. It goes well with Alsace wines.

NEUFCHÂTEL

This cheese from Normandy comes in a variety of different shapes, including hearts, loaves and discs. The new cheese is kneaded with older, riper cheese before moulding. The skin is brilliant white, the paste golden and the fat content 45%. Cream-enriched variations include Petit-Suisse.

PONT-L'EVÊQUE

Another Norman cheese which was first thought to have been made around the 12th century. It may originally have been round and possibly changed its shape to square to differentiate itself from the other local cheese, ANGELON. Originally the crust was just brushed, and washing was only adopted in the last century. Washed, the crust is smoother and more russet; brushed, it is more granular and pale fawn. It is now made from milk in all five Normandy *départements* and the Maine *département* of Mayenne –'stretching the Vallée d'Auge beyond reason and inexcusably allowing pasteurized milk' accuses Patrick Rance. It should weigh 350-400 g (12-14 oz) and be 10.5-11.5 cm (4-4¾ in) square. Unlike Brie or Camembert, the curd is broken. When young it is almost Brie-like; allowed to mature at room temperature it will get progressively stronger. The most interesting will be unpasteurized. The paste will be soft, golden, not runny until in the mouth. The flavour is rich but not sharp, with a wide edge of citrus. Usually sold in a box, it also keeps surprisingly well after cutting.

**REBLOCHON

From the Savoie, Reblochon was originally known as *fromage de devotion* as the farmers asked the local monks for their blessings on their mountain huts. The rent for the huts was paid in a percentage of the value of the milk, and the farmers came to hold back some of the milk from inspection and used the (rich) milk from a second illicit milking to make Reblochon for themselves. Until the Revolution, the cheeses were never sold. The warmth and humidity of the caves in which the cheeses are ripened were historically provided by a sheep penned in there for the winter. The milk is from the Abondance cow.

BEST BUYS Good Reblochon is golden-pink and weighs around 500 g (1 lb 2 oz). The smaller PETIT REBLOCHON or REBLOCHONNET is regarded as inferior because it does not ripen so consistently. It has a mild, soft, voluptuous flavour and creamy but springy texture.

**ROQUEFORT

The fame of arguably the world's greatest blue cheeses rests with the calcareous (limestone) caves above the River Soulzon. The romantic story is that a shepherd left his cheese and bread in one of the caves when he went off to seduce a shepherdess. Coming back some weeks later, he discovered the miraculous effects of the bluing. The 23 natural caves were known to the Romans as places to store cheese. The caves now go down eleven stories and the subterranean village is twice the size of the one on the surface.

To create the bluing, loaves of barley and rye are left in the caves for three months until they have developed furry coats. These are then dried and powdered and added to the cheese. Bluing is also further encouraged by the puncturing of each cheese with 38 needles to allow the air in.

The first month-old Lacaune lambs are weaned in December and then the numbers of cheeses rise through to April to peak and fall off again as the sheep mate. One litre (1¾ pints) of milk produces nearly 115 g (4 oz) of Roquefort, which is 45% fat. Some milk is now imported from Spain and there has been an influx in the region of British Milk Sheep. There is fierce discussion over which cheeses still use Lacaune milk. AOC states the milk must be unpasteurized.

BEST BUYS Good Roquefort is firm with large holes. The intensity of the blue (or aquamarine) is electric, giving the cheese a taste of the caves. It is best eaten with sweet wine or even sweet ale. The most commonly found Roquefort in Britain is from the **Société** co-operative. **Papillon** claims to be one of only two or three using local milk. It has pale aquamarine to dusty blue-green cratering, and has a good mild flavour and creamy texture. Other good examples are from **Constans Crouzat** and **Gabriel Coulet**.

SAINTE–MAURE

This mild goats' cheese from the Touraine is long, ashen and orange tinted, staked through its axis with a wooden axle. Quite subtle when young, it is creamy, with edges of Roquefort and hints of primroses.

*SAINT–NECTAIRE

Related to the better-known Auvergne cheese, Cantal, and just as ancient, it is made in 12 cm (4¾ in) discs, 3.5 cm (1½ in) deep. White or grey-red and mimosa-like, sometimes even jade or blue in colour, it is made with milk from Salers and Ferrandaises cows and ripened 2-4 months. Awarded AOC in 1979, the best use unpasteurized milk, have an oval green plaque on the face of the cheese and the word fermier on the label. The cheeses with pale pink rinds tend not to be farmhouse.

SALERS

One of the oldest French cheeses, Salers takes its name from the Auvergne cattle who supply the milk. It is similar to Cantal, but is less liable to short-cuts. In summer the cattle graze at over 800 metres on volcanic pastures, both of which factors contribute to the flavour. They are also moved from pasture to pasture to maintain an organic approach. The full cheese is made from the milk of at least 40 cows, weighs 35-55 kg and carries an aluminium plaque. The golden crust turns red and marbled and the paste is yellow and giving. The flavour improves wonderfully with age.

**SELLES–SUR–CHER

The traditional cheese of the Loire, it is sprinkled with a mix of charcoal and salt to preserve it. It can be eaten very young, when it is mild and lemony. As it ages it develops a bluish-grey rind and dries out, concentrating the flavour. Good examples can be strong and long-lasting, with a gummy vanilla spikiness and hints of spring flowers and nuts.

VACHERIN

Following the 1987 outbreak of listeria in Switzerland associated with Vacherin, the French government stopped exports of their own versions of the cheese made in Savoie and the Franche-Comté, while the Swiss went on happily selling theirs. The Swiss version is pasteurized (as it was at the time of the outbreak) and called MONT-D'OR DE JOUX. Both cheeses are made in the same mountains and the difference is political not natural, though the French cheeses are by general consent superior, due to the quality of the cheese-makers. To differentiate them, these French versions are now called LE MONT D'OR or VACHERIN DU HAUT-DOOBS. The Swiss version is also more expensive because it attracts a levy on being imported into EU countries.

Vacherin is made from August 15 to March 31, when the Montbeliarde and Pie-rouges de l'Est cattle are brought inside. Sold in distinctive round, wobbly, thin wooden boxes, the crust is pink, swollen and undulating as if indicating the potent forces underneath. When ripe, the paste looks like mayonnaise and the skin smells of the cobwebs in the cellar. The bark around the outside is from the mountain spruces and needs to be cut with a serrated knife. An enthusiastic Patrick Rance declares: 'If you are not in stuffy company, lick your bark after each mouthful of cheese, and do not waste what is left; put it on the fire to die in a scent of glory'.

BEST BUYS Typical flavours are smells of football socks, very vegetal, unctuous, clean taste ending in flowers, powerful. **Badoz** is a good maker. Swiss **Le Pelerin** has an intense creaminess, but lacks the depth of other good cheeses.

L'Edel de Cleron is a commercially made copy of Vacherin. If properly looked after, so the insides starts to run, it can be a good alternative at half the price – if a shade one-dimensional. Tasting notes include, 'the smell of bitter almonds, woody, lovely cream, in fact quite a gentle smoky flavour of casseroled lemons'.

The *AOC* is not definitive. A number of other excellent traditional cheeses find their way over here and often provide better value for not being *AOC*.

OTHER TRADITIONAL FRENCH CHEESES

BANON · CABÉCOU · CARRÉ DE L'EST · COMTÉ ·
COULOMMIERS · ÉPOISSES · FLEUR DE MAQUIS ·
GAPERON · MORBIER · PALET DE BOURGOGNE ·
RACLETTE · SAINT-FÉLICIEN · TOMME DE SAVOIE

BANON

Made in Provence from 90% cows' milk, but with some goats' milk added, these 7x2.5 cm (2³⁄4x1 in) cheeses are wrapped in chestnut leaves. They have a delicate greyish-blue mould. They are either matured to softness or dried to concentrate them. They may now be found in supermarkets. Good examples are firm, grainy and potent, with a sour milk and dairy-yards flavour and hints of lemons.

CABÉCOU

From Quercy, meaning 'little goat', which it is. It can be eaten fresh within 48 hours of making (as an aperitif), kept in the caves for 15 days to dry out (good in salads) or it may be even macerated in *eau-de-vie de prune*, when it is known as CABÉCOU TRUFFÉ.

CARRÉ DE L'EST

This square, pale orange cheese from Champagne is underrated and good value among the stronger cheeses. Unlike Époisses and Livarot, the aroma is in the cheese itself. It ripens quickly and is known as the 'Champagne of Brie'. Good names include **Saulxurois**. There is a white Camembert-rinded Carré on the market, which is unwashed and lacks the flavour and character of the original.

COMTÉ

The French version of Gruyère from the Comté (sometimes called 'Gruyère de Comté') is creamy beige, with a firm rind and should have a few small holes in it. The unpasteurized versions are superior and nearly all production is still farmhouse. This was a pioneering area for cheese-making in the 12th century. It is made in the summer using milk from the same cows that provide Vacherin in winter. About 530 litres, or the yield from 30 cows, goes into a single cheese. The crust should have bells and the name 'Comté' engraved in it. If not, it will have been downgraded at inspection. It should always be sold with the crust on (a device that prevented it being sold pre-packed in supermarkets, as happened to Cheddar). With its nutty flavour it is often used in fondues.

COULOMMIERS

Although in practice this is a Brie, it is sold as a different cheese. It was first recorded around the end of the 10th century and although it does not have the *appellation contrôlée* it is as good as many cheeses which do. The fat content is higher than Brie, at 50%, which has led to accusations of adultery, but the milk from the Coulommiers cattle has a naturally high fat content.

BEST BUYS **COULOMMIERS LE SAINT-JACQUES, from the Île de France, is round, 15 cm (6 in) across, with a chalky white rind (it can have a blue bloom on it which is just wiped off without any adverse effect). Tasting notes include, 'soft, voluptuous, dry meadows, hay and lemons, long finish into citrus'.

ÉPOISSES

This classic washed-rind cheese from Burgundy comes in round wooden boxes and the cheese inside is sometimes wrapped in vine leaves. The pale orange skin is washed with *marc* or wine to encourage the strong aromatic smell. Inferior versions will have just been washed in brine. It is the rind that smells and gets quite sticky. The inside is soft and white and not quite so pungent. Kept at room temperature for 2-3 days, it ripens dramatically. Some say it is the strongest of all cheeses, outdoing even Munster. Better examples are from unpasteurized milk.

**FLEUR DE MAQUIS

A fresh ewes'-milk cheese from Corsica, coated in rosemary, chilli and juniper – the *maquis* or scrubby bush of Corsica on which the sheep graze. One of the few cheeses with herbs on the outside which really suit. Soft in texture, it is a stunning cheese, with the taste of roast lamb from the rosemary.

GAPERON

A distinctive cheese from the Auvergne, hand-moulded in deep white half-ovals and flavoured with crushed garlic and peppercorns. A buttery deep yellow with grey flecks, it is really an excuse to use up the garlic of the region.

MORBIER

A mountain cheese, properly made with the milk of the morning and the evening. The top and bottom are separated by a thin filling of ash – though sometimes other vegetable fillings have now crept in. Akin to Comté, the 30 cm (12 in) rounds are off-white, solid and milder and softer than you expect. Available all year, it has a pink to orange rind, and a smooth paste with the odd hole and the fleck of ash through the middle. Soft, pungent and spongy it does have a good elastic texture and the mild hint of farmyard.

PALET DE BOURGOGNE

When older, this cheese from Burgundy is reputedly as strong as any French cheese. A pale beige round, 10x3 cm (4x1 1/4 in) which is washed in *marc*, it should change from dry chalkiness to a golden paste with age. Tasting notes include, 'skin has a silage-like smell, but inside is a slug of cream, sharp at the back of the throat.'

RACLETTE

This unpasteurized cheese, 12 cm (4 3/4 in) high by 30 cm (12 in) across, has a dusty beige rind tinged with reds and yellows. The flesh is yellow and smooth with pockets of air. It is an individual cheese, with a gamy flavour of chestnuts and long high notes and finish as in Cheddar and Parmesan. Usually used in cooking but good versions should not be dismissed for the table.

SAINT–FÉLICIEN

Made near Lyons around the Beaujolais region, this 45% fat, fresh cheese is eaten within two weeks of making. It is unattractively packed in clear children's-party-style jelly moulds and marked like soft butter. Lightly washed, it begins very curdy but becomes more alcoholic with age. An excellent cheese with Beaujolais. At its best in winter.

TOMME DE SAVOIE

Tomme means a 'big round'. Usually sold quite young here, older versions can be found in France. Usually unpasteurized, this was *the* mountain cheese, alongside Comté and Emmental. Grey-cream in colour, with a distinct mild taste enhanced by the mustiness of the rind, it will be at its best around September and October when the milk is from the richest grazing in June.

MODERN FRENCH CHEESES

BOURSAULT · CHAUMES · EXPLORATEUR · PAVÉ
D'AFFINOIS · PORT-SALUT · SAINT-ANDRÉ ·
TOURRÉE DE L'AUBER · VIGNOTTE

The new generation of French factory cheeses can be impressive, despite
their industrial parentage. A few, like BOURSAULT, GRATTE-PAILLE,
PAVÉ D'AFFINOIS and ST-AUGUR are capable of being miraculously
improved by *affinage*. Others remain themselves whatever. Also worth
looking for are BRILLAT-SAVARIN (invented between the Wars by
Androuët's father), PONT MOUTIER, VIEUX PANÉE and ROULÉ.

BOURSAULT

This big brother of BOURSIN has triple cream added to the milk for a
high fat content. The cheese is usually sold in a box and its deep yellow
sticky rind wrapped in paper. It tastes like clotted cream, running soft
with hints of lemons. Go for those near and after their sell-by dates.

Invented in 1953 by Henri Boursault at Le Perreux sur Marne, the
creamery was later bought by Boursin. The unpasteurized is sold as 'gold
label'; the 'silver label' denotes the less interesting pasteurized. Patrick
Rance says to take it out of its box and paper and keep it on straw in a
cool place, turning daily three times a week to let the pink coat develop
for up to 7-10 days.

CHAUMES

This popular mass-produced cheese is well made and well marketed. The
rind is waxy and a vivid orange colour, the paste stable but it will ripen
like Brie. First made in Jurançon in 1971, based on what was an Alpine
cheese, the original seems to have died out. About 20 cm (8 in) across,
the modern version is wrapped in orange paper with an egotistically large
logo and fattening curves bulging out the sides like a spare tyre. The paste
is silky cream with pockets of air, the flavour clean with hints of vanilla.

EXPLORATEUR

Invented in the '60s by M. Duquesne of La Fromagerie du Petit Morin at
La Tretoire and named to honour the then mayor of Coulommiers – and
explorer – Bertrand Flornoy. The rocket on the logo is said to be France's
only rocket. It is a triple-cream cheese – therefore 75% fat.

*PAVÉ D'AFFINOIS

Small white cubes of cheese which, if allowed to ripen, will become liquid in the centre. Cut them across the centre and spoon out the insides, which are like melted butter. Now sold in supermarkets, it is quite dry with a velvety skin and has a Brie-like chalky texture when unripe.

PORT–SALUT

Until 1988 Port-Salut was made by the monks of the Notre Dame du Port-du-Salut, probably since around 1830. The name was registered in 1874 and commercial imitators forced to use the name SAINT-PAULIN. The monks' hold on the cheese has been eroded since the '50s, when the marketing was put outside the abbey, and finally finished by the Swiss Vacherin-associated listeria outbreak – the monks refused to pay for their raw milk to be tested each month. With a bright orange rind, and about 15x4 cm (6x1 1/2 in), fattening out at the edges, it has a parchment-yellow paste and warm waxy smell. The taste is quite homely, fireside, with some hints of nuts and a nice short sweet finish.

*SAINT–ANDRÉ

A triple-cream cheese (75% fat) close to a Vignotte, it is made in rounds about 20 cm (8 in) across and 8 cm (3 1/4 in) deep. It has a clear white rind and a luscious, very thick buttercream paste with a long-lasting flavour that hints of meadows and acid lemons.

TOURRÉE DE L'AUBER

This cheese from Isère is another modern copy of Vacherin. About 20 cm (8 in) across and 8 cm (3 1/4 in) deep, its orange-to-brown rind, neatly lined on the surface with crevices filled with white, is ringed with conifer bark to constrain it, corset-like, the creamy white paste is bursting at the sides. Not as brilliant as Vacherin, but interesting in itself with a mildly sour, flowery flavour.

VIGNOTTE

This highly popular cheese with 72% fat, 7x8 cm (2 3/4x3 1/4 in) in size, is Camembert-white. Smaller ones are sold in red boxes. Double-cream with an edge of lime and lemons, it is almost like double cream by another name.

ITALIAN CHEESES

BEL PAESE · CACIOCAVALLO · CROTIN ·
DOLCELATTE · FONTINA · GORGONZOLA ·
GRANA PADANO · MASCARPONE · MOZZARELLA ·
PARMESAN · PECORINO · PROVOLONE · RICOTTA ·
TALEGGIO

Italian cheese-making has gravitated from the farm to the factory.
Unlike here, however, there has been no rush to diversification. The big
names still dominate, often monitored by consortia applying strict rules
for size, shape, ripening and labelling. The quality control is admirable.

BEL PAESE
Created by Galbani in the '20s, this is one of the best-known cheese
brand-names, but not to be overlooked for that. It is supple, mild and
slightly sweet.

CACIOCAVALLO
One of the original Italian cheeses. The similarities with the way cheeses
were kept on the backs of horses in sheep- and goat-skin bags in the Caucasus
and Central Asia suggests there may have been a very early trade with the
east. Caciocavallo is father to Mozzarella and the *filata* process – the curds
placed in hot whey and heated to 45°C (113°F), then cut into strips, put
back in warm whey and finally kneaded. Caciocavallo is moulded into 3-4
kg (6½-9 lb) rounds and hung for 3-6 months, or even kept for a hard
grating cheese. With a 44% fat content its flavour is mild and delicate.

*CROTIN
This cheese from Piedmont is made from half cows' milk and half ewes'
milk cheese. It is kept in – and named after – the cellar in which the
white truffles are kept and these imbue the cheese with their flavour.
Aged for a month, it can be hard enough to shave over Bresaola, or it is
served with Mascarpone.

DOLCELATTE
Meaning 'sweet milk', this modern imitation of Gorgonzola is made in
Pavia with pasteurized milk and matured for 45 days before the
Penicillium is introduced. A good version should be nutty and defined,

with a developing character that is sweeter and creamier than Gorgonzola often quite mild for a blue. DOLCELATTE TORTE is layered into a 'cake' with Mascarpone.

FONTINA

Designed for fondues, but is a good cheese in its own right eaten from the block, especially when made in summer after the cattle have grazed on the mountainous pastures of the Val d'Aosta. FONTAL is the second-grade cheese. It is the basis for the Turin dish of *fonduta*, warmed to a sweet creamy mess. The cheese has a pleasant, lactic, nutty flavour.

GORGONZOLA

Named after the town in Lombardy, north of Milan, it has probably been made in the area for more than 1,000 years. The cattle drovers stopped here, bringing the cattle down from the mountains after their summer grazing. The cheeses are matured for two months before the *Penicillium* is injected. The cylindrical cheeses, 25x20 cm (10x8 in), with a 48% fat content are usually wrapped in silver paper marked with the brand.

Typically they are smooth, bouncy white through which violent circular and serrated crevices of blue have run rampantly, as if ravaged by an alien force that has since departed. The visual aggression is in contrast to the mildness of the cheese itself. Creamy. The blue is nutty, not sharp, and develops a relationship with the creaminess that gives an aftertaste of mellow meadows, sharply herbaceous, tarragon tang.

GRANA PADANO

Grana is the generic name for all hard cheeses, invariably made with semi-skimmed milk, while the cream will often go for Mascarpone. Grana was originally made in the Padana valley but now is made across Italy, regulated by its consortium. Unlike Parmesan, it uses an assortment of skimmed milks. The cheeses may be matured from 1-2 years and can weigh as much as 40 kg (90 lb). Made all the year, with a fat content of 32%, they are cheaper than Parmesan, but not necessarily inferior. The best can grace a cheeseboard or be served with fruit as a starter.

MASCARPONE

Traditionally made in Lombardy in the winter and sold in pots, as a by-product of the grana cheeses (see above). This soft cream cheese can have a fat content as high as 70%. It is similar to crème fraîche, but has had a starter culture added. It is eaten with fruit and cognac. Cheeses with long shelf-lives tend to develop an off-tone. They can be dramatically sweet and sticky, triple-cream with very little element of cheese at all. A little goes a long way. Mascarpone is the main ingredient of *Tiramisu* 'pick-me-up', flavoured with coffee and alcohol.

MOZZARELLA

Takes its name from the cutting, *mozzare*. The curd is drawn by hand into rope-like strands and spun into concentric circles to create its elasticity. The best is made from the milk of water buffalo introduced into Lazio and Campania in the 16th century to work the rice fields, but mozzarella is now widely made with cows' milk (even in Wembley and Ireland), though much of this will go for commercial pizzas. MOZZARELLA DI BUFALO is slightly fattier at 50% to 45%. Good mozzarella will be subtle, nutty and sweet, the traditional foil for raw tomato.

Some buffalo milk mozzarella is now being made near Shipston-on-Stour in Warwickshire where Robert Palmer has imported his own herd. He sells the cheese through **Neal's Yard**.

PARMESAN

Responsibility for the birth of this great cheese is claimed both by Tuscany in 11th century and Parma in the 13th. Cheese made in the areas around Parma, Bologna and Mantua has been protected since 1954. The cows' milk is skimmed, unpasteurized and the cheeses pressed and matured for a year or more. In Italy, Parmesan is sold in different stages of ripeness, the young designed to go with fruit. Reggiano is only made north of the Po, in Mantua, where the pastures are deemed to be more lush and have more clover. About 16 litres (28 pts) of milk makes 1 kg (2¼ lb) of Parmesan and the fat content is 32%.

The cheese in the ready-grated tubs of Parmesan is, for most part, stale and poor. The best argument for grating it at home is that it will be fresher and less will go further.

There is an English Parmesan, **Avanti**, made in Sussex; often sold too young and wet to grate properly, but regarded as a distinctive cheese of merit in its own right.

BEST BUYS Tubs of grated Parmesan are sold in grams, whereas blocks are usually sold in pounds, which makes comparison difficult. In practice, tubs tend to be cheaper. New sachets of 'freshly grated' have picked up the quality considerably, but in some cases are more than £1 per 500 g more than if bought in the block. In real terms, the price dwarfs other mainline cheeses, steepling upwards to almost £10 per 500 g – or more than four times the price of Cheddar. On the other hand its usages grated on pasta are a model of restraint.

PECORINO

Made in Lazio from November to June, using sheep's milk and rennet, dried for a month and matured for eight, though some examples can be matured as long 10 years. It is 36% fat. Sold in big cylinders, weighing 8-22 kg (18-50 lb). The younger cheeses are supple, distinctly sheepy and clean-tasting. Older cheeses, known as SARDO, are designed for grating. Pecorino can be found selling for less than Grana or Parmesan in some supermarkets. A similar cheese is also made in Sicily.

Pecorinos are very salty and good for pasta, soups and other hot dishes. Nutty, with a sweet caramel flavour, the cheese needs a strong country wine when served on a cheeseboard.

PROVOLONE

Another spun-curd cheese, but using rennet from goats rather than cows, and allowed to mature. Poor examples are rubbery; the best are harder, fruity and *piccante*.

RICOTTA

Strictly speaking, this not a cheese because it is made from whey which is then cooked (ricotta, 'to re-cook'). The whey is often left over from the making of other well-known cheeses, notably Fontina. In the south it is often made from sheep's-milk whey, which is stronger. The practice of making ricotta is ancient and varies from region to region. With a 30% fat content, it is eaten fresh, though salted versions will keep two months. It is essentially a cooking cheese, for sweets and pasta.

TALEGGIO

Like Gorgonzola, this cheese is named after a town in Lombardy where the drovers rested overnight when bringing the cattle down from the mountains after the summer grazing. It probably dates back to the 9th century and is matured for 40 days. With a fat content of 48%, the large flat square orange blocks, 20x4 cm (8x1 ½ in), with a pinkish brown gritty rind have a superb texture, like spring Brie or undulating Vacherin.

SPANISH CHEESES

CASSOLETA · ETORKI · GARROTXA · IBERICO ·
IDIAZÁBAL · MAHÓN · MANCHEGO ·
MONTENEBRO · PICOS BLUE · QUESO DE
MURCIA · REY CABRA · SIERRA DE ZUCHEROS ·
TETILLA

Cheeses from Spain have increasingly been brought over here since her entry into the EU. Some are strikingly individual and artisanal. Under three month's old, soft Spanish cheeses must by law be pasteurized, but hard cheeses can be unpasteurized.

CASSOLETA

Typical of many Mediterranean coastal cheeses using goats' and sheep's milk, it is coagulated using thistle juice and the curds are moulded into volcano shapes. These are then pressed and sold in brine within a week. Often fried with peppers in Valencia, it is also used in salads in the same way as Mozzarella or Haloumi. TRONCHON is a similar cheese, but larger and usually older.

ETORKI

This Basque cheese, made from ewes' milk, is 20 cm (8 in) across by 10 cm (4 in) deep. The dappled rind is straw-yellow or rusty, the paste a shiny grey white. It is a mild dry cheese, with a strong accent of nuts and chestnuts. It can be lightly grilled.

GARROTXA

A compact goats' cheese from Catalonia with a blue-grey velvet bloom, the flavour is infused with crushed acorns, rye grass and wild flowers. It can be fried and served with olive paste and toast.

IBERICO

This variation on Manchego originally from central Castile (although now made across Spain) looks much the same but is made using a mix of ewes' and cows' milk. It is sold in four stages of maturity: after 20 days, vacuum-packed, when it will be white; after 30 days, when the outside is painted black; fully cured after three months, with a natural brown rind; and (not often found here) fully matured at six months, marked 'Anejo'.

IDIAZÁBAL

Highly expensive and revered in the Basque country, this hard-pressed ewes'-milk cheese is unlike other smoked cheeses in that the smoking is a traditional variation based on the shepherd's hut where it was hung in the chimney over the fire. It has a distinctive long flavour, 'subtle with three or four waves of hues'. It is usually only sold here in restaurants. Production of the cheese is now restricted to North-west Spain, under the EU Denomination of Origin.

MAHÓN

Eighteenth-century invaders brought the Friesian cow to Menorca and insisted the milk was used instead of sheep's milk to make a Cheddar-like cheese. Known as 'the Brit', it is flat, square, with rounded edges, it has a bright orange rind. It is unusual in that it is sold at different stages of ripeness: from 10 days, when it can eaten sliced with oil and peppers; semi-cured it becomes herbaceous and salty with a firm texture; later as it dries out it becomes hard and Gouda-like. The cheese has an EU Denomination of Origin, for island production.

MANCHEGO

A hard ewes'-milk cheese made only from the milk of the Mandega sheep, 20x10 cm (8x4 in), is brown with pretty latticework from where it has stood. Older Manchegos will be matured for up to 12 months, when they achieve an intense sourness and velvety taste. Younger, they tend to be buttery with a slightly chewy texture and a taste of apples and crushed walnuts. Such cheeses are served thinly sliced to allow to them to breathe, often with sherry. It makes a good alternative to Cheddar and Parmesan for people with an allergy to cows' milk. The cheese has an EC Denomination of Origin for the Castile La Mancha region.

**MONTENEBRO

Obscure but brilliant, only 40 of these goats' cheeses are exported here each month. The 7x10 cm ($2^{3}/4$x4 in) log is virgin white and smooth. Strongly creamy, it has sour verdant seaside notes.

PICOS BLUE

This round leaf-wrapped cheese, 9 cm ($3^{1}/2$ in) across with well-spread mottled fleck, is possibly the strongest of all blues, 'all bluntness and no cream. Interesting but foot-soldierly'. An older version was creamy but with enormous blueing.

QUESO DE MURCIA
A goats' cheese weighing about 1 kg (2 lb), it is patterned top and bottom from the olive wood mould. It is sometimes made unsalted for desserts, in which it is usually mixed with cinnamon, nutmeg and honey.

**REY CABRA
From the Ronda, Malaga, this is the king of the goats' cheeses and arguably among the finest cheeses in Europe. Hard and about 25x35 cm (10x14 in) in size, it has an outstanding and perfectly delineated taste of nuts and purified lemons and salt, not even immediately recognizable as a goats' cheese.

SIERRA DE ZUCHEROS
Andalusian semi-soft round, 7 cm (2¾ in) across, goats' cheese which is firmly pressed and drained, then rubbed with salt and paprika. It has a brilliant orange rind with a straw lattice. It is crumbly, goaty, with a hint of smoky bacon, and is usually served at home with dried pressed fruit cake. An example had an intense flavour hinting mildly of oranges.

TETILLA
Expressively meaning 'a little breast' – more politely, known as Perilla, or 'little pear' – this Galician cows' milk cheese is sold with or without the rind. It is creamy, mild, elastic and full-fat. Production is controlled under EU Denomination of Origin.

SWISS CHEESES

EMMENTHAL · GRUYÈRE

There are some very good Swiss cheeses, although they do not often surface in the UK because of punitive EU levies. The quality of the cheeses is underwritten by political intervention as the Swiss Government is committed to the idea of keeping the farms small and in family ownership. Most cheeses are therefore not produced in factories but in village dairies, most of which were built at the end of the last century. The marketing is by a national agency into which co-operatives subscribe. Originally this was a response to the closing of frontiers with the outbreak of the 1914 War. In the 1950s the Swiss Government went further by fixing the price of milk so that it was economic to go on making cheese. All master cheesemakers have to have four years' experience to sit their qualifying exam, including one year at Dairy College to study cheese. Cheeses made in Switzerland usually carry a logo of an Alpine hornblower standing on a three-quarter round of Emmenthal. Swiss cheeses will be unpasteurized unless the label says otherwise.

EMMENTHAL

Emmenthal was first mentioned by name in 1542 in the district of Langenthal where cheeses were given as donations to the victim of a fire. Its history traces back to the start of the 14th century. It was originally an Alpine cheese but production moved to the German-speaking valleys at the turn of this century. It is 48% fat and produced on large cooperatives in huge 85kg wheels. The distinctive holes should be the size of a cherry.

GRUYÈRE

Cheese-making in the Gruyère region is dated back to around 1115, though it does not appear by name until 1602. Around 60 farms still make Gruyère, always using summer milk (Vacherin, page 73, is the winter cheese) usually from still above 1,000 metres. It is 49% fat, hence the creaminess The briny dry sharpness of a good version should stay on the palate.

OTHER SWISS CHEESES

SBRINZ is a hard cheese like Parmesan and is thought to be one of the oldest Middle-European cheeses. The Swiss version of the story is that it comes from near Berne and was traded on mules across the Alpine passes to Italy. The whole cheese bears a handsome Grecian-warrior-style emblem. The delicate, spicy TÊTE de MOINE was originally called after the monastery at BELLELAY where it was first produced around 1570 and re-named after the French Revolution in recognition of how well-fed the monks at the monastery seemed to be. FRIBOURGEOIS used to be two cheeses, one variation being a notable soured cheese for fondue. Both have been standardized into one mild, young cream cheese that can develop a strong tang if matured and which is exclusive to the canton of Fribour, where it is called Vacherin Fribourgeois. APPENZELLER is a generic bringing together different Alpine traditions which shared the rubbing of herbs into the rinds as a characteristic. The louche Swiss saying sums it up well enough: 'How do you make cheese, Appenzal girl? I sit on it to make it flat and that's why it tastes so strong!'. RACLETTE derives from the Valais farmers who celebrated family occasions by melting cheese over the fire. The demand has outstripped the farmers' ability to produce unpasteurized cheeses, or to mature them, and most are now made in factories.

A SWISS RECIPE FOR FONDUE

Rub the fondue dish with a clove of garlic. Heat half a litre (1 pint) of dry white wine gently. Add a teaspoon of wine vinegar, 200 g (7 oz) of coarsely grated Emmenthal to 400 g (14 oz) of grated Gruyère. Bring to the boil. Stir in a glass of Kirsch. Season with nutmeg and pepper. Each person dunking in their dried bread should give the pot a stir to keep it creamy.

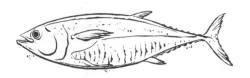

FISH & SHELLFISH

The biggest fishing port in Britain is Peterhead, north of Aberdeen. Hull tends to take the bigger ships from further afield. Billingsgate notionally takes most of the fish, but this has been a sluggish artery where fish has tended to hang around before getting to the fishmonger. For packing and presentation, the Dutch (who else) and the French at Rungis set a considerably higher standard than is commonly found here.

In recent years, however, the numbers of fish have declined. In 1948, Billingsgate fish market handled 3,800 tonnes of fish in a week, in 1960 this was halved to 1,700, in 1970 down to 1,100, in 1980 only 800 and in 1990 a mere 600 tonnes. The downward trend in white fish is worse: the 1980 and 1990 figures are buoyed up by imports of exotic fish. Just as our waters have been ravaged, so now are the tropical coral reefs.

Fresh v. Frozen Fish

There is some truth in the claim that fish frozen at sea within hours of catching may be in better condition than much of what passes for 'fresh'. Frozen fish is best cooked straight from the freezer, without thawing. This retains nutrients and flavour.

The best supermarket for fresh fish is **Waitrose**. **Asda** is probably the cheapest. **Sainsbury** is content to stock mostly frozen fish, but often at competitive prices compared to Billingsgate. Displays are spasmodic varying from cabinets of mostly farmed fish – trout, salmon – to occasional opulence in showpiece stores where the range can even extend to tropical fish.

MINDLESS POLLUTION

Whole tracts of the North Sea have been plundered into voids where familiar names like cod, sole and haddock face extinction. The North Sea mackerel is commercially extinct. EU politicians appear unable to bury parochial national interest to save the seas.

As I wrote in the first edition, the history of fishing is one of 'nationalistic greed, war, mindless pollution and contamination of the marine environment'. Now we face the prospect of that most famous of seas becoming a jellyfish eco-system as the whole structure breaks down. The massive catchings of the larger predatory white fish leave the smaller crustacea and fauna to flourish in a new balance. The main culprits are over-fishing and eutrophication – too many agricultural toxins washed into the sea causing toxic algal blooms.

The International Council for the Exploration of the Seas has called for a ban on cod fishing. Some environmental threats have been recognized and restricted. The tributyl used to paint ships' bottoms to inhibit barnacles has also wiped out whelks and snails on the sea floor. Cancers found in the livers of flat fish have also been attributed to the now-banned group of hydrocarbons.

Disaster theories are offset to some extent by a survey of harbour porpoises which estimates a population of a quarter of a million. The porpoises are a good barometer of the health of the sea because they feed on larger fish and are liable to accumulate high levels of toxins.

Faced with impending wasteseas, Britain has responded feebly, blocking EU moves to declare the North Sea a Vulnerable Zone under the EU's Nitrates Directive, on the parochial grounds that our own coastline is not as badly affected as the shallow ledge to the east, off Denmark. We have also given up traditional Cornish fishing grounds to open fishing, especially by the Spanish (who in contrast have aggressively fought their ground over tuna in the Bay of Biscay and as far as Canada).

There is no historical precedent for giving up a national resource the size of the North Sea and yet the evidence mounts up as more coastal towns are given over to mindless tourism.

The river authorities accept that UK rivers are too polluted to sustain breeding populations of healthy fish. The campaigning zeal that led to salmon being caught again in the Thames seems to have dissipated. On some salmon rivers, anglers have been buying net-men out in a desperate effort to protect the waters for themselves.

In the long term these trends have to be addressed. The inland rivers need to be cleaned up. Inshore fishing needs to be protected and revived. There needs to be a recognition that ultimately fishing has to be a small-scale industry. There is no sense in it being anything else.

The nutritional advice is that we should all seek to eat fish three times a week. How can we reconcile that advice with what is happening in the North Sea?

THE BIG WHITES

COD · COLEY · HADDOCK · HAKE · LING · WHITING

The big whites are long tubular-shaped predators that feed on smaller fish, often herring. Their numbers have been badly affected by over-fishing and the pollution of the North Sea. Invariably they are at their best when the waters are at their coldest.

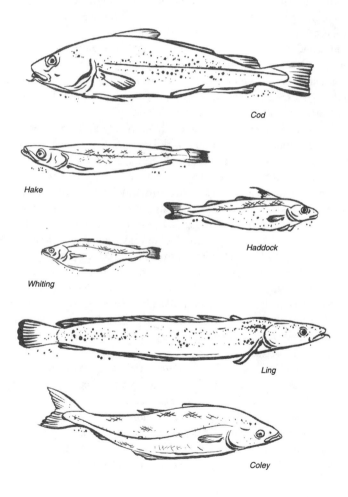

Cod

Hake

Haddock

Whiting

Ling

Coley

COD

Overfishing in the North Sea is now so critical some researchers are saying that only 3% of cod are living to breeding age and only 1% will breed more than once. The Worldwide Fund for Nature has called for people to stop eating the fish entirely, although as we have seen with other species, especially rare breeds of animals, that may not be the answer either. The Government's Laboratory at Lowestoft fears the population may be as low as 60,000 fish – or one third of the level needed to maintain the population.

In 1948, 300,000 tonnes were landed. (This figure included the salt cod sold in barrels where the boats went north for much of the summer and preserved the fish on board.) By 1987, only 90,000 tonnes were landed and in 1992 that figure was halved. Massive fishing by Russian factory ships is one potent factor in this decline.

Cheap cod is off-loaded on the English markets from the Atlantic and can be as much as four weeks old, so more than other fish it is worth checking for freshness.

Cod vary from greenish-grey to khaki in colour, depending where they come from: brownish-green with brown or yellow spots from the North Sea; the darker from near the Faeroes, and the almost black from further north, although they all seem to share the look of earnest sadness and the courtier's smart little goatee fin under the mouth. Cook and writer Frances Bissell calls cod 'the patriarch of the (big white) family'.

Most are fished off the Newfoundland Bank, a submarine plateau 800 km (500 miles) long and 500 km (200 miles) wide, but stray as far afield as Britain and Iceland. They range from 35 to 100 cm (14 in to 3 ft) in length, larger fish tasting discernibly different from the younger sweeter, more delicate smaller inshore fish, known as codling. They can grow as big as 45 kg (100 lb), but over-fishing has made these giants increasingly rare.

The trade price of cod rises steeply at the start of autumn to a peak of nearly £1,500 per tonne or 67p per lb, at port by December, against £1.70 per lb in Billingsgate.

COOKING: *Scarcity has rehabilitated the culinary reputation of the cod and it has increasingly appeared on restaurant menus. Short and plump fish are the best. Steaks are more tender if taken from nearer the tail, but shoulder cuts have more flavour. Cod deserves more attention than simply deep-frying in batter; grilled or poached, it lends itself to strong sauces, even curry. It is good cold with aïoli and is excellent in stews, like the classic French bourride.*

SALT COD

Originally these were known as barrel cod. After catching the fish were beheaded and gutted and kept head-to-tail in layers in salt on ship. After a couple of days, they were salted again, cut into chunks and put in barrels. Today, salt cod is principally prepared in Norway. The fish are gutted, soaked in brine and then kept in salt. They are then dried for export – mostly to southern Europe. In Scotland the barrelled cod were laid out on the beaches to dry. In Portugal, salt cod is still hung along the streets of fishing ports to dry. STOCKFISH is the dried variation and was a feature of the pre-war diet here as it still is in the western Mediterranean. It needs to be soaked for 48 hours to remove the salt before cooking.

COD'S ROE

Available from November to March, this is usually already boiled by the fishmonger. Raw, cod's roe is sold in pairs. Handle carefully so as not to break the outer membrane.

COOKING: *Poach for 10 minutes. Dry well, then shallow-fry or make into fish-cakes. They can be baked with strong sauces, like shrimp or anchovy, mixed with cream as a filling for omelettes, or rolled in bacon slices and grilled. For a salad, chop and mix with diced hard-boiled eggs, fresh herbs, spring onions, and diced ham.*

BEST BUYS John West tins of *soft cod's roe* from Denmark are disappointingly small and fragmented, and the brine seems to have taken on the taste of the tin. The *pressed cod's roe*, also from Denmark, is more robust, granular, and arguably a good alternative to lumpfish; there are still some hints of the tin, but its unusual strong flavour repels this well.

COLEY

Sometimes called COALFISH, BLACKJACK or SAITHE and sold still as ROCK SALMON. They are blackish or dark green paling to silver, 60-100 cm (2-3 ft) in length, best in summer. They are clean creatures, preying on other fish, notably herring. Coley was always decried as a second-rate fish, but it does not really deserve this poor standing. A good everyday fish, it can be about £1 per lb cheaper than cod, possibly more.

COOKING: *Translucent pink-grey flesh turns a more attractive white on cooking, but is dry and breaks up easily in cooking. It is best baked or braised with strong flavourings, or used in pies and fish-cakes. It is occasionally found dyed orange and smoked.*

HADDOCK

One in five fish taken from the North Sea used to be haddock, but serious over-fishing has seen catches halved in the five years from 1987 to 1992. It is similar in shape to the cod but the markings tend to be dark grey-black, with a silver underside; the head is more worldly, wider-eyed and smaller-mouthed. Legend has it that the thumb-print-like indentation on the side of the head is St Peter's mark. Smaller than cod, between 40-75 cm (16-30 in), it is available all year round, but best from colder waters from November to February. Large fish are now rare.

Some say haddock is superior to cod, especially the smaller fish which tend to have softer flesh, but the flakes are well-sized.

BEST BUYS Sainsbury's frozen haddock has matched the Billingsgate price of fresh at £2.10 per lb, a margin of about 40p. Fresh **Somerfield** fillets are £2.99 against **Marks & Spencer** at £3.98 per lb.

COOKING: *Haddock's blandness encourages bright saucing, like brown butter, and stronger flavours like mustard and cheese and the more old-fashioned flour-based sauces. Northern fish and chip shops traditionally prefer haddock to cod.*

SMOKED HADDOCK

Haddock does not salt as well as cod. Instead the fish were smoked for eight hours over peat and sawdust after being left in brine for three hours, hence FINNAN HADDIES from the peat smokeries at 'Finnan', or Findon, eight miles south of Aberdeen. GLASGOW PALES are smoked just enough to turn the colour to that of hay. ARBROATH SMOKIES are hot-smoked in pairs, originally in barrels but now in large kilns. There is still an active industry in Arbroath, which filched the idea from the tiny cove of Auchmithie further north. Smokies will keep up to two weeks. Cod treated this way was never deemed as good.

HADDOCK ROE

Available from November to March, this is usually sold raw.
COOKING: *Poach gently for 8-10 minutes.*

HAKE

Voracious cannibals, hake sleep on the ocean bed by day and swim upwards to feed at night. The mouths are hinged, like monkfish, which gives them a smug glare. They snare unsuspecting passing prey, usually herring and pilchards. Preferring deeper waters, these fish have long tapering bodies about 30-100 cm (1-3 ft), pointed heads, black mouths and ferocious teeth. Dark grey with large loose scales, they are best in the second half of the year, from June to December. Sometimes they were confusingly called stockfish.

COOKING: *The flesh is more fragile than cod: soft and creamy and less well-flavoured, so it tends to suit stronger flavourings. When*

White Fish

The effects of cooking on different white fish

	Calories	Protein g	Carbos g	Fat g	% Fat of Cals
Cod (raw)	76	17.5	0	0.7	0.8
(fried in oil)	199	19.6	7.5	10.3	46
Haddock (raw)	73	16.8	0	0.6	0.7
(steamed)	98	22	0	0.8	0.7
Plaice (raw)	91	18	0	2.2	21
(crumbed & fried)	228	18	8.6	13.7	54
(fried in dripping)	279	15.8	14.4	18	58

The effects of the frying mediums in these examples are quite dramatic.

absolutely fresh, some argue hake is the finest of all the cod family. It is also inclined to break up, however, especially as it ages. Hake is well suited to being wrapped en papillote or in leaves, cooked briefly and served with garlicky salsas or green vegetables or stuffings. Hake is good cold and in fish pies, with lots of garlic and parsley. It is much appreciated in Spain, Italy and Portugal. Smaller fish are deep-fried. Basque kokotxas are hake throats marinated in oil, garlic and parsley.

LING

Longer than the cod, ling has a green-brown mottled back and a grey belly. From 75 cm (30 in) long, the fish often goes for salting as *bacalão* in Spain. Ling has a good flavour but is inclined to wateriness.

COOKING: *It marries with strong flavours in pies or fish cakes. Although not always available, it is cheaper than better-known fish and makes a good midweek buy – but the tail cuts tend to be bony.*

WHITING

Most whiting come from the sub-Arctic, though the best are attributed to Cornwall. Slim, silver-grey with white bellies, 30-60 cm (1-2 ft) in length, they are best from cold waters in winter. The sweet flesh is versatile and used to be recommended for invalids, but is worth more than that although some cooks are disparaging. An old recipe book declares the flesh 'delicate in flavour and easily digested'.

COOKING: *Whiting can be dry, so it is best to poach rather than grill. It is useful for soufflés and mousses and may be braised in wine for 15 minutes.*

THE FLAT FISH

BRILL · DAB · FLOUNDER · HALIBUT · MEGRIM · PLAICE · SOLE · TURBOT

The great flat fish like the halibut, turbot and sole are rarely seen outside of restaurants these days. They tend to be at their best when the waters are warmer, in spring and in autumn. They are bottom-feeders, eating mostly worms and shellfish.

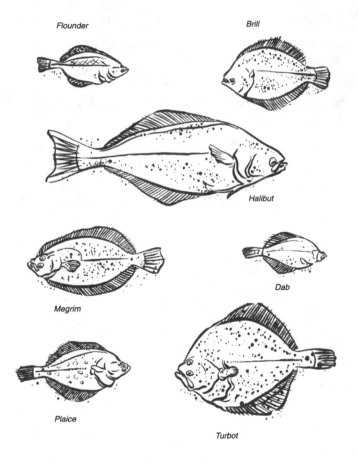

Flounder

Brill

Halibut

Megrim

Dab

Plaice

Turbot

BRILL

Brill do not have the bony bumps under the skin found on the turbot, which they closely resemble. Their bodies are ovoid discs 30-50 cm (12-20 in) in length, with light brown freckled to grey black markings and small scales. Although at their best in early summer, they are available most of the year. Sinistral fish, they lie on the seabed with their left sides uppermost and are predatory feeders, eating fry and eels.

COOKING: *The flesh is well-flavoured and makes a good alternative to turbot – it was known and derided, wrongly, as 'poor man's turbot'. The best, and most expensive, are the larger fish which can be filleted and sauced. Otherwise grill or bake. They go well with vegetables.*

DAB

Dab is the smallest but fastest of the flat fish, and so enjoys a wider choice of prey than others in the plaice family. It has a coarse, sandy brown back, white underside and is 15-25 cm (6-10 in) in length. It is at its best in autumn, when it is sweet, tender and fragile, but may be found all year.

COOKING: *Grill or shallow-fry in breadcrumbs. Larger fish are now quite a find; they can be filleted and take sauces as strong as soy, mustard or horseradish.*

FLOUNDER

Also known as FLUKE, the flounder migrates into estuaries in summer, but is found all year. Dull brown, sometimes with a blotchy orange skin, it is akin to plaice, but less good (though often passed off as such). Plaice has nodules on its head, flounder is smooth. It must be eaten very fresh or the flesh suffers.

COOKING: *Some cooks are disparaging, dismissing it as a filler for terrines; others attempt to sauce it for added flavour.*

HALIBUT

The most magnificent and largest of all flat fish, and now also one of the most expensive – even more so than turbot. Before the War, fishing boats kept the halibut alive in tanks beneath the boats or in shallow coves for up to eight weeks before bringing them back to port. Halibut feed on the floor of the Atlantic near Greenland, favouring rocky ground in the Arctic and North Sea and also the Pacific coasts of America. There they were usually caught on a line with live herring for bait. The duels of small boats landing huge fish were the stuff of fishermen's tales. Records exist in Grimsby of a halibut landed in 1957 weighing 137 kg (304 lb) and possibly 60 years old. Some report fish even larger, at six feet long and 225 kg (500 lb), although such monsters are rare now. Smaller fish, under 2.3 kg (5 lb), are called CHICKEN HALIBUT.

Halibut are best in spring but available most of the year, though some may be frozen imports. For a fish of such size it has a tiny glum boxer's face, white belly and blotchy olive-green rough skin. Halibut farming is currently being developed in Norway.

COOKING: *Its reputation has waxed and waned; most agree that the flesh is dry, but some recommend 'as little preparation as possible'. The tail end has more bones and these will conduct the heat in cooking and make it dry. What the fish needs is careful moist cooking, preferably poaching or shallow-frying, accompanied (not swamped) by other flavours. Like brill, halibut tends to combine well with vegetables.*

SMOKED HALIBUT

Usually GREENLAND or MOCK HALIBUT, a smaller fish without the white belly, with flesh that is drier and coarser. Some is sold in **Sainsbury** and occasionally mock halibut is even sold fresh in some branches of **Somerfield**, where it is cheaper than haddock.

MEGRIM

Also known as MEG, WHIFF, SCARBOROUGH WHIFF or SCARBOROUGH SOLE, it is sandy in colour with spots, ovoid and snoutish mouth, white belly and 25-40 cm (10-16 in) in length. They blanket the deep ocean floor.

COOKING: *The flesh is inclined to wateriness and needs quite strong sauces. Best suited to deep-frying or fish-cakes.*

PLAICE

From the same family as lemon sole, witch and flounder, plaice is a dextral flat fish, ie it lies right side uppermost, head twisted. The mouth is jaggedly awry, the eyes of different sizes. The plaice hunts either under cover of camouflage on the sand of the seabed or moving horizontally through the water, devouring molluscs and small crustacea. They have brown backs to merge with the sands in which they lie, with orange spots (they used to be called DIAMOND SOLES) which disappear on older fish, white bellies, and are 30-45 cm (12-18 in) in length. They are at their best from June to December.

BEST BUYS Smaller plaice sell for about 50p per lb wholesale, larger fish for just over the £1 mark. **Asda** sell them at £2.09, but **Somerfield** at £2.59 or fillets at a steep £3.29.

> COOKING: *Plaice have an iodinic smell when very fresh. Older fish are best cooked on the bone. Look for large fish and take a middle cut, using the rest for soup. 'More watery than flounder' say some, but fish restaurateur Rick Stein says, 'a fresh delicacy, I grow ever more fond of plaice, but its delicacy is soon lost as it stales'. Traditionally plaice was regarded as invalid food, steamed between two plates over boiling water. It is better grilled or shallow-fried.*

SOLE

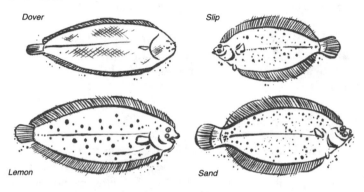

True soles are called DOVER SOLES because most destined for the London market were landed there to meet the train to the capital. Most are, in fact, caught in the North and Irish seas as well as the English Channel and around the Mediterranean. They propel themselves just above the seabed, tapping the ground with the blind side of their head in search of worms, molluscs and small crustacea. The nose is blunt, the colouring surly grey, depending on its habitat. They have coarse, tough skin, compact flat bodies, lightly blotched, white underbelly, and are 25-55 cm (10-22 in) in length. Smaller fish, 20-25 cm (8-10 in) long, are termed SLIP SOLES; smaller still – under 20 cm (8 in) – are called TONGUES. They are available all year, but are best out of mid-winter. Witch and megrim are sometimes passed off as sole.

The price of Dover soles is now so exorbitant, they have become almost entirely the preserve of the restaurant. Even supermarkets will sell them for as much as £11 per lb – three times the price of lobster.

> COOKING: *The only fish perfectly suited for serving on the bone, sole is best grilled or à la meunière. The classical kitchen offers more sauces for sole than for any other fish, but at today's price this now seems almost irresponsible. Some say soles are best left a day or two before use.*

LEMON SOLE are plump oval fish, with sandy brown backs, indistinct mottled markings, small heads and white belly. About 25-40 cm (10-16 in) in length and not related to Dover sole. They have a very good flavour, especially when very fresh, and are at their best from March to December. Underrated and good value, lemon sole cost between £1-£3 at Billingsgate, against three times as much in supermarkets. They are best bought from fishmongers at half that price.

COOKING: *Cook them simply: flour and grill them with butter, pan-fry or bake. Two people will need about 675 g (1½ lb) of fish.*

SAND SOLE, an oblong fish with a freckled sandy back and white belly, is similar to Dover sole, but mostly goes for export. The flesh is creamy, moist and very good.

WITCH SOLE, oval fish with pale-brown mottled backs and white bellies, are 30-40 cm (12-16in) in length, have white flesh and are a good value alternative to Dover soles, especially in heavily sauced dishes.

TURBOT

Turbot is the king of the flat fish. Like brill and megrim, the turbot's eyes are on the left side of the head. It was held to be the finest fish, but is now rare and expensive. Mostly from the North Sea, it has a sandy or dark-brown grey back, no scales and a white belly. It is 50-100 cm (20-40 in) long and is almost circular, with thick moist flesh and an excellent flavour. 'Two points ahead of sole,' declares fish expert Alan Davidson. Small fish, up to 1.35 kg (3 lb), are termed CHICKEN TURBOT.

COOKING: *Classical kitchens used huge diamond-shaped turbotières to accommodate them. Up to one-third of the fish is bones and waste. Bones for stock should be cooked longer than is usual – up to three hours to extract their gelatinousness. Unlike sole, the skin is eaten. So too can the bones if they are deep-fried to a crisp. Whole fish should be slit along the backbone and the bone broken to stop it curling. Cook simply: poach for 6 minutes per 450 g (1 lb). It can look quite pallid and needs colourful accompaniments. Serve cold with mayonnaise.*

THE OILY FISH

ANCHOVY · BRISLING · HERRING · MACKEREL ·
PILCHARD · SARDINE · SPRAT · TUNA ·
WHITEBAIT

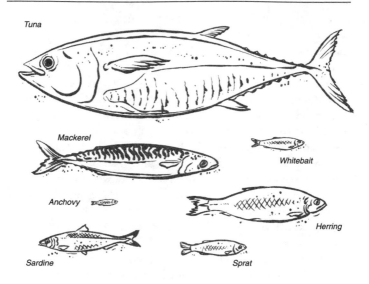

All fish have a positive effect on our bodies, but the oily fish
containing the omega-3 oils (also found in the livers of white fish) are
exceptionally valuable. These oils are believed to relax the arteries
and improve the flow of blood. With most fish, moreover, little is lost
in the cooking, although tuna is an exception. The average
recommended weekly intake of these beneficial oils is 8 g for women
and 10 g for men – or roughly three meals a week. Smoking the fish
increases the percentage of the oils as the water content evaporates,
and smokers also tend to buy oilier fish than is usually sold in the
supermarkets.

% OF OMEGA-3 OILS

Mackerel, smoked	6.6	Conger eel, raw	2
Kippers, grilled	3.2	Sardines, canned	2
Pilchards, tinned	2.9	Salmon, farmed	1.8
Mackerel, grilled	2.8	Tuna, fresh	1.5
Sardines, grilled	2.4	Trout, raw	1
Sprats, raw	2.4	Cod, cooked	0.5
Rock salmon, raw	2.3	Tuna, canned	0.1

(*Table reproduced courtesy of Miriam Polunin and* Taste *magazine.*)

ANCHOVY

One of the herring family, this silver-skinned fish about 10-20 cm (4-8 in) long is distinguished by a deeply cleft mouth and long snout. Some reach the south-west coast of England in summer, but the trade is now centred on Spain, Morocco and Italy, where nearly all the canning is done (including some imports from Peru). In early summer the fish are attracted to the boats by lights and caught in nets.

Italy packs in bottles, Spain in tins. Unlike sardines, preserved anchovies do not improve with age so look for far-off sell-by dates. Anchovies are only semi-cured in salt and, strictly speaking, ought to be kept chilled, but rarely are. The best fish used to come from the island of Gorgona off Livorno, one of the pre-war centres of the olive oil trade. The price is governed by the filleting. Hand-filleted anchovies are stripped in cold water and will often still have the skin on. Machines use hot water, which takes off skin and bone neatly. The former has personality, the other uniformity. Some arrive from Holland unsalted, but preserved in diluted sunflower oil, and are sold in specialist delicatessens. The contrast in the colouring – the one a grey white, the other a meat red – is testimony to the power of salt.

COOKING: *Fresh fish should be filleted, salted for two hours, cooked very briefly in hot oil, drained and then marinated in olive oil, garlic and lemon for 48 hours. The two types of preserved anchovy need different handling. Unsalted are ready to eat and go well with potatoes or peppers. They will be as good as the oil and vinegar in which they are kept. Usually they will be better for being rinsed out and put back in fresh oil. Brine-packed fish should be rinsed in cold water to rid them of the salt, then soaked in warm (not hot) water for 15 minutes and drained. Salted they are used as a seasoning, as they are high in the glutamates associated with the fifth taste umami. From the Middle Ages they have been used to season pies, pastes and meat and, in classical pâtisserie for canapés. In British cooking they are traditionally mashed up with butter; in French mashed with oil, lemon and garlic, then spread on toast and flashed under a grill. Anchoïade de Austin de Croze: this recipe incorporates all the flavours of Provence. Mince 1 part each fresh herbs, onion, garlic, fennel leaves, to 3 parts dried figs, stalks removed. Pound a small chilli with a dozen ground skinned almonds (or 6 walnuts), add a dozen anchovies in oil, and a dozen anchovies in brine, lemon juice and orange flower water. Slice an unsweetened brioche in half, spread the paste on one side, oil on the other, close up and bake in a hot oven for 5 minutes. Garnish with black olives.*

BEST BUYS The best tinned anchovies, *Rizzoli Emanuelle from Parma, are low in salt and have 10 fillets in extra-virgin olive oil, 'chewy, texturous, delicate, salt building at the end.'

Traditionally the Italians preserved anchovies in bottles. The best examples of these are from Iasa, in good oil and salt, still with some skin and bones but plenty of flavour and character.

Prices range from 75p for 133 g or 6p a fillet, to £1.76 for the Italian Zarotti at 30p a fillet. The big brands like John West, Epicure and Waitrose have tended to out-perform the more romantic colourful labels of smaller producers. Moroccan examples have been very scraggy and bony. Princes has also been cheap and poor, even greying. Sainsbury buy neat, meaty fillets from Spain; Tesco's from Italy are paler grey, less promising to look at but a good flavour in good oil (with an extravagant sell-by date of 18 months – nine more than Sainsbury's). The most expensive Zarotti are even poorer value on opening, with only seven fillets compared to Tesco's 12; they are bony, but with good flavour.

BRISLING

The French contested Norway's right to sell into Britain what they were calling 'sardines' under the **Skipper** label. In 1912 the name was changed to brisling or SILD. The Norwegians had their revenge by inventing the seamless tin can, and by the early '20s were selling more than a million cases a year into the UK.

The brisling is most common in Norway, coming close into the fjords in summer to feed near the surface in such numbers that the waters can seem to boil. Much of the fishing is still done by fourth-generation farmers, who form the main co-operative. The boats use fine-mesh purse seine nets, echo scanners and lights to attract the shoals. Two-year-old fish are taken at full maturity, when the fat content will be at its peak. The catch is impounded in nets in the fjord for several days so that the fish cleanse themselves of impurities. They are washed and then hung on steel rods to smoke for an hour over oak chippings. The heads are then removed and the fish packed, still by hand. Although small, they represent high sources of omega-3 oils (see page 101), as well as vitamins A, B and D.

BEST BUYS Brisling are sold tinned under the **King Oscar label. Norwegian brisling have not been sold widely into EU countries, since tariffs make them prohibitively expensive. John West sell brisling under the original Skipper label, but sourced now from Scotland. They lack the infusion of smoke and oil and are inferior to the Norwegian. Brisling mature in the tin and after two years are markedly improved.

HERRING

The scale of the herring trade at the start of the century was massive. More than 6,000 Scottish girls went to Great Yarmouth in 1913 to deal with 854 million fish. At nearby Lowestoft another 436 million were landed in the same season. A deft fish girl was said to be able to gut and grade more than 60 fish a minute. They were salted and barrelled and most went as exports to northern Europe where they held the prime market.

Once second only to cod as the most important fish in the Northern-European economy, vast shoals of herring came inshore. The Atlantic herring stocks were halved in the decade of the '50s; whether this was from over-fishing or a cyclical catastrophe – or both – is unclear. As many other fish feed on herring, the impact was two-edged. Since the lifting of the ban on fishing in '84, the catches have picked up dramatically. They remain cheap, as little as 40p per lb wholesale.

The herring has a dark blue-green back, silver sides, and a reddish tint to the eyes as if it is hungover (which accentuates as it gets older in the fishmonger's). It is best avoided in spring and autumn, after it has spawned, when it starves itself – such fish are known in the trade as SPENTS or SHOTTEN. Herring are a high-quality food with the same protein as beef and good vitamin A, B and D content. Levels of polyunsaturates alter through the year and with different species; the smaller Baltic herring being less fatty than the Atlantic.

COOKING: *As oily fish, herring can be cooked without fat, just a little salt in the pan; filleted, wiped in fine oatmeal (semolina in Norfolk) and pan-fried with the butter added at the end; or with a little bacon fat under the grill and served with bread and a mustard sauce.*

BEST BUYS TINNED HERRING John West has been putting herrings into tins, the results obscured by gunky sauces. They have also smoked small herrings and tinned them as kippers in oil. The two processes fight each other. More successful, but only available in delicatessens, are ****Liflig Gaffelbidder** from **Varefakta**; packed in Denmark and confusingly called sild, they are marinated in sherry and vinegar.

HERRING ROE

Roes are mostly taken from herring that go for kippers, or are imported frozen from Canada. They are very high in vitamin D and underrated, both in price and value.

COOKING: *Flour them and shallow-fry or bake or grill with mustard. Traditionally served on buttered toast with malt vinegar and pepper.*

BLOATER

Most famously from Great Yarmouth, bloaters are lightly smoked, which gives a silvery cast. The guts are left in, which gives a gamy flavour. The curing process is not long enough to preserve or cook them.

COOKING: *They are best grilled.*

BUCKLING

Hot-smoked herring, traditionally imported from Germany. Their smell is that of a clean kipper, but they tend to look off-puttingly squishy and soft. The flesh turns a bready dry, but is quite creamy. The little bones are irritating.

COOKING: *Eat as they are or dressed in a sharp dill vinaigrette.*

KIPPER

Kippers were reputedly invented by John Woodger, a Northumberland fish-curer, around 1843, though the history of smoking and curing haddock further north in the Scottish ports suggests it must have been earlier. Arbroath Smokies can show their history back to the 12th century and if haddock were being smoked, then surely herring were too.

The herrings are split, washed, put in brine, hung to dry and then smoked for 4-6 hours (even quite recently 6-18 hours seemed to be more usual). The disappearance of the herring meant that many smokers had to turn to frozen fish to keep up their trade. The main quality difference is between a freshly caught and smoked fish and one that has had to come from another area. CRASTER KIPPERS began in 1856 or at least the Robson smokehouse was built then. The style in the north east is to put them in brine for only 20 minutes and then smoke over white wood and oak. *Robson's* only smoke in the summer months when the fish are fat and oily. In winter they go over to salmon. Some others are artificially dyed with the controversial browning agent FK.

BEST BUYS Those cooked on the bone will have more flavour, but ironically they are more expensive – usually by 10p or more per lb – than fillets, a general recognition that the processing is not constructive. Kipper prices are elastic: Billingsgate sells for about 80p per lb, **Tesco** for £1.69, **Sainsbury** £1.31, **Asda** 89p, **Young's** fillets in butter at **Somerfield** are £1.59.

COOKING: *Kippers don't need cooking because they have already been cooked in the smoke of the cure. All they need is warming. There is intense debate over the best way to cook kippers so that they do not smell out the kitchen. The old advice was to put them in a jug and cover with boiling water for five minutes. More modern is the idea of microwaving for 90 seconds.*

BISMARCK HERRING

These are flat fillets, marinated in vinegar and white wine with onions and juniper. The French reputedly gave them the name after the Franco-Prussian War of 1870.

MATJE HERRING

The process for curing these in a light brine is credited to the Dutchman Willem Beukelzoom in the 14th century and was protected for centuries. The fish are packed in distinctive small barrels and were considered at their best in May, when the herrings returned after wintering further north. Traditionally they are eaten with French beans and chopped onions.

RED HERRING

Red herrings, originally designed for long keeping, are heavily salted and then smoked. Such fish had to be soaked overnight before use. Today the few curers still active use much gentler cures. Five minutes soaking is enough. Treat as kippers.

ROLLMOP HERRING

Fillets rolled around onion or gherkin and marinated in vinegar. Some may be frozen before marinating, which destroys the texture. The commercial recipe soaks the herring fillets in a solution of vinegar, sugar, salt, onions and spices for up to three weeks in a fridge. They are then drained and packed in bottles with a new marinade and spices.

BEST BUYS Swedish brands like **Laurel Farm** and **Konserver** are notably good. They ignore southern tradition and pragmatically cut the herring into chunks.

MACKEREL

At one time mackerel was the only fish allowed to be sold on a Sunday as it keeps so poorly. The French term for a pimp, *maquereau*, is thought to come from a 17th-century manual which described mackerels as leading young female shad, which were also known as *vierges* (virgins), to their males. Another explanation is that their glistening green-blue markings resemble the bright clothes of pimps in the Middle Ages. The fish prefer the warmer currents and swim inshore as the summer draws in, but not further than the Wash or the Isle of Man. In winter they are trawled from deep seas. These fish tend to be fatter and oilier and usually go for smoking, which is one reason smoked mackerel shows so well in the omega-3 oil statistics. Even at three and four times the wholesale price, in the supermarket mackerel still represent good value.

HORSE MACKEREL, or SCAD, are similar in flavour but are, in fact, from a different family; both are distant relations of the tuna. They have no black markings but share the distinctive dark waves, torpedo shape and white belly of the mackerel. Similarly, they will be 30-45 cm (12-18 in) in length.

COOKING: *Mackerel is best simply cooked – usually grilled – with tart, assertive accompaniments, such as lemon, rhubarb, sorrel, gooseberry or mustard. Very fresh, it can be eaten raw in Japanese sashimi, or follow ideas for tuna. Preserved, soused or pickled, it shows an affinity with white wine or cider.*

BEST BUYS Mackerel are best in the first half of the year. The rich oily meat deteriorates quickly because of the high and healthy oil content when not fresh, but is an excellent source of vitamins and minerals. The mark-up for smoked fish is steep, sometimes £2.69 per lb against 40p for unsmoked wholesale.

Mostly from Denmark, the images on the packaging of **TINNED MACKEREL** suggest clean, brilliant white, large fillets: in most cases, however, the contents tend to be grey-beige broken flakes. Either the cheap off-cuts go to brine or the brine actually breaks up the flesh. **Princes** and **Gerber** are notably guilty. The fat levels rise from around 15% for fillets in brine to 25% in soya oil. Good examples are **Marina** and **Sainsbury** in soya oil, though **Sainsbury Scottish** mackerel in brine still has the skin on and is in horizontal chunks not fillets. **John West** do an interesting tinned wood-smoked and peppered mackerel fillet in oil.

PILCHARD

The adult sardine, it has larger and fewer scales than the herring and its habits are also different: it goes out to sea in spring and its eggs survive on the surface, unlike those of herring which sink. Pilchards are caught off the south-west coast of England from July to September. It was, however, the vast shoals of Pacific pilchards massing around California at the turn of the century that were historically important. Being so rich in oil, the canners sold the fish cheap in order to be allowed to extract the oil from the rest of the catch and sell on the debris as fish meal. Demand for this oil came from the emergent margarine and fats industry, ironically taking the oil in one nutritionally acceptable form and putting it into another less acceptable compromise.

The pilchard makes great claims for health-giving attributes: more calcium than milk, more protein than beef and high in omega-3 oils. Over-fishing, as is the story the length of the Pacific coast of the Americas, destroyed the Californian industry. In the '50s, the same machinery was shipped to Peru to process another surge of fish, which in turn was over-fished and vanished. Pilchards are now usually found in tins from **Glenryck**, labelled 'south Atlantic' and arriving via Namibia. The brine does the bland breadiness little favours. They are oversized sardines without the flavour. They are one of the cheapest foods in the supermarket.

SARDINE

In summer, large quantities of sardines are caught off Cornwall. About 10-15 cm (4-6 in) long, with a blue-green back and silver belly, they are best barbecued or marinated in oil.

The trade in tinned sardines began in Nantes about 1834, although the name derives from Sardinia, off whose shores huge quantities were once caught. As the waters warmed, the fish headed north in ever-growing shoals, either towards Provence in May and June or up the Atlantic coast arriving at Brittany in July and not leaving until October. The French boats used cod's roe as bait to attract the shoals and caught them in nets fine enough just to let the head through, but not the gills or fins. The fish were gutted, salted, left to dry on wooden slats, then raised on wire nets into vats of boiling olive oil to cook for 5-6 minutes. Once drained they were hand-packed into tins. Further south in Spain, Portugal and North Africa, because of the heat, the fish were steamed and laid in olive oil in the tin. French sardines were considered better because the fish came from colder waters and the oil they used to cook was better. Often the oil in the tin was flavoured with bay, cloves or peppercorns.

Good tinned sardines are judged firstly by the quality of the oil. Signs of redness on the flesh indicate it was not freshly packed. The bones should almost have dissolved. Smaller fish have more flavour. Sardines will improve in the tin with age. All the supermarkets sell them too young, in the same year that they have been caught.

BEST BUYS   **TINNED SARDINES**   **Sainsbury** favours Portuguese, which are good by our standards, but not in the same league as a brand like **Piteu** in Portugal itself where the skins gleam unbroken and the fish are as delicate as brisling. **Connetable à l'Ancienne** from Brittany have been made in the same way since 1853, and are sold either as fillets, in red tins , or with lemon, in yellow tins. 'The lemon is very pronounced and by some ingenious trick the bones are removed leaving the whole fish intact, skin and all. Very much like a fresh product and very good..' **Waitrose** go to Italy where they have been palmed off with broken skinned fragments. The big canners, **John West** and **Princes** – and **Somerfield** – go to Morocco, which does not as yet appear to have ring-pulls.

SPRAT

Sometimes known as BRISLING or SILD when tinned, it is similar in appearance to – and often confused with – young herring. It is, in fact, a different species found mostly off the Norwegian coasts, East Anglia and

TUNA WARS AND DOLPHINS

The Atlantic fishing season runs from June to October. Tuna has become the cash crop of the year for many small boats in Cornwall and along the Galician coast. On a good trip, one boat might catch 300 fish a day, each weighing perhaps 5 kilos.

The Spanish boats still use rod and line. They carry 20-metre poles that swing out behind the boats and on each pole there will be five lines. The Spanish have vigorously defended the principal of fishing with lines rather than drift nets – the 'curtains of death'

as they call them. They have cut nets on French and Cornish boats. They argue, quite rightly that drift-net fishing, especially at night (which the French tend to do), leaves the surviving fish (and dolphins) traumatized and indiscriminately destroys all marine life. Spanish estimates say stocks of tuna will be destroyed by 1988.

The EU has stood by the use of drift nets and very little tuna sold here not does not claim to be 'dolphin-friendly – but that simply cannot be true.

previously around the Thames estuary. Catches have dwindled alarmingly in the last 20 years. With a dark blue-green back, silver sides and belly, and 7-12 cm (2¾-4¾ in) in length, they are at their best from September to March. Test for freshness by squeezing one between the fingers – it should slip out. Although a bit bony, they have very good flavour and are cheap – possibly, food writer Colin Spencer argues, because they smell strongly in the cooking.

COOKING: *Shallow-fry or treat as anchovies, using the fillets in a brine of 2 parts salt to 10 of water for 30 minutes, then dry and preserve in olive oil with herbs. Pragmatically (less smell), they are excellent smoked.*

TUNA

This is the fashionable fish of the '90s. High in the omega-3 oils, with a beautiful individual flavour, it is well suited to the cross-fertilization of Asian and European cooking and overdue for recognition. The neck and stomach cuts generally command higher prices.

Most of the European catch is from Spain where the boats use rods, long lines and live bait to catch albacore. French boats have contravened UN recommendations and used indiscriminate drift nets set out across the Bay of Biscay. These walls of death use cheap nylon monofilament, invisible to the fish, stretched across as much as 60km of sea to bring in huge numbers. The Spanish have blocked ports and captured boats in protest.

From 150 cm (5 ft) long, ALBACORE TUNA, found in warm waters only, is long-finned and smaller than blue and yellow fin, with chocolate rather than deep red flesh, which becomes paler on cooking and is not as dense. It is said to be sweetest of all tunas. It is best grilled, baked or braised.

BONITO is usually called SKIPJACK for tins, has steel stripes on a blue-black back, and is 30-50 cm (12-20 in) in length. Imported fresh from the Mediterranean or frozen from elsewhere, it is the least expensive of the tunas. Dried and simmered with konbu seaweed, it makes the Japanese stock dashi. Grill or bake the dark red flesh.

BLUE FIN and YELLOW FIN TUNA are the large streamlined fish beloved of angling photographs, from 100 cm (40 in) long, with pointed heads and deep middle body. Their rich deep red flesh has few bones and is best grilled or stir-fried – be careful not to overcook. Yellow fin is used for sashimi.

MOJOMOA, from south-west Spain, is salted like ham, then cleaned and hung to dry on the factory rooftops under great sails. It keeps for six months in vacuum or oil. Orange in hue, ham-like in taste and with a soft grainy texture, it is a cousin to anchovy in saltiness, but rather a clumsy and somewhat unsophisticated product.

BEST BUYS   In Spain and the rest of the Mediterranean, the sardine fleets also caught tuna. It was packed in large tins to be repacked after the sardine season was over in October. Today most of the tinned tuna comes from the southern hemisphere.

The canners prefer skipjack because the meat is compact and the flesh deemed too dark to fetch a good price fresh. Cooking the tuna and draining off its oils reduces the omega-3 oils drastically. **Waitrose** sensibly makes no distinction between chunks and steaks which are now in practice the same thing, varying only in price. They are all skipjack, but landed in different ports: Seychelles (**Glenryck** and **Tesco**), Thailand (**John West**), Ecuador (**Heinz**). So too are the steaks: from Fiji (**Sainsbury**), Philippines (**Waitrose**), St Helena (**Tesco de luxe**). The flesh is more benefited by canning in oil rather than brine (**John West** claim spring water), but that may be subjective. The best examples have tended to be **Waitrose** and **Sainsbury** by a short distance.

More specialized tins deal in the discernibly different albacore and yellow fin. These are confusingly called 'paler', 'deluxe' or (in **John West's** case) 'Jonggol', which does not appear in any textbooks. **Tesco** confuse the issue further by selling skipjack in 185 g tins and deluxe in 150 g. These varieties respond differently to the oil and exchange the familiar mealiness of skipjack for an intense meatiness with an edge of lemons. There are good examples from **Tesco deluxe**, **Asda deluxe**, **Connetable**, **John West**, and two Italian sources, **Medusa** and *Carluccio's yellow fin* – albeit at £3.50 for 250 g, against skipjack at 40-55p for 183 g, but as good an example as may be found on the market.

Zarotti from Italy can tuna from the Azores: the square designer tin contains

Oily Fish

	Calories	Protein g	Carbos g	Fat g	% Fat of Cals
Anchovy (tinned)	280	25	0	20	64
Herring (raw)	234	17	0	18.5*	71
Kipper	205	25	0	11.4	50
Mackerel (raw)	223	19	0	16.3	65
(smoked)	354	19	0	21	53
Pilchard (raw)	126	19	0.7	5.4	38
Tuna (canned in oil)	189	27	0	9	42
Whitebait (fried)	525	19.5	5.3	47.5	81

*The fat levels in the herring family vary from as low as 5g in midwinter to 20g in late summer. Notice also the higher level in smoked against fresh mackerel, also how smoking reduced the total percentage of fat. Much of the percentage fat in these tables derives from the canning oil.

meaty sections which are 'chunky in good olive oil'; the limited-production **oval can has the fillets of paler flesh, 'milder and more delicate, beautiful for cooking, superb for *vitello tonnato*.'

WHITEBAIT

Normally used for a mix of the fry of herring, pilchard and sprats not more than 7 cm (2¾ in) in length. Whitebait used to be caught in the Thames: the great Cockney dish of deep-fried whitebait with lemon, salt and cayenne was a notable open-air feast in Greenwich in the 19th century. They are best from February to July, though invariably now they are frozen.

COOKING: *They are very delicate, do not wash, but flour and shallow- or deep-fry.*

Fish Products

Analysis of different fish products and percentages of fats accrued.

	Calories	Protein g	Carbos g	Fat g	% Fat of Cals
Fish cake (raw)	188	9.1	15	10.5	50
Fish finger	233	13.5	17.2	12.7	49
(grilled)	214	15	19.3	9	37
Fish paste	164	15.3	3.7	10.4	55
Kedgeree	166	14.2	10.5	8	43
Taramasalata	446	3.2	4.1	46.4	94

OTHER SEA FISH

BREAM · CATFISH · GREY MULLET · GROUPER ·
GURNARD · JOHN DORY · MONKFISH · RED
MULLET · SEA BASS · SHARK · SKATE · STURGEON

With the polluted state of traditional fishing grounds, other fish have
caught the attention of restaurants. Some have lurked unnoticed in
European waters, others like grouper have started being imported from
warmer waters to fill the market. The quality is excellent.

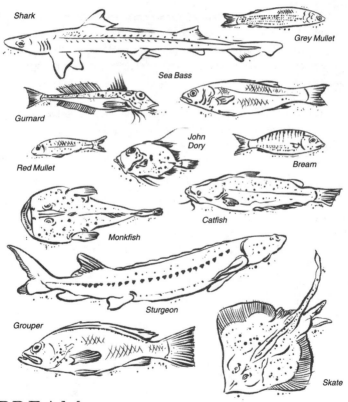

Shark

Grey Mullet

Sea Bass

Gurnard

John Dory

Red Mullet

Bream

Catfish

Monkfish

Sturgeon

Grouper

Skate

BREAM

These red and black fish live in warmer tropical waters; some come into
the west coasts of England in summer and will stray into the North Sea.
Young bream are known as CHAD. The best, GILT-HEADED BREAM
or DAURADE, are imported from the Mediterranean or the Indian
Ocean. Bream have strong crushing teeth and feed on hard-shelled
molluscs. They can prise a limpet from inshore rocks. These teeth were

imbued with mythical qualities: it was said they could make you invisible. They were embossed on tasting chalices and said to change colour on contact with poison.

The BLACK, or OLD WIFE BREAM, is actually blue-grey with gold markings; the red bream is brown to silver and coarse-scaled. The GILT-HEAD is grey-black, with sad yellow bands on its face, and can grow to 30-40 cm (12-16 in). It is much favoured in Italian restaurants; the flesh is coarse, the fins sharp and the bones large.

More tropical species are given imperial names to mark their often strikingly beautiful appearance. BOGUE is popular in Malta, where it is known as VORPA, and usually barbecued. BLACK-BANDED, found in the Indian Ocean, are 20-30 cm (8-12 in) in length, oval, silver in colour with vertical black bands and with a yellow tail and fins. They are good white fleshy fish. CAPITAINE BLANC BREAM, silver grey with an orange hue to the fins and 15-30 cm (6-12 in) in length, are from Seychelles, hence the French name. The smaller version is called 'sweet lips' due to a red mouth, but is rarely seen. These are good, full-flavoured and big-boned. The EMPEROR BREAM, also found in the Indian Ocean as well as the Arabian Gulf, is grey-green, 15-30 cm (6-12 in) in length, with red-edged gills and large eyes, and it too has a good flavour.

COOKING: *Usually dry cooked – baked or grilled, especially the black which is often char-grilled, with strong herbs – rather than poached.*

CATFISH

Also known as WOLF FISH or (in fish and chip shops) as ROCKFISH, ROCK EEL or ROCK SALMON, the catfish has an elongated shark-like body, from 50 cm (20 in) long, a blue-grey-green back with vertical bars and a white belly. The more aggressive names come from the teeth and because it is so ugly the fish is usually sold head-off, providing steaks of pinky, dense, boneless meat.

COOKING: *The versatile firm flesh has a good flavour. Fry, bake or grill – it responds well to stronger flavours.*

The AMERICAN CATFISH is another fish entirely, raised on farms through the Mississippi delta, growing to 1.35 kg (3 lb) in 18 months. It is popular throughout the southern states and has started to be used here in ready-made dishes.

GREY MULLET

Shoals appear along the south and west coasts at the end of summer when they are at their best, although they are available all year. They are thick-lipped fish, with no teeth, and feed by sucking in the sand and mud and taking tiny crustaceans off weed in harbours and estuaries. The Greeks romantically regarded them as fine fish for being vegetarian (not strictly true), and gentle for the gallantry of the males who will follow a female on sight (they were caught with lures as a result). The pollution of inland waters affected their standing, but fish caught at sea are a fine buy; not as distinguished as sea bass, but not far behind and similar in shape and size. The head is flat and pointed, the body heavily scaled (the fishmonger will usually have brushed these off with a metal brush), grey-blue-back in colour, with a silver underside and faint hoops, they are 20-40 cm (8-16 in) in length and quite princely.

COOKING: *If you have an estuary fish that may be muddy, rinse it in vinegar. Recipes for sea bass are largely interchangeable. Grill smaller fish, stuff the larger and bake them. They are also good char-grilled, in casseroles or raw in ceviche.*

GREY MULLET ROE

Mixed with soaked crustless bread, oil and lemon juice, the roe is the traditional basis for Greek taramasalata (now more usually made with cod's roe). More commonly it was called BOTARGO, the roe salted, pressed, preserved in barrels and sliced to serve as an appetizer around the Mediterranean. Popular here in the 17th and 18th centuries, it has been usurped by smoked cod's roe and other variations on taramasalata. Use it as a flavouring ingredient, or grate it over pasta.

GROUPER

Highly regarded in Hong Kong for the meatiness of the flesh, grouper is used in flamboyant centrepieces for banquets. The fish are attracted to the warm waters of the Caribbean, Mexico, South-east Asia and the Indian Ocean, but can stray into the Mediterranean. Groupers grow to enormous sizes, up to 23 kg (50 lb). There are many varieties, with evocative pretty names – CORAL TROUT, CRESCENT TAIL, LEOPARD CORAL TROUT, VIEILLE MACONDE or HONEY-COMB, VIEILLE ROUGE or RED. All are distinguished by the generosity of the flesh. They change their colour according to their habitat, often spectacularly so. Usually they will be flown in from the Seychelles within 24 hours of being caught (they can be fresher than many fish caught nearer to home). Most keep their splendid colouring after cooking.

COOKING: *The taste alters fundamentally depending on whether it is served hot or cold, and the latter is not to be overlooked. The meat is robust and adaptable, but distinctive enough to be plainly steamed and lightly seasoned.*

GURNARD

Also known as GURNET. There are three varieties: the smallest – at around 40 cm (16 in) – and the best is the RED. There are also the GREY and YELLOW (with a blue flash on the fin). The large angular bony head inhibits its swimming. To compensate it has three rays to the front which it is uses like stilts to walk across the sea bed. Found all the year, it is at its best outside of summer. Underrated and still often used for bait for lobsters, it does have firm white flesh, though it can be inclined to dryness.

COOKING: *Gurnard suits poaching, frying and baking with strong flavours, as in a cheese gratin or wrapped in bacon and grilled. The head makes good stock.*

JOHN DORY

ST PETER'S FISH, like the haddock, has finger and thumb marks on either side of its back, reputedly from where St Peter threw it back into the sea after it groaned so loudly in his hand – or perhaps because it looked so ferocious. The body is compressed, grey and ugly; 20-50 cm (8-20 in) in length, it has large grimacing lips, tough spines and fins which are swept back like an aquatic teddy boy. It is a greedy hunter, using its slimness as camouflage. It approaches its prey with a wavering motion or, lying on the ocean bed with its dorsal fin as a lure, it attracts smaller fish. It has been known to eat six times its own length in other fish at one time. It is highly regarded by the restaurant kitchen, which will make it more expensive still. The resemblance of the flesh to lobster is one attraction.

COOKING: *Allow about 675 g (1 1/2 lb) per person, or buy steaks. The percentage of flesh to bone is poor (about 1:3), but the bones and head make excellent stock and soup. The versatile flesh may be fried, poached or lightly grilled and suits sauce recipes for either turbot or sole. In Venice the poached fish is served cold with mayonnaise. In Devon it is poached in cider and served with cream.*

MONKFISH

Like the sea bass, the monkfish has risen to pre-eminence on the enthusiasm of restaurants and has become loftily priced as a result. Twenty years ago it was regarded as nothing. The enormous horny head and huge mouth, through which its unsuspecting prey are lured by the barbel on its head, was deemed off-putting on the slab. Today, hardly a self-respecting fishmonger would be without it. Apart from the occasional cheek, only the short tapering tail is sold. With its dirty brown, dark grey or browny-green skin, it is usually about 30-75 cm

(1-2½ ft) in length – though it can grow to 2 m (6 ft). Best in winter, though available most of the year, the wholesale price will be between £3 and £4 per lb. The solitary central bone makes it good for roasts. The robust flesh will take strong flavours and forceful cooking. For more delicate saucing, it must be quite fresh and cut thinly. It is nearly all meat (take off the tough outer membrane before cooking). Traditionally used as an alternative to lobster or scampi. The head makes good stock and soup if you can buy the whole fish. The liver is rare and excellent. A French company, **de Cadenet** in Brest, has developed a *foie gras* of monkfish liver. The livers are marinated, then warmed and vacuum-packed to be sold fresh (they will keep 21 days) or bottled (these will keep for up to a year). The delicate flesh is white flecked with brown, which shows well in pâté combinations with salmon.

RED MULLET

The Greeks said the red mullet was sacred, stained by the blood of the goddess Hecate. This handsome red-scaled fish, 15-30 cm (6-12 in) in length, is available fresh in summer. They migrate from the Mediterranean around June to September, one species going as far as Norway. Cornish fish are often said to be among the best, as are the GOLDEN (in fact, red with a hue). There are more than 50 species in all. They are small-boned, so the bigger fish are at a premium, about £3.50 per lb wholesale. The liver, a prime delicacy, should be left in, hence the fish's nickname of 'the woodcock of the sea'.

COOKING: *Serve the livers separately, or use to sauce. Red mullet is well established in top-class French restaurants, which does not help the price. The fish is best cooked simply: grilled or marinated in olive oil, lemon and fresh herbs for an hour and then baked in foil parcels. It is also one of the few fish that responds well to red wine in the cooking.*

SEA BASS

An aristocrat with the expression of a nun, a steel-grey chain-mail mesh of large scales (which need to be brushed off) and white underside, bass are found around the globe, but are most common in southern and western waters. They are usually 40-80 cm (16-32 in) in length, but can grow to more than 100 cm (40 in) and weigh up to 9 kg (20 lb). They are at their best from May to June, but still good until October. In early summer they come in from the deeper waters and head up river. Before pollution spread, the river fish were prized over those of the sea. The Romans claimed to be able to tell from which river a fish was caught. Farming has begun in France, Egypt and Greece.

COOKING: *Often wrongly compared to salmon, the quite delicate flesh is soft but holds up well in cooking. Best baked, grilled or steamed, it is usually served hot. The Chinese steam it with ginger and spring onions. The French bake it with fennel and pastis; or poach and serve with a classical Maltaise or mousseline sauce, or a beurre blanc.*

SHARK

The smaller shark family go by rough-and-tumble, unflattering names like DOGFISH (or its equivalent in many different languages), FLAKE, HUSS, RIGG, and TOPE. Usually this will be the SPUR DOG, a sandy brown spotted shark, 50-100 cm (20-40 in) in length. Found most of the year, the boneless, underrated, strong-flavoured flesh stands up well for kebabs, curries and in soups, making it a useful cheaper alternative to monkfish. PORBEAGLE, caught off Cornwall, come in from the Mediterranean and are classically shark-like with rough skin, deep blue backs and white bellies. They may be anything from 150 cm (5 ft) in length. Whereas the dogfish is trawled up with other fish, porbeagle is hunted for itself.

COOKING: *The dense meat goes a long way and marries well with stronger flavours like ginger, soy and chilli. It does tend to be dry when frozen, but the French term for it, veau de mer, points to its quality and cooking strategies – marinate and then casserole or grill (good on kebabs) and serve with lemon.*

SKATE

The nose on a skate is pointed, on a ray it is blunt. They both swim with graceful waving flexes of their wings, but are voracious cannibals; slow but cunning, often swimming over their prey and smothering it into their mouth on the underside. They mainly have brown skin with variations according to species and have no bones, just a cartilaginous well-fleshed skeleton to the wings and none in the nobs (cheeks). They may be found all year, but are at their best from colder waters in winter. The mottled THORNBACK ray is usually held to be the best. Freshly caught skate, unless very young, tend to be tough (they were once dragged along behind the boats to tenderize them before cooking). Once tender, after two or three days, however, they can give off a smell of ammonia which should wash off. The ammonia inherent in the fish's system seems to wear off for the first 2-3 days out of the water, but then begins to redevelop as it decomposes. The preponderance of recipes for deep-frying or with black butter is due to efforts to counter that ammonia. Wipe a finger along a fresh skate and the slime will reappear swiftly.

COOKING: *Skate are best poached or pan-fried and finished with beurre noisette – blackened (ie burnt) butter – and capers, and are excellent cold and in salads, responding well to olive oil and lemon. Braise with cider and onions; or serve in a warm salad with olive oil, tomato, shallot and onions or bacon and croutons.*

SKATE LIVERS

These used to be held to be a great delicacy, but are rare now as they are discarded at sea.

COOKING: *Poach them in fish stock, then slice and serve on toast with butter and lemon.*

STURGEON

A fanciful explanation of the Loch Ness monster is that the sightings are of one of many different species of sturgeon which have been found migrating in UK rivers, like salmon, from the Baltic. The Caspian Sea remains the epicentre of the caviar (sturgeon roe) industry, but farming is being developed in China and America. The French government has invested in projects to revive the fish in the Gironde and the Garonne, which produced caviar-bearing sturgeon before 1940. The fish spawn in the rivers and are then transferred to farms. The fish themselves are mostly sold as meat (the taste is said to be akin to veal) or smoked, but development continues on the eggs. Any caught in British waters are offered to the Queen.

CAVIAR

Iranian caviar is now the best. The mullahs have fostered their industry on cottage fishing lines, while the former Soviet side of the Caspian Sea has been ravaged by pollution and indolent management. The fish are caught in spring and autumn. The best caviar will not be older than six months. Caviar should be packed at source, after salting; though the practice of the trade – and also the black market – is to re-pack large tins into smaller at the point where they are to be sold. Some is pasteurized to extend its shelf-life. Good caviar should hold its shape firmly in the tin. Restaurants and shops which serve it straight out of the larger tin do it no favours as it quickly oxidizes. Keep it chilled on ice and in the dark.

Caviar types are named after the variety of sturgeon. BELUGA is the longest, reaching 4 m (12 ft). One fish gives about 15 kg (33 lb) of caviar. The eggs are large, at 50 per gram. Here and in America, Beluga is prized above the others, less so in other countries. Although 1% of fish caught is Beluga, a quarter of all caviar sold is claimed as such. Often it is actually OSCIETRE, which is about a quarter the price. Oscietre can reach 2 m (6 ft) in length, and there will be 85 eggs per gram. Usually black when young, lightening through to shades of brown to gold, the taste is often likened to that of hazelnuts. *SEVRUGA is the most common and smallest of the sturgeons, not growing to more than 1.5 m (5 ft) and only giving 1-3 kg ($2^{1}/4$-$6^{1}/2$ lb) of caviar, 115 eggs per gram. Distinctly less pebbled, almost a mush, these are not just the cheapest form of caviar but arguably the most interesting in flavour. All varieties are best served simply on toast with lemon juice.

BEST BUYS Caviar is cheaper in larger quantities. Sevruga is £23 for 50 g, or £399 for a kilo, saving nearly £50 in bulk; Oscietre £36 for 50 gm or £621 for a kilo, a saving of £100; and Beluga is £76 for 50g or £1,318 a kilo, saving nearly £200. Good names are **R. G. White** and **Caviar House**. **Sainsbury** do an own-label caviar at Christmas. **Tesco** also sells caviar at larger branches.

American caviar from **Carolyn Collins** is an imitation using the roes from bowfin, hackleback sturgeon and paddlefish taken from Lake Crystal in Illinois. It is seasoned with Chilli and Peppa vodka and smoked over mesquite, 'all of which translates into a weird jelly-like heat that destroys the roes'.

CHINESE MALOSSOL is a mix of eggs from different fish. Through the '80s, the Chinese have been developing a caviar industry: the first results were wayward, but recent batches have been impressive, especially for use in cooking. Lacking the finesse of Iranian caviar, but nevertheless strong fishy and ocean fresh, it is considerably cheaper and a good alternative.

MUJJOL

This not strictly caviar at all, but a mix of herring, salmon and grey mullet roes from Spain. Black, squidgy, gelatinous and slightly sweet, it is an acquired taste.

LUMPFISH 'CAVIAR'

A derided fish, named after the lumps on its thick body, the lumpfish is occasionally found off the north-west coast. The male turns red at spawning time. It is a poor cooking fish and is caught mainly for the roe.

BEST BUYS The blackness is manipulated by the addition of E110, E151, and in the case of **Marina** of Denmark, then pumped up with flavour enhancers and citric acid. Examples from **Limford** and **Glenryck**, also from Denmark, were stale, the eggs dried out and without any natural oil, although the latter had the longest sell-by date of anything on the market. *Macrae's** of Aberdeen show both up as poor: sold in plastic tubs with a greenish hue to the eggs, it is still moist with a wide taste, actually very salty and inky. Easily the best of the batch.

FRESHWATER FISH

PIKE · SALMON · TROUT · CRAYFISH

Although angling remains one of the most active past times, little or none of the fish finds its way to the kitchen or the market. The pollution of inland rivers has destroyed the natural habitats of our greatest fish, the trout and the salmon, both of which survive either through farming or the increasingly diligent efforts of enthusiastic anglers. The native crayfish and the brown trout are endangered species, their places taken by imports of different American species which have proved more responsive to farming. Perch, pike, carp, roach and other small fish have all found their way into the cooking of other nations, but they will go on being of only academic interest until a more enlightened philosophy replaces our antiquated sewers and slack pollution controls.

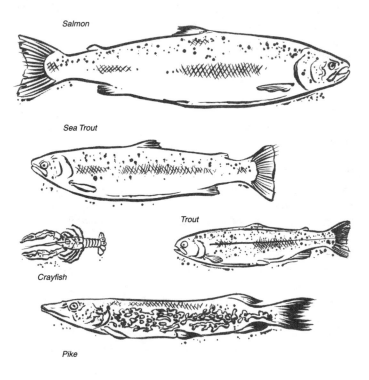

Salmon

Sea Trout

Trout

Crayfish

Pike

PIKE

These predators of fresh waters can grow from 50-120 cm (20-48 in) in length. With a grey-green back and a yellow hue to the belly, their long, duckbill mouth has very sharp teeth. Farming in Holland makes the pike increasingly available. Caught wild, it should be bled from the tail and gills to whiten the flesh. It is at its best out of spring. 'The old and very great pikes have in them more of state than goodness', Izaak Walton wrote. 'The smaller of middle-sized pikes being by the most the choicest... their life is maintained by the death of so many other fish, even those of their own kind, which has made him by some writers to be called the tyrant of the river, or the fresh water wolf'.

COOKING: *Walton recommended stuffing pike with thyme, marjoram, its liver, pickled oysters, and anchovies in a pound of butter and roasting it over an open fire (tied up so the juices do not get lost for the sauce).*

Pike has a strong affinity with the egg and butter sauces of French regional cooking. For example this recipe from Les Trois Faisans in Dijon from the '20s: Lard the fillets as if they were beef, marinate in Madeira, white wine, Cognac, shallots and herbs. Turn several times over a day or two. Bake in the juices in a hot oven with mushrooms for 20 minutes. Finish the sauce with cream or butter. The great French chef Fernand Point wiped the fillets in flour, shallow-fried them and deglazed the pan simply with vinegar and then cream. More enduringly classic has been quenelles de brochet, served with a Nantua (crayfish) sauce: add 1 litre (1³/₄ pt) cream to 1 kg (2¹/₄ lb) minced flesh, season. Add 4 whole eggs and leave for 24 hours. Roll into shapes on a floured surface, then poach in boiling water and refresh.

SALMON

The king of fish was once, as the well-worn story goes, so plentiful that workers asked not to be served it every day. The salmon is a river fish that feeds at sea and returns to spawn in the river – often the one in which it was born. The determination to return to their native spawning grounds is absolute: they will leap dams and obstacles to get up river. In 1913, millions of Pacific salmon died after a landslide blocked the upper estuary of the Fraser River in Canada – then the most famous salmon river in the western hemisphere – and the whole sockeye population was decimated.

Once in the fresh water, the sexual organs swell and the digestive tract shrinks so it does not eat again. As a result, salmon do not prey on each other in rivers. At sea they swim at great depths often 100 km (60 miles) or more in a day, migrating on a 4,000 km (2,500 mile) pattern which is still not well understood.

Salmon

The effects of different processes on the nutritional analysis

	Calories g	Protein g	Carbos g	Fat	% Fat of Cals
Salmon (raw)	182	18.4	0	12	59
(steamed)	197	20	0	13	59
(canned)	155	20	0	8.2	47
(smoked)	142	25	0	4.5	28
Compared to trout					
Trout (steamed)	89	15	0	3	30

Scottish salmon – and, to a lesser extent, Norwegian – are the finest. They can grow to well over 1 m (3 ft) and weigh 30 kg (66 lb), but the smaller fish are better. GRILSE, making their first return to the river, will be under 3.2 kg (7 lb). A good fish has a small head and large shoulders, the sleek steel blue silvery body scattered with black markings.

The Spey, the Tay, the Tweed, the Don and the Dee – the famous salmon rivers – are increasingly being bought back by the rod-and-line fishermen, who are putting a stop to netting. Wild salmon will become increasingly rare, except where caught by boat. Even now, wild represents only a few hundred tonnes a year compared with 40,000 tonnes of farmed, of which nearly a third goes for smoking. At sea, stocks have fallen dramatically in the last five years. Salmon conservation organizations have been buying out fishermen.

Wild salmon are at their best when they have just entered the river and have the sea-lice still on their backs. Farmed are said to be better in summer. The tails of the wild fish are sleeker and a more defined triangle. The main differentiation among the farmed is whether the fish are kept in sheltered waters or more turbulent sea currents. The term 'organic' is misused to describe those farmed in sea pens. The **Scottish Quality Salmon** logo indicates fish that meet trade specifications: they should not be kept at densities greater than 15 kg to the cubic metre. Pollution from the *Braer* oil-tanker break-up led to the withdrawal from the scheme of Shetland fish in the area. The trade price for farmed fish is £1.60 per lb.

COOKING: *Salmon are best slow-cooked: either poached, allowing 8 minutes to the 500 g (1 lb), or wrapped and baked slowly in the bottom of the oven for 1-2 hours. The tail cooks more quickly than the fatter belly. Vinegar spoils the coloration. There is an affinity with the acid tartness of fruits like rhubarb, and the* classic egg-based sauces. The salmon with sorrel-flavoured beurre blanc recipe from French master chefs, the Troisgros Brothers, is the dish often credited with the launch of nouvelle cuisine. Equally Raymond Blanc's salmon tartare helped establish his reputation. Traditionally, hot salmon (more effective grilled than poached) is served with hollandaise, cold with mayonnaise or, of course, it may be included in kedgeree.

GRAVLAX has come to be more about the sauce than the fish. Most commercial versions are, disappointingly, just salted salmon with a little dill laced round the edges. They bear little comparison to home-made: For 450 g (1 lb) of salmon, make a paste with 450 g (1 lb) sugar, 450 g (1 lb) sea salt, 150 ml ($^{1}/_{4}$ pt) brandy or aquavit and 3 bunches of dill. Season generously with mustard and black peppercorns. Spread over the fish and leave 48 hours. Slice thinly and serve with mustard and dill sauce.

SMOKED SALMON

Smoking was originally a means of preserving, but has now become an end in itself. Smoked farmed fish are obviously fattier, almost like butter. Wild is usually 25% more expensive, and the quality can be erratic. Much farmed is passed off as wild, or so the figures suggest. The flesh will be firmer, less oily and subtler. It will also be paler, because the fish have not been fed on pigment supplementations. A good smoker will first salt his salmon – perhaps by as much as a ratio of 2:3 salt to salmon – for up 24 hours, in which time it can lose as much as 40% of its weight. The smoke is properly from oak, not strictly a flavouring process. William Pinney of the **Butley Orford Oysterage** and smokery in Suffolk who, like many, began smoking in the '70s argues: 'The oak's volatile components are released by the smoke. Every one of the chemicals in the wood has a different boiling point. A slow heat will not be sufficient, for example, to boil the pitch latent in the concentrated sap of oak. (This pitch would impart a bitter flavour.) But it may boil the antiseptic substance that yields acetic acid, or the one for formaldehyde, both good preservatives.' The salmon is exposed to these compounds and flavoured according to the time and the heat.

Traditionally, the smoking was much slower, at around 65°C (150°F) for up to 12 hours. Commercial expediency has tended to raise temperatures and cut smoking times. Many of the old kilns have been replaced on health grounds, indeed pressure from environmental health officers nearly led to a complete ban on mail-order smoked salmon until the government relented at the last minute. While bacteria levels can be above average, these are not necessarily hazardous. There have been no recorded cases of food poisoning directly associated with smoked salmon.

COOKING: *Serve chilled, not cold, with lemon and black pepper; with scrambled eggs; as a salad with new potatoes. It has an affinity with dill, horseradish, fresh cheese and cucumber.*

BEST BUYS So long regarded as a luxury, supermarkets have found it hard not to mark smoked salmon up substantially – smaller packs of 100 g amount to two small slices. **Marks & Spencer** sell six different lines, including a London cure, each weighed – unhelpfully – differently. **M&S** Irish salmon has been more than £17 per lb against **Tesco's** at under £10; in mitigation, however, the **M&S** version has shown well in different tastings. ***Sainsbury's Isle of Skye** has shown consistently well in different tastings and is around £12 per lb. Strips and off-cuts are useful and inexpensive for recipes.

Some Alaskan salmon is smoked in Somerset, but it lacks the delicacy of the Scottish although it has a compensatory mealiness. There is little price concession.

Balik salmon, developed by Hans Gerd Kubel, is reputedly modelled on the produce of old Russian smokehouses used by the Tsars, reconstructed in the Toggenburg mountains between Zurich and St Gall. At an altitude of 800 m (250 ft), they use mountain water and three woods for the slow smoker to give a result that is tender, but hardly worth the premium.

HOT-SMOKED SALMON

Some supermarkets have been experimenting with hot-smoked fish, but the prices are giddily matched to smoked salmon rather than fresh, which makes them expensive, short-keeping divertissements for salads.

TINNED SALMON

The canning industry on the west coast of America began on the Sacramento River in 1849 and has moved north as rivers have been over-fished. Canada and Alaska began canning in 1866 and salmon canning was the first work for many immigrant Chinese. The fish are Pacific salmon. The finest for canning is the SOCKEYE, sometimes called BLUEBACK in Canada and RED FISH in Alaska. It weighs up to 4.5 kg (10 lb) and the depth of its redness has overshadowed other fish. It exudes a rich red oil – the more so after it has been in the tin for a year. They follow upstream the larger spotted CHINHOOK, sometimes called KING, which have been known to weigh 40 kg (90 lb). Chinhook's size has given it commercial weight, but it is not as well-coloured as sockeye and goes very soft in the tin after a few months. (**Waitrose** has been flying them in fresh each week from farms in British Columbia.) The smaller and more beautiful COHO, sometimes called SILVER SALMON, is more delicate but disadvantaged because the flesh tends to pinkness and the quality has varied from river to river. Also prized, especially in Asia, is the smallest of the species, the

HUMPBACK. Like the Coho, however, it tends to pinkness and the quality varies from different rivers. The cheapest and least valued is DOG or CHUM SALMON, which has little oil, loses its colour quickly on entering the river and is unappetizing. In autumn, the males' jaws become enlarged at mating time, hence the name.

The season is fixed by the return of the sockeye salmon to the Copper River at the beginning of June. Mostly reds and kings go to Japan. The big catch for the UK is that of the BRISTOL BAY REDS, on the far west point of the Alaskan shoreline, protected by the Alaskan peninsula.

BEST BUYS   Before the rise of cheap farmed salmon, tinned salmon was regarded as a luxury. Increasingly, however, it looks like a poor alternative. The brines tend to win out and create a wet salt taste that predominates. Nearly all examples include skin and bone, and are messy and lacking in oil. Pink is particularly flavourless. **Socra** from Russia has the deepest coloured oil. **Sainsbury** buy a skinned and boned version from Canada, which at least aspires to some form of status. At twice the price, say of tinned tuna, tinned salmon seems an irrelevant relic of a past era.

SALMON TROUT

A confusing term, which is strictly-speaking a nonsense. Some people hold that salmon breed with trout, but they don't. Usually the term is used to pass off pink-fleshed trout (caused by the feed) as if they were salmon. The practice does neither species a service.

TROUT

Prophetically, the brown trout is reputed to have been the first fish to have been artificially inseminated – as early as the 15th century. Before their rivers became polluted, trout were regarded as the freshwater equivalent of red mullet. Now they are almost exclusively farmed. WILD BROWN TROUT are now only caught privately, mainly in the rivers Test and Itchen and their tributaries. The sale of such fish has been banned in France since 1961. Farmed varieties are RAINBOW TROUT or STEELHEADS, imported from California and first bred on this side of the Atlantic in France at the turn of the century. The silver skin is imbued with shades of olive green, a bluish back, and flecks of the rainbow. They usually grow from 20-60 cm (8-24 in) long, and smaller fish are preferable. The flesh should be white, but will be pink when fed on shrimp-enriched diet or just a dyed diet.

The density at which the fish are held in the farms varies according to the oxygen in the water. As they tend to shoal, however, there is little percentage in offering them more space. In the wild they are voracious hunters, taking fly and smaller fish. A large trout might even go for a small bird. Domesticated, they are fussy eaters and in recent years the conversion ratios of feed to meat have dropped dramatically due to farmers going from white fish meal to herring meal, and feed with a higher oil content. Smokers also want fish with higher oil levels than the ordinary kitchen. Interestingly, the oils seem to concentrate at the head rather than the tail.

The artificial colour is due to astaxanthine, a nature-identical pigment made by **Roche** in Switzerland. The UK industry switched from canthaxanthin after (unrelated) concerns about eye problems in people who had overdosed on tanning pills containing canthaxanthin in Germany. The egg industry still uses it in their feed as does the American trout industry. The often attributed criticism of fish being muddy is more likely to be a problem with wild fish in overstocked lakes. Most farmed fish will be a year old, though larger ones can be as much as 15 months. Supermarkets mark farmed trout up by 100% over the trade price of around 90p per lb.

COOKING: *Shallow-frying remains the most effective cooking, although larger fish can be poached like salmon. However, the recipe culture, especially for rainbow, is strangely underdeveloped. The provenance of the bizarre trout with almonds is not known. Many of the regional recipes were designed for brown trout, not rainbows. It is cooked when the eyes turn white.*

SEA TROUT are not a separate species, but merely the common brown trout which goes wandering. They are caught as they return each year to their river to spawn from February to August. They do not migrate as far as salmon, return each year to the river and may only spawn once. The fish arrive at different rivers at different times, starting with the Tay in January. Once in their river they will not feed until spawning in autumn. The best are newly back from the sea at the start of each river's season.

COOKING: *These are magnificent fish and need only gentle cooking. Bake slowly in foil (with a little added butter, or olive oil if serving cold) in a very low oven for 1-2 hours.*

CRAYFISH

The largest freshwater invertebrates, they were common in the banks and holes of inland rivers before pollution decimated them. As with the red squirrels, the indigenous population has been wiped out – barring two or three protected colonies in the West Country – by an introduced variety. The SIGNAL, imported from America, is 6-8 cm (2½-3¼ in) long. Some crayfish farming is being established. They are at their best in summer and used mainly as a garnish.

SHELLFISH ETC

CLAM · COCKLE · CRAB · CRAWFISH ·
CUTTLEFISH · DUBLIN BAY PRAWN · LOBSTER ·
MUSSEL · OCTOPUS · OYSTER · PRAWN ·
SCALLOP · SHRIMP · SQUID · WHELK

The shellfish trade remains old-fashioned and individualistic. Each area still has its own language. At Billingsgate, lobsters are sold by the pound, crabs by the stone, oysters by the 100, Dublin Bay prawns by the gallon, scallops by the dozen, winkles by the hundredweight, mussels by the 25 kg and prawns by the box and whelks by the tray. The seaside stalls selling shellfish asphyxiated in baths of malt vinegar are a hangover from the costermongering of the 19th century, which has never really been thrown off. Shellfish has struggled to find a natural outlet – though some restaurants, notably the **Conran** group and the Belgian-inspired **Belgo** chain, as well as others who have seen the value of mussels, have begun to reverse the trend.

Compare for a moment what has happened here with the story in Brittany, which shares the same waters and fishing. The restaurants are famous for their platters of shellfish and attract millions of francs in tourism each summer. Until very recently much of what appeared on those cork platters was thrown back by English boats. The few sheds that survive at Leigh on Sea in Essex provide a stark illustration – a ramshackle café culture, offering tea and brown bread and rickety tables in the open air. The comparison with France is shameful.

Serious London restaurants still take their shellfish from France and Holland (better packed), where the quality standards are more rigorously applied, though often it may have been landed or caught in UK waters and sent to Paris's Rungis rather than Billingsgate.

Shellfish are fashionably low in fat – lobster 1.9%, crab 2.8%, shrimp 1.4%, scallop 1.4%, oysters 2.1%. They can, however, pick up and pass on toxins that survive in the summer in the dinoflagellate algae, so beds are monitored weekly. Paralytic shellfish poisoning is rare but potentially fatal. Less serious is diarrhetic shellfish poisoning.

CLAM

The south coast and Channel Island waters are home to some of Europe's finest clams, but only the cockle has managed to establish itself here. Until the '60s, other kinds of clam were only sold in tins. The English names for the six varieties found underlie the suspicion and unease of their transfer from scientific identification to kitchen. The French names, by contrast, are almost poetic.

Mostly imported from France, the COMMON CLAM (in French *palourde*, in Italian *vongole*) has a concave shell 3-6 cm (1¼-2½ in) across, marked with circular lines, light brown with dark mottling. The proper clam for *spaghetti vongole* or the Portuguese *cataplana* with pork.

The HARD-SHELL CLAM or QUAHOG is the clam for chowder; grey-beige, again concave with circular growth lines, it is slightly larger at 5-10 cm (2-4 in) and is best in July and August. They are thought to have been accidentally introduced around 1960, possibly by a liner from America throwing a consignment overboard in the Solent or simply carrying them attached to its hull. Older – hence larger – clams tend to be chewy and need marinating if they are to be eaten raw.

RAZORSHELL CLAMS are predictably named after a cut-throat razor because of their distinctive appearance; the shell is blue-green or beige and 10-20 cm (4-8 in) long. Widely caught off the Scottish coast and Channel Islands, these mainly go for export. Sweet and tender, serve them raw with just a drop of lemon juice, or steam them briefly. Some are smoked.

VENUS CLAMS, sometimes called VERNI, have a reddish-brown concave shell, 5-8 cm (2-3¼ in) across and are mostly imported. The smaller ones are better.

WARTY VENUS, the French *praire*, have a beige to brown shell 3-6 cm (1¼-2½ in) across, and can still be found on southern beaches by collectors. They are highly prized in Europe.

COOKING: *All clams will open and cook with steaming. Recipes tend to be interchangeable, although some varieties have associated themselves with at least one enduring dish. Clam bakes are a popular American picnic, using larger clams cooked over hot stones and covered with seaweed.*

COCKLE

The edible cockle, *Cerastoderma edule*, forms great carpets of colonies between the mid- and the low-tide points of sandy beaches, sometimes as dense as 1,000 to a square metre. The rings on the outside of the shell indicate the age, as much as 10 years. They are now harvested at three to four years, when they will be 3-4 cm (1¼-1½ in) across. They are prey for plaice, flounders, crab and starfish, as well as gulls and waders. The Thames boats suck up the sea floor with hydraulic dredges. Other commercial beds are in the Wash, Morecambe Bay and on Barra, although many are imported from Holland. The best come from the Gower Peninsula, where the extravagant tides of the Severn estuary wash over the beds with a rich supply of fresh, clean sea water. They are still harvested there by hand with cart and horse and are mostly sold in

Swansea market. The DOG COCKLE (in French *amande*) is beige with a zig-zag marking; 3-5 cm (1¼-2 in), it is larger than a UK cockle. It is not fished here, but is usually imported under the French name.

COOKING: *Beyond the boiled-in-malt-vinegar-with-pepper tradition of seaside stalls, the Welsh use the Gower cockle with bacon and laverbread.*

CRAB

The crab is more developed than the lobster and has central nerve cords. The edible crab, *Cancer pagurus*, is typically dirty rust-brown with a cream belly. It is a voracious eater and has a keen sense of smell to guide it across the ocean floor on its six legs. The male is flatter and its tail underneath is narrower, whereas in the female it is a triangular 'apron' to hold the eggs. The male has larger claws and therefore usually costs more. They must be 11 cm (4½ in) across the back to be sold. The major fisheries are Northumberland and Yorkshire, Devon and Cornwall, and the small, but well-known, area of Norfolk around Sheringham and Cromer. A crab moults to grow, shedding the old carapace and swelling up with water. Each moult may add an extra 2.5 cm (1 in) across the diameter. They mate when the female's shell is soft. She will have eggs from August to October and will be called 'berried'. The female will then move north, perhaps as much as 30 km (20 miles). Her eggs drift back to where they were conceived. Crabs are at their best between March and September, and at their peak in June when the warmer waters draw them closer to shore. In winter they become lethargic and go deeper.

COOKING: *A good crab should be heavy. If it is light it may be full of water from a recent moult. They are best eaten straight after cleaning and cooking. Ready-dressed crabs dry out quickly. To clean a cooked crab: break open the shell horizontally; take off the grey fibrous fingers around the white head (these are inedible); separate the white meat from the brown in the larger shell and from the centre of the head; cut the head in half and, using a thin knife, work from the outside in. The white shards are very sharp. The shell and trimmings make excellent stock. Underrated compared to lobster, perhaps because it is so labour-intensive.*

The SPIDER or SPINY CRAB is aptly named as the spindly claws and legs are roughly equally long, tucked under a rough cloth-cap-shaped carapace. The main flesh is in the body and legs. Wastefully, it has been thrown back by fishermen here for decades. Mostly they go straight to France and Spain, where they are more appreciated. The flesh is sweeter and more fibrous, and they are easier to clean. The ratio of meat to shell is lower than on the ordinary crab.

SOFT-SHELL CRABS are BLUE CRABS, *Callinectes sapidus*, from the American east coast, chiefly the Chesapeake Bay. They are eaten as they moult their shell – hence the soft skin – usually in summer. The males are 'jimmies', the females 'sooks'. Rarely more than 15 cm (6 in) across, they are caught in pots and kept until they moult. Most found here are frozen, and have gone out to the restaurant trade as a novelty, usually deep-fried. In Louisiana there has also been serious investment in soft-shelled crawfish since 1987.

BEST BUYS **TINNED CRAB** Canning removes the crab's greatest assets, its sweetness and freshness. **John West's** dressed crab from Scotland is 93% crab meat, extended with oil and wheat-flour. A 43 g tin might just stretch to two sides of a cricket-match-tea sandwich. It is dry, with a wheaty, biscuity and grainy filler, but at least distinct. Their white crab meat in brine comes from Thailand and has been boosted up with E621 (monosodium glutamate), sugar and salts, and then wrapped in some white paper inside the tin. The result is dry and pappy, desperately in need of mayonnaise. Worse is **Armour**, again from Thailand and again with added MSG. Much tinned crab is from ALASKAN KING CRABS, which can grow to 10 kg (22 lb) and are found round the Arctic rim of Alaska, Siberia and Greenland.

CRAWFISH

Also sometimes called SPINY or ROCK LOBSTER, crawfish like the warm waters around the Mediterranean or the Gulf Stream currents off Scotland. It has no claws – just two long antennae – and can reach lengths of 50 cm (18 in) or more. The colour changes with different habitats but, like lobster, turns bright red after cooking. Caribbean and Brazilian crawfish can be blue and reach weights as much as 14 kg (33 lb). These make a spectacular centrepiece. Crawfish are expensive, but 50% of the weight is edible. The texture is more delicate than lobster, but loses flavour swiftly after cooking, especially if the fish is kept in the fridge.

CUTTLEFISH

Not to be confused with squid, the cuttlefish has zebra-patterned skin, six long and two short tentacles, and the flat bone beloved of budgerigars and previously used to make toothpaste.

COOKING: *The shape lends them to stuffing and they may be poached, fried, or grilled. Smaller ones, around 5 cm (2 in), are prized. The ink sac is larger than that of the squid or octopus and contains more ink; it is valuable for saucing and is occasionally sold separately in sachets.*

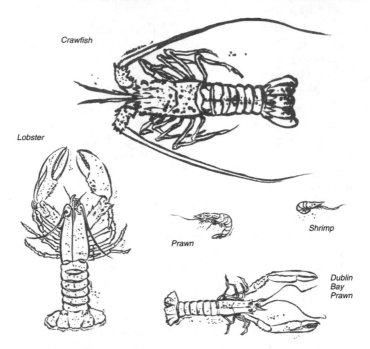

Crawfish

Lobster

Prawn

Shrimp

Dublin Bay Prawn

DUBLIN BAY PRAWN

Sometimes known as NORWAY LOBSTER or SCAMPI, from the Italian, properly they are *Nephrops norvegicus*, and *langoustines* to the French. They are found from Iceland to Morocco, but most abundantly around Norway. Shaped like a miniature lobster, with an orange hue to the carapace and hard brittle incisors, they are 7-15 cm (2¾-6 in) long. In summer they moult, making them watery. Before 1950 they were usually thrown back. Indeed, the Dublin market refused to take them and the fishermen used to have to give them away to street vendors, hence the name. They are now highly prized in French restaurants.

COOKING: All they need is two minutes in boiling water and then a quick plunge into cold. They are usually served as a garnish or on a platter of mixed shellfish with mayonnaise. The shells make excellent stock for soup.

LOBSTER

Lobster are found from the Arctic Circle to Morocco. The main concentrations are around the UK, notably the north-west coast of Scotland, Norway and mid-Channel. The female has smaller claws and a wider tail. They can live to become giant size, up to 15 kg (33 lb) – now uncommon – and 1 metre (3 ft) long. Smaller lobsters are sweeter, more intensely flavoured and better value; bigger ones have thicker shells.

Allow 450 g (1 lb) for one person, 1 kg (2¼ lb) for two; hens are a better buy than males. They are at their best from May to October. Hens from Scotland will have eggs in June and July. Lobsters moult, growing a second shell beneath the first. The shell is slipped off in 5-20 minutes and the lobster absorbs sea water and swells to its new size within 4-5 hours. They grow 50% larger with each moult. As they age this happens less frequently, perhaps every two or three years. The shell becomes rigid in 3-4 days and completely hard after 3-4 weeks. They mate when the female has just moulted and the eggs will take six years to develop to creatures weighing about 450 g (1 lb).

Attempts to farm lobsters have failed because they are quarrelsome and combative. Nevertheless new trials have released spat at 5 cm (2 in) long at Scapa Flow, Orkney; Brishagton, Yorkshire; and Aberystwyth. Lobsters share the same territory as crabs, although one species tends to dominate. The Canadians have revolutionized the trade in the last decade. Their canned lobster industry was based around Nova Scotia because of the clean sandy or gravel beds. As demand for canned lobster disappeared, the Canadians have gone into fresh. Fishing is organized on a rota system from different bays through the year and the taking of female lobsters with eggs is banned. They are rested in ponds, before being flown round the globe – notably here, America and Japan. The wholesale price of Canadian lobster is £3.50 per lb, which has brought the price below fillet steak and makes it one of the more surprising bargains widely available in supermarkets. Live Canadian lobsters are speckled down the side. They have softer shells and less colour than the Scottish. The Scottish lobster is a better quality, but the trade is less consistent and the price £2-3 more per lb.

> COOKING: *The harder shells of Scottish lobsters have more carotene, which makes them more adaptable for classical recipes like mousses where the colour infused into the stock is important.*
>
> *Cooked, the tail should be flexible not floppy and spring back to its original position. The tradition of cooking lobsters live is based on the principle that the flesh turns mushy quickly after death and does not keep well. There are different theories on how to kill a lobster humanely: place it in a carrier bag in a freezer at -10°C (14°F); put in cold water and let the temperature rise slowly to boiling; plunge into rapidly boiling water and keep there for 12 minutes to the 450 g (1 lb); or, as in Hong Kong, behead it with a cleaver.*

FLATHEAD LOBSTERS are also known by the French as *cigales de mer* (sea grasshoppers), which comes from its audible whistling underwater. Less flatteringly, they are called 'Moreton Bay Bugs' or the more southerly variation, 'Balmain Bugs', in Australia. The sandy carapace folds over and the tiny claws and legs are tucked neatly underneath.

Shellfish

The percentages of fat in shellfish against different processes.

	Calories	Protein g	Carbos g	Fat g	% Fat of Cals
Crab (boiled)	127	20.7	0	5.2	36
(canned)	81	18.1	0	0.9	1
Lobster (boiled)	119	22	0	3.4	25
Prawn (raw)	107	22.6	0	1.8	15
Scampi (crumbed & fried)					
	316	12.2	30	17.6	50
Mussel (raw)	87	17.2	0	2	20
Squid (raw)	66	13.1	0	1.5	20

They can grow to 1.8 kg (4 lb). The meat is all in the body and the smaller Mediterranean specimens go for soups. In America they are largely ignored. They have a reputation in Australia, and a few have begun to appear here frozen. A small slug of ungiving lobster-like flesh, they are still too costly to consider seriously, but likely to get cheaper as they are more widely available. Some come from the Arabian Gulf and these are highly regarded.

MUSSEL

The BLUE MUSSEL, Mytilis edulis, is highly fertile and responds to clean water by growing rapidly to 5 cm (2 in) in three years, clustering in the brackish waters of estuaries and harbour mouths by linking their beards. The shells are deep blue and opaque, the flesh creamy-beige to orange. The larger Mediterranean species, M. galloprovincialis, is sometimes found in the south-west. Wild mussels have thicker shells and less meat, 15–30% against 25%–45%. Most UK mussels are now seed taken from the wild and re-laid on prepared beds, mostly in North Wales and the Wash. The French technique of growing them on poles or ropes, known as bouchots (allegedly practised since the 13th century), is not used in UK. The story is that, in 1235, an Irishman, Patrick Walton, was shipwrecked near La Rochelle. He set nets out in the bay to catch fish on wooden poles and found colonies of mussels attached themselves to the poles.

Sold live, mussels are at their best from September to April. In summer they spawn, the males sending out a continuous stream of sperm to meet the eggs. Because of different cycles through the year, they are now also generally available in summer. They feed on the plankton in the water (hence the ban on the sale of wild, unpurified mussels, where colonies feed on sewage) and grow rapidly. They will keep in a fridge at 5-8°C (41-46°F) or covered with a damp cloth for 5-7 days. To clean mussels: scrub them under running water, pull away the wiry beards – if they have already been de-bearded (by machine) they will not keep as long. Throw away any broken shells or any which stay morosely open before cooking. Wholesale, mussels are very cheap – £15 for 25 kg. They are sometimes sold by the pint, which equals 450 g (1 lb). Mussels are saltwater creatures and will not survive in a sink of tap water overnight.

Larger, 9x5 cm (3½x2 in), green-shelled mussels have a beautiful, completely smooth, pale brown shell with a vivid green edge. Inside, the cream or orange-hued flesh completely fills the shell. They have been associated with one case of listeria in New Zealand, from where they are mostly imported, but this has been linked to bad hygiene. They are now usually sold ready-cooked at around 11p each. Meaty, not subtle but generous, these are possibly a better buy than other preserved mussels.

BEST BUYS SMOKED MUSSELS represent good value compared to smoked oysters and perform the same tasks. *John West, quite extraordinarily for a company of its size, has not gone over to ring-pull tins as yet. Once you have got the tin open, the mussels are a good size and kept in cottonseed oil, packed in China. The Danish mussels in the **Spinnaker Seafood** product are minuscule and come complete with unhelpful finger-burning recipes like heating the tin in hot water, not to mention a pungent garlic butter sauce that is rather too much of smoke, garlic and cheap butter.

OCTOPUS

This cephalopod is more advanced than other molluscs, and has a large mouth and beak and well developed 'savage-looking eyes'. Their organs are contained in the sac they use to propel themselves through the water by contraction. They are found around Britain, though mostly imported from the Mediterranean. The eight tentacles have small suckers, in either one or two rows. They feed on other shellfish and this gives them a mild sweet taste.

COOKING: *Do not over-cook (or salt) or they become rubbery. Larger specimens may need beating to tenderize the flesh. Only the tentacles are usually eaten. Coenders in his* Chemistry of Cooking *says, 'small octopus can be cooked by putting a wine cork in its mouth. This makes the octopus float and ensures even cooking. Drop in a potato. When the potato is cooked so is the octopus.' Peel off the skin and suckers to serve. The flavour is 'musky' and is best developed by slow braising. Marinating adds flavour and helps tenderize the flesh.*

OYSTER

A healthy oyster will look like a lingerie commercial, its frilly skirt edging a silken plump body. They should be chewed, not swallowed whole. Two types of oyster are reared in Europe: the NATIVE, *Ostrea edulis*, which is flat and almost round, and the elongated PACIFIC, *Crassostrea gigas*. Natives have the subtlety of texture and meatiness, whereas Pacifics are inclined to softness. The exception tends to be oysters from Ireland, where the Pacifics can be as good as anywhere, but the natives are weak. English natives are supreme, at a price, notably WEST MERSEA and HELFORD. Pacifics raised in Irish and Scottish waters are good value. Oysters grow fatter in different waters from those in which they spawn. Hence their name derives from the Greek *ostrakon*, to ostracize. Similarly, a Pacific oyster will grow much larger and more swiftly in Irish or Scottish waters than they do in France.

The Pacific was introduced from Japan in the '70s to replace the PORTUGUESE oysters which were wiped out by the perennial diseases that afflict oyster beds. More robust and less susceptible to disease and pollution, Pacifics are unlikely to spawn in our cooler waters and are eaten all year.

The **Seasalter Hatchery** at Reculver, near Whitstable, site of some of the Roman industry, has pioneered spawning techniques for Pacific oysters. The seawater is filtered and pasteurized before the microscopic algae on which the oysters feed are introduced. This enriched water is fed to the oysters until they spawn. One oyster can produce as many as a million eggs. The spat are then kept in aerated tubes until they are 3mm across and ready to be taken to outside lagoons. The hatchery supplies spat to other oyster farms.

Native oysters, badly affected in the '80s by the disease bonamia, are slower to grow to maturity, taking 3-4 years – nearly twice that for a Pacific. They can be eaten in the summer, but as they spawn they become milky (why they are not usually sold when there is no 'r' in the month). Both are cultivated on the low-water mark of a spring tide and then brought into parks or on to trestles closer to the beach for harvesting. This hardens them off and teaches them to close their mouths when out of water. (They can live for a week on a single gulp of water.) An oyster's age is told by the ridges on the shell – it will grow two a year, one in spring and one in autumn. They are graded by size and weight of the shell. The French grading system does not correspond to the English.

Supermarkets have started selling very young Pacifics for around 45-50p each.

COOKING: *You should never be poisoned by an oyster if you open it yourself. The smell of an off oyster is unmistakable. To open an oyster: place it in a cloth in your hand, hinge towards you and curved shell downwards to retain juices. Insert the tip of the knife to the side between top and lower shell and twist the blade to cut through the muscle. Separate the shells and finally cut underneath the meat to separate it from shell. Natives usually seem easier than Pacifics, which often grow razor-sharp horns.*

Oysters were a staple from pre-Roman times, mostly in stews and often with lamb. These would have been much larger and older than those we see now. Lemon brings out the nuttiness of the flesh and seems to concentrate the flavour. Brown bread and butter is the traditional accompaniment. Other accessories, like Tabasco, ketchup and horseradish have been added over the years. Black velvet – Guinness and champagne – is an uncanny match. Breton restaurants dribble cream on oysters and grill them. In Essex they were fried with butter and bacon, a less formal version of Angels on Horseback.

BEST BUYS **LOCH RYAN**: No 1, natives, 4-5 years old, 10 cm (4 in) across the neatly crenellated shell (shells on Pacifics from Loch Ryan grow razor-sharp). Meat is about 5x6 cm (2x2½ in) and fills its shell generously with a clean, smooth, beige body. Their salty, acid sourness – long in tannin – is very blunt and helped by saucing.

WEST MERSEA: Blackwater natives, 3 years old, the shell discernibly lemon and green in the greys, 8x7 cm (3x2¾ in), but a small body of only 5x3 cm (2x1¼ in). Not as neat as the Ryan, pale-beige with a gritty edge to the shell, the central bouncy pouch of meat is surrounded by a drape of frills. Aristocratic, they have more punch than the Ryan, with little salt and a delicate sweet nuttiness that comes through straight away.

*IRISH: Pacifics, 18 months old, 12x6 cm (4¾x2½ in) shell, 9x3 cm (3½x1¼ in) beige flesh with a small frill. Sweet, salty, fleshy and delicate, with an aftertaste of iodine and nuts; good value for Pacifics.

IRISH: Natives No 2, 9x7 cm (3½x2¾ in) shell, 5x4 cm (2x1¼ in) meat. Although Irish Pacifics have a burgeoning reputation, the natives do not really match up to other natives. Chewy, sweet with a slightly fizzy edge, they can be dry, musty and salty and are best cooked.

WAITROSE: Scottish, Pacifics, 45p, 9x5 cm (3½x2 in) shell, 3x5 cm (1½x2 in) flesh, very young, lime green-grey shell, possibly under a year, black edge to the frill, milky white, salty, too soft-textured, but a taste of nuts. Cheap.

**HELFORD: Natives, reputedly among the finest, still fished by sail, slightly metallic bitterness leading to a fresh saltiness, distinctive and aristocratic. Pacifics tend to be sweeter.

SMOKED OYSTERS

These barely justify the premium over smoked mussels at three-quarters the price. The smoke and oil render them equals.

PRAWN

The NORTHERN, DEEPWATER or GREENLAND PRAWN, 3-10 cm (1¼-4 in) long, is usually frozen at sea. They are encased in a water glaze that will vary from 6-40% of their weight, so buy the lowest glaze percentage or by prawn weight. Such Atlantic prawns are said to have more flavour than the cheaper ones from South-east Asia.

Larger TIGER PRAWNS, 12-30 cm (4¾-12 in), come from the Indian Ocean, the Gulf and South-east Asia. The dark-green shell with rings turn rosy red on cooking and the flesh is pale pink. They are expensive, at around £6 per lb unpeeled but cooked, but are chunkier and meatier than ordinary prawns and better for cooking. Some have extraordinarily long sell-by dates and can be very pappy and bready. Allow 2-3 per person.

SCALLOP

The scallop's fan-ribbed shell, usually 15-17 cm (5-7 in) across, is the symbol of pilgrims to the tomb of St James at Santiago de Compostela in Galicia, who eat a single scallop on arrival and wear the shell to attest to their journey.

Here the trade (which still sometimes refers to them as clams) is relatively young, gaining ground in Scotland in the '30s and in the English Channel in the '70s. The top shell is reddish and flatter, the underside is bowl-shaped where it nestles into the ocean floor. They can propel themselves across the sea bed by opening and closing the shell. The orange roes (scallops are hermaphrodites, they release the sperm first and then, a few hours later, the eggs, which are fertilized in the water or stimulate other scallops nearby to start spawning) are eaten here but not in America. Scallops are best from cold water in December to March, when they will be about 30p each wholesale, but they are available all year. Frozen in the shell, however, they are often pumped with water to increase weight.

QUEENIES are a different genus: only 5-8 cm (2-3 in) across, both parts of the shell are bowled. Available all year, they are usually cheaper and prettier, but not as succulent.

COOKING: *To open a scallop: place curved side down in a warm oven. The shell will open enough to slip a knife inside and sever the muscle. Under cold running water, separate the white muscle and orange coral from the browny – sometimes black-edged – frill and intestinal thread. Throw the latter away.*

Scallops can be eaten raw, or baked or grilled. The roe is more delicate and should be cooked briefly separately. Highly versatile, the scallop is a chameleon which will take on other flavours and comple-ment them: often rigorous ones like brandy, bacon, ginger. They are good with high-quality butter sauces or, Cantonese-style, steamed with ginger and spring onions.

SHRIMP

Almost transparent in water, shrimp are still fished around Britain. The larger variety, *Pandalus montagui*, sometimes called the AESOP PRAWN, has a pointed snout and turns red on cooking; the more delicate, but smaller and more highly prized, *Crangon crangon*, turns brown.

Found all over the world, there are many sub species and sizes of shrimp, confusingly often with conflicting names in different regions. In America, the term shrimp has also come to mean prawns. Shrimp are at their best in summer and those from Morecambe Bay enjoy a rather inflated reputation. They are still fished on horseback at the Belgian village of Oostduinkeerke. The Far-eastern fish sauces, *blakan* and *pattis*, are fermented shrimp pastes.

SQUID

Found in UK waters, squid are the tenderest of all cephalopods and good value with a wholesale price around £1 per lb. Boneless (as opposed to cuttlefish) and sweeter-fleshed, they are at their best in winter.

COOKING: *Stuff and sauté or stir-fry*.

WHELK

These small marine snails are usually thrown back by the English boats or exported. Only a few rise to seaside prominence with vinegar – usually the old rubbery ones. In Normandy, however, the young whelk is served with mayonnaise as a starter. Old recipes in this country talk of frying the larger ones. At their best in summer, they are usually (over)cooked by the fishmonger and this practice may have been their undoing. Gentle poaching in some sea water with some herbs, helps.

MEAT, POULTRY & GAME

The nightmare unfolds... a Minister's warning... a killer disease... prime-time TV... schools ban beef... protests at a port... a picket dies... the meat industry lives its own ghoulish soap opera.

As frightening has been the spectre of this huge industry hurtling completely out of control. Meat receives huge public subsidies and yet cannot clean up its own backyard (see 'For What We Are About to Receive', page xxii). Of course, our response to all this alarm is irrational and schizophrenic, because sales of meat remain for the time being high. Except for those in a few pockets of the globe, like southern India and parts of Japan, we humans are carnivores. History, however, has turned; chunks of meat now seem medieval and most people's cooking has changed.

EXOTIC MEATS

BISON are raised in large herds on the Canadian prairies. Some have begun to be imported, mostly for the restaurant trade, though some supermarkets have been conducting trials, and a farm in Dorset has been raising them. The meat is sweeter than beef, with a quarter of the fat of other red meats and lower in cholesterol and calories.

KANGAROO, usually the eastern grey, is farmed in Australia, then frozen and exported here. It is a lean red meat, low in unsaturated fat, and usually likened to mild venison or well-hung beef. It only needs short cooking because of the lack of fat.

TRANSPORTING LIVE ANIMALS

In the summer of 1994, a prophetic survey of 1200 customers for the Real Meat Company revealed that 52% of shoppers put the animal's welfare as their main concern. Not long after that the veterinary welfare groups highlighted the cruelty of animals being sold for slaughter in Europe. Ferries stopped taking live animals and so did most airports. The RSPCA-inspired concern for veal calves being exported to mainland Europe to be reared in crates was coupled with concern over how long animals were kept on lorries. Germany would only accept 8 hours without proper feeding and watering, while the UK was agreeing to 15 and southern European countries had no limit.

Ironically it was the English who first exported live animals around the world. It was English stock that sired the herds of America, of Argentina, of Australia, of New Zealand. The EU has revised its transport rules for animals. The upper limit has been raised from 24 to 28 hours for animals carried in lorries with air-conditioning and water. Younger animals can only be moved for 18 hours under this system. Conventional lorries can only take animals for a maximum of 8 hours.

The Euro-trade in animals can hardly be said to have worked to the advantage of this country anyway. For much of it the movement is marketing-inspired anyway, moving cattle to Scotland so they can be labelled Scotch beef or slaughtering sheep in France so it can be called French lamb. The standardization of breeds of beef and pigs has undermined the historical advantage this country has had in meat. The climate, the breeds, the conditions and the understanding in this country have all favoured the native culture, which is presumably one reason that we have always eaten a meat-based diet. This individuality commands a premium as is still the case with Welsh lamb.

Abandoning British breeds in favour of crosses with European animals like Simmenthal and Charolais has brought with it two results. Firstly the traditional quality of the meat has been lost, and secondly it has turned meat into a Euro-commodity that is by its nature and size offensive.

The American example illustrates well enough that, for this country in particular, there is no need to move animals vast distances. Under the Hylton beef programme, the butchery and hanging of meat is not done as whole carcasses but as individual joints. It can then be shipped across America without cruelty. The quality of the meat is also considerably better.

MEAT

BEEF · VEAL · LAMB · PORK · SAUSAGES · BACON · HAM · CHARCUTERIE

Meat is one of the most difficult foods to judge. Price is a poor guide. Conflicting advice, changing breeds and unilateral changes in farming policy leave us completely in the hands of the butcher or the grocer.

Supermarkets, notably **Tesco**, have quietly re-evaluated their policies and have introduced stricter quality and ethical guidelines across the board. **Sainsbury** has similar standards on its 'More Mature' label, where a degree of hanging has been encouraged again. The quality in other chains, especially in beef and pork, has not really kept up. **Waitrose** has innovatively been selling whole sides and half carcasses. **Marks & Spencer** has stuck with tradition for Aberdeen Angus beef, but in ready-meals has embarked on a mindless quest for novelty. **Safeway** seems to have concentrated its efforts on the more headline-grabbing lines of game and venison.

Q–GUILD BUTCHERS, set up under the chairmanship of David Lidgate of **Lidgate's** in London's Holland Park in 1986, now has more than 150 butchers nationwide subscribing to independent inspection. The aim is to provide 'something different and something better'.

BEEF

Butchers prefer the traditional UK breeds. The smaller carcasses – around 180 kg (400 lb) for a heifer that has not calved, or 270 kg (600 lb) for a steer (usually fattened on for another six months) – are as much as an independent shop can handle. The bigger chains, the processors and the supermarkets favour crosses with the larger Continental breeds, which can weigh 450 kg (1,000 lb) for a heifer and up to 630 kg (1,400 lb) for a steer. The trade judges on backsides (front carcasses are often exported) and Charolais and Belgian Blue have double muscling, a second layer of meat on the valuable rump. There has been concern, however, at the large-scale breeding of animals that have difficulty giving birth to calves with such big hips.

REARING: Calves are either suckled, left with the mother for a year, turned out in summer, and brought in for fattening when the mother is brought back into confinement; or, in the dairy method (used for 6 out of 10 calves), they are taken from their mothers at 10 days and fed on a concentrated diet of milk powder, wheat, barley and protein. They will only go outside if they are old enough in spring. Calves that have been outside will have darker flesh.

BEEF BREEDS

The oldest surviving breed of cattle is the White Park. James I knighted his host as 'Sir Loin' after a banquet around a roast of beef, and this was surely White Park. Its ancestry may go back 2,000 years – possibly more. It was found mainly on the tougher grasses of the northern parklands and moors, and was known for its flavour and its leanness. It fell out of favour in the 19th century because it was slow to mature, not reaching its prime until two years old. Its leanness was also not what the 18th-century stock-breeders wanted; they wanted big fat animals to feed the cities.

These were to be the great triumvirate of the Hereford, Shorthorn and Aberdeen Angus. They were the first cattle to be exported, and destined to be the great-grandfathers of the American and Australian herds.

The Hereford's supremacy has slowly eroded over a century. Originally it was kept both as a dairy cow and for its meat. It lost its position as a milker to the more generous lactations of the Friesian, introduced in 1922, and completely with the arrival of pasteurization, which destroyed any quality argument. The arrival in the '60s of the leaner, larger and faster-maturing breeds from Europe – the Charolais, Simmenthal, Limousin and Belgian Blue – further undermined its commercial stature.

HANGING: As well as storing, this process was used to tenderize meat from older animals. Even 25 years ago much of the beef sold was four and five years old when slaughtered. Supermarkets rejected this practice on the grounds of cost, but **Sainsbury** and **Tesco** have begun to mature meat again for 10-12 days. Some of the more extravagant claims may also include the shelf-life. Independent butchers can hang beef for as long as three weeks.

HALAL MEAT: Cattle and sheep are killed for halal butchers by cutting the throat in line with Muslim practice. Some argue the quality of the meat is therefore improved, although most halal butchers are geared to the needs of the Asian community and lack the particular skills for European butchery. They are good sources of less common cuts, like mutton, or even testicles.

HORMONES: The EU stopped the import of American beef because of their use of hormones. A small amount of prime beef – usually reared under the Hylton programme (a US version of *Appellation Contrôlée*) – gets through, but is prohibitively expensive as it carries a 20% levy. The best American beef is corn–fed and usually hung for as long as 40 days. Prime USA beef is probably now superior to Scotch.

COOKING: At 60°C (140°F), *the connective tissues in beef begin to compress and squeeze out the juices. By 75°C (170°F) a quarter of all the juices have leached. Scientifically, it follows that rare steak will be juicier and more tender. The move to leaner, unhung cuts of beef favours French-style recipes for braises and casseroles, often where the fat and other flavours are added separately; or the short sharp stir-fries and flash-grilling of Oriental cooking. The classic English roast needs a level of fat to lubricate it, and few butchers accept that the move to leanness has improved flavour.*

BEEF CUTS

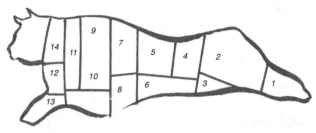

1 – Leg	5 – Sirloin	9 – Middle Rib	13– Shin
2 – Silverside & Topside	6 – Hindquarter Flank	10 – Brisket	14– Sticking (Neck)
3 – Top Rump/Thick	7 – Forerib	11 – Steakmeat	
4 – Whole Rump	8 – Forequarter Flank	12 – Clod	

FRONT CUTS are out of fashion and offer good value, especially for longer cooking and older recipes. Clockwise from the head:

OX CHEEK is a poor-quality cut, sometimes used in mince, or it goes for pies and pet food.
    COOKING: *Needs up to six hours cooking and is best in a salad.*

NECK, sometimes called CLOD or STICKING. It can be sold as stewing steak and is good value.
    COOKING: *Is good for mince, stews and curries and needs long slow cooking.*

CHUCK STEAK, sometimes called BLADE BONE, is sold as cubes or slices.
    COOKING: *Good for braising but, as the seams run through it, it is an untidy joint. Use it for* daube de boeuf, goulash *or* carbonnade.

BLADE STEAK is sold as steaks, which should not be more than 7.5 cm (3 in) across.
    COOKING: *Braising.*

*LMC or LEG OF MUTTON CUT, or sometimes POOR MAN'S RUMP, weighs 1.8-2.7 kg (4–6 lb) but can sometimes be larger in Continental breeds. A complete muscle, it is lean and good enough as a cheap steak, if cut thinly. Price should be about £2.50 per lb. If a butcher does not have this cut, he may be marking it up as topside at £3 per lb, or even frying steak.

COOKING: *Good for casseroles or flattened and rolled round a stuffing for beef olives.*

*JACOB'S LADDER is usually boned and sold as stewing steak or mince, but can be rolled and sold as boneless brisket. Very lean, it is priced at about £2 per lb.

COOKING: *Slow-roast.*

SHIN is good value.

COOKING: *Ideal for long slow stews, where the flavour has time to develop. It is sometimes used in mince.*

BRISKET is the breast, sold on or off the bone. It is good value, though bone (and fat) can account for 35% of weight.

COOKING: *It needs slow careful roasting or pot-roasting. It can go for mince, or is cured in brine and salt. It is traditionally used for boiled beef and carrots.*

FLANK is fatty and poor.

COOKING: *Mince.*

FORE-RIB is the first four ribs (sometimes five) taking one off the blade and the chuck, and weighs 4.5-6.8 kg (10-15 lb).

COOKING: *Excellent roast on the bone, but is sometimes sold off the bone. It is too tough to treat as steak or to stir-fry.*

BACK CUTS are prized and priced ahead of the forequarters:

SIRLOIN is the classic English roasting cut. The continuation of the rib, it is sometimes sold as steaks off the bone for £1 per 1 lb less. The best ribs (there are 25) are towards the back. There are a number of fanciful stories on the origin of the term sirloin. The original was supposedly from the French *surloin*. According to *Fuller's Church History* dated 1655 and repeated by **Sainsbury** in its advertising, Henry VIII christened it as part of a bet with the Abbot of Reading. Jonathan Swift credited it to James I: 'King James I who loved good eating...seeing a large loin of beef at his table, drew out his sword and in a frolic knighted it.' Others credit it to Charles II or to the *Great Eater of Kent* written in 1680: 'should presently enter combate with a worthy knight, called Sir Loyne of Beefe, and overthrow him'.

In French the sirloin is the *entrecôte* or *contrefilet*. The *aloyau* is the

BSE

As I write this, BSE is the top story on the 9 o'clock news. On the other hand, deaths this year from Creutzfeldt-Jakob disease stand at only 29, so reports of epidemics are premature. Equally, there is mounting evidence that cattle perhaps suffered from 'the staggers' prior to 1986 and it is only intensive farming that has brought the condition into focus as BSE.

BSE is transmitted in the diet. Zoo animals fed on a similar diet to cows before the 1989 ban on brain and spinal tissue in the food chain have developed the distinctive symptoms. Large cats, like puma and leopards, have died. More disturbing, perhaps, has been the rise in the incidence among ordinary domestic cats.

Isolated cases in people of the associated Creutzfeldt-Jakob disease (CJD) have been found in farmers – who might possibly have inhaled the feed. As the disease tends to strike at random, however, no real link has been proved. The incubation period is anything from 5 to 30 years. so any damage has been done

BSE was first identified in November 1986, a quarter of all farms in the UK (some 27,000) have been affected by the virus Bovine Spongiform Encephalopathy, but in nearly half the cases only one animal has been infected. Repeated predictions of a fall in numbers of reported cases have been premature. The 1988 ban on feeding 'ruminant protein to ruminants' should mean the peak of the epidemic has been reached. Last year the Ministry demanded still tighter controls on brain and spinal cord tissues in abattoirs.

The theory is that the disease began because of changes in the meat-rendering industry in the late '70s. Solvents stopped being used to extract fat when the market for tallow collapsed. Importantly, this meant a move away from high-temperature steaming to clean off the solvent. Inadvertently this may have prevented a cross-over of 'scrapie-like' infection.

Research is concentrating on the possibility that BSE may be being passed from mother to calf, possibly by the calf eating placenta in the field. Sporadic stories suggesting direct links to cases of Alzheimer's Disease are vigorously denied. The definitive studies involving 600 cows – half from infected herds, half not – will not be finished until 1997 as the animals are being allowed to live to seven years. However, Richard Lacey of Leeds University has warned that the disease may have become endemic. The biggest risk is likely to be children and pregnant women eating processed meats like burgers and sausages, he warns. The jury is still out.

BIV

BOVINE IMMUNODEFICIENCY VIRUS, or BIV, is an Aids–style virus that affects cattle. In 1993 there was an outbreak at a farm in Cheshire. The herd, which had been imported from Germany, was destroyed.

sirloin and the fillet as one cut, and this is always roasted. In beef from Charolais cattle, the grain is discernibly coarser. In American butchery three steaks are taken out of the section between the loin and the fillet: PORTERHOUSE is mostly loin, CLUB has no fillet, and the T-BONE straddles both sides.

COOKING: *It is excellent roasted on the bone (especially from British breeds); or grilled or pan-fried off the bone.*

FILLET lies inside the rib and weighs 1.35-2.7 kg (3-6 lb). The muscle is hardly ever used so it is invariably tender. In French butchery, the head of the fillet is *biftek*; the middle is *Châteaubriand* and *filet*; the third section is cut into *tournedos* or *medallions*, and the final, thickest, piece *filet mignon*.

COOKING: *Classically it is grilled, roasted or pan-fried (to make use of the juices). If stuffing it, always add a little extra fat.*

RUMP was originally only an English cut. In other countries this part was cubed for braising or boiling. Weighing about 3.5-5.5 kg (8-12 lb), it is always sold as steaks. With more flavour than fillet and sirloin, and a coarser grain (especially in Limousin).

COOKING: *Best fried or grilled. Well trimmed, it is ideal for stroganoff and high-quality casseroles.*

H-BONE is the hip bone, which used to be sold on the bone but is usually now boneless. Leaner than rib, it is equal to topside, silverside and top rump together.

TOPSIDE is the top inside of the back legs, sold off the bone. Continental breeds will be grainier and larger than 15 cm (6 in) across. Some butchers will pass off top rump or silverside as topside.

COOKING: *As it tends to be lean and inclined to dryness, cooking time is critical: 10 minutes per 450 g (1 lb) maximum for rare, 14 minutes for well done. Although it is sold as a roasting joint, it is better to pot-braise it. Use for* carbonnade de boeuf *or* daube de boeuf.

TOP RUMP is the outside of the back leg and smaller than topside at 1.8-2.7 kg (4-6 lb), with a smaller diameter at around 10-12 cm (4-5 in), tapering at both ends and usually paler. It needs good butchering as it has more seams and is fattier in the centre.

SILVERSIDE is the back of the leg, weighing 2.7-4 kg (6-9 lb). The best cut is the 'eye', a tubular single muscle 7-10 cm (2¾-4 in) across. If it falls apart, other cuts have been rolled together to imitate it.

COOKING: *Use it for salt beef.*

Beef

The effects of cooking different cuts of beef on the nutritional analysis

	Calories	Protein g	Carbos g	Fat g	% Fat of Cals
Brisket (raw)	252	17	0	20.5	73
(boiled)	326	27.6	0	24	66
Fore rib (raw)	290	16	0	25	77
(roast)	349	22.5	0	29	74
Rump (raw)	197	19	0	13.5	61
(fried)	246	28.6	0	14.5	53
(grilled)	218	27.3	0	12	49

The balance of fats in the samples of beef was monounsaturated to 50% saturated.

RUMP SKIRT, or GOOSE SKIRT, is the inside of the rump steak or the inside of the flank. The price has risen to £2.50 per lb since the ban on American imports.

COOKING: *Ideal for stews and casseroles. It is also traditional in pasties because the crumbly texture cuts easily with a fork.*

BEEF OFFAL

OX TONGUE weighs 1.35-2.3 kg (3-5 lb) and is usually sold cooked. The price has risen to £2.50 per lb since the ban on American imports.

COOKING: *Simmer for 3 hours with herbs and onions then cool and skin, or roast – from a piece that has been lightly brined (it would need soaking beforehand).*

BRAINS are no longer sold in this country due to BSE (see page 145). Ironically, old books recommend them (along with the spinal marrow, also banned because of BSE) as nutritious for children and old people.

OXTAIL is sold whole or by the pound. The butcher should cut between the joints; a whole tail should feed a family of four.

COOKING: *A traditional butchers' recipe: Trim a whole oxtail leaving some fat, and dust in seasoned flour. Sweat 2 chopped onions in a pan, add 450 g (1 lb) sliced carrots and 115 g (4 oz) chopped streaky bacon. Brown the oxtail in a little lard or butter, cover with beef stock, season with herbs, such as parsley or sage, and slow cook overnight. Check that the meat is falling off the bone. Allow to cool and skim off the fat. Thicken the liquid to taste with flour. Add 1 tablespoon redcurrant jelly and warm through for 1 1/2 hours. Serve with mashed potatoes and winter vegetables.*

It produces excellent jelly and is traditional in soup and stews.

*HEART used to be known as POOR MAN'S GOOSE. Weighing 1.35-2.7 kg (3-6 lb), it is lean It should be £1 per lb.
COOKING: *Can be used in mince. It is also excellent value as a roast, stuffed with bread, garlic and herbs.*

KIDNEYS have a very rich deep flavour. They are best used with other meats.
COOKING: *Slowly, but they can also be thinly sliced and sautéed. Traditionally used in steak and kidney pie or pudding.*

LIVER should be soaked in milk for 4-5 hours to soften the flavour. Weighing 3.5-7 kg (8-16 lb), it is very rich and pungent and is best used alongside other meats in long slow casseroles. It is widely used in commercial processing to make pâtés etc.

MARROW BONES are ideal for stocks, soups and sauces.
COOKING: *Reserve the jelly for spreading on toast or on top of steaks. Roast or boil for 2 hours and spoon out. Victorians served them with napkins. Fergus Henderson has revived the dish at his restaurant, St John, with a parsley and caper salad.*

TRIPE is the stomach lining. Initially brown, it is first boiled to blanch it. The thick part is the seam between the stomach linings, the honeycomb (from the second stomach), is usually held to be the best, as it is softer. Blanket tripe is from the first stomach.
COOKING: *If you have uncooked tripe, then boil it in salted water for 5 hours. For tripes à la mode de Caen, ox feet (not calves') and the tripe from all the successive stomachs are cooked in a baker's oven.*

COW HEEL needs to be boiled for a long time to take off the jelly: the main use for this is producing gelatine.

BEST BUYS The Argentinean practice is to use forequarter cuts for corned beef. The meat is shredded, boiled and pressed into a tin. The contents of the tins vary between dry and dense – **Fray Bentos**, **Hertford**, **Sainsbury**, **S&B**, **Libby** – and the fatty and gelatinous – **Armour** and **Princes.**

CURED BEEF

BRESAOLA is air-dried beef, cured much like Parma Ham, but with a drier, tougher texture. The practice originated in Lombardy. Bresaola is served thinly sliced, with olive oil, lemon juice and black pepper.

JERK is dried beef, usually from America and South Africa. Fibrous, it seems like an early forerunner of **Pepperami.**

VEAL

After 20 years of moribund acceptance, the full enormity of the veal crate trade has burst back into the limelight. The trade in veal calves is a necessary by-product of a milk-oriented food policy that this country has pursued since the Government edict was first issued in 1940.

What is most astonishing is that where beef is a premium product and where this country supposedly produces some of the best in the world, why is it not economic to raise male calves for sale without putting them into this cruel trade?

The animals never see daylight and hardly have room enough to move. The immobility and the exclusively milk diet preserve the whiteness of the flesh. The culture comes from southern and central Europe, often mountain areas where keeping young animals in small spaces in winter did not seem so out of place.

The other issue is one of cruelty in rearing calves for veal crates. Whether rearing calves in crates is any more cruel than some of the practices endemic in the raising of pigs or chickens is debatable. For some reason, calves seem to appeal to the public imagination more than chickens.

Selling young animals off the back of the milk quota grants into an old-fashioned, out-dated, ostensibly cruel trade is foolishness. They deserve a better fate.

Sainsbury has pursued a solitary, more humane, approach on UK farms for the last 20 years – 'large airy barns, plenty of room to move freely, natural light, fed on a diet of milk and straw'. The flesh is distinguishably paler pink, not white.

Tesco announced that it plans to switch all its veal production away from Holland and bring it back to England, and continue to rear animals to the highest welfare standards.

VEAL CUTS

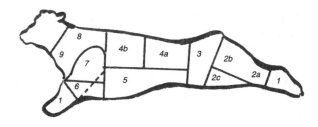

1 – Hock/Knuckle	2c – Thick Flank	4b – Best End	7 – Oyster
2a – Topside	3 – Chump	5 – Thin flank	8 – Middle Neck
2b – Silverside	4a – Loin End	6 – Breast	9 – Scrag

Veal has the lowest fat content of all red meats and is high in iron. The calves are killed at just 16-20 weeks, so the butchery vocabulary is borrowed from lamb not beef. Guernsey and Jersey bulls were the main British breeds; by-products of the milk trade.

Veal is tender because it is young; but because it is so young it lacks flavour and has come to be cooked mostly with sauces. The stronger-tasting calves' offal is correspondingly prized for its delicacy compared to that of beef.

The front part of the animal, the NECK, the SHOULDER and the BELLY are usually boned, trimmed and cubed for light stewing. Some butchers will leave the bone in a shoulder and sell it for roasting.

COOKING: Blanquette de veau.

LOIN is sold as a joint (the fillet still attached because its flavour has had so little time to develop) or occasionally as cutlets.

RUMP is sliced thinly, flattened and sold for escalopes. The prime steaks will be from the back end.

COOKING: Wiener schnitzel.

TOPSIDE, TOP RUMP and SILVERSIDE are sold as joints or escalopes.

SHIN is usually boned and cubed.

COOKING: Ossobuco.

VEAL OFFAL

VEAL KIDNEYS, weighing 115-225 g (4-8 oz), are very pale and very expensive.

COOKING: *Frying, they are also good devilled*.

**CALVES' LIVER is sold sliced and it has a marvellous creamy, aristocratic flavour.

COOKING: *Fry or grill very briefly*.

**VEAL SWEETBREADS are the neck and gut glands, weighing 115-170 g (4-6 oz). They have joined the banned list because of recent developments re BSE.

LAMB

Lamb is the last of the domesticated animals to have maintained its freedom, so seasonality retains some stock. Hill lamb will be tougher but more flavoursome; downland animals raised on the lush easy-going pastures of Southern England will be the more tender. Imported frozen or chilled lamb from New Zealand makes up the weight in winter.

The closing of local abattoirs to meet EU standards may affect the quality of much lamb. Like most animals, sheep do not like to travel; with larger and more centralized abattoirs, however, they travel further. The RSPCA has spoken out emphatically on the trade in Welsh lamb to France on the grounds of cruelty.

SPRING LAMB: at one time this would always have been a cross with a Dorset Horn. They lamb early, in October, and so the first animals can be at market by February. Now it is more likely to be a hill or mountain ewe, perhaps a Cheviot, Swaledale or Welsh mountain, put to a prolific sire like a Blue or Border Leicester or a British Milk Sheep. Their lamb would then be mated to a meat sire such as a Charollais, Texel or Suffolk. Spring lamb is tender and notoriously expensive, but most butchers hold that the lambs need a chance to get out on the spring pastures and the flavour is better in September.

By autumn, older animals start to come to market. The colour of the meat is darker – brown rather than red. It should have been hung for a week to tenderize it, and needs the longer cooking of winter braises and casseroles, not the short sharp roasting and grillings of summer. Mountain or hill lamb will have less fat because it has been running around. The back legs will be muscular and lean, but the bone-to-meat ratio is high. Downland lamb tends to be larger and is killed younger, before the fat develops – from 90–120 days.

LAMB CUTS

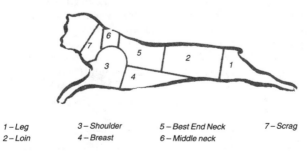

1 – Leg	3 – Shoulder	5 – Best End Neck	7 – Scrag
2 – Loin	4 – Breast	6 – Middle neck	

Few butchers label their lamb, or even know the breeds they sell. A lot of Welsh lamb goes to France, where it is better appreciated. From the head clockwise:

RARE BREEDS OF LAMB

Conservationists argue that because lamb is slaughtered so young the difference between the flavour of different breeds that was crucial with mutton has been lost with lamb. It was the great 18th-century breeders Robert Bakewell and John Ellman who wanted sheep that had good wool and large fatty carcasses to feed the growing urban populations looking for work in the factories of the industrial revolution. Before then each region had its own breed and type of sheep.

The oldest were probably the Leicester, the Lincoln and the Teeswater, and the mountain breeds like Welsh, Soay and Hebridean. The Leicester and the Lincoln had large carcasses, and were bred primarily for their wool, which was still an important industry. It was Ellman, however, who adapted the principle. His own downland sheep were more compact and easier to develop on the lusher pastures of the south. His Southdowns became the great stock-improvers world-wide. They sired the flocks of Australia, New Zealand and Argentina and only lost their pre-eminence in this century, with the advent of the supermarkets who ruled that the Southdown was too fatty and slow-growing. So it was crossed with the Norfolk Horn to produce the Suffolk, today's most prevalent breed.

As with cattle, the native animals have increasingly been sup-planted by the leaner Continental breeds, like Texel from Holland or Charollais (two 'l's in sheep, one in cattle). For British agriculture, joining the EU has seemed to have been a one-way street of importing foreign breeds, few of which have demonstrated much advantage in culinary terms.

The Rare Breeds Survival Trust has started an accreditation scheme for butchers handling rare breeds. The first award went to the Chesteron Farm Shop, Chesterton Lane, Cirencester, Gloucestershire. Marks & Spencer's lamb begins now with Cornish animals and finishes with Scottish Black Faced hill sheep.

Conservationists argue that the older, more primitive breeds may have a serious relevance over the next few years. The Hebridean is the subject of serious study to find an economic breed to revive low-intensity farming. It first came south to graze the parklands of the big country estates. Whereas most lamb is killed at 3-4 months, the trial sheep are being kept until 15 months. The meat from breeds like the Hebridean is considerably lower in cholesterol and saturated fat than the Suffolk – and higher in polyunsaturates. Genetically speaking, it is all round a healthier beast. Similar cases can be advanced for the Manx Logthan, the Soay and the Wensleydale; the last two being exceptionally lean.

MIDDLE NECK, or SCRAG END, is fatty and bony and sold as one piece or chopped.

COOKING: *It will, however, make excellent casseroles if generously spiced and seasoned and cooked slowly, for a long time.*

BEST END, meaning the best end of neck, consists of the small eye and a long rib. Sometimes called CUTLETS, the first five bones near the loin are the best. RACK is the complete set of best end cutlets.

COOKING: *Good grilled or casseroled. Classically, grilled cutlets are served cold in aspic with mint jelly or sauce.*

**LOIN is the best cut of all. Usually boned and rolled (and cut across to make French NOISETTES). When prices are cheap, look for a double chop.

COOKING: *It is best grilled or roasted.*

*CHUMP is the underrated lamb equivalent of rump steak. The CHUMP END is the small cut by the join with the loin; it is too small to make a steak and is usually sold as stewing lamb.

SADDLE is the complete top section, including the best end, loin, chump and sometimes even the tail.

COOKING: *Roasted.*

*LEG is also often known by French term GIGOT. The nearer the foot, the more sinewy the meat. The knuckle end is therefore the poorer cut on a half leg; the fillet end is the better bet.

COOKING: *Usually now roasted, traditionally it was often boiled, especially if older meat as with mutton.*

BARON is the saddle and the two legs sold as one joint.

COOKING: *It is always served roasted, usually at banquets.*

BREAST is cheap, fatty and bony.

COOKING: *Best roasted to a crisp, it is also used in dishes like* navarin, *Irish stew and* cassoulet; *or cut off the bone, egg-and-breadcrumbed and fried as* épigrammes.

*SHOULDER is the cheapest joint on the lamb. The top half, the blade bone end, is better than the knuckle end which will be fattier and more sinewy. There is as much meat on half a shoulder as on a complete rack or best end – usually more.

COOKING: *A good cut for curry. Classically, it was always boned out by the butcher and stuffed.*

SHOULDER CHOPS are cut across the bone and often found in supermarkets, although usually poor value at 80p more per lb than the whole joint.

FILLET would more properly be called neck.
COOKING: *Usually sold as barbecue or grilling meat in summer and for casseroles in winter.*

LAMB OFFAL

Lamb offal benefits from being young to a greater degree even than the meat, so it is worth buying offal from spring lamb, even at a few pennies more, though this is more likely to be found at independent butchers than at supermarkets.

KIDNEYS are likely to be fresh at small butchers because they get them as part of the carcass (he will price by the kidney). They should be cored and the pipes taken out to stop any lingering taint of urine (occasionally the taste persists, a sign of infection). New Zealand exports kidneys frozen in bulk and these are usually found in supermarkets. Processing factories sell by weight, so the temptation is to leave in the pipes.
COOKING: *Buy them in the fat for roasting or barbecuing. By and large, kidneys do not freeze well, going mushy and losing texture. Sauté or grill.*

*LIVER from spring lamb is almost as tender as that from calves, for about one-fifth the price. The whole liver tails off into a thumb shape at one end, unlike pigs (which is sometimes passed off as lamb). Frozen livers are imported from New Zealand and sold by the tray in supermarkets (check for the tell-tale pool of blood). They are usually browner or, worse, develop a green glaze. Freezing affects the texture, making it coarser.
COOKING: *Grill or sauté fresh liver. Frozen is only good for casseroles with other meats.*

HEART is an overlooked cut, too often sold as pet food or secreted away in mince, sausages and haggis. If it is crumpled and misshapen, it will have been frozen and will be the poorer.
COOKING: *A stuffed and roasted heart from a young lamb makes a good meal.*

SWEETBREADS are two separate glands – the thymus from the neck and one from the pancreas (the latter are called 'gut sweetbreads'). They are at their best from spring lamb, when all good butchers should have

Lamb
The effects of cooking different cuts on nutritional analysis

		Calories	Protein g	Carbos g	Fat g	% Fat of Cals
Breast	(raw)	378	16.7	0	34	80
	(roast)	410	19	0	37	81
Chop	(raw)	377	14.6	0	35	83
	(grilled)	355	23.5	0	29	73
Kidney		90	16.5	0	2.7	27
Liver		179	20	0	1.6	8

This sample seems to have included rather fatty chops. Lamb fat is 51% saturated.

them – but they are popular and scarce as a result.

COOKING: *Boil them in salted water for 15 minutes and then peel off the outer membrane.*

BRAINS from lambs, unlike those from calves, can still be found.

FRY, or testicles, are rarer because most animals are castrated, though in country cooking they were prized. Halal butchers often stock a few.

COOKING: *Recipes are interchangeable between the fry of different animals: poach them in stock with vinegar; slice, marinate in oil, vinegar and fresh herbs for 20 minutes, then dip in batter and deep-fry at the last minute before serving.*

TONGUES are rarely found but can be cooked in the same way as veal tongues, braising first and then skinning.

TROTTERS used to be cooked but are very rare now.

COOKING: *Singed and split open, they are then cooked in stock with vinegar, traditionally covered so they do not discolour, and then finished with a white sauce, stuffed or deep-fried.*

PAUNCH is the stomach used as casing with the PLUCK (heart, liver and lungs) mixed with oatmeal for haggis.

LAMB HAM
Unlike pork, lamb was rarely preserved, but seems to have been a prime source of fresh meat: Harry Fellows at Ashdown Smokers has developed a ham from the Lakelands sheep, which he calls Herdwick Macon. The legs are matured for up to eight months which gives it a powerful flavour.

PORK

The pig has sustained civilizations since it was domesticated. In recent years there has been a move to give it back its freedom, with as many as one in five now reared outside. Campaigners have, however, been concerned that some pigs still have rings put through their noses, which stops their natural practice of rooting for tubers and other foods below ground.

The trade and quality have become militarily uniform. The commercial vision is of a fast-growing, long-legged pig who has plenty of babies; but, most importantly, it should have a long lean back which gives the lucrative bacon cuts. Breeders make little or no distinction between bacon and pork. Pork pigs will be younger – from 16 weeks, before the boars reach maturity (and the flavour becomes tainted). By 21 weeks they weigh 50-60 kg (110-130 lb) – while full-grown, older breeds only ever reached 35 kg (80 lb) or so – and go either for bacon or pork, depending on the cut. Older animals, up to 27 weeks, will be bred on for their weight, primarily as bacon and hams.

Two countries have eradicated the disease-producing micro-organism *trichonella* from pork, the UK, since the late '70s, and Australia. The extended cooking times in most books can now be read as overly cautious, and pork cuts cooked merely to a point of pinkness (but not undercooked, because there are other problems in rare pork to worry about) improve in flavour. Allow about 20 minutes to the 450 g (1 lb) for roasting.

PORK CUTS

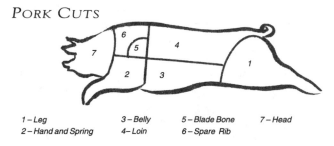

1 – Leg
2 – Hand and Spring
3 – Belly
4 – Loin
5 – Blade Bone
6 – Spare Rib
7 – Head

BATH CHAPS are the bottom half of the jaw, cut in half. Usually boiled and sold skin on, they are fatty and sold as a cheap salad meat.

SHOULDER breaks down into the HAND, a bony cut with 675 g (1½ lb) of meat and the same of bone. Lean and good value, it is often overlooked, though it tends to be sinewy and the meat is caramel-coloured rather than white.

COOKING: *'Too ordinary for anything other than the family table', said Escoffier, but it is flavoursome and good value for stuffing and for long slow roasting. Boned and salted, it is found in soups and* potées *across French regional cooking.*

HAND AND SPRING, weighing 1.35-2.7 kg (3-6 lb), may be only one-fifth bone but is fattier than the hand and makes a good roast. There is more – and sweeter – meat than on a hand, so it is even better value. It also presents a good expanse of crackling. Because the SPRING is fatty, smaller butchers will tend to use it in sausages.

COOKING: *Good value roast.*

SPARE RIB JOINT is the shoulder with the hand and spring taken out (ie the blade and the neck) and usually boned and sold as a joint, but it is inclined to fall apart on cooking. The meat is sweet and preferred by people who like a fatty cut. When the bone is left in it is called SPARE RIB CHOPS (ie the neck, but never called as such). This has a good meat-to-bone ratio when cut across as chops.

COOKING: *It is good for casseroling or roasting and serving with strong sauces, such as the traditional Oriental sweet-and-sour. Cubed meat taken from the spare ribs and the hand is good for casseroles, etc.*

BLADE BONE is awkward to carve. Weighing about 1.35 kg (3 lb), it is lean, but has sweet meat and is good value.

NECK BONES are good for stews at around 40p per 450 g (1 lb).

LOIN is primarily used for chops, but is a prime cut with a high percentage of good-quality meat.

BEST END, next to the spare rib, has one eye of meat and nothing under the bone.

COOKING: *It is good for grilling or a joint roast.*

LOIN PORK CHOPS are best as a joint or chops.

TENDERLOIN is the best-value cut, including the kidney underneath the bone, and has no fat and the best flavour. Weighing 225-350 g (8-12 oz), it is usually taken off bacon pigs and put into the pork trade because of its value.

LOIN OF PORK FILLET END, complete with the tenderloin and the kidney, is the best roasting joint. Score it finely for the crackling.

PORK STEAK is the equivalent to a rump steak. A good alternative to tenderloin, it is low in fat and is good marinated or in casseroles.

LEG OF PORK is the roasting and crackling cut, but is not as good value

RARE BREEDS OF PIG

At the end of the 18th century there was a large importation of Asian pigs, either directly into the UK or via Italy, where the influence is still seen in the Neapolitan pig. European pigs were long and lean; Asian pigs were short and fat – and prick-eared. For 150 years afterwards the British pig meant one of seven breeds. The Middle White, was the original pork pig. It was fat and compact, a beer barrel on legs with a sergeant major's snub nose. The Japanese had particularly admired it and raised a statue in honour of its physique. The Berkshire was not so rounded and needed feeding up to reach any size. The British Lop came from Devon and Cornwall and was a quiet old grazing pig, as was the Large Black which was also from Cornwall but found in Norfolk. The Gloucester Old Spots (yes spots) was the orchard pig let out to graze on the apples and feed on the whey from cheese-making. British Saddleback was found in Wessex: a docile forest pig, it was good for both pork and bacon, and an important breeding stock because of its docility. The red Tamworth was mostly a bacon pig, wanted for its lard.

The Ministry of Food ended the era of small pig farming. During rationing, farms were only allowed to kill two pigs a year – with a policeman in attendance to verify. After the War, there was enormous government encouragement for pig farmers to change from the smaller native breeds and go over to the placid Norwegian Landrace. In Denmark all other breeds of pig were taken out of production. Danish bacon had a reputation for quality and uniformity. It looked good as whole sides when it was fashionable for butchers to hang the carcasses outside their shops (the colouring of native breeds was deemed unattractive). Crossed with a faster-growing Large White, this became the bacon pig of the '50s and '60s.

The political pressure against the native breeds was twofold: to stem the tide of imports; and to satisfy larger factory processors who wanted uniformity and larger cuts off larger animals. The docile Landrace was also happy to be moved indoors while other breeds resented the confinement.

Research for the Rare Breeds Survival Trust has shown that the water loss in cooking from the rare breeds can be to up to one-quarter less than from Landrace, Large White and the equivalent American breeds, Hampshire and Duroc. Ironically Marks & Spencer has now reached the point of developing its own pigs, a Duroc crossed with an English Hampden Gilt, which are hardy enough to live outdoors. A new kind of rare breed.

as loin. Weighing 3.5-6.8 kg (8-15 lb) complete, it is usually cut into joints. With the bone in, these should be at least 1.8 kg (4 lb) or they will fall apart.

COOKING: *To ensure good crackling, score the skin as this allows the added salt and oils to seep into the fat under the skin and also helps to make it more manageable after cooking. The fat dries out and creates the crackling. One trick, not infallible, for failed crackling is to put it under a tea towel in a microwave for 60-90 seconds.*

KNUCKLE, sometimes called HOCK, is good value. It is sold on the bone, though it can be stuffed if the butcher will bone it. It usually goes into sausages, or is sold ready-cooked, often at appreciably larger mark-ups.

COOKING: *Braise, pot-roast or simmer.*

BELLY can be used as a roast. Usually the flank end, nearest the legs, goes for sausages. It produces good crackling and is sometimes sold as slices for baking or grilling.

COOKING: *Is also useful in terrines or cut into 2.5 cm (1 in) wedges as an extra source of fat in a casserole, where it lends sweetness and richness.*

CHINESE-STYLE SPARE RIBS is the end of the belly and used to go for sausages but is now cut the length of the rib to give meatier chops. These used to be thrown away, but somehow supermarkets and butchers have succeeded in raising the price to £1.59 per lb or more, disguised with dubious flavours.

PORK OFFAL

Offal from pigs tends to be among the least expensive items in most butchers' shops. They reward careful cooking.

HEAD mainly goes for processing into pies, salamis, luncheon meat; or, occasionally, it will be made into brawn (see opposite) or what the French call *fromage de tête*. Traditionally the whole head was served at banquets or at a Christmas table.

TONGUES are rare, but can be cooked like veal tongues.

EARS were esteemed in Middle-European cooking.

COOKING: *Singe, boil in salt water with vegetables and then breadcrumb.*

Pork

The effects of cooking on different cuts of pork

		Calories	Protein g	Carbos g	Fat g	% Fat of Cals
Belly	(raw)	381	15.1	0	35.5	83
	(grilled)	398	21	0	35	79
Chop	(raw)	329	16	0	29.5	80
	(grilled)	332	28.5	0	24.2	65
Leg	(raw)	269	16.6	0	22.5	75
	(roast)	286	27	0	20	62
Trotter	(boiled)	280	19.8	0	22.3	71

The levels of fat in pork are roughly equal monounsaturates to saturates.

KIDNEYS are stronger and firmer than those of lamb. They weigh 115-170 g (4-6 oz) and are rarely larger. The core and pipes should have been removed.

COOKING: *Cut them in half lengthwise and grill or fry.*

LIVER weighs 900g-1.8 kg (2-4 lb) and is usually sold sliced. Stronger and firmer than lambs' liver, it becomes cardboardy if cooked too long. Better for a casserole than lambs' liver because it retains its shape.

COOKING: *Cook for 45 minutes maximum. It goes well with potatoes, onions and bacon.*

HEART is sold whole and is larger than a lamb's heart, but leaner. It is a cheap old-fashioned cut, which now often goes as pet food but can make good meals.

COOKING: *Stuff it with bacon, bread, herbs, egg or vegetables and rice, and bake for 40 minutes. It is also good cold, sliced with ravigote sauce.*

CHITTERLINGS are the intestines, stripped and boiled. Popular in Wiltshire and Lancashire as a snack with salt and malt vinegar; they are served fried in America. The intestine skin goes as sausage skins, although these are increasingly artificial in origin. Chitterlings in a small butcher should be a sign of home-made sausages.

TROTTERS are the feet and are sold at a give-away price. They do not have much meat, but are highly gelatinous and very versatile for casseroles or extended recipes.

COOKING: *Usually poached and then breadcrumbed and grilled or roasted, they can also be stuffed.*

CAUL is the transparent cobweb of fat lining the stomach, widely used to wrap dry mixes that need extra fat during cooking

COOKING: *Terrines, sausages or even wrapping fish for baking.*

Pigs' Offal Products

BRAWN is the head and trotters (and sometimes beef shin) boiled together. Currently out of vogue, it can be excellent when well done.

COOKING: *A traditional recipe from Wiltshire: Saw the head into quarters, remove the ears and eyes, add 3 whole peeled onions, parsley, thyme, bay, salt and pepper. Cover with water in a large pan and simmer for 3 hours, or until the meat is falling away. Allow to cool, then take out the meat and chop coarsely. Reserve the liquid and add a handful of chopped parsley and salt to it. Add just enough of the liquid to give the mixture a thick sloppy consistency and pour into a mould. Cover, weight down and cool for a day. Turn out and slice.*

FAGGOTS are the lights (the lungs, liver and heart), fat and breadcrumbs, minced and fashioned into balls and then baked wrapped in caul. Small butchers' shops will omit the lungs.

COOKING: *A traditional recipe: Chop or mince 450 g (1 lb) liver, 85 g (3 oz) smoked streaky bacon, 85 g (3 oz) pork fat with 450 g (1 lb) breadcrumbs (soaked in milk and rung out), 3 onions, 1 teaspoon freshly grated nutmeg, 1 teaspoon chopped parsley and 1 teaspoon sage.*

Form the mixture into balls the size of a tangerine. Lay out on the caul fat and wrap completely. Bake in milk for 30 minutes. Add 600 ml (1 pt) brown stock and bake for a further 10 minutes to make the gravy.

BLACK PUDDING, or BLOOD PUDDING, in English versions uses pork blood, fat and barley, often in an ox stomach lining as a casing as pig's is too small. The use of rice is also credited to English butchery, brown sugar, currants and sultanas to Flemish. The fat is properly the suet from around the kidney, and is often disguised in the mincing. French versions, principally from Normandy and Brittany, tend to be smoother, omitting the barley.

COOKING: *Fresh black pudding as follows: Mix 500 g (1 lb 2 oz) pork fat with 400 ml (14 fl oz) pig's blood, 100 ml (3½ fl oz) cream, 200 g (7 oz) softened onions, and mixed spices. Fill a casing with the mixture. Then poach at 95 °C (203 °F) for 20 minutes, and allow to cool. Grill the sliced black pudding lightly to serve with mashed potatoes.*

BOUDIN BLANC or WHITE PUDDING is made using 2 parts pork fat to 1 part lean pork, though it may also be veal or chicken, pounded and mixed, in classical cooking at least, with foie gras, eggs, onion and cream and seasoned with nutmeg. The traditional British version is based mostly around oatmeal and pork fat.

ZAMPONE is the stuffed shank, a speciality of Italian butchers, and usually sold here pre-cooked to be served warm with cabbage, pulses and purées or served cold and cut thinly as a starter.

SAUSAGES

Sausages are arguably the most popular food in the country and the last surviving artisan craft of the butcher, although the craft has been allowed to diminish considerably without protection for decades. The usual contents are now 65% belly, shoulder or trimmings; the rest will be water, rusks etc.

The smoother, emulsified texture of modern sausages disguises what might have gone into the mix. In law, even skin can count as 'meat'. Good sausages have a coarser texture, a mark of the maker's self confidence. The best cuts of meat for sausages are probably the more labour-intensive cheek and shoulder.

Natural skins were often taken from sheep, rather than pigs. Since the '60s, most casings are made of collagen taken from cow hides – an accidental discovery by medical researchers working for Johnson & Johnson, the US health-care conglomerate in their factory outside Glasgow in 1962. Now collagen skins are used for 75% of all sausages. The collagen has the advantage of being a regular size, which suits factory production. Sausages tend to burst because the water in the rusk content expands and cannot escape in an artificial casing. Sausages in natural casings do not need pricking, because the skins already have minute openings. They can be spiked three-quarters of the way through cooking to drain off any excess fat.

The best sausages were always attributed to Cambridge and Newmarket. The rusk was made with freshly baked bread which was toasted for two hours and then ground (most breads today have too much yeast to achieve this), and the sausage enriched with egg.

Sausage names are applied loosely and carry less and less weight. CUMBERLAND is sold in coils; LINCOLNSHIRE will contain sage, but even this is often overlooked; and an OXFORD used to be veal with lemon. Despite the tomes written and the many competitions to find the best sausage, the essential difference is between hand-made and factory-made. Many factory-made sausages are just gristle, bone, slush and slurry. However, supermarkets – led originally by **Tesco** – have broken away,

Sausages

How cooking affects the fat levels

	Calories	Protein g	Carbos g	Fat g	% Fat of Cals
Beef (raw)	299	9.6	11.7	24	72
(fried)	269	12.9	15	18	60
(grilled)	265	13	15	17	57
Pork (raw)	367	10.6	9.5	32	78
(fried)	317	14	11	24.5	69
(grilled)	318	13.3	11.5	24.5	69

The difference in carbohydrates reflects the amount of extenders used. More extender equals less meat equals less fat.

with impressive mass-produced versions under traditional labels. London has seen a small revival of sausage-making led by the brilliant ****Bill O'Hagan** in Greenwich, and followed by a small central chain **Simply Sausages** originally in Farringdon Road and Brewer Street, which has also spawned a rival offshoot in Bath, **The Sausage Shop** and others.

Matthew Fort of the *Guardian*, who hosted a series of tastings of more than 1,500 sausages nation-wide in the search for a sausage of the year, is unequivocal, 'Good sausages are about two things, the quality of the meat and the higher quantity of meat.' Common-sense says they will likely be from a shop selling about five different types in weekly batches. They should be kept for 24 hours to settle into their skins after stuffing.

BEST BUYS Sausage prices tend to be governed by the level of pork content, ranging in most supermarkets from 65% to 85% for top grade premium. Generally the differences are infinitesimal and hardly allow for prices to vary from £1.15 to £1.90 per lb. Even a 20% difference in pork does not equate to 75p per lb.

FRANKFURTERS were originally lightly smoked sausages made from pork mixed with salted bacon fat. The kosher influence added beef. They have become up-market variations on HOT DOGS, which are further extended with cheaper chicken, even potato starch and numerous additives, from 'natural' smoke flavour to liberal dashes of water-retaining phosphates.

BEST BUYS Most tins of frankfurters claim percentages of meat which hover around 50% meat, but **Sainsbury** offers 58% in packets, 67% for premium hot dogs in tins against 70% for its tinned frankfurters. The price difference between frankfurters and hot dogs can be as great as 43p, which is hardly a true reflection of the relative costs of ingredients.

The big brand names for hot dogs are disturbingly tasteless: **Plumrose** are dark, almost purple-skinned and vapid; **Kingsford** are quite mealy; **Ye Olde Oake** are nastily vapoured; **Princes** are very wobbly and anaemic. They all reflect very little of the traditional virtues. **Sainsbury** tinned premium frankfurters have some vestige of flavour to the skin and stand out, but its ordinary range returns – not untypically for **Sainsbury**, who specialize in selling top and bottom of many meat ranges – to being dry, creamy and as near to tasting of nothing as is possible.

Sainsbury Original German frankfurters in brine, resplendent with Gothic lettering on the tin, are two-thirds of the size of their own-label, which also has two more sausages per can (for 5% more meat). They are barely worth the premium over the salty own-label.

*__Danish Sausage Co Giant__ skinless frankfurters are much closer to the traditional juicy (if fatty) ally for sauerkraut. The skinless notion is spurious as they split. As do *__Herta Skinless Continental__ frankfurters, which have enough skin to split but are reasonably solid, with a distinct Middle European flavour. **Beni Foods Frankfurter-Traditional** (pork and beef) German sausages have a stale sour, unattractive flavour.

The general quality is so poor that, for the most part, one suspects collusion with the mustard manufacturers to save the day.

BACON

Before 1940, the Berkshire pig supplied much of London and South Wales bacon. The Tamworth provided for Birmingham, where it was wanted not only for its meat but also for its lard, used as a cheap substitute for butter on bread. Pig farms had to be around the cities for safety.

To be bacon or ham the meat must be cured. A whole romance has been built up around the different cures for bacon and ham. The reality is disappointingly mundane and standard. The cure is injected and many of the old cures may have been sources of food poisoning in themselves. Hams, usually the back legs though sometimes (and less good) the shoulder, will be cured longer than the conventional 4-5 days for bacon. The first 10% of added water in cured meat does not have to be labelled. A packet of ham or bacon that declares 3% water, therefore can have 13% water. Whether supermarket hams sold as 'not more than 20% water' in fact mean 30% is an open question. Cheap bacon rashers can shrink by half in the cooking.

The nitrates in the cure react with the haemoglobin in the tissue and turn to nitrites, causing the pinkness. Saltpetre was one means, but its use is restricted. It is an explosive. Potentially unpredictable levels of nitrites can be carcinogenic. 200 parts to a million, or a combined 500 parts per million with nitrates, is the legal maximum, still higher in this

BACON PRICES

Bedlam... variations in breed, feed and age of most bacon are minimal and cures vary in only slight degrees. Yet there is a massive, incomprehensible spectrum of pricing. Take a few examples at random. **Sainsbury** charges 10p more for smoked; **Waitrose** 74p less. **Sainsbury** has been selling a low–salt extra–trimmed unsmoked bacon, a minimum of extra work and ingredients, for 80p more per lb than its normal range. **Waitrose** sell Dutch back bacon £1 cheaper than English back, **Sainsbury** 15p cheaper on the deli counter than at the chill cabinet. **Sainsbury** add a premium of 10p for cutting off the rind, **Waitrose** 50p for slicing it. **Tesco's** 'extra trimmed for leanness' suddenly prices itself in inconvenient sizes of 255 g, as against the lb for everything else, and is the most expensive bacon of all, topping even **Sainsburys'** 'traditional oak–smoked' by almost 20p. **Tesco** in the same week had a sensibly restrained window of pricing from £1.99 to £2.19 per lb for back cuts, compared to **Sainsbury** of from £1.79 to £3.38. **Safeway** complicate matters further by pricing in bands of 5 oz, 9 oz and 15 oz. Brands like **Danepak**, alongside, are in 184 g packages.

country than in Italy One gram can be lethal.

Wiltshire Cure was used for whole sides and was more to do with the cut rather than the cure, which is simply 26% salt; 0.1% sodium nitrite; 0.32% sodium nitrate. Other cures reduce the level of salt to as low as 15% and add up to 3% polyphosphate. The phosphates allow the meat to absorb up to 15% of the brine water, double the amount of a traditional Wiltshire Cure.

Ayrshire Cure means only that the meat has been skinned and boned. The basic recipe on which most regional hams are based still favours a dry cure rather than the wet brine baths of the bacon factories. It mixes 2.7 kg (6 lb) salt with 1.35 kg (3 lb) brown sugar and 115 g (4 oz) potassium nitrate. For every 450 g (1 lb) meat, 45 g (1½ oz) of this salt-and-sugar mix is rubbed in. Middles and backs are left for four days, gammons for five. Wash them off before use, but do not soak.

BACON CUTS

1 – Collar
2 – Forehock
3 – Short back
4 – Top back
5 – Streaky
6 – Long back
7 – Gammon

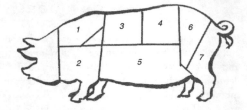

GAMMON is the back leg, weighing 6.8-11.3 kg (15-25 lb). Sold whole, as halves or as boneless joints it tends to be very lean and as a result increasingly dry.

COOKING: *Roast or boil for 45 minutes. Using kitchen gloves (not to scald yourself), cut off the skin with a sharp knife leaving the fat on. Score the fat in criss–crossing diagonal lines to make a lattice pattern. Stud cloves into the intersections. Mix brown sugar, honey and treacle and cover the fat well with this mix. Bake in a hot oven for 20 minutes to the 450 g (1 lb), basting occasionally.*

SLIPPER is a joint cut off the gammon, weighing 900 g-1.35 kg (2-3 lb). Very lean, it is the equivalent of rump steak.

BELLY is streaky bacon, half the price of back. With a high fat content, it is good for pâtés and stuffings.

BACK is the traditional breakfast cut and is always sold sliced. It includes the loin and the chump and is lean. It is more popular unsmoked. **Sainsbury** is claiming a breakthrough in dry-cured bacon 'without the use of water' and with lower salt levels. The process is said to be much quicker and therefore cheaper.

Bacon

The effects of cooking on different cuts of bacon

	Calories	Protein g	Carbos g	Fat g	% Fat of Cals
back '59% lean' (raw)	428	14	0	41	86
streaky '61% lean'					
(raw)	414	14.6	0	39.5	85
(fried)	496	23	0	45	81
(grilled)	422	24	0	36	76

Notice how the selling tags of '59% lean' and '61% lean' obscure the true percentage of fat. Grilling achieves a 10% reduction. The fat in bacon is typically 45% monounsaturates to 40% saturates.

FORE-HOCK is the equivalent to the hand and spring or shoulder of pork. Good value, it is fattier than the gammon and is sold on the bone or boned and rolled. It makes an excellent mid-week joint.

*COLLAR is the spare rib. Boned and sliced as bacon, it is cheaper than back, with larger slices though it tends to fall apart without the bone. It is also sold as joints. Fattier than gammon, it is therefore more moist and usually £1 per lb cheaper.
COOKING: *It is good for roasting or boiling.*

*KNUCKLE, or GAMMON HOCK, is usually very cheap in independent butchers.
COOKING: *If smoked, soak or boil it for 15 minutes and throw way the very salty water. Simmer for 2 hours with vegetables. Traditional in pea and ham soup.*

BACON RIBS are the spare ribs and are cheap.
COOKING: *Parboil and glaze like ham, or simply glaze and roast.*

HAM

English ham is the long cut of the back leg. It was necessarily produced in areas where the Wiltshire sides of bacon were not. Most were called York hams, though they were produced everywhere.

York hams were salted and turned every three days for a month. They were then hung in calico bags to mature for several months. In the south, they were smoked, but not in the north. Escoffier declared these as the best hams for serving cold. When he was writing in 1905, however, the breeds would have been very different and significantly fattier. A small amount of York ham is still cured in the traditional way, notably **George Scott's** in York and more interestingly because it is matured longer at **Radford's** at Sleights near Whitby, both of whom do mail order. BRADENHAM HAMS, originally from Chippenham in Wiltshire, are cured like York hams and then pickled in molasses for a month, which gives the distinctive black skin and supports the sweetness of the meat. DEVON HAMS were centred on Plymouth but seem to have disappeared.

PRAGUE HAMS and WESTPHALIAN HAMS, smoked over juniper and beech-wood, and the more highly smoked BLACK FOREST HAM can be stunning, but are harder to find.

AIR-DRIED HAMS are found across Europe, each valley claiming for itself a distinction derived from the smells hanging in the wind. Some of these are wonderfully outrageous. Parma claims its winds sweep over 'olive groves, pine and chestnut trees, before reaching Parma and infusing the hams with their scents'.

BEST BUYS **HAM PRICES** As with bacon, ham is packed to confuse: deli counters sell in ounces, chill cabinets in grams. At the bottom end are the hams filled with water. **Waitrose** Danish ham has 'not more than 20% water', which might mean 30% water (see page 165). Gradations of weight are misleading: thin sliced smoked ham is in 113 g packs, English ham in 200 g, wafer-thin smoked ham in 100 g, or in another packaging 160 g, or with honey in 60 g, or wafer-thin at the deli counter in ounces. Unlike bacon, the price banding is not so blatantly rapacious, staying for the most part between 70p and under £1 for 133 g or 4 oz. There are a few notable exceptions, however, like **Waitrose** oven-smoked at £1.35 for the same weight. Compare to **Somerfield**, where the lower prices are under 50p for 4 oz.

ITALY

**SAN DANIELLE has been a protected name for dried hams since 1970. Production is limited to the area around the village of San Danielle del Friulli in Udine. The trotter is left on and the hams are beaten into a guitar shape. It will be matured for at least nine months, in which time it loses a quarter of its weight. Production is now centred on 26 plants in the foothills of the Alps, producing 1.8 million hams a year. Each carries the 'SD' seal. The flavour is more pronounced than Parma, but is its equal. The flesh is dark and reddish, tending to be like a leather hide. The taste is sweet, with hints of nuts and an intense saltiness, 'like being at the seaside, but with bite and a great length of flavour, the sourness edged with salt and a shade of sweet'.

**PARMA hams were made in the hills around Parma from before the Roman era and have been famous for as long. The name has been protected under the same legislation as San Danielle since 1970. The pigs must spend the last four months grazing in Emilia, Veneto, Lombardy and Piedmont. The legs are salted (in sea salt) and left in drying chambers for 70-100 days. They are washed, dried and beaten into the familiar chicken-leg shape. The airing houses must be in Parma province in specified valleys up to an altitude of 900 metres. Hams of 7-9 kg must be hung for 10 months, larger ones for a year. They are then branded with the ducal seal. The flesh tends to be an opaquely pink-brown, the taste dry and meaty, not unduly salty, 'a lovely deep delicate flavour with a sweet finish... more feminine than San Danielle'.

Another consortium has been set up to link the 12 producers in the hills between Padua and Vicenza. Their products carry a lion's head seal and the words 'Veneto'.

PANCETTA is the Italian version of bacon, usually using both back and flank rolled into a round. In Italian cooking it is secondary as most pig production centres on salami. Although it looks like streaky bacon, because the pigs are older there is a different dimension of flavour. It is salty and sweet, with an intense distinctive aniseedy taste 'eau-de-vie of sea breeze'.

THE MAGNIFICENT IBERIAN PIG

The Iberian pig that grazes the scrub, oak and cork forests of south west Spain produces the finest hams in Europe (see Jamon de Jabugo, overleaf). Many of the surviving pigs can trace their bloodline back to the 1600s. It is one of three ancient types of pig native to Europe. Its physique is adapted to the poor countryside where it has established itself.

The black skin is resistant to sunstroke and its long legs let it roam long distances in search of food. The early formation of fatty tissue allow it to go extensive periods without eating. From 1955 the numbers dropped horrend-ously from half a million sows to only 67,000 in 1982, many of which were cross-breeds. The acorn diet of the forests saved them. Only the indigenous pure-bred pigs could differentiate between the (edible) part of the acorn and discard the (indigestible) husk and base.

The acorn diet was what set apart the flavour of the hams of the region. Today there are around 100,000 sows in the hills around Extremadura, western Andalusia and parts of Castile, of which more than a third are pure-bred.

The piglets are allowed to feed with their mother for two months, then given their freedom for between 14 and 18 months. The fattening period starts on November 1, when the acorns are ready.

The pigs are let out on the steep hills first and brought down to the lowlands later in the year. They can eat as much as 10 kilos of acorns a day and put on as much a kilo a day in weight. They are killed when they have reached weights of 180 kilos.

To qualify for a Denomination of Origin, the pigs must be 75% pure blood and one-third of the weight derive from the acorn fattening. The acorn diet also appears to have unusual affect on the composition of the fats producing a high unsaturated fatty acid content for both oleic and linoleic. The hams, shoulders and loins are cured for up to two years.

SPECK is from northern Italy, mostly the German-speaking parts. It is made from the legs, which are opened up, salted, smoked and matured for a few months. ROSSENSPECK COTTO is cooked to an opaque pink-hued beige and usually sold sliced, the flavour 'goes from sour to sweet and disappears into sour nuts and peas'.

FRANCE

BAYONNE ham is lightly smoked. Whereas the San Danielle and Parma hams are aristocrats that demand to be eaten alone, amber-hued Bayonne is subtler and more fragrant. Different ages of ham are sold: firstly around 7-months-old, when the hams are quite light; by 12-months-old they take on more character and in the dryness become more leatherine. Bayonne ham doesn't have the subtlety. The taste tends to be of the cure rather than of the meat. It needs accompaniments to bring out its more lyrical flavours and suits well the traditions of serving it with melon or figs.

SPAIN

JAMON DE JABUGO is arguably the finest and most expensive of all hams. Sold at around £13.75 per 115 g (4 oz), only a small amount ever comes out of Spain. It is sold with the hoof on to show its origins. Attempts to industrialize the process or to introduce different breeds of pig to the area around Huelva have failed. The oak forests are still populated by small farmers each of whom lets out his black Iberian pigs to roam wild on the mountains and feed on the acorns. There are as many curers as there are farms and the result is an astonishingly rare and brilliant ham. Bright orange with deep scarlets running to black, it has the taste of the forest. The flavour of the acorn diet comes through, with overtones of lychees, chocolate and treacle, and it is sweet like a pâté. The cure seems to create an effect as if the ham were cooked.

SERRANO comes from the mountains of Caceres, Granada and Salamanca and, like other Spanish hams, tend to be rougher. Quite a meaty product, it has unfashionable visible layers of fat. It tastes leathery and is a big chew, with saltiness that ebbs and flows.

BRITAIN

Air-dried hams may well have been a feature of the diet before the 18th century, but they have dropped out of circulation. The best examples are from **Woodall's** of Waberthwaite in Cumbria, but even with these the maturation period is a quarter that of Parma. The result is completely different. **Denhay Air-Dried Ham** from whey-fed pigs raised near Bridport, Dorset, uses apple juice and honey in the cure and is oak-smoked for several months. Closer to a fresh Bayonne, it goes well with fruit as it is juicy, citrusy and fresh-tasting. Much small production is now being done by smokers rather than the curers themselves, which may be another obstacle to pursuing the Parma tradition of pork air-drying.

CHARCUTERIE

The warmer climate of southern Europe favoured cured pork over the bacon and fresh meat of the north. The art of charcuterie began in Italy and spread north and west. Today 217 different varieties of salami are still claimed to be made in Italy.

The Italians say their salami is better than that of the French or Spanish. Their agriculture is set up primarily to produce charcuterie rather than bacon or fresh pork. The pigs have been bred from English Large Whites and are allowed to get much larger than in England – up to 180 kg (400 lb).

ITALY

The best salamis come from the Po Valley, with its strong dairy heritage, and whey from the cheese-making for feed. There are four styles of salami: fine cut, coarse cut, pure pork and pork and beef. Beef is added to give an element of hardness that pork rarely achieves.

A good salami smells fresh and pure. Held up to the light, it is possible to see the coarseness of the mincing. Poorer meats will still have hairs and edges. In the best, the tastes will evoke white truffles or bacon. In the dry cures, the flavours usually go from sweet to sour; but in the cooked products, like the specks from the north or the smoked products, this is reversed.

MILAN salami was originally just from around Milan, but is now made all across Italy. The recipe was for one-third pork (usually shoulder), one-third beef (again forequarter) and one-third pork fat (the fat should be taken from the back and the belly, while the soft fat from around the kidney goes for lard – back fat is supposedly lower in cholesterol). These are then mixed with 3% salt, a gram of pepper for each kilo, some garlic and wine. The salami is matured for a minimum 40 days. Some will be aged for eight months, in which time they can lose 45% of their weight.

CACCIATORI salamis are only cured for 20-60 days and are almost always sold whole, and Veronese is lightly smoked.

CREMONA salami is similar to Milan, but more loosely packed. It has survived because Cremona was the home town of **Negroni**. The sausage is only made in winter when it is snowing, to 'create the adhesion' they claim.

FELINO, made around Felino near Parma, is often held to be one of the best salamis. Pure pork is mixed with peppers, wine and garlic, and then matured 30-60 days. It is lean and delicately flavoured. **Fini** is a good example.

VARZI used to be made in the town of that name, but the trade has dwindled, and it is now mostly made in the north. Conspicuously low in fat, it uses 75% pork from the forequarter and 20% fat from the throat, and is matured variously for 1-8 months.

NAPOLI is distinctly bright red and sometimes flavoured with chilli. It has twice the pepper content of a Milan. The mix is pork and beef, and it is lightly smoked during the drying and matured for 2-3 months.

SPIANATA ROMAGNA is distinctive because it is flattened out, a practice typical of the area around Rome, with large visible cubes of fat and often strongly peppered.

FABRIANO from Marchese, Umbria, Latium, has pronounced higher levels of pepper (1 ½ grams per kilo) and garlic, but uses lean cuts of pork or beef.

FINOCCHIONA from Tuscany, is distinctive in being flavoured

with fennel and very salty – possibly because Tuscan bread is unsalted, unlike that of the rest of Italy.

MORTADELLA is the original sausage from Bologna, hence 'baloney' for American imitations. The name probably comes from the pounding of meats in a mortar or, more fancifully, from using up the dead horses after battle. In Medieval times, it cost four times more than ham. As with bacon, the bright pink colour comes from the action of the nitrites and nitrates. The longer cooking time for larger sausages (18-24 hours) draws out more flavour. Pork neck, shoulder and hand are the main cuts used – usually from hogs not sows – and 10% is tripe. Beef is not used in the best mortadellas, though the casing will often be from cows rather than pigs. The fat is the harder fat from the back and cheeks. Seasoning is salt, pepper and sugar. The flavourings used are garlic, wine, pistachios and milk powder. Sometimes polyphosphates are added to enhance the water retention. The resulting mass is often now frozen to make it easier to work. The fats are added later to create the distinct pink and white checks seen on the slices. These giant sausages are cooked in special ovens at 80°C (176°F), then cooled in cold water straight after to gel and left to stand for 24 hours.

COPPA from Emilia, is widely made from the neck of pork. The meat is not minced but trimmed of fat, salted and seasoned with garlic, pepper and rosemary, then rolled out in a natural casing it is matured for 4-5 months. It has no protection in its trade name.

ZAMPONE, from Emilia, is traditionally a Christmas or mid-winter dish. A medium mince of pork (equal parts lean and fat) and spices is stuffed into the skin of the trotter and dried for several days at above room temperature and then boiled for 5-7 hours. It is usually sold here pre-cooked.

FRANCE

A great many French *saucissons* are made, but few rival the sweetness of the Italian. The best known styles are ROSETTE which has a white crinkled rind and large visible knobs of fat set in a deep pink-rose flesh. It has the smell of hung bacon and is sweet and acrid in flavour, 'noticeably sour with a peppery finish'. JESUS (DE LYON) has a white rind, and distinctive oyster-shaped ridging, from a deep meaty red to beige flesh, with the sweetness of chestnuts, high *umami*, and an intense finish of pepper.

POLAND

Polish salamis have increasingly become available and offer interesting new dimensions. The long crenellated thin sticks of KABANOS offer a very true salami flavour; sweet in the centre, the taste develops in the mouth. The rust-skinned, ham-coloured MYSLIWSKA has a hint of

Meaty Fast Foods

Old fats versus new fats. How traditional meat products compare to newer fast foods in percentages of fat.

	Calories	Protein g	Carbos g	Fat g	% Fat of Cals
Beefburger (raw)	265	15	5.3	20.5	69
Black pudding (fried)	305	13	15	22	64
Corned Beef	217	27	0	12	49
Cornish Pastie	332	8	31	20	54
Frankfurter	274	9.5	3	25	82
Haggis	310	11	14	22	63
Liver sausage	310	13	4.3	27	78
Pork Pie	376	9.8	25	27	64
Salami	490	9.9	1.9	45	82

The levels of carbohydrates indicate the amounts of non-meat

truffles but a short finish. The bacon-rasher-shaped SOPOCKA is sweet. The mild KRAKOWSKA is also sold in a dry version, where it picks up a tough leathery texture and develops an accentuated sourness. The black-skinned KOLSKA is soft and sweet in taste, with a vegetable hint ending in sourness and spices. The highly concentrated TUCHOWSKA is intense in flavour. These are all worth experimenting with ahead of any German or Danish competition, which are mostly mass-produced (stripped of its pepper overcoat, the widely available GERMAN PEPPER is tasteless meat, while DANISH SALAMI is simply fat coloured with beetroot juice).

SPAIN

Spanish salamis tend to be rough and ready, lacking subtlety if not taste. The most famous is the CHORIZO, with bright red rusty skin and a pronounced fat content in the meat. The flavour has an immediate edge of chilli, with a following taste of chilli sours. It is striking but primitive and often very hot. The SALCHICHON, from Catalonia, uses gammon and strips of salted belly and is matured for 6 months. It looks like the French Rosette and is visibly fatty. It has a good dry texture and a sour taste on the edge.

POULTRY

CHICKEN · EGGS · DUCK · EMU · GOOSE ·
GUINEA FOWL · OSTRICH · TURKEY

The battery farm was introduced from America in the '40s to provide for the needs of the supermarkets. Before then egg production was seasonal, the hens laying fewer eggs as the days shortened. The best eggs were said to be laid in May or June. By controlling the light, the battery farms deceived the chicken into laying all year. Most are culled at age three, but can go on laying until well into their fourth and fifth years. Henri IV's proud ambition that every French family should have a chicken for the pot on Sundays has been subverted. The healthy image of the meat is at odds with the intensity of the production.

Chicken & Turkey
How cooking affects different cuts of chicken and turkey

	Calories	Protein g	Carbos g	Fat g	% Fat of Cals
Chicken Breast(raw)	116	22	0	3.2	24
Wing (roast)	74	12.4	0	2.7	32
Leg (roast)	92	15.4	0	3.4	33
(breaded)	242	18	15	13	48
Turkey Breast (raw)	103	23	0	1	8
Leg (raw)	114	20	0	3.6	28

The balance of fats in chicken breast meat is 45% monounsaturates 35% saturates 20% polyunsaturates.

CHICKEN

No animal has so comprehensively established its relationship with the kitchen. There are more recipes in more cuisines across the world for chicken, let alone eggs, than any other food. It may have paid a high price in crossing from the farmyard to the battery, but protagonists might argue that so have we in moving from the countryside to high-rise cities. As ever, the chicken has just moved with us. Its versatility and adaptability are outstanding.

A good chicken will have a plump breast and no bruising or marks on the chest. Glassy skin is usually a sign of age or mistreatment in the cold store. The bird should be cleanly plucked with no tears in the skin. The best value birds will be 1.8 kg (4 lb) plus, where the ratio of meat to bone is better. As it will be an older bird, the flavour will have developed more. Previously these were always boilers who had finished their stint of egg laying, but these now tend to go for processing.

There are five EU classifications for rearing chickens sold in this country: CORN-FED will have been fed on a diet that is 70% corn, maize or cereal, but will probably have been raised in a barn. The yellowing of the flesh is distinctive, but whether it improves the flavour of the meat on the breeds used here (unlike in France) is debatable. EXTENSIVE REARING means the chickens have been kept in a controlled environment in large houses, and fed on a high-protein (meat and fish) diet. FREE-RANGE BARN is tautologous, the birds are free to roam in a barn, but have no access to open ground.

Most chickens sold will reach 1.35 kg (3 lb) in 42 days, before reaching sexual maturity. (What are called cockerels are fed on a super enzyme diet that can give them a weight of 5.4 kg (13 lb) before maturity.) Free-range birds are often allowed to live longer. TRADITIONAL FREE-RANGE must be at least 81 days old and must have access to grass. TOTAL FREE-RANGE are birds which have been reared in an environment which allows a maximum of 13 birds per square metre and gives them access to pens at night, and they will be at least 56 days old. The move to free-range flocks has brought with it attendant concerns of stressed animals living in unnaturally large flocks. Mass agriculture remains in conflict with the traditional image of the cockerel and his hens in the farmyard. Often genuine free-range will be more emaciated because they have worked harder and therefore are not so plump – not the Barbie dolls of intensive breeding. The skin is sometimes rougher and the meat can be tougher and darker, but the compensation is in the flavour, or at least the genuine taste of chicken.

The most famous and distinctive are the POULET DE BRESSE, from north of Lyons, where whole tracts of the *département* are given over to freedom for chickens.

CAPONIZATION was made illegal in 1988: this practice implanted hormones in the neck of male birds to postpone sexual maturity and allow the birds to put on huge weights. In the last century around Dorking in Surrey, farms specialized in rearing capons on milk diets for nine months for the Christmas market.

BEST BUYS Whole chickens are invariably cheaper than pieces. A farmhouse chicken from **Waitrose** costs £1.25 per lb against leg quarters at £1.59 per lb and breasts at £2.19. On an ordinary chicken at £1.17p per lb whole or 89p per lb for smaller birds, however, the breast with 'part bone in' is £2.85 per lb, not just 66p more than farmhouse but a mark-up of nearly £2 on the whole bird, plus the price includes the weight of the bone. Theoretically, a 1.35 kg (3 lb) chicken bought whole costs £2.67, but the same bird bought in pieces might be more than £5. Surprisingly, in a **Somerfield** (where it might be expected that a chicken would be cheaper) the price per lb was the same as **Waitrose**, but the breast was an exorbitant £3.45 per lb. For the same price it was possible to buy the whole bird.

EGGS

Eggs have become the latest thing in advertising. Ink-jet sprays print on them adverts for Sky TV, condoms, BT, Channel 4 and even Hovis. 'Eggvertising' will be a new word for the OED. At £6,000 for a million eggs it may well be the cult medium of the year.

FREE-RANGE eggs must come from farms with not more than 404 birds to an acre. The requirements to test eggs for salmonella have made small production uneconomic.

Freshness is the main issue in eggs. Although eggs will keep for two weeks and longer in good condition, the packing stations still tend to date the boxes with the date of packing – not laying – and some packers may only collect twice a week. **Tesco** insist its eggs be dated with the laying day and claim to have eggs within 24 hours. In an old egg, the white will be loose and flaccid, the yoke will not sit up on the white in frying, and the air space at the tip will be more than 6 mm ($\frac{1}{4}$ in). Textbooks suggest it is possible to see this with a candle, but it is quite tricky to do at home, let alone in a supermarket aisle. There is no essential difference in colour either in the shell (brown or white depends on breed) or the yolk, often coloured from the feed. Larger eggs come from larger birds.

FOURGRAIN eggs from chickens fed on a diet of wheat, barley, maize and corn have shown relatively well in tastings. **Eggs from Speckeldy Hens** claim to be a move back to pure breeds, but the emphasis is probably more about marketing than quality. FREE-RANGE, as sold in supermarkets, now suffer from new problems of hens being kept in enormous flocks, which stresses them and affects the

THE SALMONELLA SAGA

The aftermath of the Gummer-Currie fiasco – thousands of birds needlessly slaughtered, farmers inadequately compensated, small producers put out of business, half the nation terrified to eat breakfast, imports of inferior (older) foreign eggs, another tier of testing bureaucracy – dwarfs the original concern. On the other hand, practices have been cleaned up: for instance, the disgusting habit of feeding chickens on the feathers of other poultry – and even chicken meal – has been stopped. Salmonella enteriditis seemingly occurs at random. A chicken may lay 50 unaffected eggs and then one that is affected. The numbers of eggs discovered containing salmonella have been minuscule, but the risk is inherent. Egg shells are porous, so can absorb infection. Salmonella is a danger that we have to learn to live with.

The official advice is not to eat eggs unless they are hard-boiled or the equivalent. It is probably preferable not to eat eggs at all as a protest against the state of the industry than to give in to such fey blackmail. Pasteurized egg mixes are now being widely adopted by the catering trade. However, the same zealousness has not infected the supermarkets where they are not stocked. Some alternatives are found in health food shops, such as a non-dairy mayonnaise using an emulsion of sunflower oil, vinegar and apple.

quality. Moreover, as John Gummer effectively stopped small flocks, the era of the fresh quality egg may have passed completely for anyone without the space for a chicken coop.

DEEP LITTER allows for seven birds per square metre of floor space and enough straw/sawdust to ensure the top layer is not damp. PERCHERY or BARN is the 3D version of deep litter with 25 birds per square metre, each with at least 15 cm of perch space. BATTERY is not a word that appears on the packaging any more, for obvious reasons.

The smallest egg is grade 7, at 45 g or less, then in gradations of 5 g to the biggest, grade 1 at 70 g or more. Grade 3, at 60-65g, is the most popular and the most used in recipes.

DUCK

Large-scale production inevitably raises questions of welfare. Specialist breeders have increasingly begun to point out that humane killing should be dislocation of the neck by hand. The ducks should be out of sight of other ducks and also of any dead ducks. The need is for tranquillity. Commercial abbatoirs string up the ducks in long lines, often unstunned.

Fresh will always be better than frozen, as the freezing affects the fat and defrosting allows the flavour to leach out. The fat was insulation for living in water, but levels seem to have fallen back with domestication.

Britain's most famous duck, the Aylesbury, became extinct some 20 or so years ago in a flurry of cross-breeding and centralization. Only one farm, **Long Grove Wood**, at Chesham, Bucks still raises the old breed on a small scale and claims to trace its progeny back to 1775. Nearly all the ducks sold now come from one firm, **Cherry Valley** in Lincolnshire.

AYLESBURY – or what passes for it – is now rather a large duck, about 25 cm (10 in) long, and pallid white in colour with blue patches. They are usually packed tightly in boxes on top of each other, which does them no favours, misshaping their long, otherwise elegant, limbs. Now a hybrid crossed with Peking and rarely the 4.5 kg (10 lb) they used to make, they need considerably longer cooking than other ducks – right at the edge of maximum cooking times, 2 hours or even more, to burn off the levels of fat and get the skin crisp. Succulent but fatty, it carves with difficulty, falling apart from the breast, but crisp skin is achievable. It is disappointing for the national duck. Expect two cups of fat from a bird. The WALESBURY is a cross with a Welsh Harlequin, bred for eggs and meat, and raised to be at table-weight within 16 weeks.

**BARBARY from the South of France, have a sallow yellow skin, usually with signs of hand-picking of the feathers. Often the innards retain large pieces of fat and are poorly cleaned out. They have an excellent ratio of dark flavoursome meat to bone. They are best well cooked (about 2 hours) to let the skin crisp up. Done like this, one bird is really only enough for two, so they are expensive. The fat content is about half a cup.

GRESSINGHAM was developed in Cumbria by Peter Dodds as a cross with a wild mallard. It was originally a strongly meaty bird. However, success has led the business into franchising, with disappointing collapse in their bone structures and a falling off of the meat-to-bone ratio. Nevertheless it is a good duck, if not the mega-star originally perceived. About 20 cm (8 in) long, with neat military configuration, it has dark meat with a good flavour and skin that crisps. The fat content is about half a cup per bird.

KHAKI CAMPBELL are bred for egg laying only.

The TRELOUGH duck was developed from a Rouen by Barry and Gay Clark near Hereford. The ducks are raised in an orchard (replanted with old varieties of apple, such as Golden Knob and Glory England, under the auspices of the National Apple Collection) with access to water. Unlike the Rouen, whose fabled reputation was undone by maturing at seven months and older, the Trelough will be ready at 10 - 14 weeks – compared to 4 weeks for a commercial bird. Since starting in 1990, the ducks have been well supported by the regional restaurant trade. Their configuration is particularly apt for separating, with a good lean breast and fattier legs. The flesh is dark and dry and the skin crisps

Duck

The effects of cooking on different cuts of duck

	Calories	Protein g	Carbos g	Fat g	% Fat of Cals
Duck (raw)	122	19.7	0	4.8	35
(roast)	189	25	0	9.7	46
Fat and skin only					
(raw)	430	11.3	0	43	90
(roast)	339	19.6	0	29	76

The levels of monounsaturated fats in these ducks were almost twice as high as the saturated.

well with a covering of honey. They do not need pricking.

COOKING: *Duck is invariably better cooked well done. The French vogue for underdone breasts is a fad. This is especially true with the more mass-produced ducks like the Aylesbury where all the fat needs to be cooked out. The best way of cooking duck is how the Cantonese do it – wind-drying for 24 hours and then roasting in vertical cylinders so the fat drips away.*

EMU

Farmed in western Australia, some of these exotic birds have started to be imported frozen. The virtually fat-free red meat is not dissimilar to ostrich and tastes and looks like prime fillet. Some goes for charcuterie, designed as a low-fat salami for Germany, but it is best briefly cooked in the pan. The Aborigines used the oil as a lubricant, but government sponsorship has created farms in the last 20 years for meat production.

GOOSE

Geese were an important part of the economy of the Middle Ages, the feathers used for arrows and the down for pillows.

Goose fat was commonly used as a medicine, especially for bronchial complaints, while long-distance swimmers used it for insulation. Reserve it for sautéing potatoes and flavouring casseroles. The low instance of heart disease in South-west France has led some nutritionists to the seemingly unlikely suggestion that the fat may have some positively healthy properties.

The main breeds of goose are EMBLEM and TOULOUSE, sometimes crossed together, or DANISH LARGARTH. Now very much a small-scale, free-range or barn business, the young are hatched between March and July for Christmas. GREEN GEESE or GOSLING were the first young geese killed in spring or at Michaelmas (September 29) for the Harvest Festival, but are almost impossible to find now.

'Long-legged' or 'New York' means weighed with the guts in. You lose one-third to one-quarter of the weight, which makes it more expensive than it appears. Most of the meat is on the breast, and one bird should do five people. Some wild geese, usually Canadian, are also shot. These will have less fat after their arduous flight and need extra basting.

COOKING: *Goose is nearly always roasted with fruity stuffings like prune and Armagnac. They are usually cooked with stock or cider, plums, apples or oranges.*

BEST BUYS FOIE GRAS The production of foie gras (goose or duck liver swollen from force-feeding) is not permitted on UK farms. A small amount is imported fresh for the restaurant trade, and this is infinitely superior to most of the tins of ready-made pâté found here. The price fluctuates through the year, from £15 to £90 per lb, hitting a peak at Christmas. The best is from Alsace and around Toulouse, but most comes from Hungary and Poland. Some very inferior examples have come out of Spain, from **Markiko of Navarra**, they are presented in deceptively beautiful sleek packaging. Duck foie gras is arguably better than goose. Guard the leftover juices for cooking.

COOKING: *The big white bready lobes need careful handling: slice them with a hot knife and pan-fry or bake in an oven which is not so hot you cannot put your hand in.*

GUINEA FOWL

Native to the Guinea coast of West Africa, the purple grey plumage dotted with white of the guinea fowl has found them favour as far back as Roman and Greek times. One theory is that they were the original bird meant by references to turkey, before being usurped by the American bird. Traditionally they were sold between February and June, when other game was out of season, and considered akin to pheasant. They used to be mainly available frozen from France, but fresh are now increasingly found. They are likely to become more fashionable and widely available, and are worth seeking out. It was said that guinea fowl was an expensive tasteless chicken, but given what has happened to chicken the roles are probably now reversed. In France there is a *Label Rouge* scheme for them to be raised on grain. Smaller than a chicken, one will only just stretch to four people, but they are more flavoursome – even if, at first sight, they look unpromisingly grey and not as voluptuous.

COOKING: *They do tend to dry in cooking, so benefit from barding and delicate saucing.*

OSTRICH

Farms are being set up to breed ostrich meat in Britain, although the trade is still mostly in eggs for breeding. Some is imported to Europe from Africa, where it has a long history as a culinary animal, especially in South Africa. Californian restaurants have also begun to sell it. The meat tends to 'look like lamb and taste like steak, with a hint of chicken'. Its nutritional advantages are low calories, low cholesterol and one-third of the fat of chicken.

TURKEY

There is only time of year to buy turkey as the entire industry is centred on Christmas. Any other birds that reach the market tend to be marketing experiments with breaded shapes and self-basting, invariably using poor-quality, abused, intensively reared birds. Even the workers are abused as cases of long-term injuries from repetitive work have ben upheld in the courts against processing plants.

After decades of obscurity the turkey industry revealed all for Christmas last year. The market was suddenly glutted with frozen birds in November selling for as little as 34p per lb, or less than the price of pet food.

Frozen food giant **Iceland** declared war on its rivals with mud-slinging press adverts declaring: 'Virtually all supermarket "fresh" turkeys aren't as fresh as ones frozen within hours. That's because these "fresh" have been blasted with carbon dioxide and deep-chilled at temperatures on or below freezing for a month or even longer. Then they are thawed and put on the shelf to catch the eye of the unwary shopper who'll pay three times as much.' To back up the claim that frozen was as good as fresh, blind tastings were held which purported to show that people preferred frozen.

Such birds sadly represent 95% of all turkeys sold each Christmas. At the other extreme are TRADITIONAL FARM FRESH birds, which have a gold triangle symbol to denote membership to a traditional breeding scheme. This covers 12 points. The birds are grown slowly without hormones, or growth promoters, fed 70% cereals and no animal protein, live in housing with natural light and ventilation, on beds of straw or soft-wood shavings which are changed regularly. Farms are independently inspected. The birds are killed on farm (to avoid stress), dry plucked, and hung for a minimum of 7-10 days, compared to the average 4 hours for an intensively reared bird to be killed and frozen.

The BRONZE variety of turkey attracts the image of the quality bird. They have tended to be the birds put out for free-range. However, the strains have so much white breeding that the differences are small. The difference is in breeding. Most birds are intensively reared, processed in the factory within four hours and then sold frozen, gas flushed or chilled – the point **Iceland** make is that, in practice, these are the same birds. Years of supermarkets buying simply on weight and price have led to a coarse-fleshed bird, coded as T8, that does not, in fact, reach full maturity until it is as big as 30 lb plus – which they never do. Specialist breeders can use as many as seven different strains of bird to ensure that each one reaches its peak for the size at which it will be sold. The differences in price are down to the feed and age – a traditional bird will convert its food to body weight at a ratio of 1 to 5, compared to a bird in an intensively reared system, which may achieve the same weight with half the food. Traditional birds should be hung for at least 7 days and specialists will say that it should smell 'as if it is going' as it goes in the oven.

NORFOLK BLACKS are rarely found these days. The flesh tends to be drier and there is a high percentage of bone. Some specialist farms still breed them in small numbers and they need ordering well in advance of Christmas. **Sarah Pinfold** (01394 383922) raises them alongside her free-range pigs at Woodbridge in Suffolk.

Out of the Christmas season, a good turkey is hard to find. Most of the smaller birds, weighing 2.3-3.2 kg (5-7 lb) at around 11 weeks, go for processing or the larger 'stags' at 16 kg (35 lb) go directly to the catering market. Most are raised in three-sided poll barns (ie with space to jump around) or broiler-like sheds, but breeding has reached such a point that they are too fat to fend for themselves so have to be artificially inseminated, and some larger birds have difficulty moving around. One of the most economical birds to rear, converting 450 g (1 lb) of meat from 1.25 kg (2½ lb) of feed. 'New York' dress means they are sold with the guts in. At 20 weeks the difference between the sexes is negligible, though hens will be slightly smaller. Traditionally they should be hung for 10-12 days, but supermarkets rarely do this now. Independent butchers will and so increasingly do abattoirs. The seeming bargains of the large legs sold in cut-price supermarkets may not have had their sinews drawn and will be tough as a result.

Most turkeys now are hybrids, based on the Broad Breasted Bronze derived from the American breed Beltsville White. The English bird until the '50s was a Norfolk Black or a Cambridge. They lost favour for their smaller breast and grey speckling. FARM-FRESH turkey, identifiable by a black triangle on the packaging, should have been fed on a diet of 70% grain and 30% milk powders. A good turkey will be white, not pink or purple, with a layer of fat all round, dry and with large breast and plump legs.

COOKING: *Some argue that stuffing a turkey restricts the flow of hot air needs to cook the insides properly, and an apple in the chest is the only thing it needs. Cook them breast-side down and turn them over for the last half an hour.*

GAME

DUCK (WILD) · GROUSE · HARE · PARTRIDGE ·
PHEASANT · PIGEON · QUAIL · RABBIT · SNIPE ·
VENISON · WOODCOCK

The fate of wild game mirrors the ravaging of the countryside and the rise of pesticides. What was once a poor-man's food has become a luxury.

And yet game like rabbit and pigeon are cheap, abundant and overlooked. Pheasant, quail and venison are extensively farmed and increasingly widely available. Pheasants in December or January can be cheaper than chicken. Yet some of the most famous game birds, notably grouse but also snipe and woodcock, are endangered – and will go on being so until their habitats are protected.

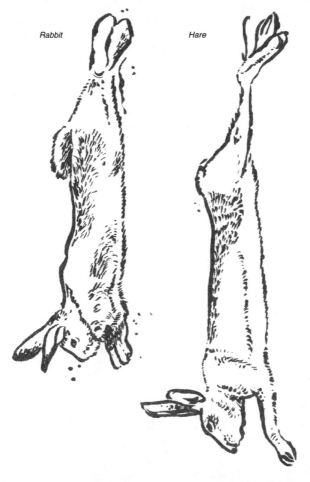

Rabbit *Hare*

DUCK (WILD)

Ducks have survived the onslaught of mass farming rather better than other game. The **MALLARD is the prime wild duck for table. With small legs and mostly dark good quality fatless breast, it has a gamier, richer flavour – sometimes said to be fishier – than domestic duck. Now mallard are often hand-reared, not as intensively as pheasant, but then released for the shoot.

COOKING: *One duck should feed two and it should be hung for 4-5 days then simply roasted for 45 minutes. Old books suggested the breast being roasted separately (it 'should only fly through the hot kitchen before being sent to table') and the legs braised.*

TEAL are small birds shot in smaller numbers than mallard, mostly in the north. In season from October to February, but at their best after the frost has set in. Allow one per person.

WIDGEON, of which even fewer are shot, are larger than teal and smaller than mallard. In season from October to February, they are at their best earlier in the year.

GROUSE

Of the 16 species of grouse in the world, four are found here, including the finest of all, the red grouse. The PTARMIGAN you will not find and the CAPERCAILLIE was almost lost to us. Hunted to extinction by 1770 and only reintroduced 60 years later in Perthshire, again as a sporting bird, capercaillie reached their peak at the turn of the century. The spoilage of their preferred woodland habitat and increasing exposure to rising numbers of predators, especially foxes, has pushed their territory back to North-west Scotland, and once again extinction is possibly looming. Three years ago it was estimated there were only 2,000 left in the wild. Moves from the Secretary of State for Scotland to ban the shooting were stopped on the grounds that estates might never be persuaded to re-plant the forests of Caledonian pine, their natural habitat, if there were was no prospect of revenue from shooting. Currently a voluntary ban remains in force and numbers are estimated by Game Conservancy to be around 3,500.

Their dark plumage is enlivened with a metallic green breast. They are shot from October 3 to December 10, and usually now are stuffed as trophies. Young birds in autumn feed on bilberries and other plants, which is one reason the shooting season is later. As the year wears on they eat the pine needles which give an unattractive turpentine flavour to their flesh.

Unique to Britain and in need of protection, the **RED GROUSE is the king of British game, but is now in serious – if not terminal –

decline from the encroachment on its moorlands. Famously, the shooting season opens on August 12 and goes on to December 10. The Yorkshire moors still have the same density of birds as decades ago, but the moorland itself has shrunk. Many of the birds go to Germany. Most grouse sold here are from northern Scotland where the numbers have been in decline. This may be down to foxes. Before myxomatosis, estates employed keepers to keep rabbit numbers down, but they were laid off in the '70s and '80s and the return of the rabbit has brought back foxes in large enough numbers to also attack the grouse.

Some 500,000 are shot a year, which represents about 30% of the breeding population in August. Despite its culinary reputation, the commercial reason for grouse-rearing is shooting. Guns pay £75-80 to shoot a brace, against £3 when sold to a game dealer. Unlike pheasant and partridge, estates have shied away from farming to preserve the sport.

A healthy bird can weigh 350 g (12 oz). They usually arrive within 24 hours and the butcher can then hang them. Peter Hudson of Game Conservancy explains: 'Hanging was designed for older birds and is really a Highland tradition. London restaurants would not dare to serve traditionally hung grouse. The taste is in the guts, which are unusually long and needed for a digestive system to cope with the fibrous heather. It is this where the flavour comes from.' The perennial debate about whether grouse can be eaten fresh or needs hanging is based in snobbishness. The only unhung grouse available are at shoots or the few that expensively arrive at London hotels for the first day of shooting. The real debate is about how long, not if. Game dealers will pluck, draw and hang the birds. Although expensive, they are a unique treat.

COOKING: *The dish for which grouse are renowned is a well-hung bird, roasted and served on croutons with game chips and bread sauce. The older birds (more than a year) are only good for casseroling, which helps counteract the bitterness in the legs.*
Modern recipes for serving just the breast are rarely so successful.

The BLACK GROUSE is larger than a red grouse. The female is grey and the cock is black. Found on the edges of moors, they are in serious decline – there are perhaps only about 15,000 birds left. One hundred years ago they were found on heathland across Britain; as recently as the '50s they were abundant in the Highlands, Devon, Somerset and the New Forest. They are now very rare south of the Border and are mostly found in Tayside. The season is a week after the main grouse season, starting on August 20 and ending on December 10. It must be well hung or it is dry and flavourless. It is as good as red grouse, but it is not necessarily as expensive because there is no proper trade. Attempts to introduce the bird into Ireland have failed.

Game

How the total percentage of fats compare in different game birds.

	Calories	Protein g	Carbos g	Fat g	% Fat of Cals
Grouse	173	31.3	0	5.3	27
Partridge	212	36.7	0	7.2	30
Pheasant	213	32.2	0	9.3	39
Pigeon	230	27.8	0	13.2	51
Goose	319	29.3	0	23	64

The levels of saturated fats in wild birds are considerably lower than the equivalent levels in domesticated or farmed birds.

HARE

Under the 1880 Game Act, farmers can shoot hare all year round except Sundays and Christmas, but they can only be sold from August to February. Hares used to be commonly as big as 5.4 kg (12 lb) and sometimes as much as 9 kg (20 lb). There are two kinds. The BROWN HARE, probably introduced by the Romans, thrives in cereal-growing areas. The MOUNTAIN HARE is probably indigenous and shares the same moors as the grouse. In the last century they roamed the fields in flocks. Brown hare numbers have dropped markedly in the past twenty years.

Unlike rabbit, they should be hung – with the entrails in and by the legs not the head – for up to a week, and sold with the blood, liver, heart and kidneys. The brown hare is larger than the mountain hare, and opinions divide as to which is the best. Nicola Cox in her *Game Cookery* sides firmly with the brown. The flesh is rich, but good value at around £1 per lb. The best cuts are the hind legs and the loin, which are sometimes cut as one piece to make a baron.

COOKING:Hare does not overcook easily and should never be served rare. They are traditionally roasted or 'jugged', using the blood for the sauce. Ideally you need a young animal, preferably a leveret being under a year – ideally only six months, otherwise the cooking time may prove excessively long. The blood should be mixed with a little vinegar to stop it curdling.

To casserole hare first marinate the hare joints overnight in a mixture of red wine and wine vinegar, with bay and orange. Make a stock from the trimmings. Put the hare and the marinade in a covered casserole, add the stock, some onions, bacon and herbs. Stand the casserole in a larger pot. Fill that with boiling water, so the casserole is completely surrounded, and bake for 3 hours in a medium to slow oven. Take out the meat, reduce the sauce to thicken it and sweeten with redcurrant jelly and Port. Add the blood to thicken it, but do not bring the sauce back to the boil.

PARTRIDGE

The devastating decline in the indigenous GREY PARTRIDGE (*Perdix perdix*) in the '50s coincided with the collapse of estate management and the introduction of herbicides, insecticides and artificial fertilizers on the land. Nor was this confined to this country: the impact was worldwide. Organized game shooting began with drives on English estates for the partridge in the 19th century and it became highly fashionable across the south. Now the concentrations of the birds are nearly all to be found in Lincolnshire and East Anglia.

The FRENCH PARTRIDGE (*Alectoris rufa*) have red legs and were introduced here 200 years ago from the south of France, expressly for shooting. They thrived in the open marshland of East Anglia. They are hardier than the grey, and less susceptible to herbicides. Since the '60s, they have been cross-bred for hand-rearing and shooting like pheasants. Numbers have risen sharply and has led to the wide introduction of new shoots across the whole country, but mostly in Norfolk, Essex and Hampshire.

Shot from September 1 to February 1, partridge are at their best early in the year. The English are more expensive and the flesh sweeter. They should be hung for 3-4 days. The French confusingly also differentiate between young birds: *perdreau*, which need brief cooking, and the older, perdrix, which should be casseroled.

PHEASANT

The most beautifully feathered of all game birds, the pheasant was originally brought here from China. The Romans may have brought pheasants here; the Normans certainly did, and there was much cross-breeding of different species in the 19th century. They are now bred so prolifically for shooting – 20 million are reared a year – they have become a more common sight in country lanes than rabbits or pigeons. The season is from September to the end of January. The first birds are often last year's. They are at their best after October, reaching their prime in November.

Check that the spurs, 5 cm (2 in) up the leg, are not long and sharp. On a new season's bird they will be short and rounded. The cock is larger than a hen, weighing up to 1.35 kg (3 lb), but the hen is considered better meat even if two-thirds of the size. They can be hung by the neck up to seven days, and in the old days longer for a green (high) bird, they waited until the head fell away. Make sure they are not badly shot. They should have plump breasts and needs a line of fat (to the side) to help keep it moist in the cooking. A large bird will feed three.

Near-domestication may not have helped their flavour, as they potter about the fields like country vicars certain of their next tea, but it has brought the price out of the realms of luxury – at around £6 per brace. The science of rearing pheasants is borrowed from the poultry industry in the early '50s. The chicks are released into pens at six weeks and are fed regularly for the first year. Woodlands managed for pheasants have recorded notable rises in the variety and numbers of other wildlife, notably butterflies.

COOKING: Traditionally pheasants are roasted, but sealing either in a roasting bag or pot compensates for the innate dryness which may also account for their often eccentric and wayward pairings with almost every fruit, liquor and cream sauce in many recipe books. One envisages long dark nights in baronial Northern castles with solitary cooks over-endowed with pheasants desperately thinking up new ways with pheasant. 'Is that Drambuie over there, Macduff?'

PLUCKING FEATHERED GAME:
Put a polythene bag between your legs (be out of the wind or draughts), put the bird's head down and pluck carefully against the lie of the feathers. Don't snap, just pull gently, taking extra care around the breast and parson's nose. Gut after plucking.

PIGEON

The number of pigeon shot bears little relation to the few that arrive at market... an unholy waste of life. In the Middle Ages, the pigeon loft was an important source of food for both the farm and the estate. They are sold whole or as breasts, the difficulty is judging the quality before cooking. In the feather, young birds will be slightly paler grey; otherwise, there are few tell-tale signs. Older birds will be fatter and age translates as toughness. Young birds can be excellent, especially if they have grazed near corn crops. Imported French pigeons, or SQUABS, from Anjou are found in top-class restaurants and are worth the enormous expense.

COOKING: Marinate pigeons and cook them slowly with vivid, fruity accompaniments.

QUAIL

The name quail used to be used of any small bird and was associated with many miracles: they may have been the manna from heaven, falling out of the sky exhausted after a long migration over sea. In Egypt, they were caught with huge nets on the shore and shipped via Marseilles to Europe in the '20s as return cargo on the ships taking cars to Africa, until the cruelty of the trade led to it being stopped in the '30s. These were the *Coturnix coturnix*, which are still shot in Continental Europe but not here in Britain, where the Japanese quail *Coturnix japonica* is farmed. The tiny birds have to be contained in confined spaces or they fly off like sidewinder missiles and crash into the meshing or the walls of a barn. Farming seems needless and cruel. At £1 per bird they are also expensive.

COOKING: *Traditionally they are roasted, and said to have an affinity with vine leaves and grapes. Some recipes suggest over 21 other ingredients, a sure sign of meekness of flavour.*

Quail's eggs with brown speckled shells should be simmered for 1-2 minutes only and then shelled. Serve with celery salt and sesame seeds. Most of the charm is in the size.

RABBIT

Probably introduced by the Normans in the 11th century, rabbits were an important part of the economy until the start of the 18th century. They were kept in enclosed warrens on estates to provide meat and fur (for hats) and only ran wild after their place was taken by developments in the breeding of other animals and imports (especially from Australia) began.

They bred in prolific numbers until the epidemic of myxomatosis started in Edenbridge in Kent in October 1953 – probably from infected imported animals – and wiped out 99.9% of all rabbits. Myxomatosis is spread from animal to animal by the rabbit flea. Some argue that its impact was the most significant event in modern agriculture, allowing huge areas to be put over to crops and cereals which previously the rabbits might have destroyed. Myxomatosis is not, in fact, harmful to humans, though the epidemic also destroyed all the trade in the meat.

But the numbers of rabbits has grown steadily and in Scotland they are found again in force. The Ministry of Agriculture, Fisheries and Food is piloting a scheme to put a contraceptive in the feed.

Rabbit are shot all year round. Good value at £1-1.50 each, they provide a good proportion of lean meat. Most of the trade is from rifle to butcher's door, and a good butcher should be able to help revive its reputation. Look for an animal around 900 g (2 lb), with clean pale-pink flesh which is not emaciated. Legs and the loin (saddle) are the best cuts; roast or casserole them. Rabbit is sometimes (or was, I have never encountered it) used as substitute for chicken in the catering trade.

CHINESE RABBIT is mass-produced and sold frozen, but has little flavour and is often more expensive than fresh.

SNIPE

There are two types of snipe: the COMMON SNIPE and the rarer and protected JACK SNIPE. Both migrate here, preferring the westerly wet reedy flatlands and moving north in spring to breed. There is some hope that the move to set aside farmland and less intense agriculture will see their numbers start to rise again. Shooting is from August 12 to January 31. They were once regarded as one of the finest of all game.

COOKING: *Are usually roasted like woodcock, with the guts still in.*

VENISON

The word venison used to cover all kinds of furred game, but has come to be used solely for deer meat. The native is the RED DEER, found mostly in Scotland where it has migrated further and further north to avoid civilization. It is the strongest-tasting meat. Older textbooks favoured it above other breeds, especially if well-hung. Young meat, say 12-18 months, is rarely hung and is distinctly different. More recently, other writers have advanced the cause of the SIKA, imported from Japan originally to graze parklands but some have escaped and are interbreeding with the red deer in the wild. There are also the woodland FALLOW DEER, again originally the deer of parkland and large estates, and the smaller ROE DEER.

Farmed venison is likely to be more tender than wild, where the quality is naturally more erratic. The deer are kept within a 2-metre high perimeter with their own dedicated raceways. There are pens to handle the stags, mainly to protect the handlers from the antlers. Most of the feed will be from the enclosed hills topped up in winter with silage, hay and roots.

COOKING: *Venison is a modern meat, almost fatless and freezes well. Haunch, loin and best end are best roasted and served rare, when they will still be juicy. Steaks and chops can be pan- or wok-fried, but need more fat than other meats. The less expensive cuts, such as neck, shoulder and shin, need marinating and then long slow braising. The liver was always a hunter's perk; it is highly valued and should be fried lightly and served pink. Except for that of young roe deer, the meat invariably benefits from marinating for at least 4-5 days (if the aim is to tenderize) in oil, red wine, vinegar and aromatics. Traditionally it is paired with sweet fruity accompaniments: redcurrant jelly, baked pears, cherries, apricots etc. Venison is always served on very hot plates to stop the fat congealing unattractively (traditionally in Scotland, spare plates were kept hot for the second helpings).*

BEST BUYS **Sainsbury** take their venison from southern parklands.
Safeway takes the red deer from the Highland herds. The rise of deer farming in
the last 10 years has made venison increasingly available. Pricing is erratic:
Waitrose sell steaks for £6.99 per lb (a considerable saving compared to beef
fillet), but haunch at £5.75 per lb off the bone is an expensive joint. Steaks direct
from the farm would be £2.50 less, haunch £1 less.

WOODCOCK

The numbers of woodcock have been kept up because they like the same
open forest as pheasants, but they are very fast and difficult to shoot and
therefore prized trophies. They are nocturnal and secretive, with long
beaks and matronly expressions. Many migrate here, especially in
colder winters. They must be plump, and are at their best in October and
November. They are not hung and are, unusually, cooked complete
with their giblets and the neck folded back around the wing.

'Scotch woodcock' is nothing to do with the bird, but a savoury of
anchovies and capers in scrambled eggs on toast.

COOKING: *Roast them for 20 minutes, covering the breast
(which should be rare) but not the legs, and place on a crouton to
collect the juices. 'There is more art in roasting a woodcock, than
any other bird,' argues '30s food writer Henry Smith. He says the
oven should not be hotter than 230°C (450°F/gas 8).*

VEGETABLES

Europe has been a collecting house for the world's vegetables. The first introductions came from China and Asia, probably with the Persian traders who sold them to the Greeks and Romans. The second generation arrived in the Dark Ages with the Moors, who brought aubergines, cauliflowers and other exotics from Africa to Spain.

The discovery of the New World was as much about finding new kinds of vegetables and fruits as it was about gold and silver. The mid-16th century sees the first mention of many vegetables, though this may be related as much to the rise of the first textbooks as to the vegetables themselves. Many still had to wait until the 19th century before there was any serious cultivation, certainly in this country.

How far the older varieties resemble what we now see is a matter for conjecture. Potatoes and cabbages are examples of vegetables that we know were very different. Gregor Mendel, a Czech, is credited with much of the early work on the genetics of vegetables and selective breeding.

We might be said currently to be enjoying the fourth great age of the vegetable, with the development of new varieties – and even new vegetables – that can be moved across the globe to markets. Some of this is obvious – aubergines, courgettes, peppers, even mushrooms were unheard of in Britain as recently as the '50s. Other changes have been more clandestine: for instance, potato varieties changed radically in the late '80s and commercial canners and freezers bought up exclusive rights on old varieties of peas and consigned others to oblivion.

All this change has brought vegetables to the front of food fashion after centuries when they were often generally mistrusted and their nutritional virtues overlooked, or they were cultivated purely for their perceived medicinal value. With this resurgence have come new ideas about cooking vegetables that have introduced strategies from other parts of the globe. The vegetable is, in many ways, the great triumph of the global food economy.

LEAF VEGETABLES

BROCCOLI · BRUSSELS SPROUT · CABBAGE ·
CAULIFLOWER · CHINESE LEAVES · SPINACH

The brassicas – cabbage, Brussels sprout, cauliflower, etc – have been somewhat unrecognized, possibly because they spent so much of this century sitting around in boiled water or smothered in a white sauce. They are cheap, nutritious and deserve rediscovery, combining well with the new flavourings like garlic and ginger. They have been excellent sources of nutrition over the centuries. Some of their uses have also been quite bizarre. On the Isle of Wight cabbage stems were left to grow 4 metres (12 ft) tall and sold cut into walking sticks. New cultivation has seen mini cabbages and cauliflowers in the supermarket small enough to fit in the palm of the hand.

BROCCOLI

Nowadays the main property of broccoli – originally spelled with just one 'c', is the texture. Any other merits it once possessed have been bred out of almost all varieties, purple or green. Where great lengths are gone to with other vegetables, say asparagus, to point out the different cooking times needed for the tips and the stalks, with broccoli the consumer is handed two almost separate and quite distinct vegetables on the same stalk and expected to cope. These mini umbrellas are too old and too big for any serious cooking. Writing only as recently as 1978, Jane Grigson said enthusiastically that broccoli was second only to asparagus in flavour. Varieties would seem to have changed.

It was always known as an untrustworthy vegetable for growing in the UK because of the climate. The first seeds were imported from around Naples.

By contrast the relatively unexploited PURPLE SPROUTING BROCCOLI, available in early spring, shows the potential for flavour from the stalk, the leaves and the florets. Cook and serve it as asparagus. There are different varieties on sale. The spindlier stalks are the best, by quite a long way.

PURPLE CALABRESE arrives at the same time from the New World. Most of its colour and flavour is lost in an inky stain in the cooking water.

COOKING: *In Japanese cooking broccoli is valued for being decorating. Lightly blanched for 3 minutes, the florets retain their vivid green and respond well to light saucing with sesame, miso and garlic. The heads need seasoning rather than saucing. In young*

VEGETABLE DIVERSITY

The diversity of Europe's vegetables is controlled and restricted under EU laws. In practice, any seeds that are not licensed are banned. The imbalance has outraged small and organic gardeners who are potentially disadvantaged. Intensive growers with research programmes can register and copyright seeds, where a market gardener cannot develop the varieties particular to his or her growing conditions.

Under the relevant Directive, 2 kg of lettuce seed is classified as equal to 2 kg of potato seeds. Alan Gear of the Henry Doubleday Research Association (see page xxxix) points out the former is enough to cover half of southern England while the latter is hardly enough to plant two rows in a garden.

The HDRA estimate more than 2,000 traditional vegetable varieties have been lost since 1950. So they launched an 'Adopt A Veg' campaign to preserve some 700 old varieties. For a payment of £12.50, the variety will be kept and maintained as part of the HDRA's heritage seed catalogue (tel 01203 303517).

broccoli the stems can be eaten raw or thinly sliced. Otherwise the best form of defence is attack – aggrandize it with classic sauces like hollandaise or maltaise as a vegetable centrepiece or use the brightest seasonings like chilli, anchovy or cumin.

BRUSSELS SPROUT

The Belgians claim the Romans introduced this relative of the Savoy cabbage, but they may be confusing it with broccoli. There was certainly serious cultivation there by the 13th century, which did not follow in England for another 600 years. Compact and tightly furled green – not yellowing – leaves are the best. Buy sprouts of a uniform size for consistency of cooking.

COOKING: *Apart from being boiled, they can be grated and then stir-fried, sautéed or puréed. The inherent nuttiness is reinforced in pairings with chestnut, hazelnuts and nut oils; or more traditionally, with cream and butter.*

CABBAGE

The motherly cabbage is one of Europe's oldest vegetables. The Romans saw it poetically as a cure for melancholy and it was a staple to the Celts and Saxons. The French expression *petit choux* is more endearing than the colloquial English use of cabbage for a vegetating person. Perhaps familiarity bred contempt... or over-cooking. In the kitchen it has the ability to surpass nearly all other vegetables and it has infiltrated the diet in ways which are often overlooked, like coleslaw, bubble and squeak, and sauerkraut.

The season of the cabbage starts in April with the first SPRING GREENS, which are all leaf and no heart, then follows leafy SPRING CABBAGE, and by July there is pointy-headed HISPI and PRIMO, with their tight bright, rugby ball shapes peaking out of stubby leaves. The first SAVOY starts in September, with the deep green SAVOY KING and the resplendent JANUARY KING beginning in November. The tight-leaved WHITE CABBAGE was originally from Holland, but the wild cabbage may well have been native to our coastline.

CAVOLO NERO is the black Tuscan cabbage, in season in November to coincide with the new pressing of the olive oil. Some can be grown here, but it is not produced on a commercial scale; some importing has begun recently.

Good cabbages are heavy, richly coloured and should squeak when squeezed. RED CABBAGES should have a grey blush on the outside, but rarely seem to. They need vinegar in the cooking to stop the colour fading. Very fresh cabbage leaves will actually weep.

COOKING: *A cabbage needs either short cooking or long slow cooking, though some dietitians favour cooking it twice: first blanching it and then braising or sautéing it to make it more digestible. Soups, casseroles with bacon or chestnuts, and stuffed cabbage are found across Europe. More modern approaches, like wilting and stir-frying with smoked haddock, grating it and dressing it with hot vinegar or pairing it with singular strong flavourings like juniper or cider, show it to better advantage. To counter the sulphurous smell produced when boiling cabbage, add a corner of stale bread to the water.*

SAUERKRAUT, pickled cabbage, is a valuable part of the diet for vegans who do not eat other fermented foods and was known as an early antidote to scurvy. For no reason that seems apparent the English pickled red cabbage where in northern Europe, especially Germany and Holland, white cabbage was used.

COOKING: *The cabbage is sliced and layered in wooden barrels with salt and usually seasoned with juniper or caraway. The tops of the barrels are weighed down to encourage the cabbage to ferment. They are then left covered in a cool place. At this stage the cabbage leaches its sulphur which makes for a very smelly process. A similar process was sometimes used where the last of the year's cabbages were trimmed and put into a hole in the ground and covered with leaves and earth. After a few months the cabbages turn white and are then taken out and kept in salt.*

CAULIFLOWER

This relative of the cabbage was first grown by the Syrians, Turks and Egyptians and only brought to Spain in the 12th century and to England in the 16th, possibly from Cyprus. Mark Twain famously said cauliflower was nothing but cabbage with a college education. He may have had a point.

New varieties have emerged with differently coloured florets. The so-called CAPE BROCCOLI, from South Africa, needs to be bought young and small; the turreted florets of ROMANESCO are disappointingly vapid compared to the traditional white curds. Eaten raw there is some redemption.

COOKING Cauliflower cheese was a highly fashionable and very rare dish in London at the start of the 19th century. Cauliflower has great potential for vegetarian dishes: with watercress sauce, with coriander, or with hollandaise.

CHINESE LEAVES

Chinese vegetables have begun to emerge from Chinatown supermarkets into mainline shopping. Most just need simple steaming.

PAK-CHOI grows amazingly quickly – from seed to plant in six weeks, thus providing two crops per season. There is a lot of white for the money – especially when older – and it tends to need the kind of strong oyster sauces that Chinese restaurants use on it. It is sold both as a vegetable and young as an extra for salad. The leaves are warming, spicy, moist and sour, with a good texture. Raw it leans instinctively towards dressings with Oriental spices or soy in them, and can be rather dominating in leaf mixtures. There is a green variety; in both this and the white the brilliance of the colour is a mark of their freshness.

More interesting is CHOY-SIM, which has to be grown quickly to stop it going stringy. Like spinach, it should have decidedly more leaf than stalk. CHINESE MUSTARD GREENS are more large-scale, with stalk and leaf. KAI-LAN looks similar to Choy-sim, but has more stalk than leaf.

Both are now being planted under polypropylene on a commercial scale in Lincolnshire and are likely to become more widely available. Huge plantations around Valencia begin to send to Chinese supermarkets from April.

SPINACH

Younger spinach leaves can cost twice as much as older, which is proper testimony to their worth. Having endured the worst excesses of over-boiling, zealous nannies giving children cups of spinach water and the bizarre inanity of Popeye, the rehabilitation of spinach is long overdue. The Arabs brought it to Europe, and it has been esteemed across the southern Mediterranean for centuries; used in tarts, with eggs, in salads, and also for its medicinal properties as the 'broom of the stomach'. It is a prime source of iron, calcium and vitamin A, although some say its high oxalic acid content works against their full benefit.

The summer leaves are round and in winter they are prickly seeded.

COOKING: *The leaves should be washed and placed in a covered pan without any extra water over a moderate heat, squeezed dry when they have shrunk and then married off with cream, butter and sometimes a very little nutmeg. Older spinach might have been designed for butter – it will absorb vast amounts. There is a famously unhealthy recipe from the great Fernand Point of Le Pyramide in Vienne in the '30s in which 900 g (2 lb) spinach are cooked with ham and bread along with 170 g (6 oz) butter, 300 ml (1/2 pt) béchamel sauce, 6 tablespoons double cream and 3 egg yolks. Today's cuisine favours treating the young leaves as salad, with strong flavouring accompaniments, such as bacon, avocado or blue cheese.*

SALAD LEAVES

CHICORY · DANDELION · LETTUCES ·
RADICCHIO · ROCKET · SORREL · WATERCRESS

The hothouse culture that has delivered fresh leaves to supermarkets throughout the year is one of the great triumphs of the past decade – even if we pay excessively for them compared to more traditional winter leaves. The mixed leaf combinations tend to be poorly understood by supermarkets and need careful sorting out. **Waitrose** now sells salad leaves still in the soil for extra freshness. Nevertheless, fresh leaves will be the tone of the next few years.

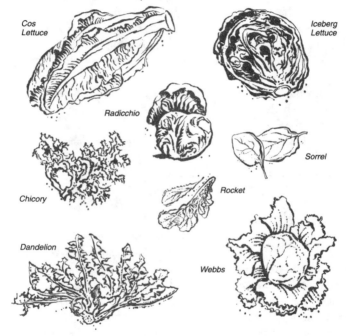

Cos Lettuce · Iceberg Lettuce · Radicchio · Sorrel · Chicory · Rocket · Dandelion · Webbs

THE RACKET IN THE PACKET

The pricing of mixed salads is wildly irrational and seems to take no account of cheaper leaves like the lollos, even cabbage, being used as bulk. Good mixes should need a minimum of dressing because the flavours and interactions should be sufficient on their own. Those with herbs therefore tend to be the most efficient and the best value. Look for contrasts of textures, say of escarole, oak leaf, radicchio and lamb's lettuce, and also flavours, say oak leaf, lamb's lettuce, spinach, radicchio and chervil.

CHICORY

Meaning now the WITLOOF, developed in the Brussels Botanical Gardens in 1850 as a forced and blanched vegetable grown in the dark, like mushrooms. There are earlier references of similar techniques being used on ships to supply fresh leaves. Before then it was a winter vegetable only, which accounts for the recipe list of warming braises. Its more modern role as a salad vegetable is botanically more appropriate. It is related to radicchio, both originally from succory.

Its infamous use as an adulterant in coffee began in Holland in 1830 and was banned here two years later. This was later relented on the grounds that some people liked it for what it was. The chicory used, however, was a different strain, sometimes called MAGDEBURG, where the roots are cut, dried in a kiln, crushed and roasted.

Much of the white chicory, with its beautiful yellow edging and precise bitterness, is grown here. As it wilts badly in cooking, it is better value as a raw vegetable than in the traditional braises with strong flavours like garlic, orange and mushrooms, or serving it with gamy meat or scallops for a texture contrast.

Equally pretty and novel is the development of the RED-TINGED CHICORY which is sweet at first bite, but becoming stronger and more bitter than the yellow.

COOKING: *Chicory makes an excellent gratin with breadcrumbs, bacon and a little cream added two-thirds of the way through cooking, or as a salad with farfalle pasta and blue cheese.*

DANDELION

Forgotten in the hedgerows and rarely making the market, this is one of the oldest native foods still running wild. The young leaves were among the 'bitter herbs' of the Old Testament and go for the regional French dish of *salade de pissenlits au lard* – with crisp bacon and the fat poured over. The *pissenlit* refers to its diuretic qualities. Related to wild chicory, the plant's roots are also used as a coffee substitute sold in health-food shops. The flowers make a retsina-ish wine. In the American south they go for 'poke salad'. Older leaves need to be blanched and treated like spinach.

LETTUCES

The cost of designer salads is now on a par with wild mushrooms and fillet steak. The mark-ups on a whole lettuce are in the region of 1,000%. The only work involved is separating the leaves from four different lettuces and putting them in a bag. This is convenience at an astronomic price. It is best to buy and make use of single plants. Try to match opposites of texture, of sourness, of bite.

EDIBLE FLOWERS

NASTURTIUMS were brought here from Central and South America, but are named after the old battle habit of piling defeated enemies' weapons in a heap – the leaves look like shields and the flowers like blood-stained helmets. Known to the Romans as *tropaeum* (trophy) hence *Tropaeolum majus*. Easily grown from seed, they are now widely sold in supermarkets and are one of the best flowers for salads. The leaves, buds and flowers are all edible. The leaves are peppery, the flowers are very pretty in salads; the pickled buds are akin to capers. It was always said chewing leaves will ease sore throats and the juice will clear pimples.

Supermarket flower mixes are often plumped up with more common petals, like marigold, pansy, viola and borage, all of which can pro-vide colourful decoration to salads, sweets and drinks.

BATAVIA, with its large handsome crenellated leaves, has a strong flavour, bordering on the sour with traces of acidity and metal. Characterful and dominating, 'very male'.

BUTTERHEAD is a good but undervalued lettuce, with lolloping large soft pale green leaves about 20 cm (8 in) across when compressed. The outside leaves are bitter and sour with hints of grass; the heart on the other hand is white and sweet. This lovely interplay produces an interestingly varied flavour that shows off dressings and other herbs well.

COS, sometimes called ROMAINE, is increasingly out of fashion, but the staple for Caesar Salad. The long leaves have a crisp texture, but not much flavour.

ESCAROLE is the primary braising lettuce. A thicker-leafed version of frisée, with thick white stalks and green leaves, it is rough, bitter and chewy, with a interesting – slightly meaty – flavour and bitterness in the stalk.

FRISÉE is sometimes called Endive. Like dandelion, this was one of the original 'bitter herbs' of the Bible. With thin stalks and wispish, brackenish leaves which are yellow at the stalk becoming green at the edge, it is sweet and crunchy – only bitter at the stalk bases. Good, grassy and clean-tasting, it is cleansing, although its content of vitamins A and C is slightly down on other lettuces. The singular flavour is good with a blue cheese dressing, and it can also be blanched and served as a vegetable.

ICEBERG is the classic crisp and crunch lettuce: clean and wet, it is mostly texture and bite and the flavour is elusive, if at all apparent. It is also not as effective a palate-cleanser as frisée. Weight for weight, whole Iceberg lettuces are considerably cheaper than leaves sold in packets.

LAMB'S LETTUCE, sometimes called CORN SALAD, has small

curly leaves with a mild peppery, floral – almost a pot-pourri – aroma. Not dissimilar to a gentler version of watercress but nearly twice the price. Use to season other salads.

LITTLE GEM is the gardener's favourite. Deep green going to yellow at the centre, it is small and bullet-shaped. Soft-textured, it has a real lusciousness from the thickness of the leaf. The taste is almost floral and slow to assert itself. A good lettuce for braising. SWEETHEART GEM, developed by **Tesco**, is a gem lettuce in which the strains of sweetness have been bred on so the leaves are distinctly sugary with minimum bitterness.

LOLLO BIONDO is the frilly light-green-leaved variation of Lollo Rosso. It has a neutral, rather sour taste, but a good texture.

LOLLO ROSSO is originally from Italy, but is now widely grown in the UK. Frilly and attractive, with a deep red fringe going to green in the centre, it has a good texture and is mildly bitter. Its popularity is more a matter of looks than flavour.

*OAK LEAF, or FEUILLE DE CHÊNE, owes its name to the beautiful large oak-leaf-shaped leaves, deep red at the rim going to green deep inside. A very glamorous leaf, a queen to the Batavia's 'king'. The outside of the leaf is soft and smooth, verging on the sweet, but with bite. It is bitter and assertive by the stalk, so there are almost two tastes.

RADICCHIO

Resplendently vermilion fused leaves paling to pure white have a beautifully crisp texture. In its native Italy it is often grilled, which does not help the colour, nor that distinctive gentle bitterness it gets from its cousin, chicory. It does not need overpowering with strong flavours, although it can handle them well enough. Go for younger plants.

ROCKET

Also known more pretentiously as ROQUETTE, the small 10 cm (4 in) long leaves are the most distinctive of all the salad leaves – indeed they are often listed as a herb when sold in pots – with a potent very sweet pepper taste and a texture that is strong and characterful, but still delicate enough to combine with other, milder leaves. It is something of a bargain in wholesale markets at £5 per kilo from France, Italy and Israel. There is a wild version which has thinner leaves. (See also page 210.)

COOKING: *Ideally suited to olive oil and Parmesan.*

SORREL

Brought by the Romans from North Africa to Northern Europe, the arrow-shaped deep green leaves have a pronounced lemon sour, or vinegar, flavour. Used as vegetable in the Middle Ages, it may be cooked as spinach; alternatively, use it in salads, in soup or to flavour fish sauces (only the briefest heating is needed or it turns khaki). It is high in vitamin C and was used against scurvy, but it also contains oxalic acid which may inhibit nutrient absorption. The commonest form is FRENCH SORREL, but BUCKLER SORREL is smaller-leafed and better for salads.

WATERCRESS

Nasturtium officinale from the Latin *nasi tortium*, 'nose twisting' (from its pepperiness), as watercress is known horticulturally, grows in lazy running rivers and springs in sandy soil, almost exclusively now around Alresford in Hampshire and in Dorset. It is a particularly good source of vitamins A and C and deserves rescuing from its ubiquitous fate as a garnish. Packets are usually poor value, containing the smaller (less developed) leaves and more stalk, and quickly going sour in their airless environment. Bunches tend to have good percentages of the better wider leaves. The pepperiness is concentrated in the stalks, which can be diverted for soups while the leaves go for saucing, salads and anything with eggs.

Salad Leaves

Comparison of different leaves as nutrition

	Calories	Protein g	Carbos g	Fat g
Butterhead lettuce	12	0.9	1.2	0.6
Iceberg lettuce	13	0.7	1.9	0.3
Spinach	25	2.8	1.6	0.8

VEGETABLES

Nutritional Values of different vegetables

	Cals	Prot g	Carbo g	Fat g	Fibre g
Asparagus	25	2.9	2	0.6	1.7
(boiled)	26	3.4	1.4	0.8	1.4
Aubergine	15	0.9	2.2	0.4	2.3
(fried)	302	1.2	2.8	32	2.9
Beetroot	36	1.7	7.6	0.1	2.8
(boiled)	46	2.3	9.5	0.1	2.3
Broccoli	33	4.4	1.8	0.9	0
(boiled)	24	3.1	1.1	0.8	0
Brussels sprout	42	3.5	4.1	1.4	3.8
(boiled)	35	2.9	3.5	1.3	2.6
Cabbage	26	1.7	4.1	0.4	2.9
(boiled)	16	1	2.2	0.4	2.3
Carrot (old)	35	0.6	7.9	0.3	2.6
(boiled)	24	0.6	4.9	0.4	2.8
(new)	30	0.7	6	0.5	2.6
Cauliflower	34	3.6	3	0.9	1.9
(boiled)	28	2.9	2.1	0.9	1.6
Celery (boiled)	7	0.5	0.9	0.2	1.6
Chicory	11	0.5	2.8	0.6	0
Courgette	18	1.8	1.8	0.4	0
(boiled)	19	2	2	0.4	0
Cucumber	10	0.7	1.5	0.1	0.7
Garlic	98	7.9	16.3	0.6	0
Leek	22	1.6	2.9	0.5	2.8
(cooked)	21	1.2	2.6	0.7	2.4
Onion	36	1.2	7.9	0.2	1.5
(cooked)	17	0.6	3.7	0.1	0.75
Parsnip	64	1.8	12.5	1.1	4.3
(boiled)	66	1.6	12.9	1.2	4.4
Parsley	34	3	2.7	1.3	8.2
Potato (new)	70	1.7	16.1	0.3	1.3
Swede	87	1.2	21.3	0.3	2.4
(boiled)	84	1.1	20.5	0.3	1.2
Tomato	17	0.7	3.1	0.3	1.3
Turnip	23	0.9	4.7	0.3	1.3
(boiled)	12	0.6	2	0.2	2.0

Vegetables are not sources of vitamins D or B12.

Carotene ug	E mg	Thiamin mg	Ribo mg	Niacin mg	B6 mg	Folate ug	C mg
315	1.16	0.16	0.06	1	0.09	175	12
530	1.16	0.12	0.06	0.8	0.07	155	10
70	0.03	0.02	0.01	0.1	0.80	18	4
125	5.5	0	0	0	0.70	5	1
20	0	0	0	0.1	0.30	150	5
27	0	0	0	0.1	0.30	110	5
575	1.3	0.10	0.06	0.9	0.14	90	87
475	1.1	0.05	0.09	0.7	0.11	64	44
215	1	0.15	0.11	0.2	0.37	135	115
320	0.90	0.07	0.09	0	0.19	110	60
385	0.20	0.15	0.02	0.5	0.17	75	49
210	0.20	0.08	0.01	0.3	0.08	29	20
8,115	0.56	0.1	0	0.20	0.14	12	6
7,560	0.56	0.09	0	0	0.10	16	2
5,330	0.56	0.04	0	0.20	0.07	28	4
50	0.22	0.17	0.05	0.6	0.28	66	43
60	0.11	0.07	0.04	0.4	0.15	51	27
50	0.20	0.06	0.01	0.3	0.03	16	8
120	0	0.14	0	0.1	0.01	14	5
610	0	0.12	0.02	0.3	0.15	52	2
444	0	0.08	0.02	0.2	0.09	31	11
60	0.07	0.03	0.01	0.2	0.04	9	2
0	0.01	0.13	0.03	0.3	0.38	5	17
737	0.92	0.29	0.05	0.4	0.48	56	17
575	0.78	0.02	0.02	0.4	0.05	40	7
10	0.31	0.13	0	0.7	0.2	17	5
5	0.15	0.09	0	0.3	0.12	9	3
30	1.0	0.23	0.01	1.0	0.11	87	17
30	1.0	0.07	0.01	0.7	0.09	48	10
4,040	1.7	0.23	0.06	1.0	0.09	170	190
0	0.06	0.15	0.02	0.4	0.44	25	16
350	0	0.15	0	1.2	0.21	31	31
165	0	0.13	0	1.0	0.04	18	15
640	1.22	0.09	0.01	1.0	0.14	17	17
20	0	0.05	0.01	0.4	0.08	14	17
20	0	0.05	0.02	0.2	0.04	8	10

Cooking appears to halve the nutritional value of the vitamins, albeit most of the cooking times in this survey exceeded 20 minutes.

FRESH HERBS

BASIL · CHERVIL· CHIVE · CORIANDER · DILL ·
FENNEL · LEMON GRASS · MARJORAM · MINT ·
PARSLEY · ROCKET · ROSEMARY · SAGE ·
TARRAGON · THYME

Many herbs are grown in hothouses here and in Holland, which has brought fresh herbs back into vogue and added wonderful new dimensions to cooking. If there is a fundamental difference between modern and traditional cooking it is that herbs take the place of spices like salt and pepper and are used at the end of preparation.

Leaf for leaf, the pots of fresh herbs weigh about the same as the packets, but are usually 25p more expensive. The advantage is that they keep, especially chives. Price differences are noticeable and subtly obscured. **Waitrose** have one price for all herbs, but different weights in the packets. **Sainsbury**'s parsley is £1.18 for 100 g and 85p for a pot, while their coriander is 59p for 15 g, or nearly four times the price. By contrast, **Waitrose** coriander is half the price of **Sainsbury**. **Tesco** fresh herbs in the pot have been 16p cheaper than **Sainsbury**. But then the mark-up on herbs can be as much as 400%. Selling in small packages is ultimately self-defeating as cooks need volumes of herbs, armfuls even. However, the way the trade makes the bunches even smaller keeps them out of mainstream cookery. For what they are, wholesale they are cheap, but retail expensive. For dried herbs see pages 306-314.

BASIL

There are different varieties and they perform in markedly different ways. Garden catalogues sell packets of BUSH BASIL, with short spiky leaves which have an intense aniseed edge, quite different from **SWEET BASIL which has a broad deep-green fragile leaf and is the true basil for cooking. There is also DARK OPAL BASIL and LETTUCELEAF BASIL. Commercial growing has introduced different strains, not all of which are successful. Some English pot-grown examples have striped ribs and hints of, 'metal, fresh cut grass, strong texture, not really what we all get excited about'. These are best used with oils in dressings. By September some of these pots can have grown enormous leaves up to 10 cm (4 in) long. There are also good examples flown in from Thailand, which has a profusion of varieties.

COOKING: *A pot on a windowsill will supposedly keep flies away and a tea made from basil leaves is said to be a sedative. Basil needs to be used generously in handfuls, not as a seasoning but as a prime*

Herbs				
Comparison of fresh and dried herbs				
	Calories	Protein g	Carbos g	Fat g
Mint	43	3.8	5.3	0.7
Parsley (fresh)	34	3	2.7	1.3
Rosemary (dried)	331	4.9	46.4	15.2
Sage (dried)	315	10.6	42.7	12.7
Thyme (dried)	276	9	45.3	7.4

flavour. The pots sold in supermarkets may suggest a dainty good housekeeping, but are a more accurate guide to portion control – use the leaves of the whole plant, and add them towards the end of the cooking – the flavour dies in the heat of the pan. They can be kept in the pot, but will shrivel if the kitchen temperature is not right.

Pick the smaller leaves, leaving the suckers and the top shoots. Tear them rather than cut to release their oils. Tomato is its main benefactor, but it is also the crucial influence of pesto pounded with garlic, pine nuts, Parmesan and olive oil. To freeze, first wipe in olive oil.

CHERVIL

This has delicate miniature fronds, looking like a green lace tablecloth, and swiftly loses its looks as it turns an unappetizing yellow. Chervil is one of the four French *fines herbes*, along with chives, parsley and tarragon, and is not out of its class in that company. It originated in the Middle East, but has become naturalized across much of Europe and can still be found in hedgerows here. Very much a favourite in restaurants, where it has displaced parsley as a more feminine and subtle garnish. It has surprising depth of flavour, 'somewhere between a rich fennel and a soft parsley'.

COOKING: *Like chives, it does not benefit from cooking and is best added at the final moment in deliberate small amounts, as if it was a seasoning. It marries well with eggs in all forms.*

CHIVE

Sometimes called CIVET, SWETH or RUSH LEEK, it is the smallest member of the onion and leek family. One of oldest culinary herbs, it was little used as a medicine and always associated with the kitchen. The flowers should be cut in June and July to keep the plant strong and can be used in salads. Use scissors to cut the fragile stems or they mush. Pots raised in Holland sell at 85p against 56p for the herb in the packet, but the pots will keep indefinitely and can be grown usefully on a windowsill. GARLIC CHIVES are a different species, *Allium tuberosum* not *A. schoenoprasum*, with flatter and wider stems than the ordinary chive, and white not violet flowers. Sometimes called CHINESE CHIVES because of their use in Chinese cooking, they are stronger than the European chive and should be used more sparingly. There is some confusion in early summer when Chinese supermarkets sell thick-stemmed but beautifully delicate fronds as long as 45 cm (18 in) to serve as a vegetable, either steamed or stir-fried.

COOKING: Snipped into 1 cm (½ in) strips, they combine well in all salads, go well with butter and have a deep affinity with new potatoes in a salad with a vinaigrette. They do not like the heat and are best used in the final preparation. Chives can substitute for salt in meat dishes and they freeze well.

CORIANDER

Possibly the world's most widely used fresh herb, dominating the cooking of the world outside Europe and North America. As recently as the '50s, English text books referred to the 'nasty, disagreeable odour' of the fresh leaf. Writers took gleeful pleasure from pointing out that the name comes from the Greek *koris*, meaning a bug (coriander was supposed to smell like bed bugs). Its main role in this country was as a seed used in gin, in pickling and to disguise less pleasant tastes like senna. The flavour of the fresh leaf is subtly addictive and has an affinity for chilli. In America it is called CILANTRO, from a Mexican and central American plant that is similar but of a different species. Coriander is a herb with bravura and demands to be used with a swagger not a limp, to galvanize parts of cooking too long occupied by parsley. Also, any highly spiced Indian dish.

DILL

This is commonly called 'false fennel', which is appropriate. The seeds are used in North-African cooking, but in Europe more usually in pickling combinations for gherkins and aromatic vinegars.

COOKING: The fresh fronds are universally stamped with the association of gravlax, where the sweet butteriness of the fish and the mustard of the sauce mute the tones of aniseed, but it can also be used sparingly in a salad and with other fish.

FENNEL

A biennial herb that can grow to more than 2 m (6 ft) in shady corners and is found across the Mediterranean. The leaves are thin green stems that form into feathers. BRONZE FENNEL is more properly thought of as purple. Stumpier in growth and with less delicate fronds, the flavour is less accentuated but in compensation it has the looks of nobility. (See also page 238.)

LEMON GRASS

A grass native to South-east Asia, *Cymbopogon citratus* is grown commercially to extract citronella oil that is used as an insect repellent, for cosmetics and soaps. The young stems (rather than the long brown leaves) are chopped for salads, and the roots crushed to add flavour but taken out before serving. It is essential to many Thai and South-east Asian dishes.

MARJORAM

In this country marjoram remains largely the province of gardeners, who grow it robustly both in the green form and the variegated golden. There is sweet marjoram, *Origanum majorana*, and the wild *O. vulgare*, more commonly called OREGANO (see page 210). The sweet combines well with pork, carrots and cucumber, but fresh should be added towards the end of the cooking when its marigold-style flavour is not lost in cooking. The stalks tend to be tenacious and should be discarded. Dried, the flavour intensifies significantly.

MINT

Mint grows wild across the world and there are many varieties. The sweet industry favours SPEARMINT, *Mentha spicata*, but more commonly found in gardens and seed catalogues is the round-leafed M. *rotundifolia*. APPLEMINT, M. *sauveolens*, has cream edges to downy green leaves. It attracts flies in the garden and is the least successful of the culinary mints, although it is said to have been the original basis for mint sauce. PEPPERMINT, M. *piperita*, has a purple stem and hue to the leaves; the oil is also used in the confectionery industry. There are other variations, mostly flourishing in different parts of the country, such as the decorative PINEAPPLE MINT or the perfumed EAU-DE-COLOGNE MINT, which have commercial applications and flourish better in some areas than others. The best use for the variations is as leaves in a salad.

Ordinary mint is pungent and dominating and needs to be used sparingly or with confidence. The hesitancy of older books seems less valid now with the emergence of more virulent comparable aromatics, like ginger or coriander.

COOKING: *Mint is a surprisingly friendly herb, combining well with fish and fruits such as orange as well as more conventional*

*pairings like that with new potatoes. For a Fresh Mint Sauce: chop
2 parts mint and add to 1 part sugar, blend with 5 parts white wine
vinegar and 5 parts water.*

OREGANO

Oregano is a relative of marjoram, and is rarely found fresh in this country.

PARSLEY

Native to the Mediterranean, *Petroselinum crispum* first reached here in the 16th century and was subsequently taken to America. All parsleys are rich in calcium, iron, vitamins A, B1, B2 and C, and deserve to be used more widely in cooking. They are too often miscast as a garnish and have been, rightly, replaced in the French kitchen by the more delicate chervil. The high chlorophyll content sweetens the breath, notably after eating garlic. Heavy parsley eaters are reputed to smell seductively sweet.

The densely curled-leaved varieties beloved of garnishes and garden centres are PARAMOUNT IMPERIAL CURLED, which looks like miniature kale, or MOSS CURLED PARSLEY, which is an unhappy relative that keeps getting rolled out for the wrong party. Raw, it is bitter and dry and one suspects its reputation is based largely on its bizarre role of livening up food shop window displays, a hangover from its brief moment of post-war fame when it came to be a symbol of a shop for serious cooks. More delicate and interesting is FLAT or ITALIAN PARSLEY, with larger fern-like leaves that have a more definite cutting flavour, edged with aniseed. HAMBURG PARSLEY, *P tuberosum*, looks like Italian parsley but is grown for its flavoured root and recipe history, associated with celery and parsnip. CHINESE PARSLEY is actually coriander (see page 208).

*COOKING: Parsley is best used as if it were a vegetable, generously
filling up casseroles, or where it can star in soups and purées, and
salads like tabbouleh. The stems are also useful in stocks.*

ROCKET

Also known as arugula, it is sold as both a salad leaf and as a herb, and, in part, it has the attributes of both. The spindly leaves are peppery and enliven salads with other strong flavours, like that of blue cheese or a very fruity olive oil. It is native to southern Europe but is easily grown here from seed. It needs to be cut before it flowers, otherwise the leaves become hairy and the flavour mustard-strong. (See also page 202.)

ROSEMARY

Rosmarinus or 'the rose of the sea', is native to the Mediterranean and will grow to 1.25 m (4 ft). 'There's rosemary, that's for remembrance,' says Ophelia in *Hamlet*. It was introduced here by the Romans and flourishes well enough in southern Britain, not necessarily by the sea. It likes full sun and well-drained soil. Commercially, rosemary oil is used in eau-de-cologne and toilet waters. In gardening catalogues Miss Jessup's Upright is neat and straight; O'Connell's Blue needs space and gives spectacular flowers which can be used in salads; there is also a creeping rosemary, *R. prostrata*, which is 'beautiful and functional'. The needle-like leaves are best used to flavour because, unless they are very young and fine and are diced small, they are quite hard to eat.

SAGE

A native of the Mediterranean and named after the Latin *salvia*, meaning to be in good health. For many centuries it was grown mainly for its perceived medicinal properties. The purple-leaved varieties are most commonly associated with healing. The leaves are harvested before flowering. Raw, they are delinquently strong, often said to have tones of camphor, but lose their pungency in cooking and have come to be used to underwrite other blander flavours, as in sage and onion stuffing, or to flavour milk dishes. They have other more peripheral uses. Fashionably they are deep-fried as a surprising garnish in restaurant cooking. Sage tea reputedly clears phlegm and was popular before China tea was imported. Chewing the leaves whitens teeth and they can be used as a scent in the bath.

TARRAGON

This may have originated in central Asia but was used by the Arabs and the Greeks. Tarragon enjoys a proud place in the French kitchen, being part of the classical repertoire in a Béarnaise sauce, in regional salads and most famously with chicken. It is also now the most expensive of herbs. In this country, however, it has been largely overlooked except as a flavouring for vinegar. There are two kinds: the paler, inferior RUSSIAN TARRAGON, which can be grown from seed but is coarse and of little merit; and **FRENCH TARRAGON which has to be cultivated by cuttings, but once established will submit to any amount of hacking around. The flavour is subtle, with elements of 'sharp aniseed, greenness and a mild fluorescent anaesthetic'. An aristocrat among herbs, like basil it can transform the mundane.

THYME

Thyme has a long history: the stalks were used as temple incense; bees are attracted to it and make an ancient dark-brown honey scented with thyme, marjoram and savory, from Mount Heymettus in Greece. Thyme was a symbol of courage, because it is supposedly mildly intoxicating, and was embroidered on the uniforms of crusaders; French republicans used it as a secret symbol of recognition. There are upwards of 50 varieties: common thyme is a small evergreen perennial, growing to 30 cm (1 ft). The leaves are tiny grey-green arrows which can either be diligently plucked off individually or, less diligently, the branch pulled through two fingernails.

LEMON THYME has a gold or silver edge, is highly perfumed, prettier and more feminine, and allies well with fish. Dried thyme is one of the most successful preserved herbs.

PODS & SEEDS

BEANS · BEANSPROUTS · OKRA · PEA · SWEETCORN

Pods and seeds are among the few types of vegetables with which freezing and canning really come into their own. Historically, corn, beans and peas were grown mostly for drying as winter staples. (See also pages 246-252). Massive plantings in Kenya have brought fresh vegetables to market all year round, but often the shelf-lives are too prolonged, and they are sold well past their superb best.

BEANS

Green beans are a modern development. Even country people would have been inclined to keep most of their crop for drying and storing as food for winter or to grind to a flour (see page 246). There are many varieties and variations, BROAD BEANS alone are known as SHELL BEANS in America or WINDSOR BEANS, FIELD BEANS and HORSE BEANS, which all pass in Latin as *Vicia faba*, with a parentage somewhere in South-east Asia.

Young BROAD BEANS, the size of a finger nail, are as fine a vegetable as young peas and maintain their allure even flown across the globe – even in February. Most broad beans now tend to come from Kenya, Egypt, Spain and Cyprus; while most of the UK crop goes for processing and PYO, where they are surprisingly early and usually finished before the full flush of strawberries begins.

Broad beans should be cooked or a condition called favism results in which the pollen from the plant creates anaemia and blood clotting. Dried broad beans are not widely stocked any more, but the price is linked to age and the cheaper they are usually the longer the cooking they need. It was these that sustained the old world before Columbus brought back not just the potato but the RUNNER BEAN, the GREEN BEAN and the FRENCH BEAN from Central America.

RUNNER BEANS were initially grown for decorative use on the walls of kitchen gardens. They were known for their scarlet flowers. The strings that bedevilled the early plants, especially the red flowering rather than the white, have been largely bred out of modern strains. As ever, however, youth is a virtue and there is little indication of varieties in markets or supermarkets so comparison is difficult.

FRENCH BEANS are so-called for their popularity in France after being introduced from America. They are the immature bean that would otherwise produce a haricot. The home-grown beans are

SPROUTING SEEDS

Seeds when sprouted offer a potent form of nutrition, as well as crunch and variety in salads and sandwiches. The best seeds for sprouting are peas, beans, alfalfa, parsley, celery and lettuce. They are best bought from health-food shops or supermarkets. Commercial industrial seed stock may have been treated with chemicals.

ALFALFA, a member of the pea family, has come to be confused with all kinds of other sprouting seed, but it was an important forage legume in many parts of the world. It originates from the Mediterranean and is sometimes known as lucerne. Two thousand years ago it was traded along the spice routes through Persia as far as China. The Spanish took it to America, where it spread across the more temperate regions and was used as early cattle feed. It is credited with many health-giving properties. The juice contains the amino acid *L-canaverine* believed to be anti-carcinogenic. It can also reputedly lower blood cholesterol.

COOKING: for *sprouting seeds any container will do provided it has clean drainage – a jam jar, colander or flower pot. Allow 2/3 teaspoons of seed to every 100ml (3 1/2 fl oz) the container holds. Soak the seeds in plenty of water overnight. Strain (the water can be used in cooking) and place the seeds in the container. Cover the container with a tea cloth or muslin so the seeds germinate in the dark. Water 3 to 4 times a day (strain off the water each time or they will rot). After 2 days, throw away any that have not sprouted. The remaining sprouts will be ready to harvest after 4 to 5 days. Most grain and vegetable sprouts can be eaten raw, but those of the pulses tend to need light simmering to make them more digestible: mung beans 3 minutes; lentils 15 minutes; peas 5 minutes; chickpeas 8 minutes; soya beans soak for 2 hours in running water and then simmer 15 minutes.*

harvested from June. Kenya supplies all year, but the quality seems to be getting increasingly slack.

Beans should snap cleanly when they are broken open and not be at all limp. All freeze well enough after being blanched.

BEANSPROUTS

These are usually from MUNG BEANS. Immigrant Chinese families brought the culture with them growing in small dustbins in their back rooms for family restaurants. They are a prolific crop, going from seed to sprout in four days. This has spawned a factory industry with warehouses able to produce 50 tonnes a day. Much is made of the nutritional advantages of sprouts, which seems in inverse proportion to their cost.

OKRA

The unripe fruit or pods of *Hibiscus esculentus*, a tropical plant that was first discovered in West Africa, okra came to Europe via Egypt around the 13th century and then migrated with the slave trade to the Caribbean and the American south. It used to be called GUMBO, (the name used in French Africa), but this is now only used for the Creole stew with oysters, fish, chicken and beef), or, prettier, LADIES' FINGERS.

It is its mucilaginous qualities that have endeared it to many styles of cooking. There are different varieties and styles of cultivation – the Middle-eastern culture uses them differently and has sought to breed out the mucilaginous qualities. There they are quite commonly pickled and in Turkey they are often found dried. In India okra is steamed as a vegetable – *bindi*.

The pods are best bought fresh and bright – older and larger ones tend to go woody. Originally it was imported into this country only in tins, but it has surfaced fresh in supermarkets and ethnic grocers. The pods should be perfectly green, not brown, and not more than 10 cm (4 in) long. They can be salted when sliced, like aubergines, to reduce the stickiness. Cook the pods whole, or sliced across to show the beautiful spokes. The seeds can be roasted and ground to make a coffee substitute.

PEA

The large commercial freezers and packers of peas have taken the copyright in their strains of pea and bought out the best seeds. What is left is found in gardeners catalogues or the few stragglers that manage to get to market. The Yorkshire blue was a highlight of the year but seems to have disappeared. Greengrocers tend to buy according to grower rather than variety. The pea has a schizophrenic history. In French and Italian courts they were eaten by hand as little snacks. The Romans reputedly ate them like popcorn as they watched the gladiators. Before potatoes, they provided the poor with a basic staple: the basis for soups such as Scotch broth.

PETITS POIS are literally young – therefore sweeter, riper – peas than those which go for splitting and drying. In practice, though, the trade glosses over the difference between young peas and the much mealier beige French varieties which just took the name. Very old pre-war varieties like Onward and Kelvedon Wonder are still widely available for amateur gardeners, who can get crops through to October – but few get to market after August. SUGAR PEAS and MANGE-TOUT PEAS are pea pods that are picked even younger, before the peas themselves have developed; the imports from Kenya and the new world have been massively successful. (See also page 252.)

BEST BUYS Price comparisons between fresh, frozen and tinned peas are complicated by the packaging which splits brands into sizes as various as 907 g, 410 g, 340 g and 145 g, and other devices that seem to offer 20% more or less. The big difference is between tins and bottles on the one hand, and frozen on the other. The other difference is between garden green peas and older style marrowfats, often with colorants, and the mealier French-style. Green is English, khaki French. In frozen peas, the gradation to 'garden peas' is essentially as much about size – they are probably the equal in flavour across the board. **Bird's Eye** has some justification in claiming to pick only the smallest and the sweetest. **Lindsey Manor** is most uniform. The difference between **Sainsbury's** 'Garden', 'Economy' and 'Peas' is so subtle as to be irrelevant. In tins, **Green Giant** 'Small peas', with added sugar and salt, are closer to the French-style petits pois, while **Morton's** look sensationally green thanks to the colouring and the use of added flavours. **Sainsbury's** tinned peas are indistinct and vapid, and a poor buy compared to frozen. Processed and marrowfat peas seem to have more liquid in the tin possibly on the argument that – because they are mealier and more distinct in flavour – fewer go further. The big brands like **Farrows** and **Batchelors** are bravely slimy and ooze gently out of their skins in a manner much closer to that of the historic pea, betraying a cousinage to something like a chickpea. **Safeway** colours its processed peas. *Sainsbury** does not, but then adds sugar to what it terms its 'marrow fats'

SWEETCORN

Whereas maize is one of the most important staple crops of middle-America, supplying all needs from liquor to cattle to grits (a gruel-like porridge), here it remains rather daintily in the realms of the etiquette of how to eat a corn on the cob. In Italy (as polenta, see page 357) and in Africa, corn is and has been an essential – the last crop before starvation, what the broad bean was to early Europe. South American corn is red, purple, black, brown. Here it is steadfastly yellow. Until the '40s, sweetcorn was only grown for fodder. GIs stationed here are credited with introducing it to this country.

Freshness is absolute, the more so with the older varieties. An old expression in the American South says to take the pot to the field and not pick the corn until the water has boiled. New varieties have, however, improved the keeping qualities. The old advice about only buying creamy coloured kernels is only relevant to older varieties (not that they are named in the shops) and new varieties can colour to golden. Fresh corn will ooze a milk if you nick the kernel with a fingernail, but as quite a few people know this trick it is worth checking that you are not buying a well-thumbed cob. Sweetcorn is invariably boiled, but it also bakes and roasts well.

MINI VEGETABLES

The rise of the mini vegetable has been a dynamic breakthrough. **Sainsbury** now stock baby Savoy cabbages and cauliflowers that fit in the palm of the hand. Also broccoli and beautifully small aubergines.

Many are ordinary vegetables picked young using conventional seeds that favour good looks at an early stage of development. They are mostly grown under plastic, sown tightly together, with the first pickings in March and the full season available from May. Such vegetables were first grown in this country in 1988 by Ron Smith at Colchester in Essex.

BEST BUYS Tinned sweetcorn, sold either as creamed or whole kernel, is arguably superior to fresh because of the steep decline that corn goes into when picked. There is really no contest between tinned and frozen, unlike peas it is the tins that win hands down. New 'light' versions have been introduced although in the case of Green Giant there is no clue as to why one is 'light' and the other not, because neither adds sugar and the label just infers that one variety is naturally sweeter. Light versions are more insipid. Supermarket own-labels boost the impact with doses of sugar and salt. **Sainsbury** own-label borders closely on the overly sweet. To achieve the creamed consistency **Green Giant** uses cornstarch and sugar, which makes the contents distinctively soupy and sweet. The best is probably the ordinary **Green Giant** and the **Safeway** unsweetened. **Citation** from France are vacuum-sealed without water, but are sadly dry as a result.

COOKING: *For a tinned sweetcorn salad: hard-boil 2 eggs, shell and quarter them. Quarter 2 tomatoes. Mix together with a 500 g (1 lb 2 oz) tin of sweetcorn, using the juices for the dressing. Season with a generous amount of freshly ground black pepper.*

ROOTS, TUBERS & BULBS

BEETROOT · CARROT · CELERIAC · GARLIC ·
GINGER · JAPANESE ARTICHOKE · JERUSALEM
ARTICHOKE · KOHLRABI · LEEK · ONION ·
PARSNIP · POTATO · RADISH · SALSIFY · SWEDE ·
TURNIP

Root vegetables have sustained populations all over the world for millennia. Attempts at different varieties in supermarkets seem half-hearted excuses for increasing mark-ups. Often the differences between varieties seem poorly understood, with the prime being sold cheaper than the everyday. Large differences in price attach to packaging – loose, in boxes, or washed. In mitigation, root vegetables start from very low price points.

BEETROOT

Beetroot originates from the southern Mediterranean region, possibly North Africa. The Greeks and Romans used it for its leaves, but it was brought on by German gardeners in the Middle Ages.

There are other beets in the family, notably SUGAR BEET, developed in the 17th century and taken on by Napoleon when his supplies of cane sugar were threatened, as well as SWISS CHARD and the fodder MANGEL WURZEL. The Victorians were enthusiastic about beetroot and reputedly even sold the juice as a hair pomade. Although the red is standard, there are occasional white, yellow (unfortunately named Burpees) and pink varieties found in seed catalogues – as well as a cylindrical variety.

Young beets are sold with the leaves from June, the main crop following six weeks later. A deeper colour indicates a longer, unforced growth cycle; too large and they become fibrous. Its public image is rather that of a throwback to a vegetable Stone Age, a yobbish and unruly vegetable that stains the kitchen and the grocer's bench and has to be constrained by tight plastic bonding before being allowed into the sanitized glare of the supermarket. It is maligned as a lost cause. Many are cooked at the farm and drenched in acetic acid which may account for their poor standing. The ready-cooked vacuum-packed, long shelf-life types are at best 'emaciated'.

Beetroot needs more cooking than one suspects, and is best baked slowly in foil until the skin comes away easily. If it is pronged, it leaches messily. Stains can be removed with lemon juice, but the betanine compounds invariably stain the digestive tract. Like artichokes, beetroot is best served tepid. An inexpensive vegetable, properly cooked it can be sublime.

COOKING: *Beetroot combines well with grown-up assertive flavours like oranges, apples, capers, anchovies, nut oils and horseradish. The way they sustain all the variations of the Russian classic beetroot soup, borscht, stresses their adaptability. For the colour, do not over-cook or just add the beetroot at the end of cooking.*

SWISS CHARD is grown for its thick white stems, and the leaves are often used in some parts of France in recipes for stuffed cabbage, or mixed with meats in charcuterie, pâtés, and in Italy also for sweet tarts.

CARROT

The carrot was found wild across most of Europe, though early varieties tended to be yellow or purple rather than the more familiar red – which reportedly came from Afghanistan. The idea that carrots help you see in the dark was first put about by the Ministry of Defence in 1940 anxious to ensure that their vitamin A content was used to counter deficiencies that might lead to night blindness. Their vitamin C content is almost as significant. Most of the nutrients lie near the surface, so carrots should only be peeled if really necessary. The pale central stalks on old carrots are worthless and tasteless, and best consigned to soup.

Carrots have become a slothful, somnolent giant occupying acres of shelf space with seemingly little enterprise behind them, content to be seen as everyday bulking agents. In 1987 **Safeway** moved towards identifying different varieties: the small, sweet Parisienne; the tapered, tangy Chantenay; the sweet, crisp Mokum; and the prime juicer Zino. This enthusiasm seems to have waned lately.

Growers' names for varieties of carrot read like the characters from a strip cartoon series. Early carrots will be Primo, Nelson, Nanco, Nantucket, Gringo or Panther. Other varieties betray a sinister laboratory hand as in PSR10480-91, about which *Grower* magazine commented, 'an Imperator type, unfortunately likely to be too long and thin for most outlets'. The names may also evoke redundant geography, like Yukon, Newmarket, Seine or Normandy. Such diversity does not seem to be the privilege of the consumer.

The round carrots featured in gardening catalogues are rarities. The old trade practice of differentiating the new season's carrots by selling them with their leaves is two-edged as the leaves suck out moisture quickly. An improvement in packaging using micro-perforations has compensated. UK growers claim to have their carrots in the shops within 24 hours, against imports at a week. Carrot prices are elastic: 19p per lb loose, 27p per lb in bags, 44p per lb for organic and a massive £2.25 for elegant little – usually badly scrubbed – dwarf carrots.

Pesticide usage has been limited to three times a year, following findings that some carrots have had high levels of residues of organophosphates.

COOKING: *The legacy of carrot jams, cakes and wines is a reminder of their dexterity and role as a source of sweetness for all cooking, as well as their endless friendliness towards flavourings like orange, lemon and lime, herbs like thyme and marjoram and coriander, and even stronger influences like Pernod and nut oils.*

CELERIAC

The other name for celeriac, TURNIP-ROOTED CELERY, explains its ancestry more accurately. It was developed in Europe by Renaissance gardeners and brought here in 1723. It is a winter root available from October. The best are younger – about 450 g (1 lb) in weight, with smoother skin so there is less waste. The leaves are sometimes used to flavour soups, but are rarely sold now. The root should be firm with no signs of softness or mushiness. Once peeled of its hairy brown skin, the flesh discolours quickly and needs to be kept in acidulated water. It is usually cheap so represents very good value.

COOKING: *Grate raw and dress with vinaigrette or mustard mayonnaise; mix with potato to a purée; use in a gratin. It is an assertive and powerful vegetable that pairs well with other strong flavours that can take advantage of its fennel/aniseed tones, such as orange, lemon and horseradish.*

GARLIC

Garlic is a cultivar and the shapes and characteristics come from the preferences of the growers in different regions. In Lautrec they favour a strong, leek-like spike in the centre. In Venice the whiteness of the skin is paramount. The heat of the flavour, it is said, derives from the length of the days. Longer growing times and colder nights mixed with hot days, as in Portugal, Turkey and Hungary, produce the hottest.

The potency lies in a compound, alicin, which comes about when the garlic is cut, mixing the naturally present chemicals allinin and allinase. For the same reason, the way garlic is cut, crushed or squashed affects its virulence. Cooking actually arrests the process; it loses its bitterness and becomes sweet, with hints of artichoke and potato, or in the rose variety, chestnut.

Early books concentrated on garlic's medicinal virtues; it was a poor man's cure-all. It was used against leprosy and the plague and was left in saucers at times of cholera to dispel evil spirits – which may be linked to its role in tales of vampires. Up to the First World War it was mixed with sphagnum moss as an antiseptic. The COMA report suggests the evidence is inconclusive, as it may be necessary to eat as many as seven cloves a day for positive effect.

Coincidentally or not, it is associated with diets where there is a low incidence of heart disease – even accommodating some of the more unexplained areas that the fashionable Mediterranean diet does not, South-west France and Korea in particular.

For centuries cookery writers rejected it: John Evelyn, Mrs Beeton, Escoffier – even, quite recently, Tom Stobart – were against it. The cult of garlic is strictly a modern-day phenomenon. The festival in Gilroy, California – which produces 90% of American garlic – started in the '60s and now attracts tens of thousands of participants each year. The Isle of Wight Festival in August attracts 30,000. Across France each region has its own excuse for a fair.

The garlic season begins with the first trimmings and wild garlic arrives from France in May. The tiny purple bulbils are as potent as whole cloves. Fresh garlic is briefly available in June and July, but rarely found here. The peak is at the end of August, when the two big French growing areas – Lautrec (for rosé, or pink) and Beaumont – have had enough time to dry on the *grappe* (plaited string) and these begin to come to market and then slowly the more northerly areas follow.

BEST BUYS The best garlics are the pink from **LAUTREC – especially **Lucien Cadayon** – and the white from **BEAUMONT. The Lautrec tends to keep its potency beyond November. Other areas produce good garlics, but most of what is sold in this country is poorly graded by comparison. Italian garlic can be as good: the **VENETIAN-STYLE is brilliantly white-skinned, heavy, strong and keeps well. NAPLES-STYLE is rounder and flatter and does not keep so long. CALIFORNIAN GARLIC is derived from Italian. Spanish is particularly valuable early in the summer, when the supermarkets are filled with very poor and brutal examples from Mexico and USA. English garlic, from the ISLE OF WIGHT, is not to be instantly dismissed; based on cultivars from the Auvergne, it suffers from peaking at the same time as everyone else but is creditable. EGYPTIAN tends to be small-cloved and does not cook well, but is chilli hot – if briefly so.

The trade buys on the size of the cloves, because restaurants do not want to pay to peel smaller ones. Solid bulbs are what are wanted. Out of season, a big bulb may not correspond to bigger cloves, especially in early summer when there is a lot of rubbish about. The age of garlic can be told from the size of the kernel and the growth of the sprout in the centre. It keeps better on the *grappe* than singularly.

ELEPHANT GARLIC is a cross between an onion and garlic. Grown in Chile, the giant bulbs are sold ceremonially boxed and are very mild, like an oversized shallot, with a slightly sour smell that becomes like sticky vanilla. It is overpriced for what it is, at five times the price of ordinary garlic.

SMOKED GARLIC is an increasingly fashionable trick. The smoke overpowers the garlic but some say that it 'adds the smell of smoking bonfires to a casserole'. Others hold that it 'smells out the shopping basket with stale farts'.

GINGER

Thought originally to have come from China, ginger is endowed with medicinal qualities as a blood-thinning agent that can carry other remedies around the body which are enthusiastically supported by herbalists and are a feature in Chinese medicine. Of all the foods listed in this book, ginger seems the most likely success story of the '90s. Just as garlic's reputation rose on the back of French cooking, so ginger's reputation gets stronger with the assimilation of Asian ideas.

Ginger is an underground stem out of which stubby hands topped with small buds form. The roots are in fact cut off before marketing. It flowers, occasionally producing a cluster of yellow and white flowers which are flecked with purple. Botanically, *Zingiber*, with variations found in Japan and Thailand, is closely related to turmeric. It likes hot weather and grows in India, Australia, Jamaica, China and Nigeria. Jamaican ginger coming into West-coast ports would have been the basis for much early English cooking of gingerbread.

Gingers from different regions are discernibly different. AFRICAN tends to be harsh and camphorous; INDIAN is, 'lemony'; JAMAICAN is, perhaps surprisingly, mild, and was regarded as one of the best; FIJIAN is a, 'melony lemon', COSTA RICAN is, 'deep citrus and tongue-searingly strong'. The best is probably from *HAWAII, first arriving in February, 'handsome long roots without gnarls, smooth-skinned and almost silvery beige in colour, stalky texture, potent, somewhere between lemon and grapefruit. Very citrus'. Or another sample later in the year, so probably older, 'knobbly, yellowing, rootoid with much stalk, lemon floral smell, not too harsh'.

Supermarket examples tend to be sparse and poor compared to those in grocers, especially Indian and Chinese shops. The price is arbitrary but as the trade deals in lbs, those supermarkets (**Safeway**, **Somerfield**) that split it up into grams are usually calculating on high mark-ups. Even so, it remains inexpensive for something so potentially influential. It will freeze for up to three months and can be grated still frozen.

JAPANESE ARTICHOKE

Also known as the CHINESE ARTICHOKE or, sometimes, CROSNE, these pretty and unusual tiny rootoid ringlets, not more than 6.5 cm (2³⁄₄ in) long, are originally from central and northern China, though the French village of Crosne adopted them in the last century. Available from October to March, they have no skin and are used raw or lightly baked or stir-fried.

JERUSALEM ARTICHOKE

A variety of sunflower (*Helianthus tuberosis*) native to north America. It was first identified in 1605 and brought to the Netherlands two years later to be cultivated. The association with the flavour of artichokes was the reason for the name, and the other is a corruption of the French word *girasole*, meaning sunflower.

The wasteful knobbliness of early varieties and their justified reputation as a flatulent, made them unfashionable. Old textbooks harshly denigrated them as 'sweet but soapy', but they do have a commercial use as a source of alcohol fructose which has sustained them.

They are easy winter vegetables to grow and available from October to March. Imported varieties take Russian-sounding names, like early, very white *Bianka* and attractive *Topianka*; while UK plantsmen favour *Fuseau*, which is almost nodule-free.

COOKING: *Peel and keep in acidulated water; then steam, bake or microwave, or roast in their skins. They go well with potatoes and asparagus, but their strong flavour needs to star in any combination.*

KOHLRABI

Introduced from Germany around 1558. Kohlrabi was regarded primarily as fodder for sheep. It is an excellent undiscovered food, high in vitamin C and with a subtle flavour. On young roots, keep the skin as this is where much of the flavour congregates. More tender than other root vegetables, because it grows on top of the soil, it is part of the cabbage family and most often likened to turnip. The leaves can be eaten but do not store well; nor do the roots freeze well, except when very small.

GREEN KOHLRABI has a thick lime-green skin and a bowling-ball shape about 8 cm (3¹⁄₄ in) across, with spooky tendrils. Raw it has a mild celery-to-turnip taste and some of the texture of good potatoes; steamed the turnip flavour develops and the texture is arguably better.

PURPLE KOHLRABI is slightly larger and nuttier, with peppery overtones. Raw, it has a flavour akin to an apple/potato. but when cooked it seems more of a marrow/turnip. A good buy.

LEEK

There are different theories as to the origins of the leek. Some texts say Europe, even more precisely Switzerland, and others think points further east. They have been cultivated for a very long time, and leeks were often a second crop in southern Mediterranean vineyards.

Most of the leeks here are home-grown, with first samples coming as early as July, grown under polythene, or from France. Most of the work on the breeding of varieties has concentrated on the keeping qualities so that leeks pulled in March can hang on in over the spring.

Good leeks are young and erect, with a good percentage of white. New washing techniques have cut out the perennial problem of flushing out the dirt trapped between the leaves. The huge allotment award-winning leeks are inedibly bitter.

ONION

Onions are the most universal of foods eaten in every country, almost it seems as far back as the Persians. Quite what happened to *Danver's Yellow*, *Nuneham Park*, *Blood Red* and *Giant Rocca* is not a matter of culinary record. *Ailsa Craig* survives in some seed catalogues, as does *Bedfordshire Champion*. However, the varieties that dominate post-war allotments have disappeared for the most part, to be replaced with shovelfuls of unidentified Spanish or obscure Japanese varieties that can over-winter. Warmer climates mean larger and sweeter bulbs.

The new season's crop is usually available by September, but the sophisticated storage methods used for onions can obscure the differences between the new and the not-so-new. In fresh onions there will be no sign of sprouting in the central core. Good onions will also be firm and well-coloured.

The skin lends colour to stocks and casseroles. Once cut, they lose their potency. Keeping them in the fridge cuts down their ability to make you cry as you peel, as will peeling and cutting under water.

The beautiful RED ONIONS seem more different than they are: the exquisite purple casing around a deep white inside offer higher notes and a sharp cleansing juiciness. As they cook, however, the true differences between onions are in levels of sweetness: the red being much higher pitched – a trumpet to a Spanish onion's bassoon – but with sufficient complexity to be served raw.

PICKLING ONIONS: the gleamingly white *Paris Silverskin*, about the size of a marble, survives as a variety for gardeners and professional growers. There is also the darker-skinned and larger *Giant Zittau*.

The SHALLOT is a small clustering variation of the common onion, cultivated originally around Bordeaux. They are stronger than onions, but have less smell. There are different varieties: grey-brown, blush-pink and – most common – bronze, which are known for their longer keeping. Unlike onions, they should not be browned or they will become bitter; braise them slowly. They are preferred by restaurant cooks as a more subtle variation on onions, with more of the positive notes of garlic without the smell,

SPRING ONIONS are merely young onions forced for their stalks. The long-standing *White Lisbon* first established itself as an early crop and remains defiant in the face of competition from Japanese hybrids. WELSH ONIONS are not Welsh at all, but from Siberia; they are coarser and longer-lasting, because the bulb does not form.

COOKING: *Onions were always poor man's food and there is a great repository of hearty recipes for stuffing them. An old peasant recipe from Provence blanches whole onions and garlic, removes the central core of the onion, pounds this with the garlic and some olive oil and puts this back into the onion to bake coated in breadcrumbs. A white sauce with onion was traditional with lamb. These ideas have been overtaken by more fashionable dishes like French onion marmalade or glazed onions.*

PARSNIP

As with many indigenous vegetables, parsnips were always said to be at their best after the first frost of the year. Native to Britain, it has been cultivated here since Roman times, although often despised as food for cattle or as overly sweet compared to other roots, like carrots. They respond well to other flavours, especially seeds such as sesame or pine nuts, and the stronger spices like turmeric and ginger, and butter – as in the saying 'soft words butter no parsnips'.

POTATO

The potato season was officially opened with the delivery of the first Jersey Royals to the Queen on April 26. Now the ceremony is gate-crashed by earlier Egyptians and Sirema from Noirmoutier followed by an unholy rush from Cornwall, Pembroke and all points south.

Potatoes were discovered in the high Peruvian Andes between 1531 and 1536. The high plateau remains a huge and largely untapped resource of black, blue and misshapen specimens that might yet again source the world for another 500 years. These first specimens brought back by the Conquistadors may well have been sweet potatoes. Walter Raleigh was the real enthusiast and planted some on his estate in County Cork. At first they were reviled and treated with suspicion, and it remains unclear just what happened to turn them into one of the world's most essential crops.

By the time of the famines of 1845 Ireland had become a one-crop nation, and when that crop failed hundreds of thousands died. It was also the Irish who are credited with taking the potato back to North America, where they were called 'Murphys'. The cultivation of potatoes began seriously in England in the 1750s, when they started to appear in large numbers on the London markets. By 1836, no less than 136 different varieties were being grown commercially. This was not a healthy and forgotten seed bank, rather it is a list of species that have evolved against blight, scab, disease and viral infections. The potato is a fickle and fragile plant.

The height of the potato's popularity was in 1870, when it occupied almost twice the acreage it does today. The potato was a common man's food and was the first expression of the allotment. The country gardener grew for himself; the commercial grower grew for the cities.

The test of an early potato is the skin, if still soft and pliable then the potato is still young.

The dry summers of '94 and '95 sent prices spiralling up to a record of 29p per lb for main crops as against a '93 average of 12p per lb. The bag of potatoes even featured on East Anglian television's Crimestoppers, as rustling became rife.

BEST BUYS Potato prices swing wildly according to bulk: Estima are 22p per lb loose, the equivalent of 17p per lb in 2.5 kg packs and 16p in 5 kg packs. Also sold as 'Baking potatoes' at a hefty premium: in 2.5 kg packs at 23p per lb – or 6p more for same potato; **Waitrose** has sold the same potatoes for baking at nearly 40p per lb compared to Estima loose at 16p per lb in the same week.

Packets affect prices too: Spanish Nicola potatoes in the box are 86.2p per lb, but unwashed in the bag or loose only 32p, or washed in the packet 45p. The premiums attached to the influx of new potatoes need to be checked against the salad potatoes carefully, as the resplendent Charlotte are often sold cheaper than inferior Maris Piper.

ARRAN COMET is one of the large Arran family developed by the great Scottish grower Donald Mackelvie. The Comet was introduced in 1956 after his death and for two decades was a major potato from Cornwall. They bulk up quickly and tend to be sold either as small new or large. The younger versions are long, yellowy-brown with darker pocks; the dense white flesh with a star-burst of sweetness. Growers now see it as a rather dated crop.

*BELLE DE FONTENAY is one of the oldest potatoes still in circulation, dating back to 1885. Although posing growers difficulty, particularly in dry years, they have been continually esteemed at the table, especially in salads. Larger and fatter than La Ratte, they are also darker with a silken smooth egg-shell skin. Soft on first bite, the flavour builds into butteriness and goes well with oils and vinaigrettes.

CARA is a highly fashionable potato among growers. Originally from Ireland, it responds well to growing conditions in Cyprus and Egypt. One of the better baking potatoes widely found, it is not quite as good as the King Edward which it is replacing.

*CARLINGFORD, introduced from Ireland in 1982, has a very classic old-fashioned sense about it. Well favoured by **Marks & Spencer**, the light brown skin turns grey/beige. The white flesh smells a little of socks, but is creamy and distinctive. It is good boiled, steamed or microwaved.

**CHARLOTTE is a new French variety first introduced in 1981 and now starting to be grown here. Pear-shaped and often slightly larger than the smallest new or salad potatoes, it is the rising star of the potato world. It is brilliant boiled, baked they taste of pure chestnuts. Use either in salads or as a main vegetable.

CLEOPATRA is a new early variety introduced in 1981. Red, like Désirée, and speckled and blemished, they have firm, dense flesh that has high flavour notes. It promises more than it delivers and is only suitable for boiling.

CORNISH used to enjoy a similar standing to Jersey Royals, which they have sought to exploit, though much of the acreage has gone over to a new variety, COLMO, first introduced in 1979. It is small round dark-skinned and white-fleshed and inclined to wateriness in the cooking. Missing the classic dry chestnutty finish, it is a side-show rather than a main event.

DÉSIRÉE is a red variety introduced from Holland in 1961 and widely grown around the world. It is liked by the trade as it is a heavy cropper and is a familiar sight at many farm shops. The flavour is pronounced and it is best used for roasting.

DIAMANT are brought in as new potatoes in January. The small examples from Egypt tend to be underdeveloped and inoffensive, with tones of chestnuts in the background – but also that 'Smashy' flavour.

DUNBAR was one of the great potatoes of the '30s, with varieties like Cavalier, Rover and Yeoman. A long wide potato, it has slightly greying skin which is cracked like that of an old man. Tending to absorb a lot of water, it seems poor in today's company.

ESTIMA is much liked by the trade because it is high yielding; the tubers bulk up early, but can stay happily in the ground afterwards. First introduced in 1973, it has established itself as an everyday potato. It is a classic example of a trade that ignores flavour. Mashed, they taste very white and institutional; they tend to break up as a roast; baking pronounces its vapid cardboard taste. A lot of very poor samples are found in spring and early summer, dumped on the market and quick to sprout.

**JERSEY ROYALS were first introduced to Jersey around 1879 by Hugh de La Haye and swiftly became the main agricultural preoccupation on the island, until eventually the Jersey States department ruled that no other potato should be grown. It is now only grown on Jersey, where the soil seems uniquely adapted. Although prohibitively expensive in early May, by June they become widely affordable. Despite the growing competition, this is still a wonderful and unique potato. Brown and kidney-shaped, with a fragile skin, it has a strong body and a distinctive chestnut flavour.

KING EDWARD enjoys a legendary reputation which has been encroached on in recent decades. It was developed originally from a seed stock called *Fellside*

Hero in Northumberland in 1902 and within four years was already well-known. For the first half of the century it was the most popular potato in Britain, second only in planting to the *Majestic* (eventually to fall victim of skin russeting and bad cracking). The King Edward was vigorous and a good cropper, but inclined to be erratic in dry seasons. Once again in this story the invidious hand of the war-time Ministry of Food is seen interceding, decreeing that the GLADSTONE, a much heavier cropper, replace the KING EDWARD. In the '50s, however, the Gladstone was beset by blight. The drought of 1975-76 inflicted a natural blow to the King Edward, followed by the threat – eventually suspended after public protest – of an EU ban on all potatoes that had no resistance to warts. From the second most-planted potato in this country in 1974, it fell back to tenth by 1984; although its presence in the supermarket is maintained by imports from Egypt. It is as a roasting and baking potato that it is primarily known, though it boils well enough. Although it does not enjoy the same status as it once did in previous decades, it remains a good benchmark against which to judge new varieties.

**LA RATTE is another very old variety, dating back to 1872. For many years it was disliked by English gardeners, who found the small tubular growths proliferating everywhere in their beds. New seeds have come over from France and imports are being revived. Outstanding and justly famous, it has milky brown, innocent-looking skin which is slightly marked; the cream flesh has notes of chestnuts and sour greens, rising to a second taste of sweetness.

LINZER DELIKATESS, introduced from Austria in 1976, was designed as a salad potato to rival La Ratte – which it does not. Tubular, going to pear shape when larger, it has a creamy, soft yellow, nutty skin, with a smell of bitter honey. It is a good minor potato.

MALAGA is large and clumsy. Usually sold washed, it is a good potato but not in the company of other new varieties.

*MARFONA was introduced in 1977 and mainly now comes from Cyprus. A beige yellow, lightly marked, it has a sour nutty flavour. Better than Estima, but...UK crops are another story. The trade still sees the variety as an early baker, but boiled or mashed it is outstanding – the rising star of the potato world.

MARIS PIPER, the favourite of chip shops, was introduced in 1963 and took up the position vacated by the Majestic, though its merits as a mainline potato are increasingly being brought into question by foreign imports. It remains the biggest planted potato here, but breaks up easily on boiling and prefers the tougher treatment of baking, roasting and chipping. It needs the right soil to be grown in gardens – neither too light nor too heavy.

MONA LISA was introduced in 1984 and comes mostly from Portugal. They tend to be large for new potatoes, fat square ovoids, beige/yellow on the outside; waxy inside with a floury texture. A good mainstream new potato, but not special, it has a well-rounded flavour of sour chestnuts.

NADINE was only introduced in 1987, is now widely found in supermarkets, and often organic. White to yellow, with a smell of chestnuts, the deathly white flesh has a cloying acrid aftertaste and breaks up easily.

Potatoes

Percentage fats of calories in different raw and cooked potatoes

		Calories	Protein g	Carbos g	Fat g	% Fat of Cals
New	(raw)	70	1.7	16	0.3	3.8
	(boiled)	75	1.5	18	0.3	3
	(canned)	63	1.5	15	0.1	1.4
Old	(raw)	75	2.1	17	0.2	2.4
	(baked)	136	3.9	31.7	0.2	1
	(roast in corn oil)	149	2.9	26	4.5	27
	(roast in lard)	149	2.9	26	4.5	27
Chips	(frozen, in corn oil)	364	4.5	41	21.3	52
	(home-made, in corn oil)	189	3.9	30	6.7	32
	(home-made, in lard)	364	4.5	41	21.3	52
		189	3.9	30	6.7	32
	(oven-ready)	162	3.2	30.3	8.2	36

NICOLA, derived from German stock, was introduced in 1973 and is now a popular potato from Cyprus, Egypt and Morocco. It is said to be a stronger version of a Wilja, which is hardly a compliment. It is best boiled as an everyday potato, and not really worth paying a premium price for it.

NOIRMOUTIER is from the island of the same name, which – like Jersey – is one of the fabled isles south of Nantes where the sandy soil and the algae produce a special potato. The island is all oysters and potatoes. The first, Charlottes, are highly prized and arrive about the first week of June and run through to September. Before that is the Sirtema, which is a little fragile to be said to be in the same class, but is neatly rounded and with good skin and texture.

**PINK FIR APPLES are the oldest potato still commonly sold in supermarkets and are enjoying a revival 144 years after they were first introduced. Distinctively elongated and shaded a pink that turns to a mellow beige-yellow on cooking, it is meant for salads and serving cold in the skin. With an excellent mealy, soft texture – like condensed clouds of potato – it also has a shrill nose and slight sourness, turning to an overwhelming sweet surge, with a long-lasting taste of clear chestnuts. A very good potato, it keeps quite well without losing its 'new potato' flavour.

ROMANO has an attractive red skin which pales in cooking into pastel shades of either mahogany in baking or mauve in boiling. The flesh is cloudy: baked it is inoffensive and weedy; boiled it has a nutty-neutral mildness. The skin is quite edible and the texture holds up, but the flavour is slightly reminiscent of dirty socks. The quality is very variable from area to area.

**ROSEVAL looks spectacular on the supermarket shelf, with its deep red – almost purple – skin. First developed in 1950, it was until recently quite rare, but is now increasingly common as an import from France. A mild version of La Ratte, the distinctive pinky to deep red/chestnut small kidney-shaped ovals, contain parchment flesh which is tinged yellow and has an alcoholic perfume, redolent of warm chestnuts. This good, well-balanced mix of flavours and skin is a good match for salmon.

SANTÉ is a new main-crop variety introduced in 1985. It is a good roasting potato, especially brushed with olive oil. Baked or boiled, it is innocuous and needs peeling. It has a good texture and a slightly sour grassy taste.

SIEGLINDE, although listed in textbooks as rare, is a 1930s variety which provided the parentage for Linzer Delikatess and was being sold in supermarkets in some volume this year from Cyprus. The long ovals with yellow skin have a chestnut smell and nutty taste; quite soft, they break up in mouth.

VIOLET, sometimes called TRUFFE DE CHINE, is brought over from France either for the restaurant trade or for upmarket **Sainsbury** stores. They are deep purple ovoids, sometimes with eyes, a rough skin and bleeding violet. We have had two examples in the last year: the one direct from Rungis in September was floury and had a superb mild taste of chestnuts; another later in the year from **Sainsbury**, apparently a snip at 99p per lb was blue-skinned, with a rough outside and a watery texture. Unattractive and unappealing, it had the looks of a drowned body and a vapid flavour... a bit of an off-putting silly novelty.

WILJA may have peaked after 15 successful years; it is now being replaced by new varieties. Developed in 1972, within eight years it had occupied 11% of UK fields, overcoming the perceived problem of the yellowness of its flesh. It is best known for its boiling qualities.

Although not even distantly related (they are actually members of the convolvulus family), SWEET POTATOES are native to tropical America and remain an important subsistence crop. They were almost certainly the first potatoes Columbus brought back, pre-dating the common potato by some decades, possibly even by a century. The potatoes Shakespeare mentions were certainly sweet potatoes, and were used in pies.

There are two kinds: the white-skinned and the red-skinned, both with yellow waxy flesh. The white are drier, not so rich and less dense.

COOKING: *Both cook in the same time as ordinary potatoes, but do not keep as well. Their rich sweetness responds to tropical flavourings like brown sugar and cinnamon. Recipes invariably seek to give an edge to them, suggesting sherry or even Angostura bitters for baked; candied with brown sugar and brandy with roast turkey; mashed with apple and orange juice.*

RADISH

The family relationship with turnip and horseradish describes them well. Radishes are an ancient food, cultivated in China and Japan for millennia for their freshness and looks. Here they have become the province of the gardener, with seed catalogues offering different kinds from the perfectly formed deep crimson globes of *Cherry Belle* to the elongated white-tipped *French Breakfast 3*. In the shops they are still just plain old radishes.

In France and Italy they are eaten with sea salt as a starter. They are rich in vitamin C. Medium-sized ones are the best; any larger and they become woody. They are overlooked as a cooked vegetable but can make attractive gratins with cream, or can be glazed with sugar or honey as a vegetable to accompany meat. They lose their crispness within 48 hours with the leaf on. Packets tend to be cheaper (they don't have the weight of the leaf) and are longer-lasting but less pretty.

The almost 1 m (3 ft) long MOOLI or JAPANESE RADISH is from the same family, but is a less attractive creamy white without the sharp peppery heat.

SALSIFY

This has enjoyed bouts of fashionability across Europe at different times, though outside of country areas it has rarely established itself as part of the dietary currency in this country. It used to be called the 'vegetable oyster', because the taste was said to be similar or more likely, as Jane Grigson argued, because it was used as an alternative to oysters in meat pies. It appears from October through the winter and the slender beige roots are surprisingly delicate; they bleed easily and discolour quickly once the skin is off and need keeping in acidulated water. They are easier to peel if first soaked overnight. Raw, they go in salads; cooked they are usually boiled or steamed and then finished with a stronger medium, like butter or chicken stock.

SCORZONERA is from the same family, but has a black skin and so is sometimes called BLACK SALSIFY. Its survival has been as much to do with its supposed medicinal qualities – against snake bites and leprosy in particular.

SWEDE

A varietal form of the turnip (as is rape), known in America as RUTABAGA, it was introduced here in 1781 via Sweden from Bohemia and usurped the place of the turnip in much of northern cooking – which is why recipes confuse them. They are a true winter vegetable and should be firm and strongly yellow to orange in colour.

COOKING: *They are best in mashes with violent flavourings, like pepper and horseradish; or roasted or consigned to stews and casseroles, where they can make their presence felt. Most famously, mashed swede or 'neeps' is traditional with haggis.*

TURNIP

The swede arrived much later and replaced the turnip in northern cooking. Today the distinction is plain: turnip is a spring vegetable when young; swede a winter stalwart. The turnip has history on its side. The Romans cultivated them – the name comes from the Latin *napus* and it was a staple before the potato and used as cattle fodder. However, it was looked down on. The French for a cock-up is a *navet*. Their poor standing comes from being too old and too big.

COOKING:*The best are small, the smaller the better, and should be cooked with flavourings that emphasise their sweetness, like honey or orange. Very young, they can be served raw with just a vinaigrette containing some herbs.*

The tops used to be sold separately; peppery leaves that can provide different dimensions to spinach recipes. While this practice is still common in Europe and the southern states of America, it has died out here.

Many recipe books suggest recipes for turnip and swede are interchangeable, but that mis-states the case for both. Any turnip that can do the job of a swede is too old.

SQUASHES
COURGETTE · CUCUMBER · MARROW ·
PUMPKIN · SQUASH

The replacement of the huge tasteless watery marrow by the petitely perfumed courgette symbolizes the transition of food shopping from one era to another. The arrival of squashes possibly heralds yet another. They provide challenging new frontiers for the cook.

COURGETTE
Elizabeth David is credited with the arrival of courgettes here, where their larger brothers the marrow had previously dominated. Seed catalogues are now expansive, with yellow and even striped variations, some of which occasionally arrive in the shops.

On a good courgette the skin will still be tough enough to resist a fingernail. The best are small, cigar-shaped and need to be eaten swiftly. They will keep for several days in the salad drawer though their flavour becomes elusive.

COOKING: *They can absorb other flavours in casseroles, most famously in* ratatouille, *but are versatile enough to accommodate strong herbs like fennel or rosemary and will soak up oil like aubergines if they are not salted first. In restaurants, they are served decoratively with the flower still on, often shallow-fried or stuffed with a light mousse.*

CUCUMBER
The cucumber originated in the Himalayan foothills, and found its way to ancient Egypt. It used to be colourfully graded as 'Fine', 'Bastards' (misshapen), 'Chumps' (big), 'Double Chumps' (seedy) and 'Spotted' (marked). There are two kinds: the familiar long thin HOTHOUSE or FRAME CUCUMBER (developed by the Romans) and the shorter stubbier RIDGED CUCUMBER, which is grown outside and usually goes for gherkins. They are at their best in late summer, when the sun has been on them. Most of their best combinations combine them with hot summer dishes.

COOKING: *They have a refreshing sympathy for strawberries and salmon. In Europe they are often paired with cream or yoghurt, as in the Greek tzatziki, or tomatoes, as in gazpacho. Earlier in the year, imports are frustratingly erratic, with high densities of pips and tough skins, especially those from southern countries. If they are to be cooked, they need salting like aubergines or courgettes.*

MARROW

The marrow comes from America where it was assiduously cultivated by the Indians, and did not arrive here until the 16th century. The huge marrow beloved of the garden show and the harvest festival possibly says a great deal about our national attitude to food in past eras. Size is not everything: a good marrow is not more than 25 cm (10 in) long, before the seeds have matured and the flesh becomes coarse and stringy. They should be cooked in a minimum of added water as, after all, they are 90% water.

PUMPKIN

Pumpkin is also native to the Americas, the Pilgrim Fathers' first Thanksgiving dinner was turkey, cranberry and pumpkin. A bland vegetable, it needs saucing. There is a lot it can do – breads, jams or bulking stews – but a soup with strong flavourings, like saffron or cinnamon, or a pie illustrate its true worth. Pumpkins will keep for a few months, which allows time to plot a strategy of recipes – the vegetarian homesteader's equivalent of killing the pig.

SQUASH

Squash look more spectacular than they taste. They belong to the same notoriously watery family as melon and marrow and need marrying off with rich flavours – but they do repay the work. The recipe repertoire is still in its infancy, although American books are far more advanced, where the focus of Halloween has given the whole field the same emphasis that turkeys get at Thanksgiving. The larger squash can be hollowed out and the shell used as soup containers.

Younger examples in summer, like the pretty little PATTY PAN in shades of green and cream with crenellated edges, respond to light cooking with herbs and butter.

BUTTERNUT is the bulbous pale beige formation most widely available, about 20 cm (8 in) or more high. Inside the firm flesh is fragrant and vivid orange, with only a small amount of seed. Cooked, it comes somewhere between swede and carrot; slightly more delicate and a little floral, it mixes well with other root vegetables and is distinctive enough to avoid the usual blandness label. Microwave or roast in oil.

GEM, a neat round deep green, the size of an orange with hard skin, is also widely found. Boil for about 25 minutes, then halve, seed, and serve with butter (quite a lot).

STEMS & STALKS

ARTICHOKE · ASPARAGUS · CARDOON ·
CELERY · FENNEL

The horticultural classification of vegetables shows how far the languages of the gardener and the cook have grown apart. Celery, chicory or fennel might as happily be listed with the salad leaves. Their unusual availability and good value – at least of the first two – contrasts with the aristocratic prices of asparagus and artichoke, both of which oddly seem to have lost ground in the English garden while their culinary fame has spread.

ARTICHOKE

Essentially a Mediterranean plant (*Cynara scolymus*) that flowers from July to November, its name comes from the Armenian *ardischauki*. There are two main strains; the stubby milky-green-leaved artichoke of which the best known is the CAMUS DE BRETAGNE (or more colloquially GLOBE ARTICHOKE), a tall plant growing to 2 m (6 ft), with a violet edge to the leaves as it gets older and deep purple silken core; and the VIOLET, which is earlier, has spikier leaves, a narrow deep heart (so is less good value), is inclined to bitterness as it ages, as well as becoming progressively more purple in coloration.

The artichoke is a perennial plant that flowers annually. The smaller heads found in Mediterranean markets are from the same plants, but have not been pruned in spring and so send out many smaller branches which produce youthful heads. The crop in Britain is marginal, the climate mitigating against producing the size of heads that most supermarkets now demand. However, they have been cultivated here from the 1500s. Usually they will be Camus de Bretagne.

Woodiness and stalkiness are signs of either an overly long growth cycle, without enough sun, or that the artichokes have been stored too long. Italian examples have tended to be the best-looking. The season starts properly in July and trade price is around 25p.

COOKING: *Boil for 30-40 minutes, then turn upside down to drain; or microwave. The lower leaves should pull away gently and the hairy choke removed. They are best served tepid, rather than hot, with a sweet herby vinaigrette. Remember that artichokes clash badly with red wine.*

ASPARAGUS

Originating from eastern Europe, asparagus was known to the Greeks and also here, especially as a wild plant. The Arabs introduced it to Spain, where it still flourishes. Modern varieties trace their ancestry back to around the 1100s. It is part of the lily family, but contains an odorous chemical, methyl mercaptan, which scents the urine and has encouraged the idea that it is a diuretic.

Beds will last 20 years in most gardens, though professional growers replant after 10. The crowns start to bear shoots from the third year and then give their best in years four and five. Quality is supremely about freshness. The asparagus year starts on April 21, with the first English from the Isle of Wight, the main crop following through May and June, supplemented with fine examples from France and then a succession of lesser imports. These start with California, Washington and Virginia in later summer; Peru in October; New Zealand, Zimbabwe and South Africa for December; and moving slowly north to Mexico by January and California again in February; with the first earlies from Egypt and Spain in March.

The development of the New World cultivation in the last 20 years has brought a uniformity to varieties that previously invoked all manner of descriptive allusions – the Danish fairy-tale goblin names like the large *Backlim*, the grooved *Boomlin*, *Gijnlim* and the fat, widely grown and ascendant *Franklym*, or else ostentatiously classical, the old French *Argenteuil* or the other English favourite, the first all-male variety, *Lucullus*. At other points growers gave up and turned to the expedience of *Connover's Colossus*, still widely grown by gardeners, or the scientific *University of California 140*. The Americans opt for the tweeness of *Mary Washington*, the forerunner of *Mary Grand* and *Mary Green*. The varieties are dominated now by Franklym and its derivations, an all-male variety (females dissipate their energy in flowering) with lime-green stems, and mauve epaulets and spears.

As important as the variety are the soil, the climate and the speed with which they get to market. In the 19th century, England grew more asparagus than any other country, mostly in the London suburbs of Battersea, Fulham, Deptford, Mortlake and Chiswick, where it was known as 'sparrow grass'. The best came from the Vale of Evesham.

Evesham has a micro-climate – an otherwise 'horrible' soil of heavy clay is topped up with river silt from the Avon when it floods, as it still does in winter. The Vale is surrounded like a horseshoe on three sides by the Malvern, Cotswold and Clent hills, which protect it from the north and easterly weather, but opens up across the river to the south-westerly. As a result, here are produced the first crops – some 11 days before, say, Derby. The height of Evesham asparagus production was in the '20s, but it has fallen back to half that amount, and other areas – notably

Lincolnshire – have come on line.

Cito is grown along with *Franklym* on the Isle of Wight. A cousin variety, with similar outside markings, the core is more substantial. It replaced Colossal and Mammoth for commercial growing on the island. It is not quite so sweet, and has a tendency to flatten out in the larger stems.

> COOKING: *When cooking green asparagus, the simple approaches are the best: lightly trimmed, the woody end of the stalks cut off (and reserved for soup), green asparagus is best steamed or microwaved and served with butter when hot or olive oil and Parmesan, or hollandaise sauce when cold. Asparagus also has an affinity with egg yolks, and good salt and individual flavourings like paprika, hazelnut oil in a vinaigrette, or herbs. To avoid asparagus soups becoming sourly sludgy, add a blend of green herbs or celery tops to give texture and colour. Use the tips as garnish. White asparagus will take more robust extenuated cooking, such as gratins.*

BEST BUYS EXTRA FINE ASPARAGUS, from South America and Thailand, is available most of the year. It is small, about 8 cm (3¼ in) long, and pistachio green with pink to white epaulets and spears. They have a good texture but not much flavour cooked; raw in salads, they are pea-like and nutty with a good crunch. Out of mainline UK and French seasons, these make a good buy, and are not horrendously expensive by designer salad prices.

**EVESHAM ASPARAGUS is the *Franklym* variety. One reason for Evesham's reputation is that it produces slender green spears – straight, neat, about 1 cm (½ in) across and well trimmed, with a sweet taste, especially at the white core. Although delicate, it has a good crunch. UK growers argue that the cooler climate allows the flavour to develop more slowly. Other growers claim that the optimum is a short fast spurt. For flavour, indisputably the smaller and more slender are the best; the macho virile varieties have already shot their bolt.

FRANKLYM, from Cambord in the Loire, is usually bigger than UK examples, being nearly 1.5 cm (⅔ in) across and slightly woodier as a result. Mild to start, but with a strong developing taste right up to a mild artichoke flavour.

*SPRUE arrive early in the growing season only, often from France. The tiny lime-white young shoots hang across the hand like a necklace. Pliant, succulent and gentle, they are very nutty raw in salads and have a superb texture when cooked as a vegetable, with no trace of woodiness.

UNIVERSITY OF CALIFORNIA 140 is an imitation of the Franklym. An example from Lincolnshire was a slightly redder mauve on the epaulets and spears, but with a similar shape and difficult to tell apart. They were curled rather than straight, and were less sweet than Franklym, tending to be green all the way through and missing out on the lack of the core.

WHITE ASPARAGUS is grown differently, with the earth ridged up on all sides to protect them from the light. White is favoured ahead of green in France, Belgium and

Germany (there is also a violet), but essentially the different approach creates a different vegetable with a bitterness closer to chicory and a meatiness that deserves marriage with other flavours, like meat. Very little is imported. Some unidentified species sampled from the Loire were dirty on the outside and needed scraping; woody and cracked horizontally, the spears were more heart-shaped than ears. Really more of a vegetable, they were succulent if stalky and bitter like chicory. Good for cooking in gratins and as a vegetable.

CARDOON

Related to the artichoke, *Cynara cardunculus* is a tasty vegetable that is rarely found these days. It is invariably earthed up to blanch the leaves and keep them white, and is mostly used in salads.

CELERY

Sometimes called SMALLAGE or WILD CELERY, this is native to the south-east Mediterranean region and the Roman and the Greeks held it as a symbol of grief. It arrived here in Tudor times and was initially seen as a medicine and for eating raw. The ground seeds are used with lemon verbena as an alternative to salt and are used in pickling or as a sedative tea. The pale green varieties are now predominant. Self-blanching, the leaves are trimmed and neatly packed. The white varieties, often still with soil attached, are the older trenched celery and can be found in specialist greengrocers, especially in the North. On market days, there were celery men and celery washers as recently as the '50s. The cliché of serving it with cheese has little merit other than providing a refreshing end to the meal. Celery's main role is is an essential ingredient in most stocks and it is also good in braises and gratins.

FENNEL

Sometimes called FLORENCE FENNEL, this is a bulbous aniseed-tasting root vegetable as well as a herb. For the Egyptians, Greeks and Romans it was primarily a medicine and the Italians are only said to have started cooking it in times of severe famine. Smaller bulbs tend to be better than large, and they should be white rather than green, and tightly configured.

> COOKING: *They may be grated raw for salads, or steamed, sautéed or even made into gratins. The flavour is pervasive and needs strong companions, like tomato and basil and olive oil – or judicious portion control.*

VEGETABLE FRUITS

AUBERGINE · AVOCADO · CHILLI PEPPER ·
SWEET PEPPER · TOMATO

The vegetable fruits are among the miracles of the story of food in the 20th century. Taken from their tropical jungles and happily transplanted into new climates, they have become ubiquitous. For the most part inexpensive, they lend fascinating new dimensions to our diet.

AUBERGINE

The aubergine has more names than a vegetable ought to have, EGGPLANT, EGGFRUIT and GUINEA SQUASH; in America it was sometimes called JEW'S APPLE or MAD APPLE, though the name probably derives from the Sanskrit, *vatimigana* – it is still an important part of Indian cooking. Its first appearance was in China in the 5th century and it seems to have arrived in Europe after the Greeks, strangely because aubergines are one of the cornerstones of modern Greek cookery. They probably came via Africa with the Moors into Spain and reached here in 1597, initially as beautifully decorative plants.

Its popularity here has mainly developed in the last decade. The UK crop is grown under glass and first go on sale in July. However, sun and water are what an aubergine needs, so imports generally have more flavour. Mostly we see the purple-to-black-skinned varieties, but there are mauve, white and striped versions – some with fanciful names like the graphically evocative *Monstreuse de New York*. The bitterness associated with older varieties seems to have been largely bred out. The skin of the aubergine is nutritious and wherever possible should not be peeled and discarded.

A good aubergine will be spongy; as it ages, it goes soft and the calyx turns brown. It is sensitive to ethylene and should be kept away from tomatoes and apples in a fridge or it will ripen too quickly. There are different opinions on the value of salting – either slice and soak them in salted water for 30 minutes, then squeeze out the brown juices and drain for another 30 minutes; or slice and cover with salt for up to three hours. Some say they absorb more oil after salting, others less.

COOKING: *Recipes tend to be influenced more by shape than variety: long and thin for stuffing, round for slicing. Above all other vegetables, the aubergine is in sympathy with the Mediterranean flavours of lemon, parsley, tomato, garlic, courgette, oregano, onions and olive oil. All of which appear in their main-event dishes, such as* ratatouille, moussaka, imam bayildi (*aubergine caviar, sometimes just with lemon juice, garlic and olive oil, but in other variations also using tomatoes).*

To roast them, they should be pricked to let the air escape and stop them bursting. Alternatively, slice them in half, brush them with oil and roast for 30 minutes, until soft. Mix the flesh with basil, garlic and oil and replace in the skins to eat with a teaspoon. The same trick works well with the Japanese sweet mirin and miso as flavourings.

AVOCADO

The avocado has been known in Central America for more than 7,000 years. The Aztec word for the plant meant 'the testicle tree', from the way the pods hang off the slender laurel-like leaved branches. In the Amazon they are eaten at the end of a meal with cream and sugar. Over the centuries it has acquired names that tell their own stories – 'poor man's butter', 'mountain pear', 'midshipman's butter', or 'alligator pear'. It was first taken to Jamaica around 1650 and arrived in England about 1895. An inhibiting agent in the leaves prevents it ripening on the tree and, like the banana, it is ripened en route – or, only too often, is sold totally unripe and as a result rock-hard.

They are high in fat and the B vitamins. In producing countries they are given to babies as their first solid. Israel and South Africa supply most of the winter avocados; Mexico the summer.

COOKING: To ripen an avocado, wrap it in foil or in a polythene bag and leave in a warm place. Unlike melons, the sides should be pliable; squeezing the tip you will damage the end. They do not freeze well. Out of the skin they discolour swiftly, which is one reason for the supremacy of recipes that use acidic dressings, like vinaigrette, or the Mexican dip guacamole, in which it is mixed with onions, tomatoes, chilli, garlic, coriander, parsley and lime juice.

BEST BUYS There are four main varieties of which the usually (though no longer exclusively) black-skinned hass is very much in vogue, though South Africa has been developing other strains which may appear soon.

ETTINGER, shiny and with a brighter green skin than the Fuerte, is almost exclusively from Israel in winter.

FUERTE was once the most commonly found. Pear-shaped, dark green, with slightly rough skin, it is available all year.

*HASS has the highest oil content and for this reason is perceived to be the best. The skin is pebbly purple to black, though some examples from Israel remain resolutely green; the flesh is more supple.

NABAI is plump, round with a shiny green skin, and mostly from Mexico through autumn.

From Israel there is also a stoneless avocado, called the COCKTAIL AVOCADO, about the size of a gherkin with quite a small ratio of flesh to skin. The BRAZILIAN GIANT AVOCADO looks the part but is, sadly, mostly stone.

CHILLI PEPPER

Chillies are always credited to Bolivia, but the profusion of varieties further south, in India, in Thailand and also in China suggests that that area may not have had a monopoly on the smallest of the capsicum family. Chillies are a sub-culture of their own, with countless variations. Recipes are prescribed for individual varieties in cuisines as different as Mexican and Indian. Their brutal heat was a poor-man's spice, making the unpalatable palatable, but they have now developed their own cachet and cult status, and exotic named chillies have begun to surface in **Sainsbury** and **Safeway** and in specialist stores.

The welcome introduction of fresh chillies in **Sainsbury** and **Safeway** might be tempered by the prices at nearly £9 per lb for Caribe and nearly £7 per lb for Anaheim. Street markets sell the 1 cm (1/2 in) long BIRD'S EYE pepper for less than 1p each; extra-hot bell-shaped PEPPERONE for 5p a piece, or the much larger, 10 cm (4 in) long, red and orange sheaths of SERENADE for 10p.

Jalapeño

Bird's Eye Chilli

Hot Bonnets

The broad rules are confusing. GREEN should be hotter than RED, because the *red* is riper and therefore sweeter. But the hottest chilli of all, the HABANERO is red. What **Sainsbury** calls green chilli is actually a box half full of red ones.

The choice is further complicated by the market. India now claims to be the largest producer of chillies in the world, with a quite breathtaking range of undocumented varieties. The very small multi-coloured chillies that come from Thailand often claim, rightly or wrongly, to produce some of the hottest recipes. The more organized information coming through Mexico suggests another scale of ratings, which is in turn compounded by a fourth, more colourful, jumble from the Caribbean. The result is that much of what reaches the market remains tantalisingly anonymous.

Sight is no indicator of heat. The only guide is a cook's instinct. Chilli is a culinary adventure playground. The seeds and membrane contain more of the heat-giving agent capsaicin than the flesh does, so these need to be handled and extracted with care – with gloves or under water. The heat is measured on a scale in Scoville units. A bell pepper will rate 0; a Habanero rates 300,000, though this is commonly now scaled down to 1-10. Without a prolonged period of building up heat tolerances, it is

DRIED CHILLIES

Dried chillies add a further dimension. Pasado is light and smoky, with hints of citrus and dried apples, herbs and celery. It is used in soups and stews. Pasilla, known as little raisins – a parody on their enormous liquorice black pods nearly 20 cm (8 in) long – have a taste of berries, grapes and liquor-ice, and are mostly used in sauces and with seafood. Cascabel is also called 'the little rattle'; beautifully decorative and round, 4x3 cm (1½x1¼ in), with black grape skin, the pips shake inside like maracas. The flavour is nutty and woody, with a rounded heat. It is best known in its own salsa, but also in slow-cooked casseroles. Guajillo continues the confusion over chillies with this large leathery red-skinned pepper. Tom Stobart writing in his *The Cook's Encyclopaedia* in 1980 called it 'exceedingly hot'. Dodie Miller of Cool Chile gives it a mild rating of 2-4/10. 'A sweet medium heat with tones of fruit, citrus, green tea and pine'. It is often used with fish. Ancho is the dried variation of Poblano, both widely used in Mexican cooking, often as constituents for cooking. Stobart says, 'rather mild and rich'. Frances Bissell says, 'hot'. Miller says, 'medium 3-5/10'. Red turning black with a crocodile skin texture and distinctive umbrella handle stalks, they are sweet and fruity, with hints of coffee, liquorice and tobacco. Chipolte is the smoked version of the well known stubby Jalapeño that underscores much of Tex-Mex cooking. The smoke fundamentally alters its impact without undermining the heat, which remains above the average.

To use, the stalks and seeds are taken off and they are reconstituted in hot boiling water for 20 minutes and then puréed ready for use. They can also be lightly toasted before soaking, but must not burn.

not possible to compare different varieties in the same way that it is for other foods. The less strong chillies invoke flavours of fruits but, as the heat rises over the midway point, smokes, liquorice, and Marmite begin to edge in. To counteract the heat, add sugar or drink some milk. The heat factor is something of a distraction from the flavour, but chillies also respond differently in cooking if they are cut, left whole or ground, and different parts of the same chilli taste different – this is part of their fascination. They freeze well.

BEST BUYS   ANAHEIM is a long fat finger, about 15x2 cm (6x¾ in), scarlet turning cricket-ball-red, sometimes sold younger when still green. Fat enough to slit open and stuff, they are relatively mild.

CARIBE is tapering at the end, 7x2.5 cm (2¾x1 in), ranging from lemony white to bright orange and deep red, going brown as it over-ripens. Quite sweet and mild, it is often used crushed or powdered in Mexico, or in *salsas* when fresh.

HABANERO is innocently pretty, a deep orange box-like lantern, 2.5x2 cm

(12x³⁄₄ in), sometimes sold green, possibly a different species from other Mexican chillies. It is the intensity which marks it out at the top of the heat scale, but also for aficionados. Fruity and intense, it is widely used in salsas, stews, most often with fish and curries. In the dried form, they are a rusty red and look like small sun-dried tomatoes, and reconstitute into a fiery tropical fruit heat.

HOT BONNETS are reputedly the hottest of the Caribbean chillies. Small and squat, as if they have been sat on, they come in yellows, greens and reds.

INDIAN CHILLIES: the green is used fresh, while the red is usually dried. The best-known is the KASHMIRI, but this is a name often invoked for other varieties. A true Kashmiri is bright red and neatly plum-shaped. Few go for export. It is more likely that the chillies here will be the more elongated GUNTUR, a bright red pepper that goes largely for curry powder because of its strong colour.

SWEET PEPPER

The rise of the sweet pepper has symbolized the supermarkets move into fresh vegetables. Sometimes called a BELL PEPPER to distinguish it from the chilli pepper, to which it is related but does not share the heat. Peppers were brought to Europe by Columbus from the Americas, but have happily transplanted to green- and hot-house cultivation.

The GREEN PEPPER is the unripe version of the YELLOW or the *RED, which is probably the best example. Other colours, such as WHITE or PURPLE, tend to be cosmetic, with only marginal differences in flavour which are mostly down to ripeness not variety. Occasionally interesting, smaller red peppers are imported from America. Peppers are good sources of vitamin C.

COOKING: *The white seeds have to be taken out as they are not nice to eat. Depending on the recipe, the skin is stripped off – grill or roast in the oven to char the skin which can then be peeled off. Heat brings out their full motherly character. The red pepper can reinforce tomatoes, adding a deceptive warmth, and provide an interesting basis for soups or can be puréed for sauces. They also freeze well.*

Slice a red pepper in half and remove the seeds and the stalk. Place 1 anchovy fillet in each half, followed by a wedge of Mozzarella cheese, and a basil leaf. Add 1 tablespoon or more of olive oil to each and bake for 15 minutes.

TOMATO

Although usually classed as a vegetable, like melons and courgettes, tomatoes are on the botanical borderline. The berries are the fruit of the annual plant *Lycopersicon esculentum*. The range has become breathtaking, but for all the manipulation of the genes, growing cycles, and the feed, it has been the flavour that has suffered. Tomatoes may look the part, but they don't taste it.

Tomatoes have been in the forefront of genetic engineering. In America the FLAV'R SAV'R tomato has been on sale in supermarkets, its genes altered to slow down its ripening. Many people have bought them for kitchen table decoration rather than cooking. The genetically altered tomato, based on the Ailsa variety, was licensed for use in the UK in January 1995. Its first application is in sauces and ketchups. There was considerable publicity given to the **Co-op's** rejection of the first samples and other supermarkets' comments on the poor taste. This was more to do with the recipe than the tomato. In a blind tasting of six formulations, four using genetically engineering tomatoes and two without, it was impossible to taste the difference.

The ENGLISH tomato season starts in June followed by PLUM, sometimes called AROMA or OLIVADE, which are worth the price difference before the brilliant vine ripened tomatoes arrive. **Trust** is a **Safeway** label for its Dutch and Portuguese imports; the better ones from Provence go under the names of FERLINE and PRISCA. Look also in **Safeway** for CLEOPATRA. **Sainsbury** SLICING, PORTUGUESE and DUTCH tomatoes have been disappointing. Better are the PROVENCE. Dutch tomatoes on the vine smell the part but are not comparable to those from further south; Good reports about MAYFAIR from **Somerfield**.

The first imports from Sicily in February are not displaced by UK and Dutch crops until May. The newer varieties are tending to be be developed with tougher skins, so they hold their own in packaging and don't collapse if left to ripen longer. Examples are Ferrari, Solario and Pronto from **Sainsbury**, though names in the tomato world are changed as often as socks. The innocuous reputation of the English and Dutch tomato was down to the practice of packing the fruit early and letting it ripen in store or on the tray. The last few year has seen noticeable moves back to letting the tomato stay on the vine longer.

BEST BUYS *AILSA is an old variety, irregularly round, about 4 cm (1½ in), scarlet to deep red in colour, with salmon-pink flesh and a good ratio of it to yellow pip. The seed pod breaks off easily, and it is good for cooking, particularly in sweet-and-sour combinations. An example from the UK had an oppressive resistant skin, and a sweetness mingled with classic sourness. At 89p per lb, it was worth its I rating for value in cooking.

BRITISH GOURMET has an orange blush, and is about 5 cm (2 in) across with 1 cm (½ in) of flesh. Handy to cook with, because the seeds slip out easily leaving a good rim of flesh for dicing, it has a sweet but vanishing flavour. Our sample from the UK were 75p per lb.

*CHERRY YELLOW show well for flavour against larger varieties, although the amount of development would suggest that cherry tomatoes are just a cosmetic affectation. Pretty, deep yellow to orange and perfectly formed inside, it is mild and inoffensive, but good looking. SONGOLD from **Safeway** has shown consistently well.

CHERRY DELIGHT is round, about 3 cm (1 1/4 in), bright orange fused with deep red. Inside the pip jelly is translucent green, the pips white to yellow, with a good configuration (as in all cherries). Examples tend to have a sharp, quick taste of sourness mellowed with sugar. Sold as sweet, it is not really. There is a confusing price ratio alteration from lbs and grams between cherry and ordinary tomatoes.

DELICE is round verging on squareness, about 4.5x5.5 cm (1 3/4x2 1/4 in), bright red fused with yellow, with red flesh, red jelly and a small white seed. The flavour of an example from France was mild, forgiving, and sweet with no acidity. Soft and fulfiling, it cooked well.

FLAVIA is a small traditional tomato, about 5 cm (2.5 in) across. Sharp, with little acidity but a high ratio of pip to flesh, it is neutral but classic, and makes a fair benchmark. Exclusive to **Sainsbury**, they are reputedly left longer on the vine to mature.

FLAVOUR TOP, previously known as ELOISE until **Tesco** changed its name, is about 5 cm (2 in) across and a very mainline red, with classic contours and a summery taste. With firm skin, it had a very good interaction of textures between the skin, flesh and the juice of the pips, to produce a mildly acidic effect.

JERSEY OUTDOOR is a squat pale tomato, meaty red hued with orange; crimson inside with yellow veins and green pips, the thick flesh is good for cooking and dicing.

MANHATTAN is a classic Maserrati red, 3 cm (1 1/4 in) across, with a conventional configuration. It has green to orange pips, pink to white sweet flesh, and a strong skin: a good combination. Another example two months later in August from Jersey was sweet, sharp, mellow and juicy.

*MELROW is round, 3-4 cm (1 1/4-1 1/2 in) across, with a red blush from translucent dark flesh inside streaked with white pith; inside is pretty configuration of deep green jelly, white to yellow pip, and blood red flesh. It is sweet, with little sourness or acidity, almost honeyed, with a lasting flavour. Good at £1.19 per lb.

MOMOTARA is large and deep cerise pink, with a good aroma and a small percentage of pip to flesh. Squattish to square, soft to cut, with a lovely smell, pale watermelon-pink flesh and yellow seed, it is juicy, with a delicate taste and low acidity. Ît was good, but at £1.58 per lb you pay for all this flavour.

ROYAL DELICIOUS, about 3-4 cm (1 1/4-1 1/2 in), has an orange blush to a deep red that darkens as they ripen, and a circle of yellow on the root. Classically contoured, with a thick skin and 5 mm (1/4 in) of flesh to yellow pip, and with a similar configuration and merits to Manhattan, it is a good juicy all-rounder, but not special.

**SICILIAN TOMATOES on the vine are fat deep red tomatoes sold with their stems still attached. The internal division of textures is almost an equality of pip, pith and flesh. Juicy, succulent and very sweet, with low acidity but still some, these are excellent.

VANESSA is squat, about 3.5-6 cm (1 1/2-2 1/2 in), firm, watery crimson in colour, with a smooth skin, a useful measure of flesh around the rim for cooking and a pretty configuration, with the few pips held in firm jelly – a vegetable version of a watermelon, with slightly woody hues.

PULSES

ADZUKI BEAN · BLACK-EYED BEAN · BUTTER
BEAN · CANNELLINI BEAN · CHICKPEA ·
FLAGEOLET · HARICOT · KIDNEY BEAN · LENTIL ·
SPLIT PEA

The dried ripe seeds of legumes are among the oldest cultivated foods and some of the most nutritious. They are good sources of both protein and fibre, and usually also of the vitamin B family. Before we began to harvest them young, most peas and broad beans were dried as staples for winter. Most pulses need soaking in water overnight before use. The exceptions are lentils and black-eyed beans, which can usually be cooked without any pre-soaking. There is some discussion over whether the haricot and other beans need soaking. While most textbooks and packets say they should be, Coenders argues in *The Chemistry of Cooking* that soaking could start enzyme changes and encourage micro-organisms to ferment. The compromise is that they need longer cooking of around 90 minutes plus. Times for cooking soaked beans vary according to how old they are.

Most notoriously, red kidney beans and soya beans build up toxins which must be destroyed by fast boiling for 10 minutes. This water should also be replaced before cooking the beans on. Allow 1.1 litres (2 pt) of water for every 115-225 g (4-8 oz) of pulses. Salt only serves to toughen the skins, so add it after cooking.

Some beans are now being imported from Spain under the **Tormesina** label, from Sierra de Gredos in Avila. They carry an EU logo for specific denomination on the grounds of the well-aerated, low-calcium granite soils and the pureness of the water. These beans are quite outstanding; the butter beans, three times the size of those in supermarkets, thin-skinned and immensely creamy, are well worth the premium.

ADZUKI BEAN

Also known as the ADUKI, DADUKI or sometimes AZUKI or FEIJOA BEAN, it is identified by the Latin *Phaseolus angularis*. Widely used in Asia, especially China and Japan where they are admired for pastes in sweet rather than savoury dishes, or mixed with rice in a ratio of 1:8, they are now grown across South-east Asia. Eastern herbalists prescribe them for kidney disorders. Usually sold dried or sometimes in tins, they can be sprouted (see page 214) or ground into flour. Their nutty flavour finds extensive use in vegetarian dishes, and they bind well in stuffings and loaves. **Sainsbury** is currently the only supermarket to stock adzuki beans, considerably cheaper (at 36p for 250 g) than some wholefood shops which sell their organic varieties at four times that price.

BLACK-EYED BEAN

Sometimes called COWPEA or BLACK-EYED PEA, this arrived in the Southern states of America from Africa with the slavers in the 17th century. Now principally grown in California, the small creamy beans with a distinctive black or yellow smudge have an earthy flavour.

A staple of Creole cooking, notably in rice'n'peas, they combine well with other flavours and are good in soups and casseroles and with salads. They are, however, likely to lose texture and have a much more defined mealiness than soya for example. Usually cheaper bought loose in wholefood shops, they can be sprouted (see page 214).

They are useful because the skins are thin and thus cook quickly. They are high in folic acid, and because they are not toxic they do not need long boiling.

BUTTER BEAN

Also known as the MADAGASCAR BEAN after the island from where most now come, *Vateria indica* was the main grocery bean before 1940. The similar LIMA BEAN is slightly smaller and sweeter, and often sold younger when still green. It is the bean from a tropical climber, *Phaseolus lunatus* or *limensis*, which is native to Central and South America.

The creamy butter bean is the largest of the pulses. The lozenge-shaped cream beans are best in individual casseroles in which they can star, and their seductive silky mealiness can be brought out – they are one of the most floury of all pulses. Some varieties contain markedly high levels of hydrocyanic acid which is destroyed during cooking.

CANNELLINI BEAN

Also known as the FAZOLA BEAN, this is the prince of pulses. Longer and thinner than an haricot, it is a staple of cooking in Tuscany, where they arrived originally from Argentina. The cooking liquid makes one of the best cooking stocks for other dishes.

The beans themselves are best in salads, especially with virgin olive oil and herbs, and in casseroles in which the liquid takes on their creamy nutty qualities. Slowly becoming more widely available, **Sainsbury** and **Safeway** now sell dried as well as tinned cannellini beans. Strangely they have yet to be priced above other pulses, which their savoury

PULSE SOAKING AND COOKING TIMES

PULSE	SOAKING	HARD-BOIL (minutes)	SIMMERING (minutes)
Adzuki bean	2-4 hours	10	50
Black-eyed bean	2-4 hours	None	60
Butter bean	2-4 hours	10	75
Cannellini bean	2-4 hours	10	75
Chickpea	2-4 hours	10	up to 3 hours
Flageolet	2-4 hours	10	60-90
Haricot	2-4 hours	10	60-90
Kidney bean	2-4 hours	10	40-45
Lentil	None	None	20-40
Split pea	None	None	30-45

Some books suggest soaking overnight, but this can affect the quality.
A better approach is a shorter soaking and, if necessary, slightly longer
cooking. Times will vary according to the age of the pulses.

flavour deserves. This is probably because the market is still young and
their qualities remain largely undiscovered when they get lumped
together with the considerably duller haricot. Some people argue that
tinned is as good as dried, because the flavour and texture survive.

COOKING: *Cannellini are the beans for minestrone or in
Tuscany, la ribollita – literally 'the re-boiling'. Soak 250 g
(8¹/₂ oz) cannellini beans overnight. In a heavy pan, sweat an
onion in olive oil. Add 1 carrot, 1 celery stalk, 1 leek, 2 tomatoes,
¹/₂ cabbage, chopped, 1 piece dried chilli and 4 garlic cloves.
Stir for 10 minutes. Add the beans, mix well, cover with 2 litres
(3¹/₂ pt) of water and simmer slowly for 2 hours.*

*Take out half the beans, purée and return them to the soup.
Sweat 4 garlic cloves with a sprig of thyme and pepper in oil and
add to the soup. Leave for 24 hours.*

*The next day, slice an onion (preferably red) over the top of the
soup and cook in a preheated medium oven, uncovered, for 30
minutes. To serve, cut a slice of country bread per person, rub
each with garlic and place in the bottom of the soup bowl. Ladle
over the hot soup and serve with extra virgin olive oil and salt.*

CHICKPEA

Sometimes known as the GARBANZO BEAN or in India the
BENGAL GRAM or CHANNA DAL, its Latin name is *Cicer*

arietinum. It arrived from India and has become pivotal in the cooking of the Middle-East, notably Greece and the Lebanon. The plants grow to 40 cm (16 in) and exude a sticky form of oxalic acid and so have to be harvested with gloves. Chickpea flour is used for *chapatis*, breads and *bhajis*. Middle-Eastern varieties tend to be smaller and darker than the Mediterranean type. Their robust one-dimensional chestnutty texture combines well with the complicated spicings of the Near East. They are occasionally eaten fresh, but most chickpeas are dried. Best with vinaigrettes, in curries, vegetarian pâtés, and in dips, notably Greek *hummus*, they can also be used to thicken sauces.

COOKING: *After overnight soaking, rinsing and boiling for 10 minutes, chickpeas need simmering for sometimes more than 2 hours and up to 3 (depending on age more than other pulses). They are best overcooked, so the skins burst allowing other flavours to mingle. The cooking liquid can make an earthy vegetarian stock. They can be cooked further into purées to accompany meat.*

To make hummus: liquidize 4 parts chickpeas with cooking water, 2 parts tahini (be generous), 1 part skinned garlic cloves, 1/2 part lemon juice, and a drizzle of sesame oil. Garnish with virgin olive oil and pomegranate seeds.

FLAGEOLET

A variety of haricot, this distinctive, attractive, slender lime-green bean is an aristocrat among pulses. The beans are harvested when still young, which accounts for the sweetness and also the higher content of positive nutrients. They are sometimes found fresh, which are excellent, but they are more usually sold dried, which deserve serving on their own, or traditionally with roast lamb – they are cooked separately, added to the pan juices as the lamb rests and served with the gravy.

They are also good in salads, terrines, in vinaigrette or dressed with the juices from a roast and some herbs. Supermarkets tend only to stock the tins, though **Sainsbury** has broken the trend with 250 g bags.

HARICOT

Sometimes known confusingly as the FRENCH BEAN, NAVY BEAN, BOSTON BEAN, NORTHERN BEAN or PEARL HARICOT BEAN, its many names reflect the size of its family. Though the name haricot was probably derived from the Aztec *ayecotl*, the Latin name is simply *Phaseolus vulgaris*. These neat, cream, oval beans tend to lack the flavour of the younger flageolet and need support in the cooking or dressing. They make a good mainline filler, lending body to soups, casseroles, cassoulets and – most famously – baked beans. **Heinz** first produced its

Beans

Nutritional values of different beans

	Calories	Protein g	Carbos g	Fat g	Fibre g
Adzuki	272	20	50	0.5	2.7
(cooked)	123	9.3	22.5	0.2	2.7
Baked bean	84	5.2	15.3	0.6	6.9
Beansprout	31	2.9	4	0.5	5.6
Broad bean (boiled)	81	7.9	11.7	0.6	1.3
Butter bean	77	5.9	13	0.5	1.1
Chick pea	320	21.3	49.6	5.4	13.5
(cooked)	121	8.4	18.2	2.1	5.1
Green bean	24	1.9	3.2	0.5	3
Lentil (green)	297	24.3	48.8	1.9	1.2
(cooked)	105	8.8	17	0.7	0.4
Kidney bean (red, cooked)	103	8.4	17.4	0.5	9
Runner bean (cooked)	18	1.2	2.3	0.5	3.1
Soya bean (cooked)	141	14	5.1	7.3	21
Tofu	261	23.5	2	17.7	0.9

baked beans in 1895 and brought them to England in 1912, although full production was only eventually established here in 1928.

The price of haricot beans fluctuates wildly from supermarket to wholefood shop. Their reputation for making people fart stems from the high levels of carbohydrate not being digested and being passed into the colon. Selective trials are trying to breed this out of commercial strains.

KIDNEY BEAN

FRIJOLE NEGRO, the black bean sometimes called the MEXICAN BEAN or CHILLI BEAN, is part of the large family of beans Columbus originally discovered in South America and brought back to Europe. Now cultivated in Thailand and China but widely used in Creole cooking, it is valued for its bulk and mealiness and also its superlative nutritional content. One cup supplies all the folic acid an adult needs daily, plus a quarter of the protein, iron, potassium and thiamin. Chinese black bean sauce is not related, coming from fermented soy beans.

The RED KIDNEY BEAN is often called the MEXICAN BEAN or CHILLI BEAN. These kidney-shaped beans are grown in America and Africa, part of the same family as the black, and the colour can be anything from luridly dark maroon to pink.

It is renowned on two counts. First, the skin contains a protein which causes red blood cells to mass, so this must be destroyed in cooking. It must be boiled hard for 10 minutes and then the water thrown away before starting the proper cooking. And then there is the question of wind. Some say this may be due to hereditary factors, but only 115 g (4 oz) supplies all the fibre an adult needs a day. One solution to the wind problem is to wash the beans in a change of water prior to cooking.

COOKING: *Historically served with hot spicy dishes, it suits chilli well – as in* chilli con carne *– as it tends to need a lot of powerful flavour around it (the sugar in the tins seems to help in the same way) as the base flavour is nondescriptly mealy.*

BEST BUYS Ironically and almost uniquely, brand names like **Princes** and **Don Mario** can be cheaper in the tin than supermarket own-labels.

LENTIL

The lentil is known in Latin as *Lens esculenta* because it is shaped like a lens; or, in other explanations, from the Latin *lentus* for slow, because the Romans said they bred indolence. Along with wheat and barley, the lentil is probably one of the oldest cultivated plants and is mentioned in Genesis. Many varieties are grown, mostly they are brown or green on the outside, cream, orange-yellow or red inside. BROWN *or* GREEN lentils are often called CONTINENTAL *or* GERMAN LENTILS and are the variety used in most European recipes. These are larger than the red because they retain their skin, and so tend to take longer cooking. RED LENTILS, sometimes called EGYPTIAN LENTILS and widely found in Indian cooking, tend to lose their shape quicker because they have been skinned.

Green or brown are usually more expensive, say 10p per 500 g (1 lb 2 oz) more than red, which are around 60p per 500 g. Organic can be three times the price. The best are PUY LENTILS, known as the caviar of Le Puy as the tiny slate-grey pods resemble caviar. **Sainsbury** have started to import these, not from France but from Canada – an interesting poser for the French *appellation contrôlée* authorities, who have approved Le Puy lentils on the basis of geography.

COOKING: *Check over the lentils before cooking to make sure no pieces of grit have evaded detection. Lentils need to be cooked in well-flavoured stock, and are often at their best with something sweet. They take on the qualities and flavours around them and, left to themselves, can taste insipid.*

For the caviar of Le Puy: cook 200g (7oz) lentils in a good stock for 20-30 minutes. Peel and dice a shallot. Make up a vinaigrette of 3 parts virgin olive oil to 1 part red wine vinegar and 1 part Dijon mustard and season generously with salt and pepper. Drain the lentils, toss them into the vinaigrette and mix in the shallot.

QUORN

Quorn claims to be one of the most important food finds of the century. The name covers the mycoprotein from a tiny plant, *Fusarium graminearium*, identified in a field near Marlow in Buckinghamshire in the '60s but now produced by fermentation as in a cheese or yoghurt, and bound with egg white. It was first cleared for sale in 1985. The nutritional composition is almost identical to tofu, except it is slightly higher in fibre and in protein. Like tofu, its blandness and adaptability have brought it into play across a range of dishes as a meat substitute. The charm is that it is fatless, even if many of the cooking mediums serve to put the fat back into it with oil and stir-fries, and even cream. The publicity brochures declare that it has a 'light savoury' taste, corporate-speak for saying that it is so inoffensive as to have no taste at all. Quorn takes on the flavours of the herbs and spices around it or the cooking medium. So it has started to appear nationally as Quorn burgers, Quorn chilli with rice; Quorn lasagne; Quorn Balti Jalfrezi; Quorn Tikka Masala; Quorn Garlic and Herb Kievs; Quorn mince etc. Quorn has enough financial muscle behind it (it was pioneered by **Zenecca**, the seed division of **ICI**) to ensure that it will be tried out on every aisle of the supermarket over the next few years. The latest diversions have been into marinating in sweet-and-sour sauces for stir-fries and inside ravioli with ricotta cheese and pesto. Oddly, it does not seem to have won over the mainstream vegetarian and, perhaps like tofu, it may prove a mycoprotein too far if it cannot find its own constituency and culinary application.

COOKING: It needs very little cooking (the oils are often added to stop it drying out), but recipes extend the times to allow the quorn to absorb other flavours. For stir-frying allow 5 minutes; for grilling allow 30 minutes minimum to marinate and then 8 minutes' grilling; in sauces allow 20 minutes to cook into an onion base. Quorn should be kept in the fridge and eaten within 24 hours of opening, but can be frozen and cooked straight from the freezer.

SPLIT PEA

Until the 16th century MARROWFAT PEAS were the indigenous peas in the British diet, of which mushy peas remains as a reminder. They need long soaking. Their sweetness is classically paired with salted meats – notably ham – for an old-fashioned but convincing strategy. SPLIT PEAS are slightly sweeter than marrowfat; the yellow grown in Britain and the green in Belgium. They are skinless, so quick to cook and do not need soaking. They do, however, tend to disintegrate and are best used as a thickener for soups and stews (for texture go for brown lentils instead). Traditionally, they are used in ham and pea soup, any vegetable soup and, of course, pease pudding. Supermarkets sell them for around 42p per 500 g (1 lb 2 oz), but wholefood shops can charge twice as much and the price of organic can be twice as much again.

FUNGI

CULTIVATED MUSHROOM · CHESTNUT
MUSHROOM · OYSTER MUSHROOM · SHIITAKE
MUSHROOM · CEP · CHANTERELLE · HEDGEHOG
MUSHROOM · MOREL · OTHER WILD
MUSHROOMS · TRUFFLES

We have had a long dread of mushrooms in this country which has only recently eased with their reassuring arrival in supermarkets in neat blue boxes wrapped in cellophane. Perhaps the packaging placates our worst fears about things that grow at random in the dark. In most other European countries mushroom-hunting is a weekend enthusiasm and laws have been passed to protect the innocent from consuming the deadly, and the enthusiast from destroying his hobby.

There are more than 10,000 varieties of fungi, of which only a tiny fraction are eaten – not because most are poisonous, but simply because they taste of very little. The main culprit for wild mushrooms' fearful reputation is the DEATH CAP, *Amanita phalloides*, which accounts for a high percentage of fatalities. Others in the *Amanita* family can also cause poisoning, but some are eaten by experts.

Hunters claim that there are upwards of 90 edible mushrooms and other fungi found in Britain. For the most part, however, their reputation survives mostly on their rarity.

Big supermarkets have begun to stock some wild mushrooms. **Sainsbury** has amazingly been importing grey chanterelles from Portugal and also *pied de mouton*. **Tesco**, too, has been bringing in chanterelles – grey and yellow – but they are not cheap.

Supermarkets unhelpfully tend to price loose mushrooms in lbs and those packed in grams; loose do tend to be cheaper.

CULTIVATED MUSHROOM

Mushrooms were first cultivated by the French in vast labyrinthine caves, dug out like mines, in the Seine region and around Paris, certainly by 1800. A cave at Mery in 1867 was 21 miles long and produced 1,350 kg (3,000 lb) of mushrooms a day. Another at Montrouge was 24 m (80 ft) below ground and 11 km (7 miles) long. 'Once more we plunge into a passage, dark as ink, and find ourselves between two lines of beds in full bearing, the beautiful white button-like mushrooms appearing everywhere in profusion,' wrote one visitor.

*BUTTON MUSHROOMS are the smallest and youngest; allowed to grow on they become CLOSED CAP, then OPEN CAP MUSH-

ROOMS, with the pink to brown gills showing; and finally the large BREAKFAST MUSHROOM, which has fully opened up to 10 cm (4 in) across or more and the gills have turned black. They are the same common mushroom, *Agaricus*, as are found in the fields, though wild tend to be more strongly flavoured. The button mushroom's role in cooking is supportive, but it is a good example of mass agriculture at work and it is hard to say that it is worth four times less than the price of some exotic mushrooms. It keeps its shape well in cooking, the texture does not collapse (it remains al dente and bouncy in the mouth), and it takes in other flavours without losing its own. It will absorb roughly a tablespoon of butter to each 30 g (1 oz) of weight. In the larger open cups, the flavour has had time to unravel into sour grass and dusty roads, and is discernibly milkier and creamier, until eventually it becomes a bready sour inkiness – in practice, too dominating for cooking with anything else.

Mushrooms do not like condensation or light. Either store them in a paper bag in the salad drawer of the fridge or take off the film from the prepacked box, if they have one, and cover with a cloth.

CHESTNUT MUSHROOM
Sometimes called BROWN or BROWN CAP MUSHROOM or PARIS MUSHROOM, this is a bulbous variation on the common mushroom. The cap is a grey brown, the stalk fatter and the whole altogether firmer and less fragile. It tends to be more absorbent than the white, perhaps taking up only 1 1/2 tablespoons of butter for each 30 g (1 oz) of weight. They keep their shape well in cooking and have a discernibly stronger flavour, which is sour when raw and stronger and more earthy and intense than the white.

OYSTER MUSHROOM
This is one of the more common finds in the wild, but it is also cultivated – albeit at twice the price of white mushrooms. They have the looks, with their silky beige-grey frills like swirling skirts, and they cook quickly but lose their shape though retain their sponginess. However, they are more resistant to taking on other flavours. They have their own delicious elusive taste. Raw they are sour, milky and bready; cooked they have some of the bounciness of white mushrooms and a sense of unacid lemons, which makes them good for bulking and providing extra dimensions of texture, especially in soups and Eastern dishes. Apart from the most common white variety, there are also YELLOW and PINK OYSTER MUSHROOMS, which attract yet further premiums of up to £1 per 1 lb again. The taste is almost identical to that of the white, but the yellow keeps its attractive colour in cooking.

Mushrooms
Effects of cooking on mushrooms

	Calories	Protein g	Carbos g	Fat g	% Fat of Cals
Raw	13	1.8	0.4	0.5	34
Boiled	11	2.4	0.3	0.3	24
Fried	157	2.4	0.3	16.2	92

SHIITAKE MUSHROOM

Shiitake have very dark caps and thin stems. In the raw they are paper-dry and bready, with distinct hints of lemon, but in cooking they lose their firmness and some of the texture and become very sweet, rich, meaty and deliciously strong. Widely used in Chinese and Japanese cooking, they are good with meats and soups. Their main drawback is the price, at nearly four times that of white mushrooms.

Their culture is ancient and was developed on the island of Shikoku in Japan. Oak trees aged 25-33 years old were felled, axe cuts were made at 10-15 cm (4-6 in) intervals and the logs left in the darkest part of the forest. 'The logs are steeped in water for a number of hours according to the dryness of the locality, and then struck with pommels to facilitate the growth of the mushroom.', wrote one observer. The growth appears in the ridges after the third year. They are now grown here and in America, where they have been highly popular since their introduction in 1972 (previously they were banned because they were thought, incorrectly, to be related to a fungus that attacked railroad ties). Some of this may be due to studies that have shown that eating shiitake can have an effect on cholesterol levels. In Japan there are three grades, *donko*, the most expensive, with thick flesh and furled edges; *koko* for medium grade and *koshin* the thinnest flesh. Here they are just graded by size.

COOKING: *Brush off any particles of sawdust and take off the stems, which are usually too stringy to use. Shiitake should be cooked slowly over a low heat. Allow about 15 minutes. The texture of a fresh shiitake should be akin to an oyster or abalone. Dried will be chewier. The liquid they release during cooking will help sauces. They freeze better after cooking than before. They should not be eaten raw as there is some suggestion of allergic reactions, as in cases of people eating more than 450 g (1 lb) per day for long periods.*

CEP

Also known as the PENNY BUN, the botanical term for this highly prized wild mushroom is *Boletus edulis*. If one mushroom embodies the spirit and cause of mushroom-hunting, then it is the cep. It looks the part, with its shiny bun-shaped cap and swollen white stalk... only the gnome is missing. In fact, it looks so perfect it might have come straight from an antique shop by mistake. They like beech woods, but have been found in other woods. The flesh is meaty and substantial, tending to be slimy if they have been bottled.

COOKING: *Ceps make first-class soup, or the caps can be baked with butter. They also freeze well.*

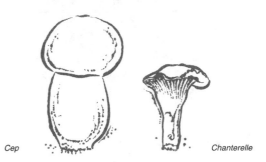

Cep   Chanterelle

CHANTERELLE

Oh for a reputation like the chanterelle! How can such a wispy, stringy choir girl be sold for such a price? At £14 per lb, it is one of the most expensive of foods. They were once so plentiful they were harvested commercially around Chelmsford in Essex and some export still goes on from Scottish pine forests. These go mainly to France, where they are known as *girolles* and have been over-hunted or their habitats chemically destroyed, if not quite to extinction certainly to serious decline. The earthiness and evocative nutty flavour – 'all moss and must' – imbues everything around it. The texture is a bit rubbery, but this makes it long-standing in casseroles.

HEDGEHOG MUSHROOM

Known to the French as *pied de mouton*, this is not actually a mushroom but a fungus found in broad-leaved woodlands from late summer. Pinky brown, it has a coarse spongy texture. It is bitter when raw, but when cooked tastes of chestnuts. Good in casseroles, they are woody and gutsy but also slightly granular. Probably because they are not as well known as other mushrooms, their price is less inflated. The little frilly honeycomb inside the cap should be rubbed off before cooking. There is also a *pied de mouton bleu*, in which the stems take on a moonscape blueness.

MOREL

Possibly the finest of all wild mushrooms, this is found in open woodland in the south of England in late spring, though not in the same numbers as on mainland Europe. Those that squeeze into Nine Elms Market are usually from the Jura and the Vosges mountains, where hunting is a cottage industry. Morels should not be eaten raw, and retain much of their potency when dried.

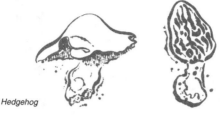

Hedgehog

Morel

OTHER WILD MUSHROOMS

The MOUSSERON is tiny, about 1 cm (½ in), with a dark brown cap. Often quite hard, they are 'expensive accoutrements'. Collectors can still find many species that were much more common until quite recently. The WOOD BLEWIT was sold freely in Midlands markets before the advent of cultivated mushrooms. The blue tends to fade on the gills as it ages. The SHAGGY INK CAP or JUDGE'S WIG is edible while it is still in the shape of a torpedo, before its umbrella opens up. The gills should still be pink, not black as the ink starts to run. It is usually found under mown grass, often at roadsides. Most PUFFBALLS are edible, and giant puffballs were served at the Freemason's Tavern in London at official occasions. They can be breadcrumbed and fried in butter or stuffed. Enthusiasts say the texture is like sweetbreads and the flavour mildly nutty.

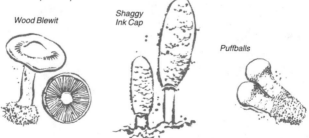

Wood Blewit

Shaggy Ink Cap

Puffballs

The HORN OF PLENTY is still abundant in patches, usually in beech woods in late summer, though they can be quite tough and are somewhat overrated. PARASOLS, both SHAGGY and FIELD, are related to the common mushroom and can substitute in most recipes. FAIRY RING CHAMPIGNON was common on lawns until the use of chemicals and was often used in steak and kidney pies. The ST GEORGE'S

MUSHROOM is supposed to appear on its namesake's day, April 23, so is one of the first mushrooms of the year and is beautifully white and can have a particularly good texture.

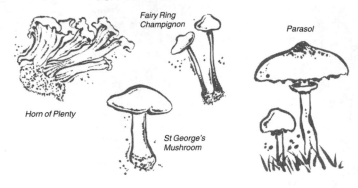

Fairy Ring Champignon

Parasol

Horn of Plenty

St George's Mushroom

TRUFFLES

Given the prohibitive price of truffles, this is a somewhat academic entry. Even most restaurants will only use shavings and trimmings, or more frequently something frozen. Amazingly, **Sainsbury** has has been selling black truffles at a relative snip of £12 for 2 whole fresh specimens, or bottled at £15.90 per 100g. Another drawback is that with the BLACK TRUFFLE, you need quite a lot of fresh truffle to create an impression. To smell a box of fresh truffles from the Périgord is a magical and convincing explanation of their reputation, and possibly as close as most of us are likely to get. Périgord truffles must be used bravely and with abandon.

The advantage of the WHITE TRUFFLE from Alba (there is a market each October) is that less goes further. A few thin shavings transform an omelette, pasta, or even the whole room with their sexual pungency. They do not respond to long cooking in the same way that black truffles do.

The SUMMER TRUFFLE is imported from Italy and there have been occasional finds here in Perth and in Avon, but it does not command the same respect. The skin is knobbly black, with pine kernel markings, and the flesh grey to black with a lighter taste that is less dramatic but not completely worthless. The vendors push their luck at £110 per kg.

COOKING: *Keep truffles in a jar with fresh eggs or rice and they will take on the aroma. There are great dishes like 'chicken in mourning', where slices are slipped under the skin of a Bresse chicken, or the foie gras of Strasbourg where it is baked in pastry filled with goose liver. For sauces, the juice in tins is a passable and necessary substitute, but even a 500 g tin of peelings may be £50.*

FRUIT

The change in the fruit we buy is less obvious than in other areas. The sense of focus on one or two varieties is stunning. The Global Food Machine wants resilient varieties that are marketable around the world and the extent to which other varieties are dispensed with is awesome. A nondescript seedless grape variety like Thompson is now almost completely pre-eminent. While wine makers around the world seek variety, fresh produce marketeers seek standardization. Sainsbury's announcement that it hopes to create new plantations for Thompson in India depressingly underscores the trend. The globalization of the strawberry has been no great step forward for this country, at least where looks and shelf-life have allowed low-flavour varieties to come to the forefront. The strawberry maintained many of the market gardens in the south of England which were recognized as producing some of the finest in the world. Sadly these growers have now gone and with them the varieties they sold.

Italian and Spanish exports of stone fruit have taken the bulk of the positions on most supermarket shelves. The French quality tends to be better, albeit it often comes late in the season. Specialist greengrocers are often the best places to find individual varieties of interest. **Harrods** and **Harvey Nichols** are particularly good at unearthing prime fruit from France and other countries.

Tinned fruits must be secondary to fresh and in the last year there have been signs that some fruits may start to develop on the chill side. Pineapples are being trimmed and peeled on the plantations before export. The variety of chilled fruit salads, notably at **Waitrose** and **Marks & Spencer** (no less than 6 variations of fruit) may be the harbinger of a new era in fruit. There has been much activity, with new plantations of exotics in Brazil which may soon manifest themselves. One of the first signs of this shift has been papaya at **Waitrose** which is left on the tree longer to ripen and vine-ripened peaches from France have also appeared in **Tesco's** towards the end of August.

NUTRITIONAL VALUES OF DIFFERENT FRUITS

	Cals	Prot g	Carbo g	Sugars g	Fat g	Fibre g
Apple (average)	47	0.4	11.8	11.8	0.1	2
(Bramley cooked without sugar)						
	33	0.3	8.1	8.1	0.1	2
Apricot	31	0.9	7.2	7.2	0.1	1.9
Banana	95	1.2	23	20.9	0.3	3.1
Blackberry	25	0.9	5.1	5.1	0.2	6.6
Fig (dried)	227	3.6	52.9	52.9	1.6	12.4
Grape	60	0.4	15.4	15.4	0.1	0.8
Kiwi	49	1.1	10.6	10.3	0.5	0
Mango	57	0.7	14.1	13.8	0.2	2.9
Peach	33	1.0	7.6	7.6	0.1	2.9
Pear (average)	40	0.3	10	10	0.1	0
Pineapple	41	0.4	10.1	10.1	0.2	1.3
Plum (average)	36	0.6	8.8	8.8	0.1	2.3
Strawberry	27	0.8	6.6	0.6	0.1	2

COMPARISON OF DIFFERENT CITRUS FRUITS

	Cals	Prot g	Carbo g	Sugars g	Fat g	Fibre g
Clementine	37	0.9	8.7	8.7	0.1	1.7
Grapefruit	30	0.8	6.8	6.8	0.1	1.6
Mandarin	52	0.5	13.4	13.4	0	0.3
(canned in syrup)						
Orange	37	1.1	8.5	8.5	0.1	1.7
Satsuma	36	0.9	8.5	8.5	0.1	1.7
Tangerine	35	0.9	8	8	0.1	1.7

COMPARISON OF DIFFERENT MELONS

	Cals	Prot g	Carbo g	Sugars g	Fat g	Fibre g
Cantaloupe	19	0.6	4.2	4.2	0.1	2.9
Galia	24	0.5	5.6	5.6	0.1	0.9
Honeydew	28	0.6	6.6	6.6	0.1	0.8
Watermelon	31	0.5	7.1	7.1	0.3	0.3

Carotene ug	E mg	Thiamin mg	Ribo mg	Niacin mg	B6 mg	Folate ug	C mg
16	0.53	0.03	0.02	0.1	0.05	1	5
15	0.25	0.01	0.01	0.1	0.05	0	11
405	0	0.04	0.05	0.5	0.08	5	6
21	0.27	0.04	0.06	0.7	0.29	14	11
80	2.37	0.02	0.05	0.5	0.05	34	7
64	0	0.08	0.10	0.8	0.26	9	1
17	0	0.05	0.01	0.2	0.1	2	3
37	0	0.01	0.03	0.03	0.15	0	59
1800	1.05	0.04	0.05	0.5	0.13	0	37
58	0	0.02	0.04	0.6	0.02	3	31
18	0.50	0.02	0.03	0.2	0.02	2	6
18	0.10	0.08	0.03	0.3	0.09	5	12
295	0.61	0.05	0.03	1.1	0.05	3	4
8	0.20	0.03	0.03	0.6	0.06	20	77

Carotene ug	E mg	Thiamin mg	Ribo mg	Niacin mg	B6 mg	Folate ug	C mg
75	0	0.09	0.04	0.03	0.7	33	54
17	0.19	0.05	0.02	0.03	0.03	26	36
105	0	0.06	0.01	0.2	0.03	12	15
28	0.24	0.11	0.04	0.4	0.10	31	54
75	0	0.09	0.04	0.3	0.07	33	27
97	0	0.07	0.02	0.2	0.07	21	30

Carotene ug	E mg	Thiamin mg	Ribo mg	Niacin mg	B6 mg	Folate ug	C mg
1000	0.10	0.04	0.02	0.6	0.11	5	26
0	0.10	0.03	0.01	0.4	0.09	3	15
48	0.10	0.03	0.01	0.3	0.06	2	9
230	0.10	0.05	0.01	0.1	0.14	2	8

BERRY FRUITS

BLACKBERRY · BLUEBERRY · BOYSENBERRY ·
CRANBERRY · GOOSEBERRY · LOGANBERRY ·
MULBERRY · RASPBERRY · STRAWBERRY ·
TAYBERRY

Berry fruits are among summer's great gifts. Their delicacy is often undermined by poor packaging. Across the board, growers have been so obsessed with yields and long-keeping that much of what gets to market is a shadow of its reputation. Looks and size have taken the place of flavour and diversity.

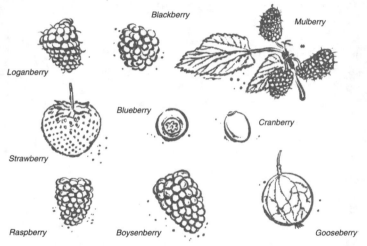

Loganberry · Blackberry · Mulberry · Blueberry · Cranberry · Strawberry · Raspberry · Boysenberry · Gooseberry

BEST BUYS Smell is probably the best test of ripeness in fruit. The quality of main-line fruits like apples and oranges tends to be consistent in supermarkets. That is less true of exotics which are poorly understood. Supermarkets retain a virtual monopoly on grade-1 fruit. Street markets can be cheaper but rarely match the quality. Any small-scale production or market-gardening seems to be a thing of the past or restricted to pick-your-own farms.

Among the big supermarkets, quality has been so standardized that there is little to choose between them. **Marks and Spencer** has the tightest range of product, but usually impeccably chosen and labelled by variety. **Waitrose** has the enthusiasm for exotic fruits and for the varieties it wants. **Tesco** has cooled on the whole idea of exotics and concentrates on main line varieties. **Sainsbury** and **Safeway** have seemed content to stick with volume. None of them seem to respond to market forces in the way that some of the smaller shops do, where there are occasional bargains to be found at peak seasons. On the other hand, bananas are often said to be the biggest selling item of all foods in the supermarket.

BLACKBERRY

More than 2,000 varieties of cultivated blackberries are credited to North America. This must, however, be a textbook aberration as, like the blackthorn, they have constituted an important part of the early hedgerows in this country. In the wild they tend to be more sour, hence their ubiquitous fate as a part of blackberry and apple crumble. When perfectly ripe, there is no finer fruit.

COOKING: *Jane Grigson argued they went better with milk than with cream, as in muesli. For cooking, include some unripe for tartness. Apple is, of course, a natural ally. Jellies have many uses; sauces for strong meats like duck and grouse are an English affection.*

BEST BUYS The first English cultivated varieties of blackberry start in August; grown under cover they have a disappointing taste but look beautiful. Sylvan, with its long pod, is one of the better varieties. Browny purple to black and hairy, it is sweet to sour in a quick flush with an acid finish. In this it resembles imports like South American Giant, which is fat like a Homburg hat, with a juicy purple/black berry, about 3 cm (1 ¼ in) long but almost square, with a very big hull. Available June to September.

BLUEBERRY

The blueberry is part of the same richly named family as the larger huckleberry, whortleberry, bilberry and the cranberry – a branch of the heather fraternity, which at the other end of the spectrum extends to rhododendrons and azaleas. Blueberries are the pick of the family, developed in America and shipped here from Oregon, although cultivation has started in Dorset. They are usually available from July to September, with a few stragglers hanging on for the Christmas market. American wild blueberries are held to be more intense in flavour.

COOKING: *Treat as strawberries with cream and sugar; in fruit mixes, especially with melon and strawberries; in stews or in pies, tarts and other bakes; prominent in summer puddings.*

BOYSENBERRY

Developed in France during the '20s, from the strawberry, raspberry, loganberry and dewberry – none of which it resembles, being mainly tart and juicy, this long berry, about 2.5 cm (1 in), is scarlet blue, with compact pods. It is sour, like an unripe cross between a raspberry and a blackberry.

CRANBERRY

The cranberry is often confused with its cousin the lingonberry. The cranberry grows in boggy ground from Cape Cod to Wisconsin, forming huge red lakes after the valleys are flooded from which they are harvested in nets. Cranberries were served at the first Thanksgiving Dinner in 1621. The name comes from the pink blossom which resembles a crane's neck. The berries first came here with the clippers to help sailors ward off scurvy, but it was only in 1974 that **Ocean Spray** took on the UK market seriously.

The European version which flourishes wild in Scandinavia is, in fact, a lingonberry. It is slightly smaller, richer and superior in flavour, though it is usually sold as a cranberry.

COOKING: *Increasingly, they have become available fresh, which is a better option for classic variations with orange or port added at the end of cooking to make a sauce.*

BEST BUYS   Ocean Spray dominates the American market, but other good brands to look for are **Original Wild Swedish** lingonberries, **Wilkins & Son**, and **Sainsbury** own-label.

GOOSEBERRY

The gooseberry was first described by the invading Arabs in Spain around the 8th century, where it was probably used as a laxative (as were many other berries, including strawberries). They were well suited to our climate and were grown as hedges too in Medieval gardens. They are, however, martyrs to mildew and most go for processing.

COOKING: *Fools, jellies and tarts are traditional, as are sauces for mackerel and veal and stuffings for goose.*

BEST BUYS   The best eaters are the red-berried Whinham's Industry and Whitesmith. The reputation of the gooseberry hangs on one variety,**Levellers, which are round and fat, almost bursting the skin, with a colour going on amber from a veined lime. This is the eating gooseberry, with sour skin and a beautifully fleshy, pippy sweetness that has lush high notes. Unfortunately, they are usually sold too unripe.

LOGANBERRY

Named after J.M. Logan, who developed it in California in 1900, it is in-clined to go mushy quickly. The long purple dusky hairy pod is juicy and sour/sweet, with a similar impact to a strawberry. Available May to July.

MULBERRY

Overlooked as a supermarket fruit, it is still found in gardens, notably of Jacobean houses. James I gave free seeds to anyone who would grow them, hoping they would expand the silk industry. Unfortunately the seeds he dispensed were for the black mulberry and the silkworms prefer the white. Luckily the black is the more edible variety. The fruits ripen from July to October and should be gathered as soon as they fall. They were originally planted for their dye rather than to eat. A German proverb says the devil used it to blacken his boots. The flavour is refreshing, sweetly acid and juicy. At first sight it looks like a raspberry but it is ripe when it turns purple to black.

COOKING: *Used to be served fresh on its own leaves, but more commonly was baked in pies and puddings. Make into a jam half and half with apples, or macerate in gin for 3 months.*

RASPBERRY

The trade tends to buy raspberries by the grower. The Scottish Crop Research Institute at Invergowrie has 500 varieties, but commercially it really is a fruit that seems to have lost its way with the decline of the market garden – which for something so prized is scandalous.

The most common is Bliss with a long pod, which is dry, tart and pippy. The pips are controversial, as is its hair. The demand of the multiples is for lipstick-pink, not the winey-hued purple berry. They are still picked by hand, another problem. The extending growing season, now up to eight weeks, has re-awakened multiple interest at the expense of pick-your-own farms and small shops.

COOKING: *An old recipe for raspberry vinegar: Bruise 450 g (1 lb) ripe raspberries in a large bowl and pour over 1.1 litres (1 qt) of white wine vinegar. Let stand for 24 hours. Strain liquid over a second bowl of fresh raspberries, let stand for 24 hours and repeat the process yet again with more berries. Do not squeeze the fruit at any stage or it may ferment. Strain through canvass, measure and add 450 g (1 lb) white sugar to each 600 ml (1 pt). Stir well and bottle.*

BEST BUYS   Supermarkets start to sell around June 15, but the first examples tend to be anaemic. The first varieties are GLEN MOY and GLEN PROSEN, before AUTUMN BLISS which can go on to October. Some GOLDEN RASPBERRIES are found in June. Among the Scottish raspberries, bravely flavoured shiny GLEN LYON compares against older neatly formed LEO from Kent, which has a grey blush on pink. It is quite dry, with a classic tartness. Gardeners suggest MALLING JEWEL and MALLING JOY are the most delicious mid-season varieties; September and ZEVA for autumn fruit.

STRAWBERRY

Never has a strawberry looked more like a strawberry, with its weight-lifter's shoulders, pretty page-boy fronds and cute yellow freckles. Deep in their salmon-pink souls, however, strawberries are not what they used to be. The strawberry has been the focus of intense varietal research over the last decade. Varieties that dominated the markets in the '30s, like The Duke, Madame Koi, and Sir Joseph Paxton, seem to have vanished. The modern strawberry may have the looks but in terms of flavour it has been emaciated. They have become the 'Stepford Wives' of the fruit world. Bigness and blandness have been breeders' watchwords, coupled with long shelf-lives. Ronnie McNichol, head of Soft Fruit Genetics at the Scottish Crop Research Institute in Invergowrie, near Dundee, argues that the move to a longer season has meant plants being grown in tunnels and being grubbed up in the second and third years, when they may give smaller fruit but the flavour has matured in the plant. 'The problem is that with a strongly flavoured strawberry, it is like putting too much sugar in coffee. If they get too much sun, the flavour goes off and an off flavour is worse than a bland flavour'. The move to all-year-round strawberries has meant many of the main-line varieties are kept in the dark in poly tunnels so they are oblivious to the seasons.

Wild strawberries grow across the world, but most cultivated strawberries can trace their lineage back to the Chilean strawberry and the Virginian strawberry introduced in the 17th century and crossed successfully by French breeders 100 years later. It is a false fruit, the real fruit being the golden pips on the outside.

Strawberries are sold in punnets – but punnets have no legal definition and are as likely to contain 6 oz as 16 oz. **Sainsbury** has begun to sell them loose. A strawberry kept perfectly in a cold store can last for up to 6 days. The cost of strawberries at pick-your-own farms is usually 80p-£1 per lb, or about half that in the shops.

Pick-your-own farms usually start selling earlier than you expect, sometimes even on June 1, though more usually by June 15. The first through are Hapil and Elsanta, followed by Cambridge Vigour and Cambridge Favourite, then Pegasus and Honeyoe (good for jam). Many varieties are selected for their ability to deal with families of untrained fingers pulling them to pieces rather than for flavour. Early commercial varieties in the shops, like Chandler, are quite poor in flavour and growers are moving towards Ossogrande. Elsanta is riding a crest of a reputation, possibly due mostly to its appearance. Sovereign is recognized as one of the best, but has less than a day's prime life after picking and so is really only the province of gardeners. The new English star is Evita.

COOKING: *No other strawberries through the year really compare with open-air-grown English in a good summer. On poor* varieties pairing with oranges or even a dash of Grand Marnier helps to reinforce the flavour; or try a salad of sliced cucumber and strawberries dressed with black pepper.

Unripe strawberries make good old-fashioned English pies and puddings, though were rarely used as such. They make a good wine and also vinegar. It is sometimes said that strawberries are the most difficult fruit to make into jam because they boil so thinly. The water content can make it tricky to judge when the jam is cooked and if it is left too long the jam becomes overly dark and tastes burnt. Gooseberries, or gooseberry juice, were often added, in a ratio of one to two. Use slightly more fruit than sugar and bring the strawberries to the boil before adding the sugar. Boil 20 minutes. Some old recipes suggest adding a little butter halfway through to stop the mix boiling over. The sides of the pan need to be scraped continuously with a knife to stop singeing.

Strawberry tea is made with the dried leaves of the wild plant (collina or vesca), sometimes supplemented with dried blackberry leaves.

BEST BUYS CAMBRIDGE FAVOURITE is out of vogue with the trade for its short keeping, but widely found on PYO farms. Annatto in colour, smaller than modern breeds, at around 4 cm (1 1/2 in), it is bright pink and flat-topped, with yellow ears and pockets. The flavour is sweet, rounded, gentle and soft, with good body. Its reputation is perhaps (wrongly) stronger than Cambridge Vigour.

CAMBRIDGE VIGOUR is scarlet turning rare-beef red, softening on the darker parts, with a perfectly formed classic shape and about 2 cm (3/4 in) – any bigger and it starts to square up into body-builder's shoulders. The flesh is salmon-coloured and loose-textured, the taste dainty, sour and with hints of watermelon, sweetening as the berries get bigger into sugary water. Much of the crop used to go for jam as it loses its qualities quickly.

ELSANTA was developed in Holland 1985. It has quickly come to dominate the market because of its resilience and long shelf-life, even if the-flavour is short lived. Ironically, it was developed for growing in tunnels as an out-of-season fruit but has come to be the all-purpose outdoor strawberry as well. All hues of red, firm and classically heart-shaped, at least 4 cm (1 1/2 in) across, the flesh has a yellow-white hue to the salmon and the taste is very deliberate and distinctly honeyed with no sours, familiar from the sweet repertory of artificial flavours. A good variety for PYO farms as the berries are firm and a good size as well as standing up well to being inexpertly hand-picked. Typically they are bright, deep ruby red with a good first bite, but fade quickly. They lack the taste of Cambridge. All looks and texture.

ELVIRA is ovoid when small, with thin page-boy-hat-type fronds off the stalk, fattening into two halves like the torso of a busty waitress. The flesh has an orange cast to the salmon and the taste is an organized sourness, like crushed lemons, especially when small, but developing a honey sweetness in the larger fruit. An example in July was neat red, long and angular, with a deep long sweet taste of lemons and a little sharpness, but lacking all-round flavour.

EVITA is a new English variety developed privately from Californian stock by Peter Vinson in Tunbridge Wells. Its acceptance has been spectacular, from three-quarters of an acre in '92 to 350 acres in '94 and rising. Well-flavoured, slightly acidic and reminiscent of a wild strawberry, it has a late season, arriving in July and August

HAPIL is predominantly red to scarlet, broad-shouldered, tapering to a point – a lifeguard's figure — eventually bulking up into two sides. The texture is a bit woody, with a poor distribution of flesh to pip and of sour to sweet. It becomes softer and very sweet, and is a bit velvety and one-dimensional.

PEGASUS is a good muscular berry, deep scarlet in colour, with page-boy looks again to the stalk, pointed and fat. It is inclined to wateriness, with a slight bite and not much acidity. It does look the part, however, and is possibly the most handsome of all strawberries.

ROYAL SOVEREIGN was always said to be the great English strawberry. It was an early variety, conical in shape and consistent. Its short keeping qualities – less than 12 hours – and susceptibility to disease have meant it never made the transfer to pick-your-own farms or supermarkets and has remained essentially a garden variety.

Other named varieties worth mentioning include: SELVA from Belgium in August, which is fat and wide, with a sweet first taste but going woody and having a short finish; RAPELLA is an interesting strawberry, but falling from favour because of mildew problems.

CAMBRIDGE RIVAL and CAMBRIDGE FAVOURITE are relatively easy to grow in gardens. ROYAL SOVEREIGN and the perpetual AROMEL, with a second autumn crop, need careful husbandry.

TAYBERRY

The Tayberry is a cross between an Aurora blackberry grown in Oregon and a Scottish raspberry. First developed in 1983, it is now also grown in France. It has the best qualities of both its parents. The long, 4 cm (1½ in), thin pendulous pale berry, has a tart raspberry-to-strawberry flavour. Again, it is usually sold too unripe. Available May to July.

CITRUS FRUIT

CLEMENTINE · GRAPEFRUIT · KUMQUAT ·
LEMON · LIME · MANDARIN · MINNEOLA ·
ORANGE · ORTALINE · ORTANIQUE · SATSUMA ·
TANGERINE · UGLI

The wonderful array of citrus fruits reaches its peak when most needed, in the dark days of January and February – a fitting counterpoint to the berries of summer. An increasing monument to the successful marriage of diversity and the global market.

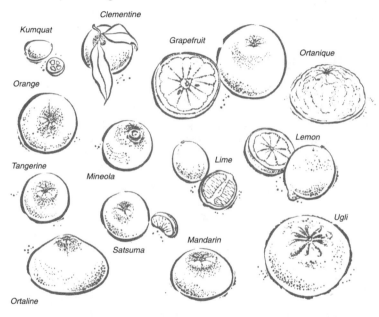

CLEMENTINE

An accidental cross between a mandarin and a sweet orange in the garden of Father Pierre Clement in Algeria in 1902, this survives where other mandarin crosses have not. Available from November to February, they come mostly from North Africa or from South Africa in early summer.

Smaller than a satsuma, at about 4 cm (1 ½ in) across, and round like an unformed orange, the thin tight skin is light orange speckled on a paler background which is almost completely hidden. The fruit has a lovely configuration, with no pips, and is firm and juicy. Fragrant, juicy and long-lasting, it has more flavour than a satsuma, but is not quite as user-friendly.

GRAPEFRUIT

The original grapefruit was probably a mutation of the exceedingly large SHADDOCK (named after the captain who took it to the West Indies), found in Thailand, Malaysia and Indonesia and which can weigh up to 5 kg (11 lb). Since its discovery in the last century it has been intensively developed using strains of different sweetness.

The POMELO is known as 'the mother of grapefruits', a cross between a shaddock and a devolved grapefruit: much larger, thick-skinned and with bitter pith. Some trials have started to develop a pink version.

Another variation – or the next generation – is the **SWEETIE from Israel: about 9x7 cm (3½x2¾ in), lemon to lime in colour, with a very bitter skin and sour thick white pith, it has an intense sour scent but a lovely sweet flavour, like an ugli fruit (see page 274).

COOKING: *The astringent abrasive quality of grapefruit matches and needs strong flavours; classically with crab; with chicory; as an edge in old-fashioned puddings and marmalades; gentler as a jelly.*

BEST BUYS The white-fleshed grapefruit has tended to be bred sweeter and to have few, if any, pips. Much of the character has moved from the fruit to the pith and they have been outperformed by the enthusiastic revival of pink-fleshed varieties. Well-known examples from **Jaffa** were poor and acidic with a high ratio of pith. Marsh Seedless, sometimes just called Marsh, turns a deeper colour – almost a pink flush – as it ripens. Widely grown and available, it is mostly notable for its juiciness and thin membranes.

By general consent, the best pink grapefruit comes from Florida, although the best American variety, DUNCAN, is not seen here or if it is then it is not labelled as such. There are different grades: 'ruby' means deeply red; then there is 'burgundy'; and 'pink' is paler still, but sweeter than both.

FLORIDA PINK has a yellow skin and, although called pink, the flesh has a rich opalescence. The long segments are very sweet, with a little sour and the texture is strong.

INDIAN RIVER has yellow skin, and orange blush to yellow flesh. It has no acidity and is sweet enough to be eaten like an orange, having good tangs of citrus.

STAR RUBY was developed in the '70s and is extensively grown in Cyprus. It could be mistaken for a squat orange from the skin, although the flesh is a corpuscular red. The pith is thin, so there is lots of juicy flesh; it is more sour than other reds, with a taste closer to lemon. Often called SUNRISE, it was conspicuously more impressive from **Jaffa** in the tastings than its white-fleshed counterpart.

KUMQUAT

Originally from China, this thumb-sized fruit with edible, slightly bitter, skin is grown around the world. Gimmicky, cocktail-party food, its flavour is quite sharp. Actually the worst of most worlds, with poor ratio of flesh to pith and skin – its single redeeming characteristic is its size.

LEMON

Lemons may not actually have reached this country until the 13th century. Only rarely do lemons carry their name, even if the difference between varieties in terms of acidity, sourness, pith levels and pip count are fundamental. **Safeway** has made some concession, importing thick-skinned Amalfi lemons in autumn and judiciously using cyrovac packaging to give its unwaxed lemons the semblance of a sheen. Price is a consistent guideline for quality, though unwaxed remain more expensive than waxed – a bizarre anomaly, as less work is done. Otherwise, one suspects the British market is probably largely a dumping ground for the undiscerning.

LIME

Originally from Malaysia, limes have proliferated in most warm climates where lemons also grow. A relative newcomer to this country, they were only planted seriously in the West Indies around 1850 and almost completely unknown in our markets until 1890. In the mid-19th century British sailors used limes to protect them against scurvy, hence the nickname 'limeys'. The distinctions between limes from different varieties and regions are blurred and information scant. The round limes of the Caribbean and Southern Europe tend to be thinner-skinned, and are likely to turn yellow and be bitter. Indian limes tend to be sweeter. Occasionally *WILD LIMES can be found – brought in via Rungis, usually for the restaurant trade. Knobbly and deep green, scratch their skin and the potency is obvious.

MANDARIN

This is a hard fruit to find these days. They were also called the 'NARCHEY ORANGE' or the 'CLOVE ORANGE' or 'NOBLE ORANGE', being distinctively flatter than taller and more perfumed. They have been widely used to cross-breed with other species. A good mandarin will be larger and darker than a tangerine, with a thin manageable skin and full fleshy segments with pips. The taste is watery and acid, but with lovely scented high notes of the kind to which commercial orange drinks aspire. The European season starts in December, although the charming practice of wrapping each fruit in coloured paper or tin foil has fallen out of fashion.

MINNEOLA

A cross between a tangerine and a grapefruit, this is sometimes called a 'TANGELO' or 'ORLANDO'. Most come from Israel. They have a distinctive bulbous nib and are easy to peel, with only a small amount of pith and the occasional pip – the segments amply filling the globe. The mild tart juiciness has hints of mandarin, verging on the sour – 'the taste of Grand Marnier'.

ORANGE

The orange was first imported from Spain in 1290; Sir Walter Raleigh reintroduced them in the 16th century. By the 19th century there were warehouses devoted to the orange trade at Hunstrete in London and at Liverpool. For oranges to flourish, the winter temperature must not drop below 4°C (40°F). Citrus fruit from the more tropical climates tends to have dirty skins, but this does not necessarily have a bearing on the quality. Pips in oranges and orange variations are becoming rare. The luminescent purple, red and green string bags in which they are sold tend to hide blemishes.

BEST BUYS FORTUNA is squat and bowls-ball-shaped. Smooth and thin-skinned, it has one pip per segment and is juicy, with tones of mandarin but gentler and duller. A very safe flavour, with high acid.

MANDORA is squat, with a smooth tight bitter skin that is hard to peel; the coarse and deeply orange flesh is juicy, fragrant and tart, a bit clumsy and unrewarding. An example from Cyprus, about 8x7 cm (3^1/$_4$x2^3/$_4$ in), with three pips per section, was very poor and unattractive.

NAVELINA is an early version of the aristocratic WASHINGTON NAVEL, beginning around November. About 8x9 cm (3^1/$_4$x3^1/$_2$ in), a perfect deep bright orange in colour and round but tending to point at the peak, hence the name. The thick tight skin is easy to peel and there is little pith. The 10 neat segments have a lovely sharp well-pitched flavour, not overly sweet to start with, but building up a great balance of acidity and sweetness. Also related, but slightly later in the season starting around January, is the Navellate, which is very juicy, round and pipless.

RUBY RED, available from Spain in January to March, is sometimes called the BLOOD ORANGE or the MALTA ORANGE. Originally grafted from a pomegranate tree crossed with an orange, the blood-red colour of the flesh develops as it ripens and eventually colours even the skin. Round and small, at about 8 cm (3^1/$_4$ in), it has a dusky, pock-marked thin skin. There are blood-red veins around the edges of the segments, which give the orange a bloody hue becoming more pronounced as they ripen. Unripe, they tend to be tart and one-dimensional in flavour. They are good in drinks, but apart from the colour have little appeal.

SALUSTIANA is sold as a juicing orange here, but also justifies its place as a sweet eating orange. Popular with growers in North Africa and Spain, they are about

7 cm (2¾ in) in size, with a thin tight pale skin which is easily peeled. The fresh neat segments have soft flesh and instant juice and fragrance. A bit underrated for juice, these are attractive and refreshing, and have no pips.

SANGUINE is spindly with a mottled orange skin flecked with red. About 7.5-8 cm (3-3¼ in) in size, it has ample skin and pith and small thin neatly formed segments. The flavour is sharp, sweet, tart, precise and to the point. They do not have the lusciousness of fruit earlier in the year, but are on the dry side, feeling more like a stored orange, a half-time football orange.

SEVILLE, usually from Spain, is almost round, about 6 cm (2½ in) across, with viciously bitter skin and pith on which its reputation for marmalade is based. It contains a small clustering of pale segments, each with 3 or 4 pips each, and a grapefruit-sour flavour which is quite arresting. The Sevillians must have been overjoyed to discover the idea of marmalade. The oranges do need vats of sugar to make them at all palatable – twice the weight of sugar to orange.

SHAMOUTI from Israel is tall and distinctively flat-topped and takes over from the Navel as the mainstream orange in March. With deep coloured, slightly wrinkled skin and thick pith, it is tricky to peel. Inside are neat segments, which are sweet, juicy and slightly tart.

SUNTINA is about 6.5 cm (3¼ in) in size and inclined to be oblong, with a deep – almost artificial-looking – orange spicy skin. Almost pithless, but perfectly formed clean segments are without pips and very sweet; like sucking a sugar cube out of an orange. Although interesting, the sugar level is way off the scale and the flavour is just a bit one-dimensional.

VALENCIA is a late orange and the handsome luminescent deep-orange ovoid is slightly deformed at the stalk. The thick-looking, pock-marked and cratered skin is easy to peel, revealing perfectly formed thin segments. An Israeli example was sweet and juicy, with a single pip to each segment or less, it was slightly pithy with a strong taste leading to sours. The less impressive examples tend to the taste of boiled sweets. At their best from Valencia: a round example, 8 cm (3¼ in) across, was luminescent, thin-skinned and strong-tasting leading to sours, chunky with no pips and quite long segments.

ORTALINE

Another of the family of tangerine/grapefruit crosses, ortalines arrive in spring from Spain. They have a flat, sat-upon configuration and a beautifully clean orange skin, quite tightly wrapped around healthy segments. Very sweet on the first bite, it is quite fragrant and tart, with a gentle and interesting flavour.

ORTANIQUE

The flat, squashed appearance of this fruit belies its superb quality. An example from Jamaica was about 7.5-8 cm (3-3¼ in) with a bitter thin skin, smooth-fleshed, flecked with black spots and occasional pips, the soft-fleshed segments filling the interior. It had a lovely texture and a beautifully perfumed intensity, building in its sweetness. Another from Morocco was more like a squat orange with a thin skin; juicy and tart with no pips. It was sweet to sticky and fragrant.

SATSUMA

A pipless variation of the Mandarin, originating from Japan and named after the province where it was first grown, it is typically the easiest citrus to peel. Early varieties from Uruguay arrive in April with very pale tight skin and fat segments. Quite scented, they are sharp and juicy with a refreshing flavour not far removed from grapefruit. Early summer varieties from Uruguay can be thick-skinned and lemony green, very juicy but low on taste and quite tart. Organic examples can be twice the price of ordinary.

TANGERINE

Along with the mandarin, one of the mothers of the new generation of citrus crosses. It is quite rare and tends to look like a rejected small orange. The tightly knit skin is speckled and a bit dirty, but easily peeled; the segments fill the pith and have two pips each. Soft, juicy, mild and not overly tart, like an immature orange.

UGLI

This is a cross between a grapefruit, orange and a tangerine first bred in Jamaica and the name was patented by **Jamaica Produce**. A dirty soft-skinned grapefruit in smudged yellows and greens, it is full-fleshed inside the skin, which peels away from its white pith. The flesh is floppy in the mouth and juicy, like an unsour grapefruit, and with an intriguing soft texture.

BEST BUYS The ugli would probably be more popular if cheaper. They can be exceptional. One from **Waitrose** was a vivid British racing green and a massive 12x10 cm (4¾x4 in), with cactus-like indentations – almost plastic looking. It was possibly under-ripe, but the orange-blushed segments sent an immediate tart zest of lemons and melons.

   UNIQ has caused some controversy among grocers. Some say it is just another form of ugli, while **Safeway – the supermarket who first adopted it – claim it is a wild variation. It is as big, with a floppy thick soft skin, opening up to reveal whole segments. A sort of relaxed grapefruit, it has a lemony smell and a beautifully fresh first mild and fragrant taste, with a brief finish. Available from January to May, it is outstanding among all citrus fruits.

TROPICAL FRUIT

BANANA · CACTUS FRUIT · COCONUT · DATE ·
FIG · GRENADILLO · GUAVA · KIWANO · KIWI
FRUIT · LOQUAT · LYCHEE · MANGO ·
MANGOSTEEN · PAPAYA · PASSION FRUIT ·
PERSIMMON · PHYSALIS FRUIT · PINEAPPLE ·
RAMBUTAN · TAMARILLO · ZALACCA

The arrival of exotic fruits has symbolized the pioneering nature of the supermarkets, although in the last two years some – noticeably Tesco – have cooled considerably. They have all experienced some difficulty with them in maintaining ripeness.

BANANA

Until the turn of the century, botanists still referred to the banana as *Musa sapientum paradisiaca*, as tradition had it that it was a banana – not an apple – that Eve gave to Adam. Hence its other name of 'Paradise fig', often still used for dried bananas in the trade. There is some confusion over the difference between the plantain and the banana, though the shorthand explanation has come to be that plantains are for cooking and bananas for eating raw. The confusion arises because not all the bananas on a bunch are fully ripe at the same time. The skill exercised on the plantations is to cut the cluster at the right time so they can be ripened on the boats.

The much smaller Canary Island banana was the first commercially traded banana in the London markets until, in 1902, the first boats docked in Bristol from Jamaica. The banana industry is sustained by international agreement, with different countries paying premiums to take bananas from underdeveloped regions. Nearly all the bananas sold here are from the Caribbean, supplemented occasionally when stocks are down by some from Central America. Although the traditional preference here – dating back to Canary bananas – has been for small fruit, Central American bananas are larger and, many hold, better-tasting, smelling more of fruit, even apricots. The Central American trade is better organized into plantations, compared to the dependent shanty industries of the Windward Islands and Jamaica. Not surprisingly, bananas do not like the cold and should not be stored in the fridge.

BEST BUYS The best bananas in tastings in the past year have consistently been *COSTA RICA, usually around 10p more expensive. The RED BANANA, usually from Cuba or India, is rarely found. Left to ripen so the claret skin has streaks of black, the flesh will be salmon pink, perfumed and creamy. The APPLE BANANA is a finger-sized miniature, perfect for neat little recipes, like fritters.

CACTUS FRUIT

The spines of this fruit are usually nicked off; if not, handle them with extreme caution and peel them on the end of a knife. The softly smooth skin is a blushing red-orange and the flesh is a brilliant vermilion, tasting like a cross between a tomato and passion fruit. There is little waste, save the tough, shot-style pips. The flesh has an attractive soft sweet mealy texture and a versatile flavour that carries over well into cooked dishes.

COCONUT

That coconuts have ended up on shies at fairs is symptomatic of the Victorian indolence towards foods. In other parts of the world the coconut has sustained whole cultures. The husk goes for brushmaking, matting and rope. The juice of the green fruit has sustained travellers in the desert and goes for palm sugar; the sap has been drawn off as a nutritious non-alcoholic drink, especially favoured by Hindus; the flesh is used in baking and to make milk; the oil for cooking. The coconut palm grows in tropical climates, usually by the sea, reaching up to 17 m (100 ft) and producing between 100 and 200 nuts a year. Part of its unfashionability has been its high level of saturated fat level, and its use in the confectionery area. In Africa, India and south east Asia its use is more imaginative.

COOKING: *A good coconut is heavy. Skewer a hole through the eyes to drain off the juice and then crack the husk on a stone or concrete floor. An average nut gives about 4 cups of grated flesh.*

COQUITO

These tiny coconuts from Chile, also known as BABY COCONUTS, are the size of marbles and are sold ready peeled. Although hollow, they are too young to have any milk. With a milky hazelnut flavour, serve these addictive fruits just as they are, like nuts.

DATE

According to an old Arab saying, dates need their feet in the water and their heads in the fire. The trees grow to about 15 m (50 ft) and open out into a cluster of 40 to 80 feather-shaped leaves, about 2.5-3 m (8-10 ft) long. From this cluster hang 180-230 kg (400-500 lb) of fruit in bunches of 9-13.5 kg (20-30 lb). They will not bear fruit until they are 8-10 years old and need temperatures of more than 38°C (100°F) and must be at least 25 miles from the sea as they can't bear any trace of salt.

The date palm can sustain a complete village, as they have done in the deserts around Tunis for centuries, where estates are handed down as dowries. The trunk supplies timber for houses, fencing and fuel; the leaves go to make baskets, bags, mats, fans, brushes, walking sticks, ropes, cords, roofs and walls; spirits like *arrak*, sugars and vinegars are made from the fruit; the young unfurled shoots and leaves are eaten as a vegetable, and the stones made into a kind of coffee or fed to the animals.

GOLDEN from Israel is a small kumquat-sized oval, 2 cm (³/4 in) tall, with a colour of burnt ochre. The skin is sweet and the white flesh is sugary sweet and crunchy, as you might imagine sugar cane to be. These are even more expensive than Medjoul, at about £4.50 per lb.

HAYANI from Israel are large smooth brown lozenges, with a long stone and a sweet straw texture. Mealy and indistinct, they are pleasantly comforting with an interesting mix of textures.

**MEDJOUL, from the Jordan River in Israel, are large, nearly 5x2 cm (2x³/4 in), morel-shaped, and translucent purple with a burgundy blush. They are dry, meaty and sticky sweet, but naturally sugared – some say they have a buttery voluptuousness. They have a small stone so make a big mouthful, but they are expensive at nearly £4 per lb. A variation are now being sold as fresh called JORDAN.

BRANCH DATES from Tunisia will keep for a year. The beige to chestnut-brown flesh has a distinct gentle nuttiness which produces sweetness, but without the cloying levels of sugar in boxed dates.

BEST BUYS As with Camembert cheese, the long boat-shaped boxes for dates have been among the finest examples of packaging art, though the dates themselves – usually the fabled DEGLET NOIR – are drenched in a glucose syrup. The original North-African trade in these is now rivalled by that of California. There is little to pick between the brands, though the quality of the dates in tubs has been noticeably poorer than that in the boxes. The best have been **Sungold** from California and the worst **Eat Me**, also from California. Price and syrup reduced everything to a singular uniformity, which does not really reflect the subtlety and richness of fresh dates.

STONED DATES from **Whitworth's** are pressed into blocks, and may be the produce of more than one country. Granulated but not over-syruped, they are useful in recipes.

FIG

Figs are so redolent of the images of sexuality – male and female – and of dreams of power that they assume a mythical significance that surpasses their more mundane fate of being battered into cellophane blocks of dense sweet stickiness or of being the butt of laxative jokes.

They are frequently mentioned in the Bible, beyond Adam and Eve reaching for the leaves to protect their modesty. It was also the flavour of Athens figs that reputedly tempted Xerxes to conquer Greece in 480BC.

The tree is native to Palestine and its cultivation has spread to encompass the whole of the Mediterranean. The finest were held to be the SMYRNA, being fatter and with softer skin after drying. The fruit from the male tree is inedible, but becomes home to a wasp which fertilizes the female. Traditionally, the female trees were wreathed in garlands of male figs from June 5-15. Smyrna figs go for drying and were also the rootstock taken to California.

The COMMON FIG does not have such a romantic aura, growing from seed and propagated by cuttings. The flavours vary from region to region, rather than by variety or colour of the skin. There can be two harvests in the year, the first to be eaten fresh and the second, much sweeter, usually used for drying, where the sugars can constitute more than half the bulk.

*BURSA figs from Turkey arrive in late autumn to a chorus of enthusiasm: 'large pear-shaped, sweet and pungent'. Traditionally, these might have been served with cured hams or stuffed with sweetmeats. The best Italian figs are *KADOTA, familiar in shape from tins. Other varieties arrive from the Mediterranean through the summer in different hues of lime-green to almost purple or jet-black, but each contain dramatic crimson tendrils sometimes touched with lemon. These are the flowers, sometimes left in figs for drying, or allowed to grow on to seed.

At the turn of the century, dried figs were always eaten on Mothering and Palm Sundays. Fig pie or fig puddings were a tradition in the Home Counties, though in other parts of the country the figs were replaced with currants – and indeed currants are still called figs by many.

COOKING: *A ripe fresh fig will be heavy in the hand and soft to the touch, as if it is filled with its own juice like a water bag. Cooking in water emaciates them, though they combine well other ingredients, especially Mediterranean flavours like anise and nuts.*

GRENADILLO

These speckled orange lanterns from Colombia have hard cardboard-like skin and white bready pith with a good volume of translucent grey pistules inside easily removable sacks. Related to the passion fruit, but not as tart, it has a better ratio of flesh and pip to skin, but is somewhat less intense in flavour.

GUAVA

When ripe, the smell of this fruit from Brazil can fill the room. The guava is often sold unripe (hence its most famous incarnations as jelly) and it has a very short peak. When ripe, however, it is an extraordinary source of vitamin C, one average fruit representing eight times the RDA for an adult. Cooking brings out the flavour inherent in the sandy and deep-pipped flesh. When the skin is still green (on ripe fruit the skin should have yellowed) it has a musky smell of elderflowers.

COOKING: *Use in ice-cream, puddings, jellies, salads or to support more conventional fruits, such as apples or pears in cooking. As a cheese, the pulp boiled down, sieved and cooled, it is sold in slices in Brazil.*

KIWANO

An orange oval from Colombia, it has small spikes like a tiny dinosaur. Inside it is obviously one of the passion fruit family, the pips held in a gel; but this is a refreshing lime version, the flavour veering towards melon.

KIWI FRUIT

Sometimes called CHINESE GOOSE-BERRY, before it leapt to universal acceptance on the back of mass cultivation in New Zealand. Most sold in this country now come from Italy. They have unseen virtues, not least their enormous vitamin C content which is 10 times that of a lemon, and they can tenderize meat in a marinade. The biggest problem is finding a ripe one: test the hairy khaki skin as for an avocado (see page 240). The ratio of brilliant emerald flesh to skin is excellent, and it is best eaten with a teaspoon. Although advocates would pair it off with anything, the high level of acidity mitigates against universal use as it will curdle cream and dissolve a gelatine-set mousse.

LOQUAT

Looking like an exotic apricot, this Israeli fruit is available from late spring to early summer. Creamy orange and speckled as it gets riper, it has a tough, inedible skin. Inside, it has a smooth lychee-style pip and the flesh is juicy and refreshingly sour.

LYCHEE

Hardly a new exotic, but this Thai fruit has still to establish itself properly. It is small, slightly larger than a grape at 2x4 cm (^{3}/4x1^1/2 in), and the horned thin pastel-scarlet skin coats a translucent, purple-hued silky smooth flesh around the smoothest of pips. Perfumed and delicious, the flavour is refreshingly chill and sweet, one of the world's great luxuries. Like mangoes, however, the stickiness lingers more than it might. The juiciness is lost quickly and they are best bought in small quantities at a time. Paler varieties tend to have a fuller flavour.

MANGO

Perhaps surprisingly, mangoes are from the same family as cashew and pistachio nuts. The dark shiny-leafed trees from which it takes its Malay name *mang* can grow to as much as 35 m (115 ft) in span and have transplanted from their native India to most hot climates. The fruits vary from the tiny egg-shaped wild varieties that taste like turpentine to the larger sweeter straw-orange with which we are more familiar. There are more than 2,500 varieties in all. 'No fruit possess so wide a range from absolute vileness to the most delicious lusciousness,' declared an early writer. In India, they are picked before they are ripe to make tarts and preserves. Here they have invariably been ripened en route. A good mango has a neon-orange flesh, oozes juice and should not be stringy or fibrous.

By necessity it will be messy to eat or to carve (see below). One easier solution is the new suckable variety from the Gambia, arriving in July and August. Some of the sense of the many differences between mangoes has started to appear in supermarkets. Most are air-freighted, but the price comes down considerably if they are sent by ship.

COOKING: *Slice down both sides either side of the flat of the stone, cut the flesh in a criss-cross pattern into squares and turn the skin inside out to allow the knife to cut underneath. Shave the remaining flesh off the stone and cut into sections.*

A Chinese delicacy is preserved slices of mango with chilli and liquorice. South-east Asia has other variations, with a spiced mayonnaise with prawn, and Indian cream with sugar, lime and milk.

BEST BUYS BOMBAY or ALPHONSO has been highly regarded for many years as among the finest of mangoes. A golden sunset-yellow, this plump oval fruit is found only during April and May. The succulent flesh is even deeper yellow – almost saffron – and can stain. Expensive at nearly £2 a piece. BANGAPALLI follow on from BOMBAY or ALPHONSO, also from India, but has deep orange flesh and is slightly larger.

HADEN from the Gambia are squat, elongated to 11 cm (4¾ in). Khaki going on red in colour, the flesh is bright yellow, smooth and rimmed light green. It has a distinctive flavour of sweet lemons with something floral, and is not fibrous.

MANGOP from Brazil is tropical green into verdant orange and smooth reds, about 11x9 cm (4¾x3½ in). The smooth deep peach-ochre flesh is fibrous to eat and slightly shreddy, but fragrant with a tart sweetness.

*RUBY from the Gambia is only available in July and August. It is unusual in that the top can be cut across and the flesh sucked out. Yellow to dusty apple-red in colour with a bright yellow flush and about 11 cm (4¾ in), it has a pure excellent taste and is very juicy.

TOMMY ATKINS from Puerto Rico is a flatfish smooth ovoid, apple green going on red in colour. Inside the flesh is vivid orange, fibrous and apricot-like with a hint of pineapple.

MANGOSTEEN

The imposingly impressive outer casing of this fruit from Thailand is like a well-worn cricket ball encrusted with hard green leaf and stalk. Inside is a lychee-like fruit in sections which is deliciously impressive. It is available from April. Tinned examples tend to be poor.

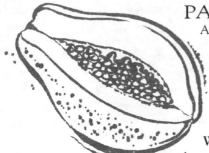

PAPAYA

Also known as the PAW PAW, this Jamaican fruit is ripe when the skin turns yellow, with just a hint of green hue. The flesh should be an intense pink that responds to lemon or lime. Some now also come from Brazil. **Waitrose** claims its fruit is ripened longer on the tree.

COOKING: *Slice lengthwise and scoop out the black seeds which are also said to be a laxative. The fruit contains the enzyme papain, so it cannot be used to form jellies or mousses; it can, however, be effective in a marinade.*

Slice open and sprinkle with lime juice; blend with yoghurt and honey as a drink; serve with cold hams, especially Parma. Papaya responds well to ginger and even chilli. It bakes well and can be a surprising feature in an upside-down pudding.

PASSION FRUIT

The passion is religious rather than sexual, christened by missionaries in South America who thought the cluster of the flower and stalk resembled the crucifixion. The round fruit, about 4-5 cm (1½-2 in), has a wrinkled rhino skin which breaks up like parchment to reveal the generous filling of yellow black pods. The flavour is tart and direct, but the sweet aftertaste is the attraction. Now mostly from Zambia, they are considerably cheaper than most other exotics.

COOKING: *They make good soufflés, hot or cold, and also a drink mixed with cane syrup and rum macerated for 6 weeks.*

PERSIMMON

Examples of persimmons are usually quite small in supermarkets here, but Italian and Spanish top-grade fruit can be as large as a beef tomato. The persimmon has such a high tannin content that it is virtually inedible unripe. The SHARON FRUIT is a variety of persimmon, developed in Israel, which is tannin-free and can be eaten like an apple, before it has matured. The smooth shiny skin is slightly fragile and bursting when ripe, with a distinct shade of dirty orange, and the stalk decoratively encrusted with its leaves. The flesh is beautifully and uniformly streaked in shades of deep orange; if it is apricot-pale then it is not ripe. It has a delicate, quite elusive, honey-sweet flavour, in a silky smooth and richly fibrous texture which is its great attraction. However, the skin is viciously bitter.

PHYSALIS FRUIT

Artistically wrapped inside its own resilient paper-like leaf, this small golden berry the size of a small cherry, is tart, sweet and custardy. Also known as the CAPE GOOSEBERRY, its tiny pips are edible. Very decorative and now mostly imported from Colombia, it has a distinctive taste, like a sour cherry or the first taste of a strawberry. Beautiful in tarts.

PINEAPPLE

Like the strawberry, this is a false fruit, ie made up of lots of little fruits which form the scales and eyes on the skin. The Spanish discovered the pineapple in the 15th century in Paraguay, where the Guarani Indians had already developed a considerable trade in the 'beautiful fruit'. As early as the beginning of the 1700s, pineapples were being grown in European greenhouses to sell to the rich. The French in the late '40s encouraged the cultivation across Africa.

Fruit still with the long leafy stalks are easier to judge for ripeness – the smaller inner leaves will come away with the pineapple's weight. Fully ripe, the stalk will give and move around. Yellow pineapples tends to eat sweeter, but are twice the price. Smell the bottom to gauge almost precisely how fresh it is. Some say the sugars accumulate at the base of the fruit so it should not be cut in circles, but in vertical boats.

Pineapples do not travel well, having only a short period of ripeness. **Necta** has been importing ready-cut sections from Costa Rica in clear plastic containers. They claim that most cooks will only get 30% flesh off a pineapple so it is cost-effective. Unlike the tinned versions (pineapple is the third most popular tinned fruit), the nutrients are not lost in heating.

QUEEN PINES, from South Africa, are smaller at about 8 cm (3¼ in) square, with deep blistered orange skin and are very sweet. They have a fragrant smell and are intensely rich, but quite dry. CAYENNE are said to be medium-sized, sweet and sharp. SUGAR LOAF is larger, whiter-fleshed and mild.

COOKING: *Pineapples contains an enzyme, bromelin, which breaks down protein and is useful in marinades, but for the same reason will not allow the setting of gelatine.*

RAMBUTAN

The most spectacular of the lychee family, with its mad monstrous tendrils, the fruit is ripe when the skin is bouncy and turns a violent crimson, and the tendrils are fused red, not brown. The flesh is drier than a lychee.

TAMARILLO

An elegant, deep red, heart-shaped fruit with a woody stalk, opens to reveal a stunning inside of black-to-purple seeds set in deep orange flesh and translucent juice. The flavour is almost savoury, somewhere between tomato and plum. The skin is very bitter, the seeds small like passion fruit. A tomato/passion fruit cross, with no acidity and luscious flesh around a central jelly pod with black pips.

ZALACCA

Another in the lychee family, this fruit is very rarely found here. Looking like a bauble-sized armadillo, it has inedible pips and sharp, tart juice which is quickly lost as they get older.

STONE FRUIT

APRICOT · CHERRY · NECTARINE · PEACH · PLUM

The beauty of stone fruit lies in it being perfectly ripe. Too often it is sold hard and ungiving. The supermarkets' problem with it is that what looks good does not necessarily have much flavour.

APRICOT

The old English word for this fruit was 'apricock' from the Latin *praecox*, meaning early ripening. By June, they are one of the heralds of summer proper. Apricots have been grown in kitchen gardens since 1542, but they do need the sun. Any frost at flowering time and there will be no fruit.

Most apricots come from France and Spain, though they originally came from Armenia and China and are widely grown around the Mediterranean rim, as well as in America, Australia and South Africa – much of this only surfacing here in tins. There is currently great enthusiasm among growers in France for giant apricots, twice the normal size. Known as Jumbocot, Lambertin, Hargrand and Orange Red, they began to be grown around Nîmes in 1989. The biggest apricot growers, centred in the Rhône valley, used to grow mainly the Polonaise variety until 1989 and have now switched to the Bergeron, and this has been said to account for the increase in sales in the UK.

COOKING: Jane Grigson accepted defeat in her Fruit Book over fresh apricots, 'As things are in this country, you will probably be wise to regard apricots as a fruit for the kitchen, then you will not be disappointed'. Tarts, fillings, jams, glazes, bakes and puddings were their destiny in English cooking. On their travels around the globe, however, apricots have been assimilated into an extraordinary number of different preparations, from meat stews to low-fat baking substitutes.

The kernels of apricots are worth the labour of cracking and adding to a salad. The culture of glacé and crystallized apricots comes from the south of France.

BEST BUYS A great many apricots are still sold without reference to their variety. If the celebrated English MOOR PARK is still grown commercially, it is being passed off under a pseudonym – though saplings are still sold in garden centres. Good apricots will be warmly coloured and rosy-cheeked, but will only keep a few days before wizening. Store them in a bag in the salad drawer of the fridge.

CASTELBRITE from Spain, is about 4x6 cm (1½x2½) with a rosy blush to the soft orange, light fur, and a stone that is less than one quarter of the fruit. It has a bright pleasant sunny taste and a good texture, although it tends to be uneven for ripeness rather than quality.

ORANGE RED from France, is one of the new larger breeds at 5x5.5 cm (2x2¼ in). Apricot-orange to mauve-pink in colour, it is long and thin, like a half-egg shape. The sweet flesh is mango-yellow, soft, luscious and juicy, but can have threads of woody filament. With an elusive flavour, it tends to dry up in the mouth, and although generally good, they are nearly 40p each.

PEACH APRICOT from New Zealand is large – almost the size of a small orange – with an orange flush to the pink fur. The crevice is about as accurate a representation of the human bottom as the fruit world possesses. Very dry and grainy, it is missing the subtle elements of a good apricot, it is possibly tired out from the journey.

RED ROYAL from France is about 4x6 cm (1½x2½ in), with a white to yellow sheen and peach-mauve blush. The flesh is an even-coloured orange, sweet, juicy, with a good mellow flavour.

DRIED APRICOTS

It is often said that some of the world's best apricots go for drying. Some of the brighter and seemingly attractive replicas of fresh fruit have, in fact, been doused in sulphur dioxide (E220) or glossed with oils and glucose to extend their shelf-life. Left to dry naturally, they will go fig-like brown. The high level of iron and vitamin A make them valuable in a vegetarian diet and to detoxify the system.

The best are HUNZA, which look more like soft walnuts, dried on the roof tops of Kashmir and Afghanistan. They need soaking or poaching for five minutes with a little lemon juice. Other varieties from Persia are often mentioned as well, although the trade is spasmodic.

CHERRY

Lucullus, the Roman general and *bon viveur*, brought the cherry tree from the city of Cerasus, hence also the French *cerise* from the Latin *Prunus cerasus*. These would have been sour cherries and the sweet *P. avium* developed later. Cherries are prolific across Europe, especially in France, and date here back to Henry VIII. The orchards were centred around Sittingbourne, but have almost disappeared in the last 40 years. They have dwindled from more than 3,000 acres in the '50s to less than 2,000 today, and now most cherries are imported. As a trade, it just seems all to have been too much trouble. Cherry picking was an unwieldy industry, and the tall trees susceptible to the climate, badly hit by rain damage in poor summers and wasps and birds in good weather.

For all the 200, or perhaps more, varieties of cherry there are only two basic types: the sweet, heart-shaped black, white or red Géans or Guignes; and the round or oblate, more acid, Griottes, which includes most of the famous cooking varieties like Morello or Reine Hortense, the latter usually going for eau-de-vie and for drying. The Géans are very much in the ascendancy.

BEST BUYS BING is a term for a hard-style sweet cherry commonly used for catch-all labelling, rather than more specific variety names like Burlat or Washington. The best are flown from America and can last up to a week, which accounts for the premium prices — usually double that of the same cherries from Italy. Washington State is largest producer of cherries. They start picking on June 25 and the season lasts until mid-August. American varieties are susceptible to having the shoulders of American footballers and the taste of tap water. Of the European varieties VAN, BING, BURLAT and NAPOLEON will dominate in the next few years, because that is the way plantings have gone. Consistently, the French have been producing the best cherries for the market. A good cherry is told by its stalk, which should still be green and pliant; as it ages, the stalk dries and withers.

BING, from the USA, is mostly looks and little substance. With lockets of pink to purple and juicy, it is short on taste. An example, called *Extra* was big, at 4 cm (1 1/2 in) across, fat and expensive. Saffron-coloured with bright red cherub cheeks, it was almost box-shaped and the white flesh was very juicy with a gentle flavour.

EARLY BURLAT, in season in November, is about 3x2 cm (1 1/4x3/4 in) and deep cerise going on brown. The flesh is soft purple with a small stone and a short juicy cheeriness, although slightly watery. Not a special variety.

FERROVIA from, Italy, is fat, at about 3 cm (1 1/4 in) across, heart-shaped, and a shiny evenly coloured purple-brown. Inside, the flesh is a vivid red, and is juicy and sweet with a lingering tastiness.

GAUCHER, from Britain, is lantern-shaped and cerise to purple in colour, with mauve flesh. It is soft and sweet to sour. A good variety, but unpopular with the trade as they do not keep.

LARIUM, from France, has perfect medallion contours. Long and about 2 cm (3/4 in) across, it is dusk-red to mahogany and sold with its stalks on. An all-round good quality variety, it is slightly sour, even-textured, with a bouncy texture and large stone (helpful in a cherry).

LITTLE GEM, from Sittingbourne in mid-July, is a quarter the size of an ordinary cherry. Black and juicy, with a large stone, the flesh is red and has a good flavour.

NAPOLEON, from Britain, is traffic-light yellow to red and beyond. Round, with yellow flesh, it is tart and sharp.

RANIER is a luxurious orange-gold, scarlet and cream cherry, which is packed by hand. The season lasts until mid-August.

STELLA is a new variety developed from Canadian rootstock. Crimson-pink to mahogany in colour, it is almost square and about 3 cm (1 1/4 in). The white flesh is juicy, with a pure flavour that is rather neutral — nice but noncommittal.

VAN is another new variety, like Stella, from Canadian rootstock. Red-mahogany to chestnut-brown, or even deeper, it consists of two buttocks. The flesh is sweet, with a pink hue and a distinct, gentle flavour — 'a lullaby'.

NECTARINE

A strain of peach, akin to the almond and apricot, the nectarine differs mainly in the skin, which is smooth. Many are frustratingly out of condition and only hint at what pleasures they may have to offer. As a rule-of-thumb, the French varieties are better looked after, but the Italians and Spanish have more sun and the silken red and yellow skins now seem an increasingly familiar sight through late summer. Varieties are remarkably uniform in size, invariably between 6.5-7.5 cm (2¾-3 in).

BEST BUYS FIRE KING, from Spain, is coloured deep orange-red to black flecked with yellow. The flesh is deep apricot with red marks by the pip: juicy, fleshy, with a short taste and hints of sourness, it is a pure example of the mainline nectarine.

*HONEYGOLD, from France, has a smooth lemon skin with odd pink clusters; the flesh is rich and buttery sweet, very honeyed with no acidity.

INDEPENDENCE, from Italy, is coloured golden sunset into a deep delicious red.

*SILVERY, from Spain, is yellow-lime going on scarlet to deep purple; white-fleshed, the flavour is soft, floral, herbaceous and luscious like soft apples. Very good, but they are expensive at nearly 80p each.

SNOW QUEEN, from Spain, is deep red, almost apple-like colour, with hints of orange sunsets and streaks of lime, like pictures of the cosmos: it has a good sweet floral, apple-like scent and the flesh is white hinting at lime.

TASTY FREE, from France, is coloured an orange, honey-yellow to a broken veined red, looking like a moonscape. The example tried was dry, woody and off.

VENUS, from Italy, is cherubic red with yellow streaks, like sunsets and freckles; the creamy beige flesh was tough although sold as ready to eat. Meaty, and juicy when ripe, they have little flavour and are mostly texture.

PEACH

Once called 'Persian apples', after their Latin name *Prunus persica*, they probably originated in China and Japan. They need so much daylight to flower, they are grown only between latitudes ranging from northern France to southern Europe, though much is also grown in America and the equivalent latitudes in the southern hemisphere across South Africa and Australia. In France, there were many small orchards mainly centred around Montreuil, which sent peaches across Europe.

The common peach tree grows to around 6 m (20 ft) and flowers in pink blossom, like the almond, which it resembles closely. The way to judge a good peach is by smell – brush the fur and if it smells good then it will taste good. On a ripe peach the skin should peel easily and the pip should rattle freely in the centre. As with much skinned fruit, the colour of the flesh will be the same as that of the palest colour on the skin. The supermarket problem is that what tends to look good on the shelf is not necessarily fully ripe.

COOKING: *Peaches and nectarines are largely interchangeable. Good for breakfast meuslis; gentle sauces for poultry; famous as Melba or with strawberry ice cream; poached in Kirsch and under the grill with a sabayon; hot slices grilled with brown sugar and served with ice-cream; baked and spiced with ginger.*

BEST BUYS CLING STONE, from Italy, about 6.5-7.5 cm (2¾-3 in), is marked with ruddy red veins opening to a deepening yellow. They have a perfumed, eau-de-cologne smell and distinctive flavour.

FAYETTE, from Italy, about 6.5-7.5 cm (2¾-3 in), has a creamy yellow, soft downy skin, with patches of purple; the yellow flesh is dry, fibrous and disappointing.

MAY CREST, from Italy, ranges in colour from dirty yellow (under-ripe) to an almost black purple, with fiery-furnace markings on the sides and a clean yellow cleavage; the yellow flesh has a floral orange flavour. It has a better flavour than Spring Crest, but is less juicy.

REDHAVEN, from Italy and about 6-6.5 cm (2½-2¾ in), was developed in America, but is now grown world-wide. With a yellow to purple blush and clean yellow flesh, it is crunchy when unripe, but clean — 'probably good when ripe'.

RED TOP, from France, about 7-8 cm (2¾-3¼in), has good fat looks, coloured with deep scarlet clouds on yellow. The white-orange flesh is woody in texture, juicy, sweet to sour and low on flavour — sweet on first bite, but the flavour disappears quickly.

SPRING CREST is round, 5 cm (2 in) across, and was developed in Spain as an early crop starting in May. With deep yellow-to-red colouring, its velvet skin is dappled purple and orange. An example tried from Italy had a mild, juicy taste which was not fully developed, but full of brilliant textures and a good ratio of pip to flesh. Another example from **Safeway** was firm and unripe when bought, softening up — even wrinkling — after a day on the window-sill. It was larger, at about 6 cm (2½ in), with creamy, buttery yellow skin, speckled with red sunset colours going to deep fiery purple; the flesh was bright yellow to ochre, fibrous and with sharp notes and edges of citrus — OK, but not really very brilliant.

SPRING LADY, from Italy, about 6.5-7.5 cm (2¾-3 in), is butter yellow streaked with orange and purple; the yellow flesh is soft and juicy, with good sour notes and caramel tones.

YELLOW CLING, from California, has an apricot blush and the flesh is a faithful mango yellow. It is used in tins because it is hard and doesn't go soft with ripeness. It is a lovely individual peach when eaten fresh — not dissimilar to the tinned varieties (which is a tribute to the canning industry).

PLUM

The northerly cousins of the family that also includes peaches, apricots and almonds, these are supposed to have first been cultivated from the sloes, wild plum and blackthorn of hedging and woodland, though there is a view that they were brought here from around the Caspian or possibly even China. At their peak they are lush and juicy, one day off their summit and they remain a closed world. The old saying was that a plum was ripe if the fruit could be picked from its stalk, but this is only partly true. They are one of the most various fruits in the grocers.

BEST BUYS BELL, shorthand for BELLE DE LOUVAIN, is an old Belgian variety now grown here. It is tall, 6x3 cm (2½x1¼ in), coloured green to deep purple mahogany, with a crease down one side. Dry, tart and coarse, fibrous and pippy, it is somewhat insipid according to some texts.

BLACK DIAMOND, from Israel, is buttock-shaped, about 5x5.5 cm (2x2¼ in), with a smoky blue sheen over a deep brown to purple; bright watermelon-red flesh goes orange near the stone and cuts cleanly; crunchy and solid, it has a good distribution of juice and a precise delicate flavour.

CASSELMAN, from the USA, at about 5 cm (2 in), are favoured by **Marks and Spencer**. With bright crimson skin and orange flesh, they have lots of texture, but small flavour. More expensive are the Israeli versions, which are smoky blushed grey/blue and generally riper, the gentle juicy sweetness going to lushness.

CZAR is half the size of a normal plum. Blushing pink to dark red black, they are mostly grown in northern Europe for cooking and available from August. The flesh is lime-coloured, with a feathery texture, and juicy, neat and pleasant.

DAMSON is a cultivated form of the wild plum, named after the city of Damascus, and used exclusively for jams, jellies and cheese. Like Seville oranges, it owes its place in cooking to its bitterness. Intensely flavoured, but short on juice, they are available from August.

FRIAR, from the USA, is fat, about 6 cm (2½ in) square, and almost black all over. A product of the 'big is beautiful' philosophy, the blood-rose flesh has little flavour — all looks and no character.

GAVIOTA, originally from Italy but now adopted by the New World, is shaped like a square apple, about 5 cm (2 in), translucent yellow to deep red in colour; the flesh is yellow to white, fibrous, soft and sweet, with a lasting taste and melon flavours, getting stronger round the pip. With a good ratio of flesh to stone, it is good for stewing. Available from America from June and from South Africa from January.

GOLDEN JAPAN is widely grown but most on sale here are from Spain. About 4 cm (1½ in), it is golden, primrose yellow and bell-shaped; the yellow flesh is soft and loses out to the bitterness in the skin eventually vanishing. It is an unhappy combination, which is a pity as it is so pretty. Available from Europe from June, from the New World from January.

GREENGAGE is properly the REINE CLAUDE, dating back to the 16th century and said to be named after the consort of François I. There are varieties, like the larger, reddish-brown *Reine-Claude d'Althan*, developed in the 19th century in Czechoslovakia, or the still larger *Reine-Claude d'Oullins*, which is a bright green that turns brown. In markets the inferior GAGE plums sometimes will be passed off as greengages. The proper greengage should be going mauve, with the flesh a deep yellow and tart. The season is from August, but of all plums the fruit must be ripe and then it becomes honey sweet.

*MARJORIE SEEDLING is green to purple, about 7x5 cm (2¾x2 in), with grape-yellow flesh that is sour with a sweet edge. An example from **Marks & Spencer** was oval, purple with a smoky hue and scratch lines on the skin, about 4x5 cm (1½x2 in); the lime-green, translucent white-veined flesh was juicy and mellow, with a very pure plum taste.

OPAL, like the Czar, grown mostly in northern Europe, but increasing in its appeal, Small and green to yellow red, it has yellow flesh with a good clean taste.

POLISH SWITZEN is purple, almost black, about 3x4 cm (1¼x1½ in), it has soft yellow vapid flesh.

RED BEAUT is an early variety available from Spain in June. About 2.5x4 cm (1¼x1½ in) and deep red to purple in colour, it has a smooth firm texture and a small stone. Although sour and refreshing, it is fairly one-dimensional.

ROYSTON is bell-shaped, about 4 cm (1½ in), and coloured red to purple to black; the juicy flesh is a lovely purple to orange and sweet — with the sour skin, a classic interaction. Available in June.

*RUBY NELL, from South Africa, is fat and dark mauve plum in colour, 6x8 cm (2½x3¼ in), The lurid, luminescent orange flesh, has a soft texture, little moisture like soft straw, but is sweet with elements of melons. It is a good plum, with a high ratio of flesh to stone.

**SANTA ROSA, originally from America, now mostly come from Israel. Bell-shaped and about 5x5.5 cm (2x2¼ in), they are coloured a tawny speckled red to mahogany-blue, with a smoky blush. The flesh is unevenly coloured, with a red rim to yellow-white interior, purple in places. Soft, juicy and delicate, they have a good clear taste, very sweet and wet, but not long-lasting. An example later in August was lantern-shaped, deep reddy black, with sweet pink juicy flesh, tart around the pip. Another example was sweet, gentle, attractive, with a good lasting flavour, not cloying. Available June to September from Europe, but from South Africa in December and January.

SONGOLD are deep yellow in mid-winter, plum-coloured in early spring. The pale yellow flesh is juicy, with a good ratio of flesh to stone, and an attractive mild but lightly soured flavour.

**VICTORIA has a reputation as one of the great plums of the world, possibly as a result of its scarcity value due to its very short storage time. The season starts halfway through August and lasts just four weeks. Bronze, orange, opaque rust in colour, about 5x3 cm (2x1¼ in), it has pale yellow flesh which is sweet, the perfect mix of juice and texture.

PRUNES

Prunes are dried plums, and take their name literally from the Latin Prunus. Drying concentrates the levels of vitamin B6 and iron. They are also good sources of the trace mineral boron, which helps calcium absorption. Prunes from Agen in France have been the best known for centuries, supplying most of the Californian stock. Their high sugar content makes them better suited to drying. They are sun-dried and then stoved gently for six hours at temperatures under 93°C (200°F), allowed to cool and then warmed again.

The Japanese take a different approach. Umeboshi plums are pickled and sun-dried. They are used to season rice dishes and have a history of use in herbal medicine as an antibiotic.

COOKING: *Prunes are supremely more efficient with savoury foods: as stuffings for goose; as a sauce with pork; in a pie with chicken, a variation on cock-a-leekie.*

TOP FRUIT

APPLE · PEAR · QUINCE

From a nation that prided itself on its apple heritage, we seem to have accepted complete surrender. The supermarkets, initially **Safeway** and more recently **Sainsbury**, have capitalized on the publicity to be had in bringing back old varieties. However, this is mere lip service to an idea. **Safeway** hoped to move 1,000 tons of old varieties of apples. To put that into context, that represents 1/145th of the market still existing for the last main-line surviving English apple, the Cox.

Orchards are not being replanted and a few bijou packets with olde-worlde labels do not represent a realistic attempt to reverse the decline, just a cynical exercise in exploiting an emotional response. It was the multiples' desire for uniformity, for colour above all other virtues, and for mass standardization that undermined the British apple market in the first place. It was the supermarkets that created the catwalk for the ambitions of apple growers in other countries which now parade themselves monthly in all their glory along the first aisles of the supermarket.

APPLE

There were 1,545 different varieties of apple shown at the Apple Congress held in the Royal Horticultural Gardens in 1883. By 1950 only 22 English varieties had established themselves as 'commercially viable' mainstream crops. What happened to Gladstone, Miller's Seedlings or Devonshire Quarrenden and most of the others in this list of 22 is clear. They were grubbed up and replaced by foreign trees as huge imports washed across the supermarket shelves. Why they should have been forsaken so readily is less clear.

Were these old varieties of English apple of any value at all? Who, now, knows? It is not unreasonable to suppose that this country had the climate, the culture, the seed stock, the knowledge and the producers to grow great apples. We threw it away. Even what we are now tempted to believe is a traditional British apple, the first of the new season on August 10, the wide shouldered lime-to-vivid-red Discovery is itself a modern apple, developed only in 1949 and its name changed in 1962 to fit some marketing whim. The first commonly available genuinely old English apple is, in fact, the Worcester which arrives in September. Common Ground (41 Shelton Street, London W22H 9HJ) is a campaign to save old orchards and holds an annual Apple Day on October 21 which it wants to inaugurate as an annual holiday. The

COOKING APPLES

Bramley's Seedling, stands supreme in this country as the cooking apple, a triumphant vindication of the quality of English apples and a monolithic symbol of mono-culture. What became of Annie Elizabeth, Bismarck, Crimson Bramley, Grenadier, Lord Derby, Lord Grosvenor, Lord Suffield, Monarch, Newton Wonder, Sterling Castle, Warner's King, Emmeth Early, Pott's Seedling, Gascoyne's Scarlet, Edward VII, all of which were freely available as recently as the '50s?

The Bramley has a fanciful history. The original tree was reputedly the work of a young Ann Brailsford who potted up some seeds accidentally in 1809 in the back garden of her house in Church Street, Southwell, Nottinghamshire. Forty seven years later, a young nurseryman, Henry Merryweather, then still aged only 17, spotted the fruit from the tree and began to cultivate them commercially. Mr Bramley was the owner of the cottage at the time but although he gives his name to the apple he was never involved in its development.

It was first shown and commended by the Royal Horticultural Society's Fruit Committee in 1876. The original tree is preserved and still stands. The Bramley has survived, mainly as a gardener's apple, mostly in Kent, around Wisbech, Notting-hamshire and Northern Ireland.

COOKING: *The Bramley's acidity is a seemingly well-established part of English cooking, though modern cooks have tended to favour the French Reinette family, especially* Clochard, *or* Golden Delicious. *The quantity of dry matter in the composition differentiates the Bramley from eating apples which also have more sugar in them.*

Brogdale Horticultural Trust at Faversham, Kent holds the national archive of apple trees and offers guided tours from April to November as well as workshops. Along with the Royal Horticultural Society, it offers a fruit identification service to name any odd trees in your garden.

BEST BUYS BEAUTY OF HAMPSHIRE is credited to Mrs Eyre Crabbe, before 1850 at Colston, Southampton. Big and ovoid, it has a lovely contrast of orange-red cheeks and pistachio green, with good crunch, and intensely acid white flesh.

BERTANNE is a small russet from France said to be nutty in flavour. Arriving in March, it has rough olive skin and white juicy sweet flesh with a clean bite. Without the acidity of an egremont, it is an inoffensive apple which is good with cheese.

*BRAEBURN, from New Zealand, is one of the brightest stars of the New World. Well liked by the trade for its long keeping qualities, it is nevertheless a good apple in low seasons. About 6 cm (2¾ in), it is squat to ovoid — as if someone sat on the flat side. The skin is lime green, pistachio to orangey-red with yellow flecks, and the flesh creamy white to pistachio. They are crisp, Cox-like, juicy, with a good hard texture and a flavour of melon.

CALVILLE, from France, has a ribbed quince-like shape, lime green skin and hard pistachio-coloured flesh. It has a distinct russety, aristocratic flavour with hints of grapefruit. The finest can be as expensive as £1.40 each.

**COX, originally the *Cox's Orange Pippin*, was bred by a retired brewer Richard Cox from a Robston's Pippin in Slough around 1825, though not cultivated commercially until the 1920s. Difficult to grow and notoriously erratic from year to year, they are picked around September and peak at Christmas. Round, with a sat-upon configuration, about 6.5 cm (2¾ in), they shade from lime to mahogany-red like a Constable landscape. A late-picked example was crisp, lime-fresh, with a brilliant impact and excellent balance of acidity and flavour. It is also parent to new apples like dull green-yellow SUNTAN, developed in 1955 and found from November, and the juicy orangey-yellow green KENT. It has a notably high pectin count in the skin.

COOKING: Use in salads with celery and walnuts. Store in the fridge (in a warm room they soften after a few days).

EGREMONT RUSSET was first recorded in England in 1872. There have been recent signs of a revival in russet apples, which has encouraged new planting. Khaki in colour, with rough unshaven skin, the crisp white flesh has a distinct smell of pears and butter, with a rich and nutty sweetness that builds up, like the taste of cooked apple. Available from October to February.

ELLISON'S ORANGE RED is originally from Lincolnshire around 1900. About 6.5-7 cm (2¾-2¾ in), its colour varies from pistachio-green to bright mottled sunset red. It is softer to bite than Cox, the crumbly flesh having a creamy melon flavour, with hints of orange.

ELSTAR was first bred in Holland in 1955. A cross between Golden Delicious and Ingrid Marie, it is now widely planted in the Netherlands. Heavy in yield, it is larger and redder than a Cox, but less interesting.

FIESTA There are different versions of the story about the breeding of the fiesta, the most authoritative credit it to Kent in 1972. A cross between a Cox and the heavy cropper Idared, it is held by many to be the most interesting variety bred in the UK in recent years. With red and yellow coloration, a soft example tried was sharp with a distinct flavour like the end of blackberries. It is a improvement on the otherwise bland idared.

FUJI from New Zealand is, along with the braeburn, one of the more interesting apples from the southern hemisphere in early summer. Yellow with binding streaks of red, it is squat, 7 cm (2¾ in) across, with a dimpled top. The yellow flesh is crisp, honeyed and immensely sweet with no acidity, close to tropical fruit.

*GOLDEN DELICIOUS is not an English apple but was developed in West Virginia in 1916 and introduced here in 1926. For many years it has been picked under-ripe and green to imitate the success of Granny Smith, but its true glory only comes out when it has turned yellow. Encouragingly, growers seem to be recognizing this point.

BLUSH GOLDEN DELICIOUS is a large fragrant variety of Golden, 7-7.5 cm (2¾-3 in), which arrives in March. Lightly speckled and with a crimson streak, the white flesh is sweet and mild. It is a very temperate and good apple, if a bit sugary and lacking acidity.

EMPIRE, from the USA, is a good example of the American breeders' obsession with looks. About 6.5 cm (2¾ in), it is a soldierly red with clouding in neat stripes, from vermilion to deep pink. Although lovely to look at, the crisp, juicy, white flesh, collapses after the first mouthful. Nevertheless, it has some flavours of lemons and a good first bite.

GRANNY SMITH is named after Annie Smith who was born in Sussex in 1800 and emigrated to Australia when she was 38. When she was in her sixties, she accidentally discovered the world's most famous apple growing from seeds that came from some discarded fruit. First exported to Britain in 1930s, it needs a warmer climate than northern Europe can provide. It has a distinctly green skin, but the flavour is indistinct and acid — it is really just the crunch. An example from South Africa in May was pale green to yellow with a melony smell, short finish and good texture. Another from South Africa a month later was bright yellow, with a saffron hue to the creamy skin, the texture was softish, bursting ripples of mellow caramel flavour, sugars to the fore. By August, all the South African imports were completely yellow. Some brilliant examples in November from **Paille** in France were fully ripened to a deep yellow, with a red sunset flush, about 8 cm (3¼ in), tapering to a small crown, the flesh a cream-hued orange, with a smell of melons, perfect texture and a bready citrus sweetness. Magnificent to look at, this was what it was supposed to be — bravo **Paille!**

IDARED is sold as a traditional variety, but was bred by Leif Carner in Idaho in 1942. Known for its texture and crispness, it is plump, round and well shaped, coloured with beautifully soft shades of pinks, crimson and yellow. The flesh is white, with a good first bite, but low on juice and with very little actual flavour, only mild distant notes of citrus, although the reputation for texture is well founded.

JONAGOLD was first raised in New York in 1943, a cross between Golden Delicious and Jonathan. Large, 8 cm (3¼ in) across, speckled, turning when ripe to smooth yellow to red on opposite sides. Juicy and sweetish it has a soft texture. Jonagored is a clone of JONAGOLD raised in 1980 in Belgium.

*KIDD'S ORANGE RED is a good example of an overlooked British apple, although it originates from New Zealand as a cross between a Golden Delicious and a Cox. About 6 cm (2½in), it is bright lemon going to deep red, flecked with parchment — sunset colours. There is an orange hue to the flesh, which has a soft bite, but a full wide flavour tinged with flowers, almost spices or vanilla. Available from October to Christmas and on.

LAXTON FORTUNE is available from September. About 6 cm (2½ in) and streaked with red on lime yellow, the sweet white flesh, although a bit soft, has plenty of crunch and is juicy, with a pleasant buttery flavour.

LAXTON'S SUPERB was first bred at Bedford in 1897, a cross between Wyken Pippin and a Cox. First picked late in October, it lasts through to January, although crops tend to be biennial. About 6.5 cm (2¾ in), it is usually speckled green with areas running to polished mahogany red. The greeny cream flesh is soft, very neutral, with muted edges of flavour; the texture is that of cotton wool. Who called this superb?

M. FRIADISE traces its history back to before 1760 as a Dutch variety known as *Knoop Tubular* and resembling a pear in shape and texture, it is scarred from mahogany to lime with clouds of russet. The white flesh is firm-textured, dry, and highly acidic.

PRINSES IRENE is a cross between *Jonathan* and *Cox's Orange Pippin* dating back to around 1925. One of the most brilliant-looking apples, streaked from bright yellow to crimson reds, it is a bit dry and soft-textured, but has a swelling sweetness mixed with acidity, almost a citrus intensity.

RED CHIEF, from France, is large, about 8 cm (3¼ in) in diameter with a fat base. Strongly redded, with occasional breaks of yellowish cloud, it has crisp, melon-coloured flesh, and the flavour is clean, juicy and mainstream, which breaks down to a buttery sweetness.

RED DELICIOUS comes from New Zealand, Chile and the USA. The colour ranges from a bright orange hue to the deepest red/purple. The shape is ovoid, with five pinnacles forming a crown around the stalk. An example tasted in May had strong skin and the flesh was mild and inclined to mushiness; one in June had flesh which was disappointingly quick to disintegrate; another in August had white crunchy acid flesh which was pleasantly sour. With a mild to cardboard edge, it had elements of crab apple in the flavour.

REINETTE ONTZ is a mid-season dessert apple, which can also be cooked. Flat and wide, with a Cox-like blush from mahogany to melon, the flesh is white, friable and soft with a light melon taste. The crunch in the skin disappears in the flesh.

ROYAL GALA, from New Zealand, is about 5 cm (2 in) across, with attractive orangey-green skin, speckled with red and lemon and a small crown on the top. With a fresh floral smell and a tart, fruity flavour, it is soft in texture with a Cox-style bite but not the acidity. Handsome examples are available in September from France, about 7 cm (2¾ in) in size and red with yellow to lime flecks round the core, the flesh is lime-white, crisp, sweet, crunchy and juicy with a hint of melons.

SPARTAN was bred in British Columbia, Canada in 1926 from a MacIntosh and a Yellow Newton Pippin and produces a high proportion of class-1 fruit. With smooth dark red/purple skin, it is at its best from September to December, after which it deteriorates. Good examples hint at strawberries and melons, others are vinous.

SPLENDOUR, from New Zealand, are about 7 cm (2¾ in) across, and are lime-yellow to bright red in colour, with a lime hue to the flesh. They have a good bite and sweet honey taste, with no acidity. A bit one-dimensional, but it does have a lovely first bite.

STURMER ORANGE PIPPIN, from New Zealand, is lime yellow to busted orange green-brown in colour, with a pale green hue to the flesh. They are crisp and intensely sour, with Cox tones, and a big distinct flavour.

WASHINGTON RED, from the USA, is a deep red that polishes up into an almost unreal varnish that reflects everything around it, like a soldier's boots. The red skin is streaked with runs of crimson and mauve and is a bit tough; the flesh is lime-hued, crisp and fragrant, with a slight vegetable taste, like sweet cabbages.

**WORCESTER PEARMAIN, often just called a WORCESTER, is one of the great English apples that has survived in the market since 1876. The seed was from Devon but raised by a Worcester nursery. At its peak for a month after picking in September. Pistachio-green to deep red and 6-7 cm ($2\frac{1}{2}$-$2\frac{3}{4}$ in), it has juicy white to lime-coloured flesh and a soft texture which tends to wooliness, but still with bite. The excellent and distinctive flavour has a beautiful mellow edge. A newer variation is the KATY, with bright-red skin, found in September and October.

PEAR

Related to the apple, pears were introduced here by the Gauls. There are more than 3,000 varieties of tree, many of which are extremely long-lived, up to 400 and 500 years old. The wood was an important part of the economy for joiners, wood turners and engravers.

Until the 16th century pears were exclusively a cooking fruit, stewed or baked and sold by street sellers. They were also made into jams and marmalades. Many of the old cooking varieties like Fertility, Bartell, or Beurré Hardy seem to have disappeared completely, although they could still be found in the '50s. Ironically, the quince has survived as the root stock for grafting pear trees. The first eating pears were grown in Italy and France and known as beurré for their sweetness, a tag that survives in variety names. Before that – especially in Roman times – they were grown for their medicinal virtues, particularly for stomach ailments.

The original gritty woodiness of the pear has inexorably been bred out in new varieties. Conference has become the dominant variety grown in this country to the exclusion of all other kinds. Pears will take on other flavours from things stored nearby and are fragile and easily bruised. **Marks & Spencer** has taken the forward-looking step of creating special polystyrene cases to protect them.

BEST BUYS *ABATE FETEL is tall, 6x13 cm ($2\frac{1}{4}$x$5\frac{1}{4}$ in), although developed in France is now available from September from many parts of Europe, and in the early spring from South Africa. Initially rather large and lumpy but now more elegant, it is lemon-yellow to brown with strong freckling; the white flesh has a good crunch and is sweet, clean and juicy — a good all-round pear.

ASIAN PEAR, or *Nashi*, are usually grown in Italy, Chile and New Zealand. The skin is rough and prickly. They are best served chilled, often with cheese. They tend to be innocuous when not fully ripe but the flavour builds up. A pretty example from Italy, with mottled deep yellow skin turning to brown paper, was 7.5x5.5 (3x$2\frac{1}{4}$ in); its white flesh is crisp, juicy, and rich in its sweetness, developing a flavour of honeyed lemons but with a mild aftertaste of something plastic/off. Another example from New Zealand was large, 8 cm (3$\frac{1}{4}$ in), with a russet skin speckled with white dots; the white flesh had some yellow hues and a taste of ice-cream and crunchy texture — a lovely mellow wet/dryness, but £1.29 each. They are at their best early in spring.

BEURRÉ BOSC from South Africa and Australia, is russet-beige with a yellow undercoat, varying widely when ripe from lime-green to leather-brown. With a wide squash-style base, crenellated not perfectly round, it tapers to a volcanic tip from 7 cm (2$\frac{3}{4}$ in) across at the base to 2 cm ($\frac{3}{4}$ in) at the tip. The stalks are usually left on and it has a very small core, only 3 cm (1$\frac{1}{4}$ in) high. The brown-hued flesh is refreshing, citrusy, light and crunchy, with watery features; some refer to it as a pear equivalent of a watermelon.

*COMICE or, more accurately, *Doyenne de Comice*, named after the *Comice Horticole* at Angers where it was developed in 1849 and introduced here nine years later. 'Incomparable', says **Sainsbury** and the 'finest of all dessert pears' according to **Marks & Spencer**. The European season starts in October, but South Africa supplies in early spring. The best tend to come from Holland where orchards grade and pack better than the English. It has the classic attributes of a pear, a good crunch, not overly woody texture, and a juicy, mild cool flavour. A squat English example, about 7.5 cm (3 in), with rough speckled khaki skin, and translucent white flesh was well-textured and juicy, with sharp notes and good body.

COOKING: Usually used raw with cream cheese and walnuts, or poached with wine and served with cream or (small amount of) chocolate sauce.

CONCORDE, a cross between a *Comice* and a *Conference*, is being tried by selective branches of **Sainsbury** and is getting enthusiastic support in the trade.

CONFERENCE is named after the Pear Conference held in Chiswick in 1885, when it was the only fruit to win a first-class certificate outright. It was developed by Thomas Rivers in 1874, from a cooking pear *Léon Le Clerc de Laval*. It is well known for its long keeping, which leaves it on the market from September through winter. Crab-apple-green, long and spindly with a very thin core and seeds at the bottom. Crunchy and dry, like an apple.

COOKING: Holds its shape in baking; also its bite in creams, sorbets and ice-cream.

FORELLE, from South Africa, is lime in colour with red freckles creating the blush. Elongated, it is about 8x6 cm (3$\frac{1}{4}$x2$\frac{1}{4}$ in). Juicy and in good condition for May, they have a fresh taste of grass and hay; crisp outside and juicy inside, with a swelling of sugars that rinses the mouth. **Tesco** call it a Red. Another example from **Safeway** was pretty, hump-shaped, yellow with orange speckles and blush turning bright fire-engine red in places; woody in texture, is sweet with a sour skin.

PACKHAM or *Packham's Triumph*, originally developed in Australia, is squatter than the Bosc, almost square at 7 cm (2$\frac{3}{4}$ in) across. Some from South Africa were bright lime green speckled with brown/grey pin heads; the mild gentle and sticky flesh had a green/lemon hue with a small core only halfway up the fruit — it is inclined to graininess by the core. Another example, from Italy, was slightly smaller and squat, a dusty pistachio green, lightly marked; the flesh white to melon-coloured and crisp, releasing its juices slowly — a good classic pear taste.

PASSE-CRASSANE, developed in France, is squat and dumpy, speckled russet, the stalks waxed red. It has juicy white flesh, and a good ratio of meaty flesh to rough skin; it had a watery, almost sorbet-like texture, and slightly sour and gritty skin.

**RED ANJOU is firm, mahogany-coloured, with a square configuration. It is a beautiful-looking pear. Examples from the USA still have their short stubby stalks; skin colours shading from a deep cerise to a mottled scarlet in definite streaks. It is sweet and juicy, like distilled sweet wood, superior in all regards.

*RED WILLIAMS, properly *Williams' Bon Chrétien* and originally favoured for canning, is 10x6 cm (4x2½ in), almost rectangular or coffin-shaped, with a beautiful redwood finish and dinky stalk. The creamy white flesh of a French example had soft bites, but perfect pear notes and a bready texture. Another smaller example from Italy was deep yellow/beige, with creamy sweet flesh and a rough skin, giving plenty of high notes.

ROCHA, about 8x6 cm (3¼x2½ in), has the classic look of a small Conference, brown at tip and base and a pronounced pale green speckled brown on the sides. The white flesh of the example from Portugal was crisp and juicy, having refreshing sour edges mixed with sweetness. A new season example in November was slightly smaller and sweet yellow, yet 38p each more than the coveted Comice. It has a granular translucence, with hints of yellow on white flesh, and a soft instant intensity, honeyed and sticky.

QUINCE

This large yellow-marked fruit about the size of an orange, 11x7 cm (4½x2¾ in), has a smooth, lightly furred skin, somewhere between the pear and lemon. It has an intense smell of melons and chocolate and hard white dry granular flesh, with a straw-like texture and a flavour of lemons and almonds. It needs to be baked to bring out its flavour, as in the ruby Spanish *membrillo* paste, which is more usually sold on the cheese counter.

OTHER FRUIT

GRAPE · MELON · POMEGRANATE · RHUBARB

GRAPE

Grapes for the table have become the poor relation of those used by the wine trade. For all the hundreds of different varieties, only a handful surface in the supermarkets. The wonderfully named heritage of Muscat of Alexander, Buckland Sweetwater, Black Hamburgh and others have been relegated to the province of the gardener. Thompson – originally cultivated as the grape for sultanas in California – has been pre-eminent, leading the move to seedless grapes. **Sainsbury** has even been encouraging new plantings in India. White grapes with pips are seemingly being phased out as seedless variations arrive from all corners of the world. Prices consolidate around £2 per lb, but can tumble dramatically in gluts.

BEST BUYS   ALPHONSE LAVALLÉE, from South Africa, are handsome round black marbles, about 4x3 cm (1 ½x¼ in), with a purple hue reflected in the green stalk. Inside there are three pips, and the smooth flesh has a well-delineated crunch, although the taste is a shade muted.

BIEN DONNE is fat with thick olive skin, lime flesh and two pips. The taste is innocuous, if not dull.

**BLACK MUSCAT is round, about 1 cm (½ in), with a dark blue — almost sloe-black — skin with a smoky blush. The flesh is opaque limy, sweetly Muscat, with three pips. This is a delicate, refined grape with a lovely muscat flavour — a lady among grapes and expensive at £4.50 per lb.

*DAN BEN HANNAH, from Chile, is tall and elongated. The smooth skin is black and the juice sweet, with one or two pips. This is a very good grape, with a lovely sense of balance and contrast of skin, the slightly sweet flesh almost tasting of lychees.

DAUPHINE, from South Africa, is thumb-sized and white to opaque golden, almost translucent. Sweet, with a tough ungiving skin, there are one or two pips per grape. With a satisfying taste of good wine, this is a good — if not outstanding — grape.

FLAME, from the USA, is small at 2 cm (¾ in), rounded, red-brown and slightly sweet with an over-strong skin. The taste is insignificant, but they are fun because they are so small.

NAPOLEON has opal, dark red to black thick skin. The soft, pale flesh, with a single pip, is sweet and lychee-like.

PERLETTE, from Israel, is lime in colour with clouds of white, oval and about 2 cm (¾ in). Crunchy and sweet, it has more fibre and texture than flavour and is good for fruit salads.

RED GLOBE is large, round, plum-coloured and hard, with two pips. As they ripen they become translucent crimson, with a sour edge, good juice and texture, and a soft edible skin.

RIBIER, from Chile, is black and clusters tightly. There are three pips per fruit. Juicy and sticky, with a crunchy skin, this is a very good everyday grape.

SEEDLESS SUGRAONE, from Mexico, is a translucent lime ovoid, about 2 cm (3/4 in) firm and tart, with a strong bite and little taste.

SUPERIOR, from Israel, is oval, about 2 cm (3/4 in). Sweet, with a Muscat ring, it has a short precise flavour and is better than Perlette.

THOMPSON is now universally grown as if there was no other variety. An example from Australia was a seedless ovoid, pale lime in colour, with tough skin and soft and inclined to pulpiness inside. A batch from Mexico were firm and crunchy, but with not much flavour save a hint of lettuce and a tart finish.

WHITE ITALIA, from Brazil. is large, at around 3 cm (1 1/4 in), with a melon-lime skin. They are fat, soft, good, sweet and juicy, with a single pip and muscat-style flavour.

MELON

There is more variety in the melon family than with any other fruit. The abundance of different varieties reflects the ease with which they can be cross-bred. The Honeydew family alone changes from green to white to orange through the winter.

In southern Spain and Portugal the piles of melons stacked for sale by the roadside suggest the easy abundance growing in the sun. Here – although they have been cultivated since 1570, introduced from Jamaica – they need glass, nurturing and water. Unlike their close relation, the cucumber, these domestic varieties cannot really aspire to the supermarket. Buying melons is about climate: Spain for honeydews; France for the more delicate cantaloupe family. When a melon is ripe the base will yield readily to pressure and the flesh will smell through the skin.

CANTALOUPE is both a family and its own variety, but the distinguishing marked ribbings have tended to be bred out. The word cantaloupe is from *Cantalupo*, one of the Pope's country homes near Rome, where they have been extensively cultivated. Usually round, about 11 cm (4 3/4 in), and smooth, with shades of lime-green skin and pale marrowy-orange flesh, the circular pod is about 4 cm (1 1/2 in) across. It has softer flesh than the Charentais and is juicy and sweet.

CHARENTAIS are round, about 11 cm (4 3/4 in) across, with a very pale-green skin streaked with thick white rivulets as if marking where to put the knife. The flesh is markedly orange, with a deep orange rim at the inner skin, and a triangular pod, 4 cm (1 1/2 in) at its widest. Richly honeyed, its ripeness is easily judged by smell. They need to be eaten swiftly as they do not keep well.

GALIA is a modern variety named after the daughter of the Israeli farmer who first developed it in 1976. Squat, like bowls balls, green going to yellow in colour, and streaked with contour-like white craters, they are quite petite by melon standards at 11 cm (4¾ in) across. Greenness of the skin denotes unripeness, yellowness maturity. The flesh is green and the bowl of pips about half the size of the fruit. Creamy and sweet, these melons are plentiful and cheap in late summer.

HONEYDEW encompasses many different varieties of the fruit, notable for their zeppelin shape and size and, for the most part, their disappointingly neutral-tasting flesh; the more so if not perfectly ripe. The percentage of pip hollow in the centre is high. At their peak early in summer, the best come from Spain.

OGEN are grown in Holland – and here – though they are named after the Israeli kibbutz where they were first developed. The English season is late autumn, but they are available from the Mediterranean through most of the summer. The ribbed skin goes an attractive mottled yellow, but the green flesh inside is dominated by the large crater of pips that occupy most of the space. Ripeness is judged by smell and important, because a few days either way and they are wishy and then washy.

PIEL DE SAPO (meaning 'skin of the toad') from Spain are large and oval, about 20 cm (8 in) long. Green in colour, turning yellow with light cratering, which distinguishes it from the honeydew, they have thin skin, white flesh and a large pod about 5 cm (2 in) across and running most of the length of the fruit. They are mild and gentle in flavour with a little tartness.

WATERMELONS are from a different part of the family and have been cultivated in India for millennia. Round, elongated, marrowesque, mottled green or even black, the variety tends to give way to distinct red sorbet-like flesh and myriad pips, varying mostly in the ratio of pips to flesh. There is no sure way to judge the ripeness of a watermelon except by cutting it in half. They are best eaten chilled.

SEEDLESS WATERMELON The seedless watermelon was first identified as a natural mutation at the turn of the century. Japanese and American farmers experimented with it in the '30s, but the big investment came from Spain two years ago. Using seed from Chile, they pioneered trials using 84 varieties around Valencia and finally arrived at a single variation which they christened Queen of Hearts.

The melons are strictly-speaking not seedless, having small white edible pips and up to seven black seeds. The skin is lighter green than conventional watermelons, with dark green stripes. The first crop is grown under glass and comes to market from late April. The outdoor crop begins in mid summer.

POMEGRANATE

These fruits enliven the autumn with their vivid pips. Along with grapes and figs, they are one of the mythical symbols of prosperity, fertility and wealth. They owe their longevity to being desert foods. The hard crimson shell retains the moisture for long periods. The juice stains badly and was used to colour Persian carpets. The best fruit, from Iran, can measure 10x8 cm (4x3 in), looking like giant apples with deep red skin. Use as garnish or pick over with a pin, discarding the bitter white pith, or make into pomegranate water, as the French do, for grenadine.

RHUBARB

The Victorians popularized rhubarb in fools and crumbles. Previously it had been grown for its medicinal properties across Asia. Most of what we find in the shops is forced over winter, grown in candlelit sheds (mostly in Yorkshire), to preserve the pinkness. Inside the sheds, the rhubarb grows at an extraordinary rate of up to 5 cm (2 in) a day and can be heard eerily popping out of its sheath in the dark. The top of the stem may be yellow rather than green. The outdoor varieties tend to be stronger and need the outer membrane to be skinned off.

LARDER

The arrival of the fridge and the freezer have almost made the larder redundant. There are a few essential staples that still occupy shelf-space rather than chill-space, most of them with long histories that reflect how the Victorians set about using the trade routes to create an empire. Most of the items are so familiar that most of us have come to accept them as basic commodities. The move into Europe has galvanized these foods and brought many more interesting variations into the shops.

Good larder staples, like oil and vinegar, offer the easiest, cheapest and best value returns for the cook. The larder is an area where economy is foolish. Some of the new lines, like flavoured oils, are just frippery, but the essential generics are increasingly excellent. The **Sainsbury** Special Selection is a significant step forward. **Tesco** countered with a range of Italian products from small producers.

HERBS & SPICES

ALLSPICE · ANGELICA · ANISEED · BAY ·
CARAWAY · CARDAMOM · CINNAMON ·
CLOVES · CUMIN · FENNEL SEEDS · GINGER ·
JUNIPER BERRIES · MACE · MANIQUETTE ·
NUTMEG · OREGANO · PAPRIKA · PEPPER · POPPY
SEEDS · SAFFRON · SESAME SEEDS · STAR ANISE ·
THYME · TURMERIC · VANILLA

By comparison to good fresh herbs, most dried herbs are a waste of time and money, except in long slow winter casseroles where they can revive in sympathy with other flavours. Only bay, oregano and thyme can really be said to dry to advantage. The best mixes of dried herbs are invariably from Provence. Other coastal Mediterranean markets sell comparably excellent reminders of their regions, but these are not commercially developed. The small jars of, say, dried mint show none of the attributes of the fresh except in teas and tisanes. Many dried herbs are also too often disappointingly old and anaemic. At the other extreme, today's new freeze-dried herbs are wet and lifeless.

Daregal package herbs in neat little boxes for the freezer, which can then supposedly be poured straight into dishes. Predictably, the herbs are wet and cold which rules them out.

Spices were what made food palatable in the old days. Today their role has been taken by fresh herbs and other seasonings like chilli. Nowadays spices are used for what they are rather than what they can disguise. Ready-ground powders will lose their potency in a matter of weeks.

**ALLSPICE

Also called 'Jamaican black pepper', is not to be confused with black pepper itself (see page 310). The trees from which the tiny berries come are tall, growing to 9 m (27 ft), and the berries are not so much black as dark brown. They are, 'very hard, with an instant smell of flowers and the obvious affinity – from which they take their name – for cloves, cinnamon and nutmeg'. The berries have to be picked under-ripe or they will turn to a mush. Plantations are known poetically as 'Pimento Walks'. The trees flower white in July and August, the berries picked when they are still greeny-purple and then dried in the sun. There are false and inferior varieties called 'allspice' from Mexico and America, but they lack the powerful and underrated pungency of the original.

ANGELICA

This is the stalks and stems of the upper branches of the large umbelliferous *Angelica archangelica* found in wet banks and ditches across northern Europe. There is a long history of confectionery working with angelica, both in candying and in crystallizing. Like juniper, angelica is one of the main aromatics in some gins. The juice is the prevailing flavour of Benedictine liqueur and the seeds go for vermouth and Chartreuse.

ANISEED

Also known as 'anise', *Pimpinella anisum*, is a part of the parsley family. Older books refer to its medicinal virtues as a carminative, and also to disguise the flavour of early drugs. It grows widely across a band running from Malta through Germany to China, which is always said to produce the best. The seed is tiny, the size of a pin head, and produces a blueish-tinged oil. Often used with other seasonings, especially coriander and fennel, to which it is related and from which anisette is made.

BAY

This is the leaves of the sweet bay tree, *Laurus nobilis*, found across the Mediterranean belt, which will grow to 10 m (30 ft). The younger leaves are more acid, so the mature leaf is prized. Bay has sustained its place in trade because of the hydrocyanic acids, which repelled weevils and other grubs from destroying dried pastas, pulses, rices etc. They are still used in boxes of figs and liquorice. The bitter-sweet flavour seems increasingly old-fashioned and unwieldy, but it is one of the basic herbs in a bouquet garni and in a faggot of herbs, also finding its way insidiously into casseroles, soups, fish, marinades, milk puddings and with rice – but always fished out at the end of the cooking.

CARAWAY

The deep brown seeds of *Carum carvi*, which grows wild across Europe but is also cultivated in Germany, Holland and North Africa. The root, like a small parsnip, can also be eaten. The best seeds are said to be Dutch, with a distinctive blue hue to the brown. The oil is extracted and the residue is sold as 'drawn caraway', but this is much darker.

CARDAMOM

The perfumed seed of a reed found originally in Southern Asia, growing as high as 3 m (9 ft), there are a great many varieties of cardamom and they are often mixed together. The three-cornered pods are green unless they have been bleached. They have sustained their reputation as an early therapeutic food and survive pungently in curries and most famously in coffee. Bought in the pod, the sides should be tightly sealed.

CINNAMON

The inside bark of the young shoots of *Cinnamomum zeylanicum*, found especially in Sri Lanka but also on a belt from Borneo to Jamaica. The tree, one of the laurel family, grows to 8 m (25 ft) and will be fertile for as long as 200 years. However, the best is taken from young trees after about four years. There are two harvests, the best of which is in summer. The outer skin is scraped off and the pliant bark left to dry, initially in the shade and then in full sun, when it curls into quills. Sometimes CASSIA bark is passed off as cinnamon, but is coarser, thicker and darker. Good sticks of cinnamon are light yellow, no thicker than cartridge paper and pliant enough to go soft in the mouth. It should be 'sweetly pungent' and 'leave no aftertaste'.

CLOVES

The dried unopened buds of the *Eugenia caryophyllata*, a kind of myrtle, cultivated across tropical latitudes, principally in East Africa. The tree is slender, growing up to 10 m (30 ft) and it flowers in clusters like honeysuckle. The flowers are white, becoming green and then red, at which point they should be hand-picked and dried swiftly in the shade of the tree for a week, or smoked over wood fires. Good cloves should leave an oily film in the hand and will exude a sticky substance if pierced with a nail. A clove where the oil has dried out (or been extracted) will float in water. The best were said to come from Penang and are red.

CUMIN

The cumin is an annual, not dissimilar to wormwood, found in China, India, Morocco, Sicily and Malta. Although its most famous use now is as part of Indian cooking, it has long been found in European cooking. The Romans used it as an alternative to pepper in cheeses and breads, notably in Germany, and to season anchovies in Norway. In shape and size it is similar to caraway – with which it has often been confused by the French who refer to caraway as *cumin des prés*, and the Spanish who call it 'Dutch cumin', and by the Indians in whose cuisine the two are often found together anyway. The hue is greener than caraway, in both the black and white variations. Some equate the assertive flavour to that of aniseed. Browned in a pan, the flavour becomes more gently nutty.

FENNEL SEEDS

Fennel seeds were used by the Egyptians and Greeks to make an infusion to stave off hunger and as an early slimming aid. In Germany and France the aniseedy seeds were often chewed. Otherwise they were used in pickling or ground to flavour apple pies and vegetable dishes, notably carrot salads and beetroot.

COOKING: *The flavour is strongly aniseedy and, like rosemary, it is best used to burn up on a barbecue or in the oven to lend its scent to fish or, less often meat.*

GINGER

Perhaps indelibly cursed by being sprinkled on melon, dried ginger, like fresh, varies dramatically depending on where it comes from. Naturally, it is black, with a green hue, where the white version has been bleached. It has another life as a medicine against gripe or headaches. It was widely adulterated and has been superceded by the arrival of the freezer. Fresh rhizomes will grate straight from frozen. The powders lose their potency swiftly.

CRYSTALLIZED and STEM GINGER are made from fresh ginger that has been cooked in sweet acid solution several times, topping up with brown sugar: sold in a syrup it is crystallized, or the pieces are taken out and rolled in more sugar to make stem ginger. Stems are obviously more delicate than roots or chips, which tend to be coarser and hotter.

JUNIPER BERRIES

The prickly juniper is related to the cypress and grows wild on heaths across Europe. There are upwards of 50 varieties, but the common juniper is the one used for gin. The berries are originally green and turn purple when they ripen in the autumn. Fresh they should be round and fat, not shrivelled and wizened. The pungency is in the skin, the sweetness in the flesh, and the bitterness in the three stones. Mostly it finds its way into pickles and marinades; very useful with game, and also sympathetic with fresh herbs and any sauce or marinade using gin, say for pork.

MACE

The outer casing of the nutmeg (see below), which when harvested is bright red. It is then pressed between blocks of wood and dried in the sun, which turns it a browny-yellow. There are different grades, of which the smaller are said to be the best. The flavour should be of a more delicate form of nutmeg.

MANIQUETTE

Also known as PARADISE SEEDS or PARADISE GRAINS, these tiny brown seeds are possibly what old books refer to as MELEGETUA or ALLIGATOR PEPPER, originally imported to France from Ethiopia in the '40s as a substitute for ordinary pepper, but later ingratiated itself for its hard mild-scented heat.

NUTMEG

The kernel of the tropical *Myristica fragrans*, which is similar in shape to a pear tree. They will bear about 4.5 kg (10 lb) of fruit after 10 years. The fruit is peach-like and can be eaten. The nutmegs are dried systematically in the sun until the shell can be broken off without breaking the inner kernel. Price is determined by size, the larger being the more expensive.

OREGANO

Today, oregano has been replaced by fresh thyme in many recipes. It was always its drying qualities that made it a favourite of Mediterranean recipes. In Greece and Portugal it can still be bought with the flower heads on. It is not a thyme but a wild marjoram and will vary in flavour wildly according to where it is grown. The most pungent varieties are from the calcareous soils of the Mediterranean.

PAPRIKA

Many of the dried powdered spices have lost their place on the shelves to their fresh counterparts. Paprika survives probably on the affection for Hungarian stalwarts like goulash and chicken paprika. As with other powdered spices, it stales quickly. Paprika is, in truth, the furthest outpost of the pepper and chilli family and links up in a chain that might also include Spanish *pimenton*, the hot chilli bottled sauces of the Caribbean and Mexican gulf and across the Pacific, to the use of chilli sauces in Szechuan, Thai and Malay cooking. The Turks are credited with bringing a pointed-shaped bell pepper to Hungary which was then dried and ground. Although ground and dried pepper mixes come from other parts of the globe, the Hungarians seem to have singularly protected the individuality of theirs and its role.

PEPPER

Pepper is becoming increasingly defined as an ingredient in its own right, whereas in the Middle Ages the term passed for all manner of spices and was used as a currency, hence the term 'peppercorn rent'. Pepper comes from the vines of the *Piper nigrum*, which thrives in low valleys in hot climates. It is a vine propagated by cuttings and trained either along saplings or stakes to some 3-6 m (9-18 ft) tall. A single fruit will produce 20-50 corns of pepper twice a year, the main crop from January to May and a second smaller crop in September. A good vine can expect to yield upwards of 2.7 kg (6 lb) of pepper in a harvest. The berries are green, turning red when fully – in fact, over- – ripe. Drying in the sun is preferable to kiln-drying. Heat wrinkles and turns the corn black.

Pepper has been accepted in nearly every cooking of the world, and seemingly also into most manufacturing practices. In the '50s it still accounted for half the spice trade to this country. Its pre-eminence is being eroded by other means of preservation, faster transport of foods and the arrival of other, more dynamic, forms of seasoning, notably garlic, chilli and ginger.

The full intensity of flavour comes either from freshly grinding pepper or using good quality berries. Ground pepper stales more quickly than whole peppercorns, so represents a poor buy.

STEAK PEPPER is an expensive affectation, as are the packaging promotions for refills. Given the price and how long pepper lasts it is hardly an area that bears economy. The very pretty bottles of differently coloured peppers are mainly designed for recipe dishes, like a colourful mild *steak au poivre* or lending colour to a casserole.

Good black pepper should be like 'scented Doc Martens, granulated, hard with elements of cloves'. The mainstay of the trade to London was from Jamaica which has led to some confusion with Jamaican pepper or allspice (see page 306). The south of India also produces excellent black pepper.

WHITE PEPPER is left on the vine until the black pepper turns white inside. The black husk is taken off the berries, often in London, in a process called decorticating and this dulls the flavour – it also made it more expensive. 'The heat of good white pepper builds slowly from a scent; the heat comes from the destruction of the cell walls with vicious, tiny crevices of heat filling the mouth and getting sharper and sharper'. The traditional plantations for white pepper are in North-east India, Sarawak and Singapore, which produce a harder pepper, called muntok, which used to be known as coriander white. White pepper was famously liable to adulteration and is today looking increasingly arcane compared to freshly ground black pepper.

GREEN PEPPERCORNS are completely unripe, but have been preserved in brine or freeze-dried. They are strong in flavour, but the brine diffuses their heat. Good versions, 'smell faintly of herbs, basil even, certainly thyme. The heat is warming, building to a point of fire.'

COOKING: *Good for sauces, as in the classic nouvelle cuisine dish of steak with cream and green peppercorns, and also in marinades.*

PINK PEPPERCORNS are not, in fact, a peppercorn at all, but from another tree found in South America. They are a pomegranate pink, 'sweet on the tongue, mild but with a hit at the back of the mouth'.

RED PEPPERCORN is the riper version of the pink, milder and subtler than Asian pepper, 'aromatic with lemons'. Good with fish and mousses, they are usually sold in brine or freeze-dried.

BIRD'S PEPPER is a wild pepper, the seeds carried and distributed by birds in the Cameroons. Larger than white, they are beige to cream balls, with a pure floral smell, not biting. 'Hard, nutty, mealy strong, building with dusky sour essences.'

BEST BUYS The leading brand of pepper **Schwartz** is consistently and embarrassingly undercut by own-labels, which can be a quarter of the price.

**Parameswaran's Finest Wynad Pepper from Kerala, is grown on a 5,000 metres-high plateau and commands a higher price than other peppers. It is, 'perfumed, paler and hotter' because it is left to ripen until fully red and the berries picked by hand each day to ensure the proper ripeness. It is said to improve with age. 'The heat is slow to eke out, quite spiced like cloves mixed with a fire that builds and lasts for a considerable number of minutes'. It is best used to finish dishes rather than in cooking.

POPPY SEEDS

The principal use of poppy seeds in Europe has been in Scandinavia. The tiny grey-blue specks of seed are used to decorate, mainly by bakers. The flavour is bland, sweet, almost almond-like. There is also an oil, of which the white is the best, the red being the second extraction.

SAFFRON

The dried thread-like stigmas of *Crocus sativus*, this used to be widely cultivated in this country, especially in Cornwall where it was well known for colouring bread. It is thought to have been introduced in 1339 and was highly popular for 300 years. Saffron Walden in Essex took its name from the cultivation, though production seems to have died out around 1750. In other parts of Cambridgeshire cultivation continued until the late 19th century. There has been a revival on a small scale in Clwyd, but the best now comes from Spain.

Saffron was valued not just for its vivid yellow colouring but also for its medicinal attributes. Unlike the common crocus, the purple and violet flowers bloom in the autumn, yielding just three stigmas per plant. An ounce of saffron comprises the flowers of 2,000 plants and each has to be hand-picked. It was often adulterated (usually with safflower or marigold), but a pinch in water reveals its characteristic bitterness and aroma. For cooking it is best first infused in tepid water.

SESAME SEEDS

These have picked up various wacky names over the years from 'gingelly oil' to 'banglo' and 'wanglo' to 'teel'. Although their use here is very modern, sesame has been accepted in other parts of the world for centuries. The long-keeping qualities of the oil have led to it being used for cooking in India and at the turn of the century it was used in margarine because it provided a quick test of adulterated butter. In Japan seeds are mixed 8 to 1 with salt as a condiment *gomashio*. Closer to home there is the Middle Eastern TAHINI paste.

Marseilles was an important port for extracting the oil, which can be as much as 50% (see page 349). The plants are vigorous annuals growing to two metres tall. They are cut down and dried upside down and the seeds left to fall. There are two kinds, the white seed and a black seed.

COOKING: *Their role in vegetarian cooking is being seen as increasingly important, added to salads, breads, bakes, stir-fries and as an all-purpose garnish. They are best bought unroasted and warmed for several seconds in a hot skillet to release their pungent nutty smell.*

STAR ANISE

Illicium anisatum, is a member of the magnolia family, related to – but different from and more bitter than – aniseed, It is native to China, where it is one of the basic five-spices. The star-shaped pods are dried before they are fully ripe. The Japanese variety *I. lanceolatum* is poisonous.

THYME

Advocates of dried thyme argue that its finest role is in long slow casseroles where the more concentrated flavours in the dried versions are more potent than fresh. Thymes vary substantially according to variety (see fresh, page 212) and geography. One theory has it that the worse looking, the better the flavour. Provence and Tuscany lay claim to the herb, although Greece and Portugal have equivalent progeny. They need a limey soil. There is also an oil which has been used for a long time in veterinary prescriptions and in cosmetics. In Spain it is also used to flavour the oil for olives.

TURMERIC

Turmeric is similar to and from the same family as ginger, but without the fierce heat, and found mostly in South-east Asia. The rhizomes are boiled, peeled and dried for as long as ten weeks. They are usually too hard to sell in their whole state and are commercially ground into a yellow powder; the flavour is bitter and musty. The powder is used as an adulterant in mustards, as a cheap trick saffron and as a colorant.

VANILLA

A trailing orchid which attaches itself to any nearby tree and bears greeny yellow flowers followed by slender three-lobed pods up to 25 cm (10 in) long, which curve and become yellow when ripe. The name is from the Spanish *vaina*, meaning a sheath or scabbard. It is only after curing and fermenting that the pods turn black and give off their brilliant clean humid smell. The best comes from Mexico, where vanilla was first used with chocolate, but there are different varieties cultivated further south along the continent and in Africa across the Tropics. Research has shown that the organic compounds of vanilla change according to where the plants are grown. Madagascan Bourbon vanilla is said to be rich and mellow; Mexican sweet; Tahitian beans to be musky and aromatic; Indonesian woody and smoky. Some adulterants are used in the extractions, notably coumarin, which is banned in America.

The pods are harvested in November and December, but may not reach the market for four or five months, depending on how they are cured. Vanilla pods must be kept in a sealed bag or container – or in the sugar jar to make vanilla sugar.

FLAVOURINGS

CAPERS · CHILLI SAUCES · CHOCOLATE ·
HONEY · HORSERADISH · LIQUORICE ·
MUSTARD · SALT · SALT SUBSTITUTES · SOY
SAUCE · SUGAR · SUGAR ALTERNATIVES

Flavourings are ridiculously cheap, given their long-lasting value in the kitchen. In all these categories extravagance repays itself many times over.

CAPERS

The flower buds of the long trailing shrub, *Capparis spinosa*, usually grown along old walls, or even on rubbish heaps, though it is sometimes kept as an ornament in the garden around the Mediterranean rim. It is low and bushy with oval leaves and beautiful flowers, a waterfall of purple stamens against four white or pink petals. The buds have to be picked daily from May as the flower withers quickly in the heat. They are left to dry for 24 hours and then put in good quality vinegar or occasionally (and very good) in salt. Capers used to be graded in seven different sizes: with the smallest, the *nonpareils*, being the most expensive and prized. The acidity comes from the capric acid which is a similar substance, albeit in much smaller quantities, as that which gives goats their distinctive smell.

The best capers were always considered to come from the South of France, though much of what reaches here today seems to come from Morocco, or better, Turkey. The best sell for as much as £9 per lb wholesale. They benefit from decanting if the brine is suspect.

**EXTRA FINE CAPERS from Turkey are small, barely 2 mm ($^{1}/_{12}$ in) across, and slate grey in colour, they are crunchy and floral.
TORNATORE, the Ligurian olive-oil-producing estate, also imports very young capers from Morocco and bottles them in wine vinegar: 'Tiny lentil-sized, quite tart from the vinegar. A treat'. **Noel's are the most widely available brand in supermarkets, bottled in Lancashire, they are conservative, fair-sized, not too tart, restrained, but OK.

The CAPERFRUIT or CAPERBERRY is a variation where the fruit grows on after flowering. These are then pickled in vinegar with herbs. They are eaten on the stalk like a cherry without a stone. Most come from around Seville.

COOKING:Capers were originally imported almost exclusively for sauce to go with mutton or for tartare sauce. The Romans used them for fish sauces. They are also a startling addition in salads and purées, as are caperberries.

CHILLI SAUCES

Chilli sauces go under different names as they stretch languorously across the globe from Mexico, through the Caribbean, North Africa and down to South-east Asia. The main difference is whether they are designed for use in the cooking or, as in the Caribbean variations, for the table like ketchups.

BEST BUYS The hottest of all are **Koon Yick Wah Kee's Soy Chilli Sauce** from Hong Kong, reinforced with garlic and sugar. Close behind is the enterprisingly **Gramma's** top-of-the-range **Very Hot**, made in Hainault, Essex, rivalled by the West Indian pair of **Encona** and **Grace**, which are both used as table sauces and not as background heat for cooking. In this company, the fabled MOROCCAN HARISSA is only tepid, its heat diluted by cumin and equal in strength to **Gramma's Mild**, and the well-known **McIlhenny's Tabasco sauce**, beloved in Bloody Mary's. Slightly stronger for drinks is the West Indian **Pickapeppa Sauce**. The international brand names have opted, predictably, for moderation and safety in the heat stakes but without really compensating in terms of developed flavours.

CHOCOLATE

The Chocolate Society states good chocolate should be more than 50% cocoa solids, and cocoa butter should be used, although labelling allows 5% of substitute to be used without any reference (even though these are saturated fats); natural vanilla not artificial, and sugar should be used as a seasoning like salt, in small amounts only.

Chocolate as sold in this country has more sugar, saturated vegetable fat and powdered milk than chocolate. Pure chocolate may have as much as 70% cocoa solids, where most Cadbury bars are closer to 20%. Purity is perhaps not the only virtue but it does mean that we have come to call something chocolate that is really only chocolate-flavoured.

Chocolate was first classified in 1720. The wild trees grow to almost 40 feet tall. The cocoa tree – or *Theobroma cacao* (*theo* meaning god and *broma* meaning food) grows in the rain forests either side of the equator and not outside of a band 20 degrees to the south or north. They need the shade and humidity often provided by banana trees, or by coffee trees in Cuba. The trees bloom brilliantly but will only yield up to 10 golden-yellow pods, 30 cm (1 ft) long and 10 cm (4 in) round. The best variety is the *criollo*, known as the king of beans. It is discernibly fruity and often likened to the chardonnay grape. *Forastero* is more profuse but blander. There are hybrids ,of which the best-known is the mellower *trinitario* from the Caribbean. Tasting notes compare it to newly moan hay, oak, honey and balsamic vinegar.

Chocolate tasters look for a chocolate that melts easily on the tip of the tongue. An unusual characteristic of cocoa butter is that within a

Chocolate

Percentage of fat in calories of mainline chocolate bars

	Calories	Protein g	Carbos g	Fat g	% Fat of Cals
Bounty	473	4.8	58.3	26.1	49
KitKat	499	8.2	60.5	26.6	47
Mars	441	5.3	66.5	18.9	38
Milky Way	397	4.4	63.4	15.8	35
Smarties	456	5.4	73.9	17.5	34
Twix	480	5.6	63.2	24.5	45

The aerated fillings and biscuit tend to dilute the fats.

In pure 'chocolate' bars

	Calories	Protein g	Carbos g	Fat g	% Fat of Cals
milk (average)	529	8.4	59.4	30.3	51.5
plain (average)	525	4.7	64.8	29.2	50

The carbohydrate figure reflects the level of sugar – usually around 95% of the published figure.

Tesco reveals the saturates and sugars in its chocolate

	Calories	Protein g	Carbos g	Fat g	% Fat of Cals
Tesco Plain Fine	501	3.7	57.7 (total sugars 55.7)	29.8 (sat 18.1)	53

expressed another way the level of saturated fat is 32%.

temperature range of only 1° (33-34° centigrade) it will turn from solid to soft. The crystalline structure should snap like 'the bark of a tree' and the fine texture should come from tiny particle size.

Chocolate-making is an advanced process, a tribute to Victorian engineering rather than any gastronomic inspiration. The word derives from the Aztec *chocaltl*. The Indians may have attributed great powers to chocolate, but they would have consumed it as simple infusions. The chocolate bar is a 20th-century innovation.

There is more speculation about the effects chocolate has on the brain than with almost any other food. Debra Waterhouse, an American nutritionist, makes sweeping claims in her populist book *Why Women Need Chocolate* (Vermillion). The case rests on the argument that chocolate (a) boosts serotonin levels in the brain, which is supposed to be calming (a claim also made for bread this year) and (b) contains phenylethylamine, reputedly the chemical released in the brain when we fall in love. However, chocolate also contains tyramine, which is linked to migraine, especially in combination with red wine and cheese.

The quality of chocolate depends on a number of key processes. The harvested beans are split open and left to ferment for up to six days, traditionally under banana leaves but now more likely in boxes. They are then sun-dried for between 10 and 20 days. It is only then that they are bagged and shipped to the factory. The first process is to roast them and then separate the shells from the nib. The debris will be pressed to form cocoa butter or dried to form cocoa powder. The precious nibs are ground into a liquor sometimes called 'cocoa mass'. Here it is mixed with sugar, vanilla and either extra cocoa butter for dark chocolate or milk chocolate.

Drinking chocolate was first commercially manufactured in this country by **Churchman's**, later taken over by **Fry's**, at Bristol in 1728, but eating chocolate did not appear for another 100 years. It was **Van Houten** in 1828 who discovered that he could press out the fat from the ground nibs and create a butter that would not only give a balanced flavour but also allow the chocolate to be moulded. The first chocolate bars were made here in 1847 by **Fry** and two years later by **Cadbury**. These would have been PLAIN CHOCOLATE. The addition of milk to make MILK CHOCOLATE was not developed until 1876 by a Swiss, **M D Peters**, a well-known brand before 1940. The moisture in the milk destroyed the balance of the chocolate. The Peters factory was next door to **Nestlé**, where condensed milk had just been discovered. That was what he used. In practice, milk chocolate still uses evaporated milk or, more often in this country, a milk crumb which has been pre-mixed with sugar and dried cocoa liquor. Labelling allows 55% sucrose to be used in milk chocolate. Equally it demands a minimum of 23% cocoa solids and 14% milk solids or an even ratio of 20% milk and 20% cocoa. Conching didn't come in until 1879 when the Swiss maker **Lindt** discovered that he could make a much smoother product by grinding it, originally in a stone pestle and mortar.

WHITE CHOCOLATE simply omits the cocoa liquor and is cocoa butter, milk and sugar.

One reason Swiss chocolate enjoys such a good reputation is that the early plants had access to cheap electricity from the mountain waterfalls

THE CHOCOLATE SOCIETY

The CHOCOLATE SOCIETY is sponsored by the French company **Valrhona**, whose factory is just outside Lyons. Being a member has the advantage of having regular access to **Valrhona** chocolates, which are among the best in the world. There is a newsletter, events, recipes etc. (Membership is £30; phone: 01943 851101).

which allowed the chocolate to be ground finer and for longer periods.

The romance of chocolate suggests that it is all about the subtleties of different blends of cocoa, whether it be from Venezuela (usually held to be the premier producer), Madagascar or Sri Lanka. To this should be added the grinding, which accounts for the smoothness. The skill of the chocolatier is to blend. 72% cocoa solids is about as high as it goes for something the equivalent of a chocolate version of espresso coffee, so bitter it is almost almonds, any more points on the scale and it becomes almost tasteless. There is a subtlety here beyond the reach of what is found in the shops.

BEST BUYS Specialists like *Coco Barry, **Valrhona and *DGF will sell variations of climate and intensity that match the recipes – a lower solid percentage for a mousse, higher for the casing. Milk comes in as a welcome diffusion at around 32% solids. To compare the **DGF Le Louis** white couverture (coating chocolate) to **Sainsbury's White Chocolate Drops** is like comparing a Derby runner to an old lag.

Sainsbury sells a Belgian version **Deluxe Continental**, at an astonishing 75% cocoa solids, an almost incomprehensible black void of nothing... the culinary equivalent of a black hole – compared to **Sainsbury** ordinary at a mere 51%, made in the UK and distinctly less smooth.

Green & Black make a great play of their organic product and pioneered the first laudable Fairtrade Foundation food endorsement for their **Maya Gold** from Belize (the cocoa crop is bought directly from the plantation and the proceeds are guaranteed to go back to the villages), which is 70% cocoa solids (as is their mainline bar, but with beans from Togo in West Africa) but tempered wisely with allspice, vanilla and orange. Another Belgian maker, **Martougin** sell a deluxe bar at only 70% cocoa solids, which is still a resounding thwack of chocolate but again underlines the importance of grinding in the sticky smoothness.

The legendary **Ménier**, which claims gold medals dating back to 1832 – now owned by **Nestlé** and their chocolate made in Switzerland rather than France – balances its cocoa solids at a sensible 52%. It remains an outstanding benchmark of a finely orchestrated chocolate, much subtler than some of the brash new competition. It is as happy as an eating chocolate as for cooking, where its long-standing monopoly is only seriously threatened by the variations of the specialist professional couvertures.

Bonnat produce a range of chocolate bars from different regions which reflect the styles and character of the region – the perfumed tonic of Venezuela, or the mild warm Sri Lankan. These are more of an educational course. **Scot's is actually produced in West Germany and, despite boasting cocoa solids at 55% and a sell-by date of 18 months ahead, was very poor and stale, quite nasty.

Valrhona might well claim to be the king of chocolates. The packaging is in neat deeply coloured tin boxes. There are tasting boxes covering the main areas of definition – Manjari, made from Criollo beans harvested around the Indian Ocean;

Caraibe, uses only trinitario beans from the Caribbean, often described as feminine and sultry; and the more individual Guanja, which in the professional variation is regarded as the best of Vahlronna's couvertures. The professional chocolates, although designed for cooking, can also be eaten raw. Jivara is unusual in that it is a white chocolate made using malt and brown sugar and has an extremely high cocoa content at 40%.

Other cooking chocolates in supermarkets, **Scotbloc** and **Supercook**, are flavours, not chocolate itself.

HONEY

Bees pre-date man by about 50 million years and were thought to have come from Afghanistan. By Egyptian times the cultivation of honey was advanced, with hives being moved along the Nile to keep pace with the seasons and the different flowerings on the bankside which imbued the flavour of the honey. Christian countries kept bees through the Dark Ages to supply the beeswax for church candles as well as an original form of sweetener and, equally important, as a medicine or as a dressing for wounds. The honey, along with pollen, is the feed for the young bees. Fields pollinated by bees have been shown to be more productive – examples on rape fields have shown a 53% increase in the yield. Bees will fly within a radius of six miles and, depending on the habitat, may well stay with a single type of flower.

Good quality honey is defined by its region or more specifically by the flowers the bees are likely to have pollinated. Brand names are something of a generic aberration that has been used to mask the destruction of the environment. CLEAR HONEY has a higher percentage of fructose rather than glucose, which depends on the kind of flora the bees have been pollinating. Dandelion or rape flowers provide most of the pollination for bees in this country and this honey will set more quickly because of the glucose, whereas honey drawn from bees that have pollinated acacia blossoms is nearly all fructose. Essentially there is little difference. Bees that have pollinated rhododendron flowers produce a honey that can cause dizziness and sickness, while those that have pollinated hemp flowers will produce a honey containing cannabis. Scottish HEATHER HONEY was always well regarded but now seems rare. SET or SOLID HONEY can be returned to liquid by standing it in warm water for an hour. Honey is hygroscopic and attracts water so in cooking the amount of liquid used is reduced.

Apicoltura from **Devalle Danille** do a range of specialist honeys from different regions – a light granular curd yellow to orange sunflower honey from Aquitaine: lime flower honey from the Auvergne; chestnut leaf honey from the Cevennes, mountain flower honey from the Savoie, and Lavender honey from Provence. In markets in Portugal it is still possible to buy honeys from quite obscure herbs.

ROYAL JELLY, sometimes added back into honey or sold as a supplement, is secreted into queen cells in the hive and its extra nutrients account for the same bees becoming queen rather than worker bees, however there is some doubt as to whether this works in the same way on humans.

The best HONEYCOMBS are VIRGIN COMB, taken from a young hive where the honey flows spontaneously. The bees will not have swarmed. In succeeding years the comb will become brown, or even black.

HORSERADISH

Horseradish is mentioned by the Egyptians as a medicine and a condiment. At the time of the Exodus the young leaves were one of the five bitter herbs – with coriander, lettuce, horsehound and nettles. It is not clear how it came here or if it was indigenous, though it was probably native to Persia but transplanted happily across Europe and America. It was popularized in Germany, though perhaps only brought here as a medicine by the 13th century. The confusion lies in the definitions of radish. Waverley Root recalls eating them plain with salt as a starter in restaurants in France 'until vanquished'. English plants were said to be among the best. The cream-coloured roots were shaved or made into early sauces with sugar, mustard, pepper and vinegar and were used with beef from an early point, certainly the 16th century and perhaps before It was often dried, too, and incorporated with mayonnaise-style sauces for fish and chicken. It is in season from October to June. The lack of enthusiasm for its development stems from the potency of the root. At **Wiltshire Tracklements**, who produce probably the best and fiercest horseradish, rather than the over-vinegared and emulsified creams of other makers, they have to use gas masks to protect the mixer's eyes and senses. The Japanese equivalent is the green *wasabi*, usually served with raw fish sashimi.

LIQUORICE

Liquorice was sometimes called 'black sugar' in Scotland or 'Spanish juice'. Although it has fallen almost completely out of use, it qualifies as one of the more important English culinary seasonings. It is native to the Mediterranean, but was widely grown here from Elizabethan times, mainly around Mitcham until the 1920s and more famously between Pontefract and Knottingley in Yorkshire, where cultivation died out finally in the 1960s. English liquorice was deemed to be among the best, but vulnerable to damp and early frosts and deemed, sadly, to be too labour-intensive to survive.

What it needs is deep loamy soil and plenty of digging. Liquorice is a root related to the pea family. It will flower pale purple, violet and white and grow to about 1 metre (3 ft). Below the ground the thick roots will bury down to 1.3 metres (4 ft). The root can be chewed raw but mostly it was crushed and boiled. There was a considerable trade in the juice for many centuries and the practice of adulterating it with rice, gelatine or potato flour was so endemic that it was an early example of labelling, graded as Cassano 70, meaning 30% adulterated.

To make cakes or allsorts, the juice was evaporated to leave the uniquely black malleable strips. Proper Pontefract cakes should be 5 parts sugar, to 7 parts liquorice to 2 parts starch.

MUSTARD

There are two principal types of mustard seeds: the WHITE (in fact yellow) *Sinapis alba*, and the more expensive and volatile BLACK, *S. nigra*, in fact brown. The white is said to be inferior, but has properties which bring out the fieriness of the black. This may have had to do with the seeds being much smaller and more difficult to harvest. The blending of mustards has been such a preoccupation that, before the War, whole tracts of Lincolnshire and Yorkshire were given over to black, and acres of Cambridge and Essex for white.

Mustard powders are credited to a Mrs Clements of Durham around 1720. She reputedly discovered that if you let the mustard plant bolt and then sieved it through silk screens the resulting mustard was hotter. She made annual pilgrimages to big cities to take orders for her blends, but these Durham mustards seem to have disappeared. Seed and powder are innocuous when dry and only acquire their potency when water is added.

The origins are almost certainly from the Italian *mostarda*, from the Latin *mustum*, unfermented grape juice. The sell-by dates are important on mustard – the later the better. Citric acid or acetic acid dissolved in water cost about 2p against 90p for good wine vinegar, which is why better mustards start their ingredients lists with vinegar, not water.

DIJON MUSTARDS account for half the world production of mustard. Mustard-making was introduced to the area around Dijon by the Romans, and in the 15th century monasteries popularized its use. Most labels suggest Dijon to go with meats, but it is also the classic vinaigrette mustard.

BEST BUYS Benedicta à l'Ancienne is made using water and spirit vinegar and has a 'creamier texture, searingly single-minded, very one-dimensional, lacking the subtlety of the Maille as the cheap vinegar betrays it'.

Colman's Dijon is sandy in texture and colour, and uses water and spirit vinegar. It is all about the delivery of heat rather than flavour. Hot, it is slow to start but builds into a resounding explosive crescendo.

Maille claims to be the oldest mustard firm in the region, established in 1747. **A l'Ancienne is their grain version, made with spirit vinegar. It is sharp, with an immediate bite on the tongue, crawling all over the taste buds like jumping beans, different impact from different grains, plenty of vinegar. It is good for saucing: mix with cream and pan juices.

**Poupon was established around 1870 and uses white wine vinegar. It is a distinctive saffron yellow and creamy, with shards of heat like a lightning storm striking different parts of the mouth and then cascading down to all parts'.

Supermarket Own-brand Dijon Mustards:Tesco is quite a spicy mix, involving turmeric, pimento, pepper, cinnamon and cloves. The impact is 'sweet to begin with a fiery edge… interestingly developed'. **Waitrose**, **Asda** and **Sainsbury** adopt a dis-appointing one-dimensional approach with variations, mainly in the level of vinegar, water, mustard seed, spirit vinegar and salt and little to choose between them.

ENGLISH MUSTARDS are dominated by **Colman**, which may account for the monocultural nature of the definition. The fashionably touristic mixes with whisky or beer have very little history and are mainly affectations, often sometimes quite unpleasantly so.

BEST BUYS *Colman's Dried Mustard** is still sold in the imperial-style tins. Invaluable and without competition for the range of old English recipes, it is all the more adaptable for its purity as a powder.

Ginger Mustard from **Leatham's Larder** is a mild mix of mustards with a considerable debt to the dill mustard sauce served with *gravlax* (**Leatham's** *gravlax* sauce is one of the best on the market) but in this case invigorated with 17% root ginger for a resounding marriage, 'a creamy warm foil to the pungency and resonating root ginger'.

Gordon's English Vineyard Mustard is, surprisingly, made with malt vinegar. The wine component is considerably smaller. It is a sludgy grainy, very hot to begin with, tones of curry, quite bizarre and out of step with what mustard is supposed to be.

Tesco Tewkesbury is a sludgy gruel reinforced with horseradish and white wine vinegar. Its very wide flavour is a bit imprecise but has more variation than its English. Shakespeare mentions Tewkesbury mustard, so it is certainly traditional.

Sainsbury makes a similar mustard using horseradish that it is very sandy and sludgy, the horseradish very much to the front and only a mild edge of mustard at all.

Cumberland mustard is drenched in honey, but with some fire left in the grains. It is not really a very good idea.

Urchfont was an invention in 1970 by William Tullberg, a sausage taster who got bored and who went on to create ****Wiltshire Tracklements**. His **Original** is all white mustard with chilli and black peppercorns and allspice. His **Spiced Honey**

uses black and white, chilli and Mexican honey. His **Strong English** is a more conventional – but still hand-made – mix.

Taylor's Original English claims its recipe dates back to 1830. Made with mustard flour and water, it is conspicuously English: intense, bitter, granular, almost sandy, akin to that Victorian taste of patum peperium... woody, strong and individual.

Taylor's Medieval is made with cider vinegar, mustard flour mixed with honey and turmeric, and olive oil. It has a tight sucking sandy texture, and is sweet with edge of fire, really more honey and turmeric than mustard. Good.

Supermarket Own-brand English Mustards: All the major supermarkets take a searingly saffron mustard that appears to come from **Colman** and, 'betrays the family culture of heat first and flavour second'. *****Waitrose** stands out from the crowd, having added pimento, 'which may well be chilli' and turmeric, which gives more heat and more interest in the flavour.

FRENCH MUSTARDS seem to be a breed apart, a brand and colouring without much progeny. The French tradition was to grind the seeds more gently on stone mills, like olives for olive oil. Of all the dark brown mushes, **La Favorite** might claim the parentage and justification for the genre. The wine vinegar is diluted with water and spirit vinegar, but is evident nevertheless, and is reinforced in some instances with herbs like tarragon. It has, 'a sour, damp heat with a sandy texture and an inner sweetness'.

BEST BUYS   ****Beaufor Moutarde en Grains**, from Reims, is a black mustard mixed as a semi-paste. It is like an aristocratic version of Dijon, with a sharp heat and a smooth texture with flecks and very good vinegar. ****Beafour** is the smoother version and is equally good.

*****Moutarde Violette** is an unusual and rarely found variation, using the must of grapes which creates a purple paste. It is made in Brive and it is claimed that the recipe has not been changed since 1839. Mildly vinous with a shallow fire at the back, it is unusual but good, although a bit cloying. It needs something moist to go with it. (**Chalice** do an equally interesting mix of **Mustard with Black Olives**, which might, in time, attain the same curiosity value.)

Moutarde de Meaux Pommery has a long romantic history of how it was first served to the King of France in 1632 and then handed secretly to the Pommery family in 1760. Sold in the kind of stone jars beloved of street markets, the contents sealed in with cork and wax, it is, 'granular and sour, familiar from steak-houses, almost a thick sauce in texture, it tastes very old-fashioned and seems to have become more porridgey in the last 20 years'. It needs using swiftly after opening the seal, or its heat disappears.

Supermarket Own-brand French Mustards: Both **Asda** and **Sainsbury** colour theirs with caramel, stabilize it with xanthan gum and flavour it with tarragon, (ground dried tarragon, in the case of **Sainsbury**). **Waitrose's** valediction about the high percentage of black mustard seeds, the wine vinegar, tarragon and dill seem almost to have moved the mustard into the confectionery aisles, and the result is very poor.

GERMAN MUSTARDS are diluted versions of Dijon with different seasonings – as are AMERICAN MUSTARDS. **Buckaroo**, a Jalapeño mustard from Texas, is not really a mustard but a Jalapeño pepper mix, using vinegar, water, turmeric, onions and colours. Chilli curry piccalilli might be a better name. Very gloopy.

SALT

Salt is an example of a market that has expanded to serve its own purposes. Cooking salt is far and away the cheapest and most expedient form of salt to use in the kitchen. The idea of salt cellars on the table is just an echo of a once brilliant marketing scheme. Although most salt grinders claim to have long lives, eventually the machinery softens. Premium salts may seem expensive for the table but, in practice, the investment is long-standing and, compared to other foods, is very cheap.

Salt is the only pure mineral we eat. Excessive salt intake has become increasingly implicated in raising the blood pressure, which is in itself one of the four major risk factors in heart disease. The dietary advice is to eat less than 6 g per day. A teaspoon amounts to about 5 g compared to a teaspoon of soy sauce at about 3.5 g. Much of the salt we actually eat is hidden. For example, a slice of pizza can contain nearly 5.3 g; a tin of baked beans about 2 g. Ready meals, potato crisps and other savoury snacks are notoriously high in salts – as are convenience foods, like breakfast cereals, for example, and also more traditional cured products like bacon or ham. The salt market is also sustained by its wide use in cosmetics, medicine, water softening and road gritting.

Salts take their name from how they are harvested. Most comes from underground lakes where the rain water has filtered through the salt strata. ROCK SALT is mined as blocks, mostly in Europe now from the enormous reserves on the Austrian side of the Alps. SEA SALT is either evaporated on natural beds, as at Maldon in Essex, or pumped inshore across shallow reservoirs. The size of the crystals depends on how much the brine is heated. At boiling point the crystals will be pin-head size. Lower heats for evaporation will produce larger crystals. Most English salt is pumped out of underground reservoirs in Cheshire in a process that has hardly changed in 1,000 years. The old Celtic word *wych* or *wich*, meaning a salt spring is still attached to salt towns like Nantwich, Droitwich, Northwich and Middlewich.

The best salts are the FLOWER OF SALT, which is the top crust of sea salt imbued with the flavours of the breeze, and RASSOL, which is rarely seen and is the salt left by the intense cold on the surface of ice fields at the Poles.

*COOKING SALT is the best value salt on the market, differing from TABLE SALT in that it does not have added magnesium carbonate and sodium hexacyanoferrate to help it run smoothly through the cellar. Sometimes the colour errs on the grey side, but in terms of cooking it is as effective as more expensive and better packaged table salts.

BEST BUYS **Cerebos British Salt** is an amalgamation of 64 small salt mines in Cheshire, formed in 1888. The main plant is, in fact, on the site of the old Cerebos packaging station. Chiefly notable for its deep-red packaging and the addition of iodine originally intended to supplement a post-War diet.

La Baleine is from the northern Spanish and western coast of France. The sea water is pumped on to inland reservoirs for evaporation. The grits are tighter and smaller than Maldon. It also contains iodine, which is still currently fashionable in France.

**Maldon Salt comes from Essex. The Romans established Maldon as a salt town and it remains a family business, following traditional slow evaporation giving crystals that are soft and wide, 'perfectly fragile'. It claims to be purer, less bitter and, therefore, stronger.

**Salines de Guerande is packed in neat white cloth bags which declare chauvinistically that salt from Guerande is *'autre chose'* (something else). Most usually found here is a small-grained mix with the dried seaweed of the estuary, specifically designed to season fish. 'Intense, characterful, it is almost a self-contained sauce.'

Tidman's was originally developed principally for its supposed health-giving properties. Up to the '20s, salt baths were thought to be effective against rheumatism and other illnesses as various as measles. It was taken under the **Maldon** wing in 1973.

SALT SUBSTITUTES

Originally developed for low-salt diets, these have grown substantially on the back of more ordinary health concerns. All use potassium chloride, which is part of the same family as sodium chloride but much more bitter. Ironically, where the Government's *Health of the Nation Report* recommends a reduction in salt intake, it actually suggests an increase in potassium chloride, which is more usually found in fruit and vegetables. Increasingly it is being used to create low-salt convenience products, like baked beans. **Lo Salt** is made by **Klinge** who deal in potassium chloride for the drug industry, where it is used to help kidney patients. The bitterness is offset by 33% sodium chloride, so it is strictly not an alternative but a diluted form. **Ruthmol** is a genuine alternative which adds a minute amount of ammonium chloride to ease the bitterness. Both claim that people can't tell the difference in cooking, even if they can at the table.

SOY SAUCE

The soya bean is native to China, Java and Japan, where it has been cultivated from the very earliest civilizations. For soy sauce, the cooked soya beans are mixed with roasted wheat flour and salt, and fermented in casks. Two kinds of soy sauce are sold – LIGHT and DARK – though, in some cases, the one seems to be a diluted version of the other, with only the salt levels remaining consistent. The lighter versions are designed for fish and poultry and salads, the darker for more meaty dishes. Many recipes call for both. Good soy is a reasonable substitute for meat stock in cooking. Mainline supermarket own-labels have the colour reinforced by caramel. There are surprisingly different elements to other brands.

There are also properly thick versions to be found in Chinese stores. **Elephant** brand is a first-class example, or else **Natural Thick No.1A** which is not, in fact, as thick as **Elephant**.

Soy sauce was a fundamental flavouring ingredient of the first generation of commercial sauces of the last century, from WORCESTER to what was called CAB SHELTER'S SAUCE, although there was an English derivation made with malt syrup, mushroom juice, treacle and salt. Interestingly ****Lea & Perrins Worcestershire Sauce**, which is now such a distinctive product and one of the oldest foods made in this country having started in 1837, does not contain soy but still claims to be a Worcester sauce. This is probably a fair historical perspective on what would have been the most popular of sauces for the Victorians. **Sarson's** also do a **Worcester Sauce** designed for the Far-east with similar ingredients, again ironically without the soy, which is somewhat sweeter and less mellow.

BEST BUYS Sharwood's Rich is 'meaty' but with tones of a flavour-enhancer and their **Light** version comparatively 'fishy'. **Lotus Light** has, 'poignant sour sharp notes' compared to **Amoy Dark**, 'a deep swelling of the sea, like a liquorice oyster'. ****Kikkoman** is, 'a vegetabley treat, like a non-meat Marmite'. Chinese imports also show well. ***Pearl River Bridge Superior** is, 'nutty, burnt, sharply sweet and sour', while ***Fo Shan Superfine** is, 'burnt old vegetables, the smell of the bottom of the junk, very salty, edges of sea breeze with a honey richness at the back of the throat as a second wave'.

OTHER SOY PRODUCTS

In Chinese and Japanese cultures the soya bean is almost as fundamental a staple as rice or wheat. Products like tofu, natto and miso are made by different applications of the same process as that for making soy sauce. The soya beans are first soaked and then cooked. For TOFU, the mix is then strained and cooled and then mixed with salt. For NATTO, the beans are boiled longer until soft, then pressed into cakes while still hot and wrapped in straw, and then – like cheese – left in a cellar for 24 hours to allow the enzymes in the air and in the straw to work on the flavour. For MISO, the cooked beans are pulped and mixed with salt and boiled rice and put into a vat to ferment for two months. The strained-off liquid from these processes goes to make SOY MILK.

Or more variegated still there is PARMAZANO, a dairy-free alternative to Parmesan seasoning, made of soy milk, soy protein, vegetable oil and sea salt which works hard to create a glutamate effect.

SUGAR

Sugar cane is a tropical reed, *Saccharum officinarum*, that will grow to 6 m (20 ft) in a zone 25° either side of the equator. It needs sun and up to 2 metres (80 in) of rain. The first sugar canes probably came from Polynesia and by 1,000BC they were cultivated in India. The Crusaders brought back the first samples of sugar recorded in Britain in 1099. There was sugar at the court of Henry III by 1264, but the first substantial shipment is recorded in 1319. It was Columbus who took the canes back to the Caribbean.

The refining of sugar is credited to the Arabs and reputedly the recipe was bought by a Venetian merchant who started the industry in Sicily in 1503. It was introduced here in 1565, though sugar was punitively taxed and regarded as a luxury until the 18th century. The biggest producers of cane are India, Brazil, China and Cuba, but Europe takes its supplies from Mauritius, Fiji, Australia and the Caribbean.

In 1747, a Prussian chemist, Margraf, discovered that sugar could also be extracted from the white Silesian beetroot, but it was Napoleon who encouraged the widespread planting of beets during the war with England in 1806, when cane sugar could not be got in to France. It was lavish subsidies from the Treasury in the '20s and '30s that established the sugar beet industry here. Europe is the largest producer of sugar beet, but under the Lome Convention it is committed to taking £1.3 million worth of cane production from African, Caribbean and Pacific countries.

The sweetness of sugars, whether raw or refined, tends to be more or less equal. The difference in taste is said to be down to the size of the crystal: the larger the flake the slower the dissolving. Hence granulated sugars work over a period of time, whereas icing gives an instant perception of sweetness. There are thresholds to tasting sweetness and, say, hot puddings need less sugar than cold and ice-cream mixes need much more. For the most part, **Silver Spoon** will be beet and other labels cane.

GRANULATED SUGAR is ordinary refined crystalline sugar and accounts for 8 out of 10 bags sold. It is the cheapest, but must be used where there is enough time for it to dissolve completely.

CASTER SUGAR consists of crystals which are half the size of

SUGAR AND THE EMPIRE

The ruins of the Victorian pact between sugar and flour can still be found in Silvertown, east London. Part of the Millennium mill is still standing, the last wing only finished in 1953. It is 13 floors high. Each floor runs for perhaps 200 yards along the front of the dock, and another 200 yards down both side sections. This was just one of the giants that took all the cane from the New World and milled it for London and the south. They collapsed almost overnight when the new generation of containers were too wide to use the old docks. Now they have all been pulled down to make way for the new urban village and the Olympic water-sports centre.

Across the road **Tate & Lyle** occupies still nearly a mile of prime Thames waterfront. Silver-town was not just a powerful agency in the food industry, it was the food industry. The doughnut, the jam tart and the sticky bun were mutually beneficial to the giants of an industrialized imperial food policy. They represented the urban face of international trade. The third stanchion, which they could not move into the towns, was the dairy industry.

How far sugar has penetrated the UK diet in that period is awesome. It is not always even labelled as such, but goes under pseudonyms like sucrose or as part of total carbohydrates. Politics and sugar went hand in hand. It was only under European pressure in 1993 that the Gov-ernment lifted the decree that all soft drinks should contain 5% sugar to 'ensure children would gain energy'.

Sugar is an unseen hand in what we eat. It is there visibly in breakfast cereals – another product of the alliance between miller and sugar merchant – and invisibly in milk chocolate which can be 55% sugar, plus a further dose of sugar in the filling. It is there in a form of maltodextrin in dried baby foods. It is there in everyday things we take for granted, like jam and jelly and soft drinks. It is in the cure for ham. It is in sweets. It is in fast foods. It is in tins. It is added to tea.

Looking back down the century it is plain that this country existed on a diet that for the most part relied on wheat and fat made palatable by the addition of sugar. Older English recipe books seem singularly devoid of recipes that do not contain at least one and usually two of these ingredients. The sheer might of these industries obliterated anything else. They were the economy and they were the price paid for industrial-ization and moving people off the land and into the new cities.

granulated and this makes it more versatile for cooking, say in cream mixtures, whisked sponges and meringues, or for sprinkling on fruit or for flavouring with vanilla, cinnamon or rosemary.

ICING SUGAR is best used for quick and easy dissolving, such as cold drinks and uncooked desserts, or to decorate cakes and sweets. It should be sieved first.

CUBE SUGAR was invented and pioneered by Henry Tate around 1890, and it is on this that much of his fortune (including enough to fund the Tate Gallery) was to be based. Designed to go with hot drinks and for ready portion control, they are still useful to grate off the essential oils of the zest of (unwaxed) citrus fruits.

PRESERVING SUGAR is designed to help make jam, jellies, marmalades and chutneys. It consists of large crystals which dissolve slowly, avoiding layers in the jam and also producing less froth in boiling, preventing discoloration.

JAM SUGAR is preserving sugar which has added pectin to support fruits which are naturally low in pectin, like strawberries and cherries, or fruit which in a wet year may be low in pectin or just over-ripe.

REFINED BROWN SUGARS, unlike white sugars where any differences are almost imperceptible, will vary because they are white sugar on to which the molasses are sprayed back.

BEST BUYS Billington's deal exclusively in unrefined raw cane sugar from Mauritius, a reviving craft industry over the last 20 years while many Caribbean plantations have been neglected because of tourism. They claim their product is purer. **Golden Granulated** is sold as the all-purpose sugar – free-flowing, grainy and less intense than refined sugars. **Golden Caster** is the cooking sugar for biscuits and baking, and it is claimed to be better than refined sugar in the microwave. Their **Demerara sugar** is for coffee, for toppings and glazes for ham. **Molasses sugar**, the unrefined dark sugar, has a treacly flavour designed for Christmas cakes, puddings, chutneys and savoury sauces. The **Muscovado** is both dark – for fruit cakes and spicier things like gingerbread or barbecue sauces – and light for other baking.

SUGAR ALTERNATIVES

Enormous effort is going into developing sugar alternatives. There are different kinds of sweeteners. The intense versions like saccharin and aspartame are used at lower levels because of their strength. The bulk sweeteners, listed as E 420 and E421, are used at the same levels as sugar. ASPARTAME is the best known, a dipeptide sweetener made up of two building blocks of protein – aspartic acid and phenylalanine – sold out through its trade name **NutraSweet**. It is found in more than 300 products in the UK and 5,000 world-wide – mainly in soft drinks, yoghurts, chewing gum and confectionery, table-top sweeteners, dessert mixes and frozen desserts. It is 200 times sweeter than sucrose and can be used in a limited way in cooking. It does not have the bulk of sugar, but can nevertheless sweeten sauces. **Tate & Lyle** have developed a new product **Sucralose** from cane sugar in Canada, which is said to be 600 times sweeter than sugar but is still waiting clearance. **Dietade** is a pure form of fructose that claims to be 174% sweeter than sugar. **Canderel** is sold as the all-purpose alternative to sugar, being less bitter than other variations. One tablet contains one-third of a calorie, a teaspoon 1/10th the calories in a teaspoon of sugar. **Half Spoon** is the first concession from the sugar giants **Silver Spoon** to the rise of the aspartame sweeteners. The formulation is half sugar and half artificial sweetener. The effect is to double the sweetness and therefore, it is argued, allow people to use half the amount. It is recommended for coffee, tea and cereals.

GOLDEN SYRUP was pioneered in 1883 by Abram Lyle as a by-product of cane refinery, and was originally just given to staff. There were golden syrups before this, but Lyle came from Greenock where different forms of treacles and molasses were known, though it may well be that none were as pure and that he developed the process that made them palatable raw, not just for use in cooking. The sucrose is broken down (inverted) into glucose and fructose and the flavours come from the 'impurities' and the acid agent or enzyme invertase. It is less sweet than sugar and contains 20% water.

BLACK TREACLE is a blend of molasses and other by-product liquids. The molasses by-product from refined sugar is largely considered too unstable to sell on – different harvests and different crops providing widely different, and often very bitter, results. The result is 65% sugars, 4-9% minerals (and the rest water) and is high in calcium and iron. This was probably one of the earliest replacements for honey in the making of gingerbread, parkin, rich fruit cake and treacle toffee, though the sugar histories do not fully tally with the baking histories.

NUTS & OLIVES

ALMOND · BRAZIL NUT · CASHEW NUT ·
CHESTNUT · HAZELNUT · MACADAMIA NUT ·
PEANUT · PISTACHIO NUT · WALNUT · OLIVES

Britain, one suspects, is not one of the first countries in the minds of traders in nuts. Despite our long history of cooking with nuts, much of what is sold here is at best second-grade or, in the case of cashews and almonds, the stale nibs and broken bits at the bottom of the barrel.

ALMOND

Native to Africa, the Romans called the almond the 'Greek nut'. It flourishes in countries where the average temperature is about 14°C (58°F). The tree grows to 10 m (30 ft) tall and flowers before it leaves. The fruit is covered with a thick green shell which dries in the autumn and opens to let the almond fall out. Almond trees will flower here, but will not fruit, and the blossoms were once prized as wedding bouquets. The first GREEN ALMONDS – sometimes found still with the green shell – begin in May.

There are two kinds, SWEET and BITTER; the difference is indiscernible to the eye, except the kernel of the bitter is thicker. The bitter usually goes for oil, confectionery and cosmetics, and in large quantities can be poisonous. ALMOND MILK and the derivative blancmange figured widely in the public cooking of the Middle Ages. Almond soup was crushed almonds mixed with blanched onions, spices, wine and water. Given the price of sugar and the long distances the almonds came, such dishes must have been precious and revered. Almonds have performed an unusual flip from the end of meals towards the front, graduating out of the Victorian sweet and sugar repertoire, up into garnishing and more inspired combinations with vegetables, eventually into breakfast muesli.

COOKING: *The skins come off easily if soaked overnight. The milk is an interesting diversion for vegans and people with allergies. Allow 125 g (5oz) of peeled nuts to 600 ml (1 pt) of water. Blend and strain. Drink as it is or combine with banana or other fruits. Their place in baking is established, but they can also be used to thicken sauces and relishes. Nobody seems to have an explanation as to why they are supposed to go with trout.*

BEST BUYS   Most packet almonds are American. Predictably FLAKED ALMONDS are poorer than whole. **Sainsbury** has sensibly adjusted the idea to selling them either toasted or chopped and are of considerably better quality than other brands.

BRAZIL NUT

The Brazil nut comes from the giant Para tree, native to the Amazon uplands. The trunk can be as wide as 2 m (6 ft) and the highest branches reaching 50 m (150 ft). The nuts are segments encased in a round thick shell, the *ourico*, up to 15 cm (6 in) across. The rainy seasons of autumn blow them off the top branches and they fall and embed themselves in the soft jungle soil where they are gathered, broken open and washed in the rivers, where the lighter unfertile nuts rise to the surface and float off. Liverpool was the prime port for their importation. They have a higher oil content than walnuts, at nearly 60%, but it is a bland and little-used oil. In fresh nuts, the kernel will be white and the taste still sweet.

CASHEW NUT

The great walnut-style trees proliferate in a horseshoe on either side of the Indian Ocean, but were originally found in South America by the Spanish and colonized by the Portuguese who took the word *caju* from the native *acaju*. The nut is encased in a very hard, bluish shell, which also contains an oily black liquid that can blister the skin but is neutralized by drying in the heat. The nuts were said to improve the flavour of chocolate. The oil went for a blue marker for linen. Most cashew nuts now come from India in the spring, and some from Brazil's autumn harvest. They are increasingly sold untreated for cooking in stir-fries and curries. When they have been roasted and salted the price leaps into the stratosphere for tiny packets sold in pubs and off-licences, as indeed do the calories. Less than £1 per 100 g is a mean average for the supermarket price. Size is everything – good cashews are big, but many packets are filled with broken pieces of small nuts. The pear-shaped casing that envelopes the nut is the CASHEW APPLE, slightly abrasive but still eaten in Brazil with sugar or in jams and fermented into a sweet wine and a vinegar.

CHESTNUT

The most farinaceous of the nuts and containing the least oil. Ground to a flour, chestnuts were an important staple, especially in Central France around Lyons, in the Alps and the Auvergne. Small quantities of the flour can still be found in specialist shops. The more export-led trade is in the sweeter MARRONS, peeled chestnuts cooked in syrup and flavoured with vanilla. Different varieties were recognized until the

'50s, the best being the almost round **Marrons de Lyons**. Most chestnuts sold here are now from Spain and Italy. The difficulty of peeling chestnuts has doubtless contributed to their decline in popularity, but it is interesting to see how many tasting notes for other foods refer complimentarily to the tones of chestnut.

COOKING: *Chestnuts should be nicked, blanched, kept in hot water and the two skins peeled off, then simmered slowly in a good stock or syrup.*

BEST BUYS Vacuum-sealed peeled chestnuts are being imported from France, which is a real convenience. **Le Gourmet Français**, in fact a Liverpool firm, sell tins of chestnut purée which is purely chestnuts, water and salt.

The familiar tins of purée with green emblems of **Clement Faugier** is a diluted form mixed with water, but no salt or sugar, at half the price of the newer English competition from *****Bridge House** vacuum-packed **Peeled Chestnuts** which, short of the quality of the stock, are pretty much as good as can be done at home.

HAZELNUT

The fruit of the *Corylus avellana*, a supple hardy bush named after the town in Italy where they were first cultivated. There are about a dozen varieties.

Also known as the KENT COBNUT, this is among the finest nuts found in this country, although only a few hundred acres are now left growing. The Kent Cob was first cultivated by Mrs Lambert of Goudhurst, hence it is sometimes called a LAMBERT. Although it is called a cobnut, it is in fact a FILBERT, *Corylus maxima*. Filberts are longer and the husk completely covers the nut.

The crop is usually harvested in two sessions, at the end of August when the nuts are formed but still green; and then at the end of September when the shells will have turned shades of deep bronze and smoky grey. The best will have a deep red pellicle. In hop-growing districts, they were always harvested very young while still green to stop the migrant hop-pickers taking them. They should be picked on the tree and not taken as windfalls. The outside may even have gone black, but the kernel inside is nevertheless pristine and unaffected. In the 17th century, sailors took them on long voyages as a source of fresh food, while the Victorians savoured them as a delicacy at the end of a meal, with salt. Fresh, they will keep for up to two weeks.

The FILBERT itself was grown in Wiltshire from around 1810, but was an improved version imported from the more benign climate of the Mediterranean.

MACADAMIA NUT

Claimed to be the finest of all cocktail nuts, which might be a moot point, it was first discovered in Queensland, but has been cultivated in the past century in Hawaii. It has been groomed as a gourmet nut, with the qualities of a milky brazil and a hidden propensity for a grassy sourness. The packaging in vacuum-sealed bags commendably keeps them very fresh.

PEANUT

Peanut is the American name for the vine otherwise known as the groundnut or earth nut, originally grown in West Africa, India, China and along the topical belt before being adopted as part of the American food culture.

Although now mostly known as a snack food it was for animal feed and for the oil for margarine that chiefly led to huge plantations being sown. The vines are fat and large and spread across the ground. The pods are initially white. The first-grade nuts were always referred to as 'fancy'. Another trade was as a substitute for burnt almonds, to colour and flavour drinks, or mixed with sugar as a cheap sweet.

Peanuts have been linked to cases of anaphylactic shock (see page 363). Sufferers can be so sensitive that they do not even need to eat the nut themselves – shock has been brought on merely by kissing someone who has eaten peanuts by ingesting other foods prepared in an area where peanuts have been.

PEANUT BUTTER is an American innovation. The nuts are shelled, roasted and then ground to the characteristic putty-like meal, which is then salted. The darker variations, like that from **Waitrose**, tend to leave the skins on. The best are the original American varieties like **Schmukers** and **Skippy**.

PISTACHIO NUT

Once called the BLADDER NUT or GREEN ALMOND, this is native to Western Asia, but particularly favours the high rolling tourist idylls of the Seychelles and Mauritius. It has also been notably adopted across the southern Mediterranean rim, from Sicily through Greece into Turkey and Iran where it has been a central fixture of the cooking for centuries. The tree is an evergreen, growing to a height of 10 m (30 ft). The nuts cluster on the branches and are a beautiful hue of blue, the more so from southern climates. They are ripe when the kernels split. Drying destroys much of their visual beauty, but develops the flavour. Marseilles was the major trading port for their entry into Europe and also into French cooking.

WALNUT

The common English walnut, *Juglans regia*, is native to Iran and the northern mountains of India. There are many different kinds of walnut, some of which are quite coarse. In Iran, the tree will fruit within eight years, in Spain after 16 years, in England perhaps 24 years – and it may be 60 years old before it reaches its full production. The tree will be 100 years old before the wood is hard enough to be used for engraving. The best nuts are young, when still green, though traditionally many of these went for pickling. The shell should be thin and the skin of young walnuts is quite bitter, but becomes milder as they age. Older walnuts are pressed for their oil which can constitute as much as 50% of their weight. The oil will turn them rancid if they are kept on through the winter. The quality varies substantially from region to region and many will be sulphured to make them last longer.

WALNUT KETCHUP was made with the brine in which young walnuts were kept for pickling, boiled for half an hour with ginger, pepper, cloves and chilli mixed with malt vinegar.

PICKLED WALNUTS are a singularly English product, cured usually with a boiled infusion of malt vinegar, pepper, ginger, mustard, cloves, mace and bruised garlic.

Nuts

Percentages of fat in nuts

	Calories	Protein g	Carbos g	Fat g	% Fat of Cals
Almond (ground)	612	21.1	6.9	55.8	82
Brazil (kernels)	682	14.1	3.1	68.2	90
Cashew (roast)	611	20.5	11.8	50.9	74
Chestnut	170	2.0	36.6	2.7	14
Coconut (block)	669	6	7	68.8	92
Hazelnut	650	14.1	6	63.5	87
Macadamia	748	7.9	4.8	77.6	93
Peanut	564	25.6	12.5	46.1	73
Peanut butter	623	22.6	13.1	53.7	77
Pine nut	688	14	4	68.6	89
Pistachio	331	9.9	4.6	30.5	82
Walnut	688	14.7	3.3	68.5	89

OLIVES

Table olives are sometime picked when they are bright green, but more usually they are allowed to start to darken on the tree so the flavour mellows. Olives are inedible on the tree and have to be immersed in salt brine with soft water for weeks to render them palatable. Traditionally they were kept in water or a light brine until the bitterness leached out, as long as a year later in some parts of Spain. Today the brines are more sophisticated using caustic soda for an alkaline solution that will in mature one to two months, or the point that the sugars break down. Usually the flavourings will be added at this point and reinforced later.

Few of the best olives are sold here and even those that carry the right names are often much smaller than in their native countries.

The difference between BLACK and GREEN OLIVES is that the black are left on the branch longer. Olives deserve to be bought by their name, because anything with just a brand generic term is likely to be low-quality. Usually table olives are distinct from olives grown for oil, except in areas where the agriculture is backward or olives are a marginal crop.

STUFFED OLIVES need to be treated with even greater caution. Stoned green olives tend to be very mushy and lose their texture. Particularly nasty are **Sainsbury's** marinated pipped olives in sunflower oil with garlic. *Taylor & Lake** sell bottles of *tanche* olives.

The best olives are sold loose. They will have been taken out of the brine – usually just a plain salt solution – and just washed off. The brine for olives in tins and bottles is necessarily very watery, because the olives will absorb liquid and their flavour is diluted.

FRENCH

**COQUILLOS NIÇOISE* are the very small, 1 cm ($^1/_2$ in) long, black olives found wild along the coasts of Provence. The colour is purple-black and the skin shines with the ripeness. The season is later and they will be kept in salted brine for six weeks; so later in the year they will have spent much longer in the brine and they will get progressively softer.

**LUCQUE* are large, ungainly, long and thin olives which are emerald green in colour. They are picked early and given a short cure. They are held to be grander than the *picholine*.

**PICHOLINE* from the Vallée des Baux, are oval, dusky green olives, 3 cm ($1^1/_4$ in) across, with a good ratio of flesh to pip. They are picked early in September/October and cured for only three weeks. The flavour is sweet and meaty, hammy, bacony.

GREEK

KALAMATA or *CALAMATA* are usually kept in brine and red wine vinegar to reinforce the colour, which can vary from deep beigey-green to deep black. The flavour is without subtlety, it is a meat flavoured with salt in various degrees.

Gaea is a Greek brand with a typically 'salt-to-the-front' brine but big olives. **Sainsbury** has opted deliberately for a milder cure and smaller olive. **Chalice** are good olives, very much as you might expect to find in Greece, with the pronounced sourness at the back – probably left to ripen longer. They also do an excellent paste, sold as a pâté, of just *kalamata* olives and virgin olive oil – a wonderfully pure and meaty example of the true merits of *kalamata*.

SPANISH

In Aragon and Catalonia the cures for olives tend to be left fairly simple, with only the addition of thyme and sometimes fennel. In Andalusia, whole basketfuls of flavours are brought into play, invariably garlic and oregano and sometimes cumin, Seville oranges and lemon. In Seville chilli may even be used and in Extremadura smoked pepper. The Teruel district of Aragon leaves the olives on the tree much later, so they are wizened and black. They are then dried in the sun and salted. More than two dozen varieties of olives are sold in Spain. The main eating olives are the fleshy, small-stoned *manzanilla* and the *gordal*.

MANZANILLA from Seville, can be excellent, but absorb the brine and go watery in the bottle if poorly handled. They are also used for making olive oil.

**QUEEN from Seville, are the largest of the Spanish table olives. Deep, almost khaki-green, they can have a 'superb sourness melting into sweet crunch, large pip, but a large olive. Excellent'.

Unusually a handful of types of olive are sold both as table olives and for oil – the *arbequina* from Catalonia and the *verdial* from Extremadura. Some oil refiners have started to export varietal table olives. The black *bajo aragon* olives are lightly cured in a brine with thyme for as long as year. Some *arbequina* are also coming to the market.

AROMATIC OLIVES

Adding aromatics was a way for market-stall holders to add value to their olives. The traditional Provence seasonings were fennel, thyme, rosemary, bay and garlic – but these have now been widened to take in more southerly influences, like chilli and other peppers. Often the olives will now be imported from Spain.

The **TAILLADÉE** is a good mixing olive because it is quite sour, picked half ripe when it is a soft mauve. They are machine-slit, which allows the marinade to go right through to the stone. They blend well with the juicier Spanish *manzanilla*. The Ligurian olive oil estate **Tornatore** also exports mixes of the small Tagiasca olives with different blends of herbs.

OILS

GRAPESEED OIL · HAZELNUT OIL · OLIVE OIL
SAFFLOWER OIL · SESAME OIL · WALNUT OIL

Culinary oils divide cleanly into two categories: those for cooking and those for flavouring. The only oils that might be said to cross this divide are olive and, to a lesser extent, the more pungent sesame.

VEGETABLE OILS tend these days to be made from rape seed, but are largely deliberately denatured to make them as inoffensive as possible to as many people as possible.

Some SUNFLOWER OILS buck the trend and retain enough vestiges of character to be useful in making milder forms of mayonnaise, but perhaps that is just an illusion fostered by the sunny label?

NUT OILS far from being outré kitchen accessories, were born of the necessity of making use of good harvests before the oils turned the kernels rancid. **Taylor & Lake** sell an ALMOND OIL, which is quite rare, and is mainly seen as helpful in baking. Chemists also sell almond oil under the **Care** label, which hopefully suggests that as well as being a good bath oil it can be used in baking, although the intensity is muted and the effect diluted. GROUNDNUT or PEANUT OIL is much favoured in Chinese cooking, where many books suggest it ahead of other oils especially for stir-frying, and also by fish-and-chip shops because it does not break down when subjected to high temperatures over long periods of frying.

PISTACHIO OIL is a newer product, which is warmly aromatic for use like the other nut oils judiciously in salads, though both command premiums for their rarity.

PALM OIL and COCONUT OIL share with cocoa oil the distinction of having the highest saturated fat of any vegetable oil, in some cases as much as 90% saturated. Palm oil is mainly used here in margarine and by fast-food chip-fryers. In Africa it is a prime cooking medium, tasting fairly neutral with just an edge of violets to it, and a reddish colour which is used as a dye.

GRAPESEED OIL

Once used to light street lamps before electricity, this now resurfaces as a cooking and salad oil, possibly somewhat happier in its new more respectable guise. The centre of crushing being Modena in Italy, its composition is similar to olive oil, except the polyunsaturates are considerably higher and the monounsaturates much lower, with only a trace of cholesterol. The label promises that it can be used for everything from shallow-frying to making salad dressings and baking, which makes it an expensive alternative to sunflower or rape oils. It can, however, be heated to higher temperatures. It is possibly best seen as an alternative to cheap olive oil with a pleasant distinctive grapey bite which can add interest to salads. It is invariably sold in clear bottles, most of which are tinged lemon, except **Dufrais** which is distinctly green.

BEST BUYS **Sainsbury's** grapeseed oil from Italian grapes, is 'neutral but drinkable, more pleasant than say sunflower with just an edge of the grapes left'.

*Dufrais** is a lovely deep green oil sold in clear bottles. The taste is of, 'summer, quite buttery and distinct, not oily, but that hint of something vinous...'. It tends to be expensive against supermarket own-labels. **Cuisine Perel** from California illustrates the potential of grapeseed. Sold in designer bottles, one example was delicately flavoured with orange, lemon and coriander, and in another a very pungent chilli. **Safeway's** is French and more expensive than other supermarket brands, and 'very creamy, not very subtle, one-dimensional, not very grapey'. **Asda's** is from Italy and 'very thin and poor'. **Tesco's** is also from Italy and 'probably from the same source as **Asda**, same bottle same country, same taste', but cheaper.

HAZELNUT OIL

Why supermarkets package hazelnut oil in clear glass 250 ml bottles is not obvious, for in most kitchens 250 ml will have gone rancid before it is ever used. A small drop is all that is needed to pervade dressings and sauces. It is only stocked by **Waitrose**, **Sainsbury** and *Asda**, whose is slightly cheaper and the pick of three good examples, 'clean-tasting, slightly toasted'. Mix hazelnut oil with other oils to extend its use and so as not to overpower other flavours.

OLIVE OIL

Suddenly yards of supermarket space have been given over to olive oil. Much of this is a real mish-mash between horrible and sublime. There is a real choice now between supporting small farms as against highly industrialized petrochemical factories.

The olive oil season starts in November and the best oils will be made before mid-December. The first oils will be unfiltered and fruity. Those for export and for longer keeping will be filtered. Most oils mellow and flatten out with age and will be past their best within a year. The olives are either hand-picked or left to fall into nets on the ground.

The traditional stone press crushes these olives along with some leaves (which add colour and bulk). The paste is then laid on circular mats and these are piled one on top of each other around a central axle. The pile is then wheeled into the press and the oil allowed to exude gently under pressure. Finally, oil and water are separated.

More modern machinery has speeded up the process by using centrifugal force to clean, wash, crush and separate the oil from the olive in a continuous process. These machines can produce more oil from premium olives at the height of the year and have been widely adopted in the top Tuscan groves. These first olives have considerably higher percentages of vitamins and antioxidants which are lost as the nights get colder.

VIRGIN AND EXTRA VIRGIN OLIVE OIL come from the first pressing, but as with wine the term can cover a multitude of anonymous blends. True quality virgin oils come from single estates where thought and effort has gone into the blend of olive varieties and the timing of the harvest.

FIRST or COLD-PRESSED OLIVE OIL is a hangover from washing the paste with hot water to extract more (but diluted) oil. In a few rare instances, like **Affiorato** from Umbria, the olives are left to stand under their own weight before going into the press. This yields a small amount of oil which is scooped off by hand. What is commonly sold labelled as OLIVE OIL, previously often known misleadingly as PURE OLIVE OIL, is made from the paste out of which the virgin oil has been extracted. This is treated chemically to extract more oil and then mixed with an undeclared amount of virgin olive oil.

The northern Mediterranean produces smoother and more elegant oils. Some of the more westerly oils, notably from Portugal, Spain, North Africa and some from Provence, have sharp metallic, petrolly overtones. Greek oils have been largely overlooked, but represent terrific value for the middle of the market. Their reputation for being heavy and greasy stems from the practice of leaving the olives on the trees too long, but the top-quality oils are reshaping this image with fresh, green apple, asparagus-style flavours close to Tuscan and Riviera oils but with softer finishes.

The health-giving reputation of olive oil is centred around the low instance of heart diseases in regions where olive oil is the predominant cooking medium. The level of fat in the oil is high, but three-quarters of it is monounsaturated. There are complementary associations with high levels of vitamin E and antioxidants, and it tends to be used with other positive foods like garlic, pulses and fruit as well as drinks such as red wine. The best shops to discover a good variety of serious olive oils are **Harvey Nichols** in Knightsbridge, and **The Oil Shop**, part of Sir Terence Conran's **Gastrodome** complex at Butler's Wharf.

COOKING: *Most kitchens need two types of olive oil: one for everyday cooking, and one for finishing salads or saucing. It needs to be stored in the dark or the light will turn the oil rancid. In Tuscany, for a light meal a piece of bread would be toasted, rubbed with a clove of garlic, the surface wetted with oil and then seasoned with sea salt.*

FRANCE

There are very few single-estate producers of any size in France, possibly because inheritance laws have split up the estates over the years and dictated that villages go over to the co-operative system. The main areas are around the Vallée de Baux, the Bandol, and Nyons, where it is mostly tanche (also an eating olive) that is grown. This has an *appellation contrôlée* although little seems to get over here. Mostly it is single olive production and there is some pressing of Spanish olives. Rarely is there any sign of the pepperiness associated with Tuscan oils. By and large French oils tend to be a bit of a mixed bunch reflecting different styles. There are a great many Moulins which should not be confused.

BEST BUYS **À l'Olivier** is a good commercial blend, typical of the Provence style: catty, buttery, spicy finish, slightly bitter, hints of grass clippings, it is unobtrusive but has character.

Alziari is made by Nicolas Alziari, former friend of Jacques Médicin, the legendary Mayor of Nice, and owner of an olive oil shop in Nice, where the olives and the oil are sold loose. He owns some groves above Nice and presses his own oil. The style is closer to Liguria than Provence: sweet, delicate, some pepperiness... herby, fresh.

****Domaine de Souviou** is one of the finest examples of any olive oil, let alone French. It has a character and vitality that surpasses any other French oil available in this country and is as good with mashed potatoes as with salad.

Les Alpilles from **Taylor & Lake** is orange-hued like castor oil, and comes in clear bottles. The label recommends it for vinaigrettes, with champagne vinegar. It has an intense more direct impact than Vaucluse (see below)... it is lighter, softly buttered, a scratching of itchiness, perfumed.

***Moulin de Bedarrides** from Helon Belon is the product of a cooperative into which olives from Sir Terence Conran's estate also go, hence it appears here, albeit at a premium price. It is grassy-green, piquant, with a good young hit but little depth save some tones of vanilla.

Moulin de la Garrigue, from Moulin de Gassac, Verdale, has a petrol smell, is pale lemon, with hints of citrus peel, grapefruit, metallic, closer to Portuguese or Spanish style.

Provence Regime from Emile-Noël is a first-pressing organic oil, quite thick and with a flavour that is 'sour lemons tinged with ice-cream'.

****Vallée des Baux** is among the most expensive of oils to be found, selling for as much as £22 per litre. The olive bouquet is striking, the flavour has sunshine edges, and is distinct, smoky and lemony.

Vaucluse from **Taylor & Lake** comes from the hills above Orange. Sunset yellow in colour, it is like thick grassy meadows, hay and lemons, with a hint of pepperiness, it is quite forceful but lacks the delicacy of Italian oils... quite heavy and unctuous.

***Le Vieux Moulin** from Alain Fournoux is made in the southern Rhône on a single estate, Mirabel aux Baronies, from a single olive variety, the tanche. A popular first stop for initiates, it is characterful and good for cooking with ... sweet, musty in this case from age, earthy, hints of cracked walnuts, green oil, very fruity with little pepper. Other tasting notes included 'Very eggy', 'Not really typical of the Nyons style' and 'High price for the fancy bottle'.

Good all-purpose French olive oils include **Puget** from **Vitrolles**, which – like its plastic bottle – is lemon-yellow in colour and is bright, grassy, one-dimensional but viscous, sweet... with a little pepper and shades of vanilla; and **Plaignol**, in the fancy fluted bottle, which is not quite first division but makes a good mayonnaise.

*GREECE

Much Greek oil is pressed too late. The kalamata olive produces good oil (some are being planted in Tuscany) but only if picked early. The koroneiki olive also produces a good oil, which is notably good value for everyday use and so far unexploited. Many of the best Greek olives go to Italy for processing. Shops also tend to keep them past their sell-by dates. A good Greek oil should taste of torn salad leaves. With the above riders, Greek oils represent excellent value and sensible cut-price alternatives to Italian. **Safeway** first, and then **Sainsbury**, picked up on this, but their prices are still excessive compared to Greek brands in specialist shops.

BEST BUYS **Chalice** is made from Kalamata olives and sold in dainty clear thick-glassed carafes with handles and cork seals (which don't fit very well). Almost emerald-green in colour, it is creamily thick and verdant, with edges of petrol and primroses, silky thick, some pepperiness. An interesting oil, it is about as thick as any I have tasted.

Aegean Heritage is a good all-round oil imported from western Crete.

Cypressa is the own-label for the Cyprus-based importer, it is deep yellow to sun-scorched grass, and is buttery with big floral notes, with mild pepperiness on the finish. Creamy. It is very good value for an all-purpose everyday oil – half the price of **Safeway's**.

*__Iliada__ is made from Kalamata olives and is deep yellow in colour, luscious, floral, winey, with hints of vanilla... it is excellent and good value.

Kolymvari from Crete is sold through an Italian wholesalers, which is a mark of respect. Floral and buttery, it holds it own well in the Tuscan company as a very good cheap oil. The price of about £3 per litre wholesale suggests some supermarkets are marking up 400%.

Kydonia from the Co-op Kolibari, north-west of Crete, is good value and tastes of fresh clear apples.

*__Mani Organic__ from the Mani Peninsula is mill-stone pressed and has, plenty of body and apply fruit, warm earthy, 'Chardonnay and orange. Sweet, rounded and grass', compare the price, at £9 for 750 ml, to Kolymvari. **Safeway** and **Sainsbury** have been selling **Mani,** the non-organic version, which is one of the best buys in the supermarket.

*Solon is widely available in Greece, but to date its sale has been restricted to Greek specialists. Hay-green in colour, it is fruity, luscious, mildly creamy, herbal... with a slight bite... very good for the money. You could not say that top Tuscan was four times better. At £1.89 per 500 ml in specialist shops, it is excellent value.

Sparta comes from three villages south of Sparta. It is suggested for use in *taramasalata*, onion fritters, cheese and eggs with Feta. Linseed, Castrol, texturous, viscous, lime-flecked gold, it is an everyday oil, reminiscent of Portuguese and Spanish oils.

Commercial blends of note include: **Athena** which is, 'sweet and creamy, hint of aniseed' and uses kalamata olives as in the **Iliada**. **Safeway** has pioneered the introduction of mass-market extra-virgin oils in which area the Greeks have been particularly impressive. 'This variation smells of lemons and cut spring mountain flowers, full and viscous, lacking a little of taste compared to the good Tuscans, but a good all-round oil that responds to lemons.' **Sainsbury** followed up this year impressively with a version that is, 'pure ice-cream... unctuous... lovely'

ITALY

The Italian supremacy in olive oil is down to the use of three or more blends of olives to create a single oil – either by design or by accident, the groves tend to be mixed. The frantoia is the olive of Tuscany, although the frosts of '85 wiped out many old groves. It is only in the last two years that Tuscan oil has come back on the market. Many more estates are about to come on line, encouraged by the sudden interest. Tuscan oils typically tend to be soloists, best used in salads or on pulses, or just on toasted country bread with garlic and salt. Ligurian oils are more mellow and inclined to be used to create simple sauces for grilled fish or even meat. They are more almondy and closer to the Provence style or vice versa.

Sicily tends to upset the easy rule that the best oils come from the north, where the cooler evenings slow down their growth. The olive there is nochelara del belice, famously good at the start of the season in December but tending to flatten off through the year. Other isolated examples from different areas suggest there is no monopoly on great olive oil in one region or one style.

BEST BUYS *LIGURIAN OILS: The reputation of LIgurian oils is more for cooking than salads; eg simple sauces to be poured over grilled fish at the final moment. **Canto** is organic and unfiltered and so is aromatic and expensive. A beautiful pure yellow, it is very pale, delicate lemony... an ultra treatment for a grilled fish.

Carluccio from Villa Nova is sold in small clear wine carafes and is a strong yellow hued with green, sweet and apply... ice-cream soda... brilliant for cooking. Add a little tomato and it creates a velvety sauce. Try it with grilled lobster and lemon.

Prela from Raineri family estate comes in elegant tall slim numbered bottles. The oil is buttery green in the style of old-fashioned Riviera oils and closer to a fine example of Provence than Tuscan, 'warm finish, nutty'. The estate also makes a second oil sold under the family name, **Raineri**, which has little pepper but good body, for half the price. One of the best oils found here while the Tuscans were replanting, it now has some serious competition.

Tornatore is, unusually, unfiltered and comes in imposing large triangular bottles, pale deep lemon in colour it is lightly peppery, sweet... an excellent everyday oil for improving cooking. The same estate also exports superb capers from Morocco and sells the aromatized small Tagiasca olives.

****TUSCAN OILS

Tuscan oils are the aristocrats of the olive oil world, the finest of all are best served just on warmed bread or in a salad. Their vibrancy far exceeds that of the oil any other region.

BEST BUYS **Ardoino**, from Vall Aurea, is sold in distinctive gold foil and green bottle. Made from late-harvested (in January) olives, it is light and delicate, with a golden green colour and a smell of peaches and almonds. Use for salad dressings or marinades.

****Avignonese**, from Montepulciano, comes in elegant slim dark glass designer bottles and is a deep burnt yellow in colour. It is sweet and creamy, with hints of peppers, luscious, mellow.

Badia a Coltibuono is often held up as the benchmark for Tuscan olive oils, but since the frosts of '85 some olives have been bought in. 'Full of style and character, it is herbaceous, bitter evergreen.'

****Carluccio** from Pistoia, is emerald-green in colour, 'My perfume,' says Carluccio. Delicate... with shades of rocket and mild saffron, the pepperiness building.

****Colonna** comes from Molise and is said to be one of the most scientific of all the olive farms. The oil is a mix of different olives, predominantly Coratina, each grown and picked by hand separately and then blended after crushing. Neat carafe-style bottles with sell-by dates sensibly marked for the end of November. Lemon, hues of grass, it is thick and creamy, with some pepperiness and hints of green leaves and grass. The estate also produces an oil imbued with lemons crushed with the olives in the press which has its enthusiasts. A mass-produced imitation for **Collavita** is destined for the market using essences.

****Dell'Ugo** from between Sienna and Florence is unfiltered. Not part of the Laudemio consortium (see overleaf), it is similar in construction and uses the same olives. Antony Worrall-Thompson named his Soho restaurant after it. Cloudy green apples, pure olives, vivacious, it responds well to the addition of salt, pepper, chilli or lemon.

Frantoio di Santa Tea from Reggello, Florence, sells two oils – one, **Fruittato-Intenso**, is a marked green, picked early (in November) it is, 'youthful, assertive, crying out for garlic'; while **Dolce Delicato** is picked in December and the oil has become a pale sunset yellow. Cut grass and peppery, it is very typical of Tuscan oil.

Gemma from Arrezo is a good everyday restaurant oil. It is clean, buttery, with a hint of pepper, fruity and full-flavoured.

Laudemio is a form of *appellation contrôlée* self-imposed on a group of now more than 50 Tuscan olive producers, led initially by Marchese Frescobaldi and the Antinori family. Half a dozen are imported here – the **Sonnino estate was the first major olive oil in a supermarket at **Waitrose** last Christmas at a knock-down price of £9.95 against the usual £13.95. In different ratios according to the estate and the year, the olives will be primarily frantoio and the maraiolo, with the fattier lecchino as the make-weight. To carry the Laudemio (meaning 'the tithe given up to the landowner') label the olives must be hand-picked, pressed within 48 hours and submitted to independent analysis before the middle of December. The younger they are the more peppery. **Frescobaldi** is, 'green leaves and green bananas'. 'The **Sonnino** and the **Torre de Caltrona** are not really typically Tuscan. They are great oils but surprisingly different to the others.'

**Monte Vertine from Radda, Chianti is made using the correggiolo, maraiolo and leccino olives. Production is still limited because of the damage from frost in '85, but the groves have been replanted. Stone-milled, it is emerald yellow in colour and comes in fat green wine bottles. 'Thick viscous, peppery, taste of meadows lemons and peppers. Brilliant. Very fruity.'

Ornellia from Marchese Lodovico Antinori who is better known for his wines and who also produces a fine **Laudemio. The groves are near the sea and, unusually, escaped the '85 frosts. The trees are 80 years old, mostly frantoio and leccino, and the olives are hand-picked before the end of November and traditionally mill-ground. In a tapered and embossed glass bottle, the oil is mown grass yellow-green, pure, clean smell, sweet, nutty, luscious combination, outstanding oil, lightly peppery... with a long, long finish.

**Podere Cogno comes from groves which date back to the Middle Ages. At 500 metres high, the soil is stony. The unfiltered oil comes in clear bottles, syrupy yellow, mild, intense citrus fruits, powerful peppery... not typically Tuscan.

Ravagni from Arrezo is a thick deep emerald-green oil, which is fresh and powerful. Very persuasive.

OTHER REGIONS

Although not well-known, or well-regulated, there is more than enough evidence to suggest that other regions of Italy can produce superlative and distinctive oils.

BEST BUYS   **Tenuta di Saragano** from Saragano near Perugia in Umbria, comes in numbered and dated bottles and, although Umbrian, uses the same olive varieties as Tuscan, it is 'soft, buttery, delicate pepper, sweet'.

**Ravida from Menfi on the south coast of Sicily is made using three different local olives harvested young, which gives it a warm smooth assertive style, which has been consistent, reputedly, since production began in the 17th century. Herbaceous, with an aroma of tomato skins, the taste of freshly mown meadows, it is expensive but widely regarded in Italy as one of the best non-Tuscan oils.

Other Sicilian oils worth looking out for are the organic **La Biotecha** and

Nochelara, back to rhubarb, greenest of green; **Bottarelli* comes from the west side of Lake Garda and Garda oils have a good reputation but possibly not deserving over Liguria, This is a fine example. Sunset-yellow in colour, it comes in a wine bottle, It is dry, fruity and thick, with a hint of bananas.

*Montiferru comes from a hundred-year-old business in the mountains in the north-west of Sardinia. Orangey-yellow in colour, it is wide, peppery and precise.

Gastrum from Bari, comes in a straw-covered bottle and is pure, very thick, mealy, almost a food, peppery on fish – good second-division oil.

Casa Bini from Reggello comes in an opaque designer bottle and is yellow to burnt umber in colour. 'Tart, short, ice-cream, pepper', it is an unusual and not bad value second-division oil.

Fior d'Olivia, from Bari, has been used in Italian embassies and is pale yellow. It is a smooth, mild minor oil.

Harvey Nichols own-label from Italy, is a deep yellow, sharp, peppery oil, with a short finish.

**Carluccio from Gioia del Colle in Apulia, is sold in a suspiciously fancy ceramic reusable jug and is bright yellow, like all the Carluccio choices, with hints of almonds and chocolate. Thick and bready, it is sweet rising to a serious pepperiness that vanishes swiftly into a creamy sweetness. Revelationary.

Worthwhile brands include **La Nonna**, a mix of olives from Tuscany which is sweetly buttered and £3.45 per litre wholesale, which puts into perspective the prices of olive oil in supermarkets where tiny phials of less good oils are sold for twice as much. Good examples of widely found commercial brands include **Filippo Berio**, based in Lucca the centre of oil blending, which consistently heads the tasting tests of mass-market oils, and they have introduced a new 'mild and lighter' olive oil which seems a regressive sop to the culture of other oils. Not to be outdone, **Sainsbury** introduced a mix of sunflower and olive oil which further complicates the polyunsaturates question. **Dante** is widely used in Italy and regarded as a good starting point. **Menucci** is sweet and grassy and well-balanced.

PORTUGAL

The Portuguese tend to leave the olives to ferment and this creates a distinctive, very gutsy muddy petroleum style, which can be off-putting. 'Burnt farmyard' is a common description. As with Portuguese wines, there is a lack of precision.

BEST BUYS **Gallo** from Victor Guedes Abrantes is extra virgin (bought in Portugal as it is not available here as yet). A good example of what Portuguese oils might be: damp yellow grass, mellow nuts, very thick, mild pepperiness, fairly harsh, good body... metallic notes muted here. Compare that to the widely sold **Damatta** from Envendos. An olive oil, rather than a virgin, it is metallic, tough with no fruit... very poor.

La Rosa, from the Douro Valley, comes in a clear wine-style bottle. Sunshine yellow in colour, it is cleanly filtered and has a petrolly smell and metallic hints... acid. It bears out the idea that most Portuguese and some Spanish oils have different applications to the Italian and French – they are not really for salads, but should rather be used as a flavouring for thick mealy dishes and for cooking large quantities of onions.

SPAIN

Most Spanish olive oil is from single olive varieties, making them emphatic but simplistic. Some argue that they are underrated. The best tend to nuttiness, lemon hints and freshness. In principle the more northerly estates produce better oils.

BEST BUYS **Lerida**, from the Vea family estate in Catalonia, is one of the finest examples of Spanish olive oil made from arbequina olives: burnt almonds and bitter chocolate, buttery, dark chocolate.

*L'Estornell** is single estate from Lerida and made from organic arbequina olives: herbaceous, sweet, hints of chocolate, walnuts and softness. A sample in September was sunset-yellow with some pepper, a very good example of Spanish style.

Nunez de Prado has been made on the same estate at Baena near Cordoba since 1795. The olives are still stone-milled on the same days as picking to ensure low acidity. Sold unfiltered in distinctive square bottles, this is probably the supreme example of Spanish olive oil. It is unusual for Spain, in that they use a blend of three different olives and only the flesh – not the stone – is milled. About 11 kilos go into each litre, rather the usual five. With hints of passion fruit, lemon rind, hints of petrol, unripe nuts, it is rustic, and intense with a fine peppery finish. A September sample had hints of grapefruit and nuts.

Sabor d'Abana from the Ebro valley, is bright yellow, with primrose edges... OK.

Siurama, from the Agrana Co-op in Catalonia, comes in gold and red label varieties in clear bottles. A clear oil, it is deep yellow tinged with green and gold in parts, With a sweet smell, it is thick, gummy, light but solid, grassy... unusual'. Tomato skins... could be Italian, not typical.

Good brands to look for include **Lupa**, which is from a single estate in Malaga but is bottled in the UK. The flavour of sweet almond, nuts with passion fruit, is typical of the Spanish style and good value. **Safeway** own-label has high petroleum notes mingled with sweetness, some fire, good texture, very metallic, meant as a support not as a soloist. **Carbonel** is well known and considerably more interesting at the start of the year; it is good for cooking and tastes of ripe melons.

OTHER OLIVE OILS

A few American-made oils sneak into specialist shops. The labels and bottles tend to cleverly slick. For comparison: **Olio Santo**, from California's Napa Valley, is thick and cool, like vanilla ice-cream.

Australia also makes good olive oils. Like the wines, they tend to be big and powerful but clean and know what they are about. The following two examples illustrate the range of different styles, although telling them apart from the label is more difficult than tasting them:

Oils
Percentage of saturated fats in different oils.

	Calories	Protein g	Carbos g	Fat g	% Fat of Cals	% Sat Fat
Coconut oil	899	0	0	99.9	100%	85%
Corn oil	899	0	0	99.9	100%	12%
Olive oil	899	0	0	99.9	100%	14%
Palm oil	899	0	0	99.9	100%	14%
Peanut oil	899	0	0	99.9	100%	45%
Rapeseed oil	899	0	0	99.9	100%	5.3%
Safflower oil	899	0	0	99.9	100%	10%
Sesame oil	881	0	0	99.9	100%	14%
Soya oil	899	0	0	99.9	100%	14.5%
Sunflower oil	899	0	0	99.9	100%	12%

Joseph Foothills Extra Virgin '94: 'Like an Australian Chardonnay, brash, very up-front, all cleavage and bosom, a belt of pepperiness on the nose.' **Joseph Cold-pressed Extra Virgin '94** is 'sharply sweet, vanilla, grassy, very clean'.

SAFFLOWER OIL
Mostly from Holland, this oil is only stocked by **Asda** and **Harrods** – which must be some kind of first – priced on the same level as grapeseed at £1.09 per 500 ml. It is recommended for salads and shallow-frying, and claims to be good for, 'delicately flavoured dishes', but probably is not, and should not be used for deep-frying. It is neutral-scented, seedy and quite creamy.

SESAME OIL
Excessively sold in 250 ml bottles, most of the contents of which will likely oxidize before they are used, a small amount of sesame oil is all that is needed to pervade salads and other dishes. The vogue has been to toast the seeds before pressing as this gives a wonderful aroma and edge but a discernibly different effect of 'autumn bonfires'. This is a fairly superficial effect that begins to pall in the kitchen.

BEST BUYS It is usually the product of more than one country, though **Safeway** claim Japan. **Asda** and **Sainsbury** own-labels are markedly superior and evocative, 'beautifully potent roasted smell and pervasive power'. **Waltrose** is milder and subtler. **Tesco** and **Safeway** have been poor, weak and vapid, with a late nagging taste. The best are from Chinese supermarkets, such as **Koon Yick Wah Kee's**, which has a powerfully potent, rich, deep aroma, and a strong nutty element.

WALNUT OIL

The profusion of walnuts in France and Switzerland led to the crushing of the nuts for their oil. Fresh nuts harvested in late September will turn rancid by the end of the year because of the amount of oil they contain. Walnut oil is sold with the health message to the front – flashes denote that it is high in polyunsaturates and low in saturates. However, as such tiny quantities are involved the benefits can only be marginal. In any case, it is best mixed with another oil so its flavour, though less pronounced than hazelnut or sesame, does not go rampant. It should be kept in dark bottles to stop it oxidizing, but unilaterally supermarkets sell it in clear glass.

The taste is mild, meek and virtuous, reassuringly homely, with nudges of autumn, a good housekeeperly taste. There is surprisingly little difference between any of the own-brand supermarket oils.

PASTA, RICE ETC

PASTA · RICE · POLENTA

The word pasta is simply the Italian for a 'paste', but that is rather a brutal description for something as old as bread that has evolved into hundreds of different shapes each of which seems to have developed its own school of saucing.

Good pasta must be made with durum wheat, which is high in the gluten that provides the stiffness and elasticity, or semolina which is the same thing but more coarsely ground. Durum's other advantage is that it does not soak in water. The best was always grown in southern Italy around Abruzzi, but now even the Italians import it from America. The hardness of durum wheat needs different milling technology from bread, which is one reason why pasta was not assimilated here earlier. The technology here now is probably as good as that in Italy, which suggests that the more outré and packaged designer pastas imported from Italy are no longer worth the kind of premiums they demand.

Pasta has become high fashion. The range of shapes, the range of packaging – from the see-through cellophane to the deep regal blues – and the designer names like **Cipriani** or **Lucio Carofalo** have arrived like a visiting football team to play the English squad of Bachelors and the own-labels. There is a bravado to 'how much egg does your pasta have?' Something of a minor issue because the home cook can always add an egg as if making carbonara anyway. Different brands have their enthusiasts, but the grand opera of it all is perhaps all too seductive and may be there is not so great a difference between the brands as such to command the kind of designer premiums that some labels have been asking. **Buitoni** has held up its position in most stores, but **Lily** and **Sitoni** have lost ground.

The real innovation has come from own-label. Here the choice is becoming more miraculous by the week and much of it extremely good. This has tended to replace the more ridiculous idea of selling pasta ready flavoured. Only spinach seems to be surviving. Much of this is still off-the-peg stuff and the real innovation around the corner will be the arrival of unpasteurized, short shelf-life fresh pasta.

The supremacy of dried pasta over fresh is as much about flavour as it is about convenience. The bigger packets are conspicuously cheaper – and spaghetti is the cheapest shape. The supermarkets have standardized the price.

Cooking times for dried spaghetti have been slashed from 10-12 down to 5-7 minutes, simply by making the pasta thinner. Most use durum wheat from Italy, though **Tesco's** value range – which almost

Pasta

	Calories	Protein g	Carbos g	Fat g	% Fat of Cals	% Carbos of Cals
Macaroni						
(raw)	348	12	76	1.8	0.4	87
(boiled)	96	3	18.5	0.5	0.5	86
Egg noodle						
(boiled)	62	12.1	13	0.5	0.7	83
Spaghetti						
(boiled)	104	3.6	22	0.7	0.6	84

The balance of percentage fats and carbohydrates shows there is a wide margin for potentially fatty sauces like pesto or bolognese with pasta without breaking any dietary strictures.

plus **Parmesan**	452	39.4	0	32.7	32	65

An average serving of Parmesan would be likely to represent perhaps just 10g not 100g or 3.2g of fat.

halves the price of dried pasta – combines durum with plain wheat. The **Tesco Italian** ranges are very good. **Sainsbury** claims a first for its **Pasta Fresca** label – fresh pasta that will keep in its sealed packets for months until opened. QUICK-COOKING PASTA is the same price as a regular, so the saving is not passed on. ORGANIC PASTA attracts a big premium: **La Biotecha** costs £1.15 for 500g, or almost 75p more. Other good names to look out for are **Ferrare**, from Modena, which is sold in designer plastic bags together with some above average sauces in bottles. **Buitoni** tends to attract a premium.

COOKING: *Pasta should be cooked in generous amounts of water to rinse out the starch. There are differences of opinion on when to add oil – if at all. Some say it should go in at the beginning to stop the pasta sticking, but if you use enough water this is less of a problem. Others use oil after draining to separate the strands before saucing. Pasta should not be over-drained. Allow up to 75 g (2^1/$_2$ oz) per person for a starter, about 100 g (3^1/$_2$ oz) for a main course.*

LONG PASTAS, *like spaghetti and its variations, and the EGG-BASED FLAT PASTA like lasagne are designed for oil-based and tomato sauces. The thicker the spaghetti the stronger the sauce should be. Egg-based pastas are designed for meat sauces, often made with softer more absorbent flours that can benefit from taking in the sauce.*

Canned Pasta

Comparison of different canned pastas as with fat as a percentage of calories

	Calories	Protein g	Carbos g	Fat g	% Fat of Cals
Macaroni cheese	178	7.3	13.6	10.8	54
Ravioli	70	3	10.3	2.2	28
Spaghetti	64	2	14	0.4	5

Manufactured pastas vary widely in composition. The low calorie levels allow for fattier sauces on the pastas.

SHORT PASTAS, like penne which, in itself, comes in six different variations of thickness, are robust all-purpose pastas. As the shapes become more pronounced, say for macaroni or farfalle, the tendency is for cream sauces. The coiled fusili or the shell-like conchiglie, need to have thicker and more texturous accompaniments, such as vegetables and nuts.

STUFFED PASTAS are often best par-boiled before stuffing and need bright fresh sauces so that they do not become bland. Their blandness is meant to take in combinations of seasonings and heavy sauces.

SOUP PASTAS come in a bewilderingly amusing range of shapes. The smaller ones are for texture, the larger designed to pick up the soup. They should be cooked separately from the stock and added at the last minute so the starch does not cloud the soup. Good stock, fresh vegetables, pasta and Parmesan or Pecorino to grate are the watchwords of great soups.

RICE

Rice has stormed up the supermarkets aisles, from the back of the store right into the first aisle. There is an increasingly large choice of indigenous rices such as arborio and basmati in different-size packages. The best value is probably the biggest bag you can carry. Alongside this welcome advance is the equally dynamic high-value-added sector of flavoured rices. Most supermarkets have invested heavily in neat packages of Savoury, Risotto, Chinese Five-Spice, Vegetable Biryani, Pilau, which all compare very unfavourably in terms of price or value.

There are more than 1,300 varieties of rice and several thousands shades and forms of those according to the climate and soil. No other grain is so widely eaten and rice is still the staple for more than half the world. Rice is a grass, *Oryza sativa*, growing from 25-200 cm (10-80 in)

tall, which is similar in shape and colour to oats. It grows in flooded fields and will yield two crops a year. The paddy fields need constant back-breaking weeding. Before harvest the fields are drained to let the sun ripen the heads. The rice is then cut, tied into bundles, sun-dried briefly and then threshed and milled to remove the two outer husks, leaving 60% of pure white husk.

Rice is infinitely flexible and interchangeable in cooking. The general principle is that long- and medium-grain rices are for savoury dishes and short-grain (in the West at least) is reserved for puddings. The Japanese use short-grain rice for *sushi* because of its stickiness and *paella* contradicts the Western rule by using short-grain. Graders grade by length, although size is no indication of quality. Soaking helps to stop the grains from sticking.

COOKING: *Allow 55 g (2 oz) per person. The usual ratio for cooking is 450 g (1 lb) of rice to 600 ml (1 pt) of water simmered for 8-30 minutes, depending on the type of rice. Take off the heat, pour a fresh kettle of boiling water over it, then drain, add butter and allow to stand, covered with a wet cloth. Another wet cloth underneath the pan helps to stop the rice sticking to the bottom.*

AMERICAN LONG-GRAIN RICE is the classic boiled rice and akin to basmati (see opposite), although it does lack the aroma. A good general all-purpose rice, it is used in curries and savouries because it separates well and is half the price of basmati. Cooking time is 12-15 minutes. **Froqual** produce a frozen five-minute rice – although it only takes 10 minutes to cook dried rice – made from American long-grain and acquiring a rather luminescent yellow colour en route, which lingers in the pan/palate. It is remarkably tasteless,

AMERICAN EASY-COOK RICE is American long-grain parboiled with the husk still on. This processing makes the grains less brittle and fewer nutrients are also lost in milling. It is also supposed to stop the grains sticking and some brands argue that it cuts the cooking time, but this is questionable. It does lose some flavour and pureness of colour. Cooking time is 10-15 minutes. **Tilda** does a boil-in-the-bag version which stops the rice sticking to the pan, but at a considerable premium.

*AMERICAN WHOLE-GRAIN RICE has the bran layer left intact, leaving much of the fibre untouched. To compensate, cooking times are longer – 20-30 minutes. 'More texture, chewier, nutty flavour.' Soaked overnight, however, the cooking time shortens. Less processing marginally shortens the shelf-life to around 12 months. It is best for soups, salads and vegetarian loaves. Looked down on in many rice-eating countries where white is supreme, it is worth rediscovering and not only for its nutritional virtues. Despite brown rice's association with the health culture it remains three times more expensive in wholefood shops than in

Rice

How cooking affects the carbohydrates and fats in different rices

	Calories	Protein g	Carbos g	Fat g	% Fat of Cals	% Carbos of Cals
Brown rice						
(raw)	357	6.7	81.3	2.8	0.7	91
(boiled)	141	2.6	32.1	1.1	0.7	91
Savoury rice						
(raw)	415	8.4	77.4	10.3	22	74
(cooked)	142	2.9	26.3	3.5	22	74
Easy-cook white						
(raw)	383	7.3	86	3.6	0.8	89
(boiled)	138	2.6	31	1.3	0.8	89
(fried)	131	2.2	25	3.2	2.1	76

supermarkets. However, they seem to grade the price up according to the increase in nutritional value. Bizarrely, the boil-in-the-bag brown rice does not seem to attract the same premium as does easy-cook.

**BASMATI RICE comes from India, mostly from the area around the Punjab. Basmati, meaning 'the fragrant one' in Hindi, is also known as the 'prince of rice' as it is generally regarded as the best. It has the longest of rice grains, thin and opaque at one end. Traditionally used for curries and most Indian dishes, it is also right for Middle Eastern cooking. Own-labels are cheaper, but the quality of *Tilda argues well for a few pennies more.

BROWN RICE has a more intense flavour and aroma than American, harder to find, as there is no own label, unfortunately. Treat as American whole-grain. The main brands are **Tilda** and **Veetee**, although **Uncle Ben's** does an eccentric tin of ready-cooked weighing an unhelpful 277g. Unlike American rice there seems little difference in brown and white basmati prices. EASY-COOK BROWN RICE is parboiled brown rice, which is very rich in nutrients and has grains which are well separated. Cheaper than whole-grain, it is well worth looking for, although it has slightly less flavour than whole-grain.

*FRAGRANT THAI RICE, sometimes called JASMINE RICE, is cultivated in Thailand. Its aroma is slightly less pronounced than basmati and it is widely used in South-east Asian and other Oriental cooking. With a slim grain like basmati, it does tend to stick together more on cooking. Also available from specialist stores are broken grains, which have been damaged during milling; since fragrant Thai rice is a slightly sticky rice, however, the broken grains make little difference to the final texture. Cooking time is between 8-10 minutes.

JAPANESE RICE is short-grain and glutinous. Due to the roundness of the grain, it becomes sticky on cooking and has a slightly sweet taste. It is traditionally used for *sushi*, mixed with vinegar and sugar then wrapped, usually with raw fish, in *nori* seaweed.

POPPED RICE is a short-grain cooked with sugar and subjected to high pressure. The water inside the grain turns to steam and smashes the outside hull. This is then toasted and the result is **Rice Krispies**.

PUDDING RICE is American and was originally called CAROLINA RICE, although it is often now grown in Italy and in Spain. Pudding rice is a white short-grain rice with very plump grains, intended to produce smooth creamy puddings. It has a similar texture to arborio but a much blander flavour, and is therefore better for a sweet pudding. Cooking times is 10-15 minutes. It is one of the cheapest rices in supermarkets. There is also FLAKED RICE, in which the white grains are flattened to thin opaque leaves. However, this takes away all the texture of the grains so it is only suitable for creamy puddings. Cooking time is 6-10 minutes. GROUND RICE is for creamy puddings and bakes in place of flour. Cook in milk or water for 6-10 minutes.

RED RICE is a wild rice peculiar to the Camargue. It is a pretty dark garnet in colour and cooks slightly differently from other rices. Add it to boiling water for half an hour, drain and cover for another half an hour. 'Nutty, chewy… very chewy… almost a fragrant wadge.' Use sparingly to add texture and interest.

RISOTTO RICE is a blanket term that means Italian fat white grains which can absorb up to five times their weight in liquid, against three times for ordinary white rice. The plump grains stick together and produce a smoother result. The final textures vary according to the rices. Cooking time is 20-30 minutes. An important phase in risotto is to whip in some butter at the end, and be generous. Risotto rice is also useful for rice balls. Prices for risotto rices tend to be higher than those for other rices. **Tesco** does an Italian easy-cook rice parboiled to stop the grains sticking. It still produces a thick risotto, but the texture is not as creamy as a normal risotto. It is best for seafood risottos.

The best rices for risotto are sold under their generic names, but attract premiums of three and four times the own-labels ARBORIO is the most frequently found of the risotto rices. **CARNAROLI rice produces a risotto with, 'a slightly nuttier texture'. This is sold exclusively in Italian specialist stores, but is very good quality. A good example is **La Gallinella**. **VIALONI, the plumpest grain of the family, arguably produces the best and creamiest risotto because of the grain thickness. It is available only from Italian food stores. As with carnaroli, a good name is **La Gallinella**.

WILD RICE is not a rice but an aquatic grass, *Zizania aquatica*, harvested from August to October and mostly imported from Canada. The grains are green and they are cured for 4-14 days to develops the nuttiness. When the grains are brown or black, they are roasted to reduce the moisture, then hulled, cleaned and graded.

> COOKING: *Cook it in three times the volume of water (the grains can expand to four times their size). Cooking times vary according to the different dishes: from 45 minutes, until swollen and split showing the white centre, for salads and stews; or longer, 60 minutes, for bakes. To fluff the grains, leave them in the water for a few minutes after cooking. Cooked it will store in the fridge 2 weeks, in the freezer 6 months. It is mostly used in salads, stir-fries or as a side dish.*

There are also mixes, usually with long-grain rice, to get the price down. **Safeway** and **Tesco** do an interesting box of long-grain brown *wehani* (a variety of brown rice, amber in colour, which is grown in eastern America) and black *japonica* (another variety of brown rice, grown in California, which is a very dark brown treacle colour). *Tilda* do a mix of basmati and wild.

POLENTA

Corn meal was first brought back from America by Columbus and adopted in northern Italy, where at times it has been a staple as important as pasta. Variations are endless, although only two kinds are sold: coarse and fine. The end results do not differ enormously, though fine is predictably smoother. Buy maize meal rather than maize flour, which is properly for bread. The consistency of the polenta depends on how much water is added: 1 part water to 2 polenta for stiff (hard work); 1:4 for frying and grilling; 1:6 for creamy; 1:8 for a soft custard. Extend the cooking times as you increase the water. It is cooked when it comes away from the sides of the pan. **Aurora** sells polenta in tubes ready-mixed for frying, baking or microwaving. It tends to come out of the tube as rather wet and spongy, almost scented. It is a bland mix with a strong back-taste of eggs and milkiness. It is pragmatic and easy to use, if lacking in character.

VINEGARS

BALSAMIC VINEGAR · CANE VINEGAR ·
CHAMPAGNE VINEGAR · CIDER VINEGAR · MALT
VINEGAR · RASPBERRY VINEGAR · RICE
VINEGAR · SHERRY VINEGAR · WINE VINEGAR

Rather than wine, early civilizations may well have drunk vinegar in diluted form to purify the water – or used it as a dip for bread, as is still the custom in Asia. The Egyptians thought of it as medicine, Moses mentions it and Roman legionnaires certainly drank it. Beyond culinary uses, vinegar has been used as a bactericide, as a balm to soothe wasp stings, sunburn or shingles. Cider vinegar mixed with honey is an old therapy for arthritis, and is used to rinse washed hair to make it shiny. Around the house it has been used to clean burnt saucepans, to clean marble, to break down limescale corrosion and to remove stains.

Good vinegars of whatever persuasion will have gone through two fermentations, the first where the alcohol is lost and the second where it acidulates. The character of the original liquid should remain, which is why short-cuts using acetic acid are self-defeating, just acidity for its own sake. Lemon juice is invariably more natural and successful. Vinegar has, however, managed to slip back into fashion and might claim – along with garlic and ginger – to be in the forefront of modern cooking, either souring sauces and gravies, or in its most glorious form as a flavouring like balsamic. Given the quantities used in cooking, it is inexpensive and the investment in good-quality vinegars is worthwhile.

BALSAMIC VINEGAR

Made for about 1,000 years in Modena and Reggio, it is only since the '40s that it has been sold at all. Before that, it was a dowry and a gift for friends and sipped as a liqueur after banquets. Most of what is sold here is a diluted or adulterated form of the original article, which takes decades to mature and might well claim to be the finest – and certainly the most expensive – individual food product in the world. **Fortnum & Mason** and the **Conran Oil Shop** sell small phials of **Giacobazzi's** balsamic at around £65. It is genuinely aged balsamic, otherwise we are dealing with scaled-down versions, house claret not Lafite.

The trebbiano grape is harvested at its peak of sweetness and then dried out in the sun. It is then pressed and the juices simmered into a concentrate over 24 hours. Unlike wine vinegar, which converts alcohol to acid, balsamic converts sugar to acid. The liquid is cooled and put in a barrel in the loft. Some families use a vinegar mother, while others discard it in favour of some of the cooked must to start the fermentation. The barrels are chestnut, oak, cherry, mulberry or ash, with holes in the top to allow evaporation and the concentration of flavours. The steamy hot summers and cold winters of the region allow for a cycle of loss and rest. Each year the vinegar is transferred into a smaller cask. There must be at least three transfers to different casks. The saying is that one generation makes vinegar for the next.

The artisan-made balsamic vinegars of Modena and Reggio must have been aged 12 years. Each one is judged by a panel of five and the bottling is done by the consortium so it cannot be adulterated. Modena bottles are small globes, Reggio bottles are vase-shaped like small decanters with three quality levels denoted by the colour of the label – gold (the highest), silver and then red. Each year there is a competition for the best balsamic vinegar at Spilamberto on San Giovanni's Day, June 24.

Good-quality balsamic is really a seasoning to be used like salt, sparingly and deliberately. Artisan-made vinegars should not be wasted in cooking, but just used to adorn dishes from pasta to fruits – half a teaspoon will go a long way. The flavours of balsamic vinegar are of browned meats, old port, wood, herbs, wild flowers and new hay...

Imitation balsamics are made in Naples and often shipped out in bulk for bottling in other countries. Commercially made balsamics can be good especially in cooking for sauces, soups, stews, salads and marinades. The best are a blend of good-quality wine vinegar, grape must and some balsamic (and sometimes caramel) aged in a balsamic cask. Others are just wine vinegar, caramel, herbs and no balsamic or must at all. The acidity should be 6%.

BEST BUYS **Five Barrels Balsamic Vinegar** is bottled in dinky carafes with metal flip-over tops by **Guidetti Fine Foods** and labelled 'extra mature'. It has a fierce nose, giving way to burnt treacle toffee, sweet and caramelized with lovely tartness. It is a good example of above-average commercial balsamic.

Torrione, from the Carndini family, makers of balsamic since 1836; their 'cask 1**' has the sweet taste of red wine, more like a high-quality red wine vinegar tinged with balsamic process. Distinctly different, it is good for salads and dressings, although it is unfaithful to the pure balsamic idea or too young.

*Luigi Ugolotti & Figli from Modena, is sold in **Waitrose** in lovely clouded glass corked bottles. It has a sweet smell of caramel, harsh, but authentic velvet tones, a generous dose of the real thing in there. Its good measure represents good value for the second division. It is easily the pick of the supermarket balsamics.

Fini from Modena, is usually sold boxed with an opaque fluted bottle inside. Aged about five years, it is a good commercial blend.

*Mazzetti from Modena is noticeable by the elegance of the 36 cm (15 in) tall thin dark glass bottle, with a cork stopper. With a deep coffee colour, it is sweet, treacly, crackling... very fine.

One of the best examples of balsamic at a reasonable price is **Fondo Montebello** from the **Fresh Olive Company**, a deep, luscious, viscous toffee.

Sainsbury Balsamic Vinegar is poor, runny and acid, like balsamic added to tart low-quality caramelized vinegar. The Speciality Sections in showplace stores now sell a much better version as well, albeit at a much higher price.

CANE VINEGAR

Datu Puti from the Philippines is opaque, the colour of diluted pastis, all acidity and sugar in almost equal parts, sharp, indistinct. Interesting uses to surprise, say with fruit.

CHAMPAGNE VINEGAR

The sugars and yeasts in Champagne create a sediment which forms around the neck when the bottles are stored for the first year. This sediment is taken off by freezing the necks of the Champagne bottles, which can then be extracted and the Champagne given its formal mushroom-shaped cork. The frozen sediment is what goes for Champagne vinegar – one year old in non-vintage and three years old in vintage.

BEST BUYS **Benedicta's Vinaigre de vin blanc de Champagne** is 89p per 250 ml, and is sweet, not bad and cheap. It is a good alternative to their wine vinegar, but not representative.

**Edmond Fallot is tart, sharp Chardonnay butter, supremely invigorating.

CIDER VINEGAR

The apple juice has yeast added to convert the sugars into alcohol, so cider vinegars tend to be sweeter than wine vinegars and have a lower acidity.

BEST BUYS Own-labels come in around 65p per 350 ml. **Dufrais** is £1.39 for 500 ml. The best examples come from France.

**Vinaigre des Côteaux Nantais is outstanding, even the version filled with shallots designed for serving with oysters, Mild and sour, it has the beautiful taste of cidre bouchée. Other variations seem to lack the same purpose in life.

MALT VINEGAR

The reverse of the process for wine vinegar is used to make malt vinegar, creating the alcohol in the first place. The grain is steamed with water to create a starch, the barley malt is added to convert the insoluble starch into sugar, then pumped into vats. Yeast is added to convert the sugar into alcohol and fermentation takes 3-4 days. The liquor is then filtered and bottled and the colour added as caramel. Its solitary valid domestic use today is for pickles. The alcohol can be taken off and distilled and is widely used in processing to preserve and retain the colour. **Sarson's** dominate the market, managing to hold a reasonable parity, around 50p per 250 ml, with own-labels.

RASPBERRY VINEGAR

Traditional in the North of England as much as in France, it is made by macerating raspberries in white wine vinegar (though presumably more likely malt vinegar in England), for a month and then filtered. (See **Raspberries**, page 265 for a recipe.)

BEST BUYS Unfortunately **Benedicta** smells like boiled sweets and is about as acid as a cream cake, and **Martlet** has met with flavours rather than fruit. It also uses cider vinegar as a base and claims to be the 'inspiration behind *nouvelle cuisine*', though it is unlikely the Troisgros brothers used cider vinegar, let alone an English version. A more genuine example is **Taylor & Lake Fresh Raspberry Wine Vinegar** which is unpasteurized and sells at £4.59 per 375 ml – admittedly nearly five times as expensive, but it has a, 'real hit of raspberries backed by a lashing rounded acidity'. **Womersley Fruit Vinegars** are outstanding. There is a raspberry and also, according to season, blackberry, loganberry and mulberry.

RICE VINEGAR

Made by adding a starter to sake and this is then matured in cedar-wood kegs for 8 months and finally filtered through cotton.

BEST BUYS **Amoy Red Vinegar** is sold as a dipping sauce with ginger for Peking-style food. Brown, diluted malt colour, it is very thin and acid, like an off red wine. Made from rice, E150 and spices, it is not very good.

*****Chinkiang Vinegar** is soy-black, with some of the sweetness and caramel of a balsamic. It says 'gold plum' on the label which is appropriate. Good and very interesting, it is made from glutinous rice and is not expensive and no worse than some of the rubbish passed off as balsamic vinegar for a fraction of the price.

Koon Yick Wah Kee's Red Vinegar is flavoured with star anise, just a light boiled sweet sourness, very direct, very refreshing, little complexity just the edges of acidity.

Mitsukan is natural vinegar distilled from wheat, sake cake, rice and corn. Pea-yellow in the bottle, it is fragrant with wheaty overtones, gentle, pleasant and sharp but low on acidity.

Yokoi Brown Rice Vinegar claims to be, 'uniquely mellow' but is actually sharply sour, mellow but distinct and powerfully influencing flavours to the east. The acidity corresponds to wine vinegars but the heaviness of the brown rice is evident.

*SHERRY VINEGAR

This is aged in old oak sherry casks. The **Xérès is revered by French chefs, being mellower, caskier but with the cutting bite of wine vinegar that lends acidity to sauces and dressings, especially those with nut oils. *Sainsbury own-label sherry vinegar is £1.15 per 350 ml, nearly twice the price of the wine vinegar, but infinitely superior. Likewise Dufrais at 95p per 250 ml is a better buy than their white wine vinegar. A good first step in buying quality vinegars, especially when there is not much else around.

WINE VINEGAR

Prices for red and white wine vinegars are interchangeable. Red wine vinegars should be aged for at least six months. Own-label wine vinegars undercut brands like Dufrais and Benedicta by one-third or more. The rage for flavouring cheap white wine vinegars with garlic, herbs or anything else does not bump up the price, nor the quality. Better to do it at home. Check the label to see if it is flavouring rather than flavoured – either way they tend to be meek.

BEST BUYS **Edmond Fallot makes old wine vinegars in Beaune: red and red with cassis. 'Very good with the taste of the burgundy still prominent', normally good value too at under £3. The quality of this vinegar stems from its origin and method of production, declares the label and so it does. Mellow like good burgundy, the cassis gives a wider accent.

Peloponnese traditionally aged red vinegar is more than 12 months old and sold for £1.29 in larger supermarkets. Vigorous, grape skins and wood in flavour, it is good for marinades, a bit brutal for salads unless the sun was very hot.

*Martin Pouret in Orleans was always known for the quality of its wine vinegars. Pouret also make La Favorit mustard (see page 324). Very pale, the vinegar is like thin cheap white wine, but mild and rich-tasting.

**Doktorenhof from Germany are wine vinegars made from good German wines, matured in oak or beech and filtered through a second barrel of beech, oak, cherry and mulberry shavings and then matured on for up to a year. The bottles are hand-blown glass and the labels from original oils painted on the estate. The vinegars are intense and sabre sharp, the marketing suggests they might be used as an aperitif, but probably they need a big fat wild duck to go with them. Superb but witheringly sharp. The rosé is from Spatburgunder, there is a very good and faithful Reisling and white from the Weisser burgunder. Exclusive to Harrods, they are outstanding for dressings and saucing and, despite the designer price, not bad value.

GLOSSARY

ACETIC ACID is the strongest of the kitchen acids, and is now widely used in manufacturing as a preservative. Its most famous applications were as an adulterant to vinegar or as the alternative 'non-brewed condiment' found in fish and chip shops. Unlike malt and wine vinegars, there has been no fermentation. Its addition inhibits bacterial growth in vinegar. It is made from a dry distillation of wood. Naturally occurring, it provides the tang in yoghurts and some cheese.

AGAR, sometimes known as AGAR-AGAR or listed as E406, is sold as a vegetarian alternative to gelatine. Found as a powder, sheets and shreds, it is obtained from boiling different seaweeds and straining off the resultant jelly. It melts at a higher temperature than gelatine – at 90°C (194°F) compared to 27°C (80°F) – and sets at about 45°C (112°F) rather than 20°C (68°F). It tends to perform erratically, as does gelatine, and there is a residual aftertaste. Allow 1 teaspoon per litre (1³/4 pt) of water. Do not boil too long with an acid food or it will not set. Agar can be used to make fresh papaya and pineapple juice into jellies, however, where gelatine cannot.

ALUMINIUM reacts badly to salt. It is used in some foods as a cheaper alternative to silver – in confectionery especially – and listed as E173. Aluminium saucepans are good conductors of heat, but foil should not be used with salty foods or in a microwave. Links to the wasting Alzheimer's disease have been suggested, but are not proven.

ANAPHYLAXIS is a trauma brought on by a food allergy. Some estimates suggest that 1 in 100 people may be susceptible. Symptoms include breathing difficulties, increased heart rate and unconsciousness. In extreme cases it can be fatal, if a victim does not receive an injection of adrenaline within three minutes of the onset of an attack. Sufferers often carry a syringe with them. The range of foods associated with such reactions is wide. Peanuts are most commonly quoted. Other nuts, sesame seeds, dairy produce, fish and eggs have all been linked, as have insect stings.

ANATTO is a bright orange/yellow dye that originates from tropical South America but has long been used to colour butter, margarine and cheeses like Cheshire. It is the red arils around the pod that give the colour and, in South America, the seeds are used as a spice in cooking. Found also in Sri Lanka, it comes from a shrub, *Bixa orellano*, which is an evergreen 2-3 m (6-9 ft) tall but sometimes twice that, and bushy from the top with a single stem. The fruit pods are heart-shaped, about 2.5 cm (1 in) long, red and covered with stiff prickles containing 30-50 seeds embedded in a reddish yellow waxy pulp, which – after the pod is rubbed or brushed off – settle in a tub of water. It contains two colorants: orellin (yellow) and bixin (cinnabar red).

ANTIOXIDANTS are labelled E300 to E321. They are used to stop foods going rancid and to preserve some of the vitamin content. Some are actually vitamins themselves. Invariably their usage suggests there may be hidden fats in the foods.

BOTULISM is one of the most lethal forms of food poisoning, usually associated with poorly sterilized food in tins. It survives at a temperature of 120°C (250°F) for up to 10 minutes. Symptoms of dizziness, weakness, breathing difficulty and paralysis come on within 3-36 hours. It is fortunately now rare, the most recent case being connected with contaminated hazelnuts in a consignment of yoghurt.

BSE see page 145.

BST, or bovine somnatotropin, is a drug that encourages cows to give more milk. The EU has stopped its use on the grounds that cows are already producing a surplus of milk and there have been welfare concerns about the genetic manipulation of animals. Britain was the only European country to oppose the renewal of the 5-year ban in 1994. In America the more aptly named BGH (bovine growth hormone) is licensed, which has led to the ban and punitive taxes on the import of American animals.

CAFFEINE is found in tea, coffee, chocolate and cola-nut derivatives. It raises the blood pressure and the sense of alertness, hence its reputation for stopping people going to sleep. In large quantities it can cause tremors as well. Coffee beans contain less caffeine than tea, but as more is used the effect is greater. Instant coffee has the same caffeine as fresh, but cocoa powder has considerably less – an almost negligible 0.1%.

CALORIE is the unit of energy needed to heat one gram of pure water by 1°C. It is usually short-handed up to units of 1,000s as kilocalories or Kcal on labels and, in fact, this is what most people mean when they use the word Calorie. A balanced diet for an adult, depending on the level of activity, would vary from 1,500 to 3,000 Kcal a day.

CAMPYLOBACTER is one of the more common forms of food poisoning, leading to vomiting and diarrhoea, usually spread from pets to food. New research has shown an uncommonly high link with drinking milk from bottles where the tops have been broken by birds. One study of 550 people found 17% of patients had drunk milk from infected bottles.

CHORLEY WOOD PROCESS was developed in the '60s at the laboratories of the Flour-making and Baking Association in Chorley Wood and allows mechanical kneading of softer flours. The level of yeast is doubled, but then fed with ascorbic acid and extra water. The main advantage is the speed of factory production.

CLING FILM will leach its plasticizers into fatty foods over a period of time – as much as 60% in five days on cheese.

COLOURS for food form the E numbers 100-200. Natural colours do not necessarily have to be natural to the food they are colouring. Synthetic dyes, including the azo dyes – notably the yellow TARTRAZINE E102, widely used in soft drinks – which are a by-product of petrol refining, have been found to cause allergic reactions, especially in people sensitive to aspirin or suffering from eczema or asthma, and hyperactivity in children. Confusingly, the numbers give no indication of progeny, so the equally controversial azo dye BROWN FK used in kippers is listed as 154, while E153 is a carbon-black derived from burnt plant material. Fifty colours are permitted. There are gaps in the numbering to allow for future additions. E100-110 are nominally yellows; E120-128 are reds; E131-133 are blues; E140-142 are greens, E150-155 are browns and blacks. E160-163 are from plants or copied from plants; E173 is aluminium, E174 is silver, E175 is gold.

CO-OPERATIVES to buy your own foods can qualify for grants from local councils to cover training and even set-up costs. The Greater Easterhouse Consumers' Project (Unit 12, 19 Blairtumnock Road, Glasgow G33 4AN) has a free (plus sae) starter pack for people looking to set up a new co-operative. Most rely on volunteers. They buy direct from cash-and-carry outlets and pass on the savings to members at a nominal mark-up of around 10%, which can be a significant saving on a household shop.

DRIPPING is rendered-down beef fat.

EMULSIFIERS are used to mix oil and fat and by definition they are used where fat is present. They are labelled E322-495. This includes stabilizers (to keep the emulsions together) and thickeners.

FAIR-TRADE FOUNDATION awards its label to foods avoiding social and environmental damage. The first food product to carry the logo is **Green & Black's Maya Gold** organic chocolate, with an agreed price to organic cocoa farmers in southern Belize for three years.

FREEDOM FOOD is an initiative started by the RSPCA to encourage animal welfare. Any foods carrying the logo will have been inspected and the animals found to be raised without 'discomfort, disease or distress'. The first stores to carry the symbol were **Tesco** for its pork and the **Co-op** for its bacon and eggs.

FOOD INTOLERANCE: Surveys suggest that one in three adults believe they are allergic to a type of food. Allergies are a reaction to an otherwise healthy food by the body's immune system. Food intolerance on the other hand is when the body cannot digest certain compounds. The most common example is not being able to digest the lactose in milk. Proper intolerance only affects one person in 50. The most common foods associated with intolerance are milk, peanuts, eggs, fish, shellfish and bread via the gluten in the wheat.

GENETIC ENGINEERING of foods is the new frontier. Only a tomato and a strain of yeast have been allowed, although the rennet for vegetarian cheese uses a genetic blueprint to synthesize a non-animal alternative. Coming up soon will be genetically altered rape seed for vegetable oils, reduced sugar potatoes for crisps, and other potato varieties more resistant to blight.

Most of the research has been pioneered by **Zenecca** seeds, an off-shoot of **ICI**. Working with Nottingham University, **Zenecca** identified the key point in the ripening of Ailsa Craig tomatoes by analysing their DNA print. They found that ripening was the action of the enzyme polygalac-turonase breaking down the pectin walls (hence why you can't make jam with over-ripe fruit). By taking the polygalac-turonase gene out (literally cutting it in half and putting it back again), the ripening process was slowed down.

The advantages are essentially commercial: the market gardener has longer to pick his crop; supermarkets have longer shelf-life; processors get a higher percentage of flesh. The higher pectin levels also give a better viscosity for use in ketchups or sauces. The stickiness of the genetically engineered tomato is probably its most noticeable feature. Any flavour difference in recipe formulations is undetectable.

The genetic engineering of yeast cultures has concentrated on removing off flavours from combinations that achieve a low calorie (and coincidentally frothier) drink.

The more important work is being carried out on developing crops that may be disease-resistant and can be cultivated in parts of the world where it has not been possible before. Trials into rape seed, again with **Zenecca** – this time in conjunction with the University of Leuven in Belgium – have taken out blight protective genes from radishes and put them into rape seed. Crop losses to blight, even in the UK, can be as high as 30%.

HYDROGENATION was invented in 1911. It allows liquid vegetable fats to be converted into fats that are hard at normal temperatures by exposing them to hydrogen with a nickel catalyst. Widely used in biscuit and margarine manufacture, the process changes unsaturated fats to saturated (see Trans-fatty Acids below).

INULIN is the fructose (fruit sugar) naturally present in Jerusalem artichokes and some pulses. It is not digested in the stomach and ferments, causing wind.

IRRADIATION by gamma rays is widely used to sterilize hospital equipment, but has also been used to preserve and inhibit growth in foods, notably to stop potatoes sprouting in store in Russia and to clean consignments of pepper. Its use is only allowed by licence, but it is only labelled where the ingredient is a component part.

Despite public commitments not to allow irradiated food into the country without clear labelling, some examples are getting in. The former Minister of Agriculture, William Waldegrave took the position that it was not his department's role to police foods for such malpractice, something of a climb-down on the commitment from his predecessor who allowed it in the first place, John Gummer. Tests by Trading Standards Officers in Suffolk on random batches of herbs, spices and soft fruit found one in ten may have been irradiated and were not labelled as such.

KOSHER indicates food prepared according to Jewish religious rules, i.e. insisting that meat is killed by bleeding. Pork, game, eels, scaleless fish and shellfish are not allowed. Meat and dairy products must not be eaten at the same meal (the favoured Jewish cooking medium is chicken fat not butter). Cheese must use vegetarian rennet.

LECITHIN, labelled as E322, is found naturally in egg yolks and vegetable – usually soya – oils and is used as an emulsifier and stabilizer. The best example of its natural properties is in making mayonnaise.

LISTERIA was first identified in a laboratory rabbit in 1926. The bacteria are commonly found in the ground, but only cross over into the food-chain through poor hygiene. Until 1982 it was believed that the disease spread directly from animals, but an outbreak in Canada showed that it was invariably a food-borne disease. Then 34 pregnant women and seven adults were poisoned by a batch of coleslaw, 16 of whom died. The vegetables came from a field with known listeria associations, had been inadequately washed and had been mixed with a mayonnaise with too little vinegar to kill off the bacteria. Three years later in California, 48 people died in the worst recorded outbreak to date after eating a fresh Mexican cheese. The difficulty with detecting listeria is that symptoms may not appear for 4-6 weeks. The notorious Swiss Vacherin cheese epidemic only came to light four years after the first deaths had occurred. Then seven died in early '87 and the cause was identified as a pasteurized Vacherin Mont d'Or. It was only revealed later that 24 others had died of similar symptoms in the region. In '92, an as-yet-unattributed epidemic killed 32 people in 46 départements in France between April and August, suggesting the agency may have been some widely distributed food product.

Foods most likely to be carriers of listeria are soft cheeses (where the bacteria will tend to be in or near the rind), chilled salads and prepared meats. The case against unpasteurized cheese is largely discredited and hard cheese is not a risk. Particularly susceptible are pregnant women, the elderly and those with poor immune systems and low-acidity digestive systems. Microwave cooking poses particular risks if the food is spot-cooked. Research is concentrating on the possible link between listeria and spontaneous miscarriages. Cures remain rare and awareness appears to have cut numbers. Two senior government ministers, Virginia Bottomley and Gillian Shepherd are being sued by victims and their families for signing gagging orders to suppress information on the dangers. A High Court judge overruled the orders. The papers show that in 1989, although the Government was fully aware of the risks, it failed to issue any warning. In that time 26 babies died and dozens of others were brain-damaged. At the same time in France there were more than 1,000 cases, one-third fatal. But 528 kilos of Lanark Blue cheese were destroyed last year when bacteria was found in the cheese.

MEAT AND LIVESTOCK COMMISSION is funded from a levy on all carcasses killed in the industry. Most of its resources go into meat promotion, but it has developed quality-control schemes for lamb, beef and pork.

MECHANICALLY RECOVERED MEAT, sometimes shortened to MRM, is the gristle, cartilage and fat removed from carcasses by centrifugal force, etc.

MONOSODIUM GLUTAMATE, or MSG or E621, is the salt from glutamic acid, found naturally in foods high in the glutamates like soya, milk, aged hard cheeses and tomatoes. It is used as a flavour-enhancer in the same way as salt. However, excessive dosages – above 0.3% – can lead to adverse reactions (Chinese Restaurant Syndrome).

NITRATES are more of an issue in produce from northern countries where they are used to stimulate growth in vegetables, notably in the UK in glasshouse-grown butterhead lettuces. The EU has sought to set maximum levels of 2,500 mg per kilo for the summer against 3,500g per kilo in winter. The UK Government, supported by the National Farmers Union, has opposed this proposal until 'there is scientific evidence to demonstrate a risk to health'. Levels of nitrates used on vegetables in Mediterranean countries are likely to be considerably lower because of the better climate.

OMEGA-3 OILS see page 101.

PDO, or Protection of Geographical Origin, was introduced by the EU in July 1993 for co-operative producers whose craft and product is unique to their area. PDI, or Protection of Geographical Indication, is the slightly lesser recognition for co-operatives that can claim their process is unique, even if the materials are brought in from outside the region.

PRESERVATIVES are given the E numbers E200-283.

POLYPHOSPHATES are labelled as 544 and 545 and are used to for their water-retaining properties to bulk up the weight of frozen fish and chicken.

QUINOLINE is a yellow synthetic coal-tar dye, E104, used in smoked haddock and Scotch eggs. Some doctors warn against its use for anyone with a history of asthma or who gets a reaction to aspirin.

RDA is the Recommended Daily Amount of vitamins and minerals, usually worked out as a percentage of 100 g, or a notional portion size which is more relevant to meat, say, than it is to butter. The calculation is based on raw as opposed to cooked foods, because cooking destroys vitamins.

TRANS-FATTY ACIDS are found naturally in meat and dairy products, but their widest application has been in the fats industry as a result of hydrogenating oils to harden them. They are believed to have worked to increase levels of cholesterol.

A 30-year study of 85,000 American nurses by Walter Willet, published in 1993, revealed the link between heart disease and the kind of trans-fatty acids found in margarine. The report suggests that the trans-fats actually increase cholesterol levels. There is further concern that there may be a link to breast cancer and that breast milk may be diluted in mothers who eat a high percentage of trans-fatty acids. Further studies by Lisa Litin and Frank Sacks at Harvard School of Public Health argue that the so-called health benefits of not eating butter are almost completely negated by a diet reliant on foods with high trans-fatty acids. They quote, as an example, someone who might eat a doughnut for breakfast, a small portion of fries at lunch, two teaspoons of margarine with bread at night and two biscuits.

It is widely predicted that margarine manufacturers may reformulate their products as a result. The only non trans-fatty margarines on the market currently are **Granose** and **Whole Earth's Superspread**, both using soya oil, and **Vitaquell** from Germany, which uses palm oil. Going one step further is **Apri-Bake**, only usable in cooking, which is a blend of apricots, fructose and lecithin, claiming to be 98% fat-free. The COMA recommendation is not to exceed the recommended maximum 2% of dietary energy.

UMAMI is said to be the fifth element of taste, associated with the glutamates found in soy, beef stock, tomatoes, mature Parmesan cheese, anchovies and ketchups.

VITAMINS are food constituents essential for complete health. Claims should not be made for foods having any given vitamin unless they contain at least 1/16 of the RDA (recommended daily allowance) of that vitamin; that the foods are 'an excellent source' of it unless they contain half the RDA; and only if they contain the complete quota of vitamins for a day should any health claims be made.

A is formed in the body from dairy foods, fish, leaf and from the carotenes in some root vegetables and pulses. Livers are a good source. Vitamin A deficiency is rare now, except in very poor areas. Pregnant women are usually advised against taking too much vitamin A because large quantities can adversely affect their babies. Children, on the other hand, need slightly more to help the growth of bone and tissue.

B is a complex series of vitamins, found mainly in wholemeal cereals, yeast products and meat. B1 (Thiamin), B2 (Riboflavin), Niacin and B6 are usually easily sourced in a balanced diet. B12 is exclusive to animal products and lack of it leads to anaemia, a problem for vegetarians. Folic acid is important during pregnancy and lactation, and also for the elderly on limited diets. Although widely available, it is harmed in cooking and by nitrates, either used as preservatives in processed foods or even present in the water, and can be at a premium.

C is an important antioxidant and good for all-round health. It is found mostly in fresh foods, fruit, green vegetables, root vegetables and sprouted seeds. The highest concentrations tend to be in citrus fruits, chilli and sweet peppers, blackcurrants, fresh milk (in the darkness of cartons rather than clear bottles). It is destroyed by long cooking and canning. Levels must be sustained when pregnant and during breast feeding. Smokers and older people on restrictive diets should seek to ensure higher levels.

D is the sunshine vitamin, added by law to margarine originally to compensate for the lack of daylight in winter. Deficiency was a major health issue in the North and in Scotland until 1940, when the idea of cod liver oil supplements first gained ground. In children, a lack of vitamin D can cause rickets. Equally, too much can lead to kidney stones. Requirements for pregnant and breast-feeding women increase, which is why doctors usually recommended a diet rich in the oily fish, liver and (pre-salmonella) eggs.

E is the most fashionable of the vitamins, for its protective antioxidants which underpin the enthusiasm for much of the Mediterranean diet. The body tends to store it up, so supplements are rarely used. Ironically, it is found in fats as well as grains, vegetable oils and eggs.

INDEX

SUPPLIERS
AND BRANDS

PRODUCE

GOOD FOOD FEEDBACK

Every effort has been made by the team working on the book to ensure
that all the information it contains is as accurate as possible. We
apologise in advance for any inadvertent inaccuracies; some are
inevitable and we cannot be held responsible for them... but please let
us know if you spot any so we can put them right next time.

Also, if you have comments on foods, would like to endorse or query a
rating for a food, notice a significant change in what is happening, can
fill in a history from your own experience, or are a food producer and
would like to register your product(s) on our database then I would be
very interested to hear from you. Please write to:

Drew Smith
c/o Department BH,
HarperCollinsPublishers,
77-85 Fulham Palace Road,
Hammersmith,
London W6 8JB